Legal Theory Today

Consent in the Law

# Legal Theory Today

## Founding Editor

John Gardner, Professor of Jurisprudence, University College, Oxford

TITLES IN THIS SERIES

*Law in its Own Right* – Henrik Palmer Olsen and Stuart Toddington
*Law and Aesthetics* – Adam Gearey
*Law as a Social Institution* – Hamish Ross
*Evaluation and Legal Theory* – Julie Dickson
*Risks and Legal Theory* – Jenny Steele
*A Sociology of Jurisprudence* – Richard Nobles and David Schiff
*Costs and Cautionary Tales: Economic Insights for the Law* – Anthony Ogus
*Legal Norms and Normativity* – Sylvie Delacroix

Forthcoming titles:

*Law after Modernity* by Sionaidh Douglas-Scott
*Law and Ethics* by John Tasioulas
*Law and Human Need* by John Stanton-Ife

# Consent in the Law

Deryck Beyleveld and Roger Brownsword

·HART·
PUBLISHING

OXFORD AND PORTLAND, OREGON
2007

Published in North America (US and Canada) by
Hart Publishing
c/o International Specialized Book Services
920 NE 58th Avenue, Suite 300
Portland, Oregon
97213-3644
USA
Tel: +1 503 287 3093 or toll-free: (1) 800 944 6190
Fax: +1 503 280 8832
E-mail: orders@isbs.com
Website: www.isbs.com



Hart Publishing, 16C Worcester Place, Oxford OX1 2JW
Telephone: +44 (0)1865 517530 or Fax: +44 (0)1865 510710
E-mail: mail@hartpub.co.uk
Website: http://www.hartpub.co.uk

British Library Cataloguing in Publication Data
Data Available
ISBN 13: 978-1-84113-679-4 (hardback)
ISBN 10: 1-84113-679-0 (hardback)

Typeset by Hope Services (Abingdon) Ltd.
Printed and bound in Great Britain by
TJ International Ltd, Padstow, Cornwall

# Contents

## PART TWO: CONSENT IN THE LAW I: QUESTIONS OF ADEQUACY

# Table of Cases

**United Kingdom**

**European Court of Human Rights**



**Australia**



**Canada**



**Germany**

## United States

# Table of Legislation

**International Legislation**

## EU Legislation



## National Legislation

*United States*

# 1

# Consent in the Law: A Preliminary Examination

## I Introduction

In his *History of the Pleas of the Crown*,[1] Sir Matthew Hale famously stated that, under the common law of England, a husband could not be guilty of raping his wife (whether or not the wife actually was, or reasonably appeared to be, consenting to intercourse was thus immaterial). For much of the eighteenth and nineteenth centuries, Hale's view was accepted as an accurate statement of the legal position. However, towards the end of the nineteenth century—effectively from *R v Clarence*[2] onwards—the courts began to express reservations about the scope and basis of the so-called marital exemption. Nevertheless, lip service continued to be paid to the exemption until, in 1991, in the historic case of *R v R*,[3] time was called on what Lord Lane CJ referred to as 'a common law fiction which has become anachronistic and offensive.'[4] Putting the issue in a broader context, Lord Keith said:

> The common law is . . . capable of evolving in the light of changing social, economic and cultural developments. Hale's proposition reflected the state of affairs in these respects at the time it was enunciated. Since then the status of women, and particularly of married women, has changed out of all recognition in various ways which are very familiar and upon which it is unnecessary to go into detail. Apart from property matters and the availability of matrimonial remedies, one of the most important changes is that marriage is in modern times regarded as a partnership of equals, and no longer one in which the wife must be the subservient chattel of the husband.[5]

If, during the last century, social perceptions of familial relationships were changing with regard to the role of wives, the same was true with respect to the rights and responsibilities of children in families. For example, in *R v D*,[6] the House of Lords rejected the nineteenth-century view that a father has

[1] 1 Hale PC (1736) 629.
[2] (1888) 22 QBD 23.
[3] [1991] 2 All ER 257 (CA); [1991] 4 All ER 481 (HL).
[4] [1991] 2 All ER 257, at 266.
[5] [1991] 4 All ER 481, at 483–84.
[6] [1984] 2 All ER 449.

absolute and paramount authority over his children (another anachronism which, if applied, would create an exemption for a father who took away his unmarried child by force or fraud);[7] and, in the landmark case of *Gillick*,[8] the majority of the House accepted that a mother's right to determine whether a child below the age of 16 years should have advice and treatment concerning contraception must yield where a (*Gillick*-competent) child clearly has the capacity to make such decisions for itself.

These three cases have more in common than their exemplification of judicial decision-making geared to keeping the common law in line with cultural change: for, in each case, it is the emphasis placed upon individual consent that is striking. In *R v R*, the House underlines that sexual relations within marriage, no less than outside marriage, must operate on the basis of ongoing and particular consent; and that a husband cannot take such consent as read simply by virtue of a particular woman's status as his wife. Similarly, in *R v D*, Lord Brandon is unequivocal in treating the child's consent as pivotal: 'I see no good reason why in relation to the kidnapping of a child, it should not in all cases be the absence of the child's consent which is material, whatever its age may be';[9] and, foreshadowing what the House would say the following year in *Gillick*, his Lordship treats the focal question as whether 'the child concerned has sufficient understanding and intelligence to give its consent.'[10] As for *Gillick* itself, it has, of course, become a watchword for respecting the decisions of those children who have the maturity to make up their own minds about whether or not to receive medical treatment.

These remarks suggest that where a society (and this, it should be emphasised, means *any* society, English or American, African or Asian, common law or civilian-based) takes individuals and their choices seriously—particularly so, perhaps, where social relationships are framed by a respect for human rights—the concept of consent will come to play a key role in its

[7] According to Lord Brandon (at 456–57):

> During the greater part of the nineteenth century I do not doubt that the position of paramountcy in the family accorded to a father, both by generally accepted social conventions and by courts which buttressed and enforced them, would in most cases at any rate, have afforded a father, who took or carried away by force or by fraud an unmarried child of his under the age of 21 without the latter's consent, a lawful excuse and that, by reason of the existence of such lawful excuse, the prosecution of a father for the common law offence of kidnapping such a child would have failed. Since the nineteenth century, however, the generally accepted social conventions relating to the paramountcy of a father's position in the family have been progressively whittled away, until now, in the second half of the twentieth century, they can be regarded as having disappeared altogether.

[8] *Gillick v West Norfolk and Wisbech Area Health Authority* [1985] 3 All ER 402.

[9] [1984] 2 All ER 449, at 457.

[10] *Ibid.*

practical thinking.[11] Concomitantly, as relationships become less guided by paternalistic considerations or by status and, correspondingly, more guided by notions of individual freedom and right, the importance of consent will be increasingly voiced. And, where politicians and judges are sensitive to such cultural changes, the importance of consent will be registered in legal doctrine (in precisely the way that we have seen in our trio of cases).

The story of consent and the law, however, is not simply one of doctrinal adjustment, albeit an evolutionary phenomenon that reaches far and wide in the modern law. What is missing from this account is the idea that parties may enter into wholly new relationships by consent, relationships specifically recognised and regulated by institutional sets such as the law of contract or the law of marriage. In the case of the former, the regulative law (the governing law of contract) treats a contract as a consensual transaction; but, more interestingly, it is arguable that consent is also the key to engaging the law of contract itself as the regulative institutional set. In other words, it is arguable that consent, first, brings the law of contract into play and then, with this body of regulative law in play, consent (as defined by the regulative rules) is required for the formation of a binding contract.[12]

If consent authorises the application of a regulative set such as the law of contract or the law of marriage, we might suppose that consent goes beyond this to larger questions of authority. For, with the rise of the ethic of individual rights, liberal political theorists from Locke onwards encourage the view that consent is the foundation for the entire politico-legal order. Consent, it might be claimed, is not just *in* the law; consent goes deeper than this, pointing to the basis of legal authority and perhaps to the essence of legal order itself.

Even if it is relatively uncontroversial to characterise modern legal systems as to a considerable degree codes for consent (or for rights and consent), the pervasiveness of the idea might give us pause for thought. Even if it is now taken as read that consent counts, do we really understand this idea as well as we should? Do we fully understand what consent does, who can consent, under what conditions consent will count, for what it will count, why it counts, and so on?

In this preliminary examination of consent in the law, we can begin to see the complexity of the idea as well as the contours of the ethical landscape in which this outstanding feature of legal doctrine is applied, interpreted, and rejected. First, in section II of this chapter, we introduce a range of issues—pertaining to the functions of consent, the capacity to consent, the

[11] Compare George P Fletcher, *Basic Concepts of Legal Thought* (Oxford, Oxford University Press, 1996) at 109 for the view not only that 'a doctrine of consent testifies . . . to the existence of personal rights' but also that '[no] idea testifies more powerfully to individuals as a source of value.'

[12] Compare Randy E Barnett, 'A Consent Theory of Contract' (1986) 86 Col LR 269.

adequacy and effectiveness of consent, and the like—each of which flags up questions to be considered in the main body of this book. Secondly, in section III, we give a general indication of how three competing ethical approaches (namely, utilitarian, rights-led, and duty-led ethics) relate to the part that consent plays in the law. Broadly speaking, we can say that, if each of these ethical approaches were to have its own internet site, it would be on the home page for the rights-led approach that we would find consent highlighted. Thirdly, in section IV, we declare our ethical colours together with our larger aspirations in addressing this topic. Put shortly, in order to have a defensible perspective on consent in the law and its ethical environment, we must have a background moral theory upon which we can draw. For us, that theory is based on Alan Gewirth's seminal work,[13] and the general purpose of this book, as we explain at the end of this preliminary chapter, is to subject consent in the law to a philosophical critique based on Gewirthian moral theory.

## II What is there to Understand about Consent?

It is tempting to think that consent, as it operates in the law, is a fairly unproblematic idea. After all, it clearly does plenty of doctrinal work—pretty much every area of law relies on consent to some extent—and lawyers are not commonly to be heard complaining that they really do not know what to make of consent. However, a moment's reflection suggests that there are uncomfortable questions hiding behind this doctrinal mainstay. To take some examples from English law, why was it that consent was not accepted as a defence to assault and wounding in the case of *Brown*,[14] where the context was consensual sado-masochism between adults, yet was accepted as a defence in *Wilson*,[15] where branding was inflicted by a husband as a token of his love and affection for his wife? Why was it that, in *Blood*,[16] the implicit prior consent of a now-deceased husband was not accepted as the basis for lawful retrieval of his sperm and posthumous insemination of his widow whereas, in *R v Collins*,[17] an open window and a gesture in the dark might suffice to furnish a defence against what would otherwise be trespass with intent to rape? Why was it that, in *Re A (Children)*,[18] the killing of one Siamese twin in order to save the life of the

[13] See Alan Gewirth, *Reason and Morality* (Chicago, University of Chicago Press, 1978).

[14] *R v Brown* [1993] 2 All ER 75; and Law Commission Consultation Paper No 134, *Consent and Offences against the Person* (1994).

[15] *R v Wilson (Alan Thomas)* [1997] QB 47.

[16] *R v Human Fertilisation and Embryology Authority ex parte Blood* [1997] 2 All ER 687; and Sheila McLean, *Consent and the Law*, DoH Consultation Paper (London, Department of Health, 1997).

[17] [1972] 2 All ER 1106.

[18] [2000] 4 All ER 961.

other was held to be lawful notwithstanding the fact that the child's parents refused to give their consent to the separation and the fact that the child itself was incapable of consenting or refusing? And, going beyond English law, why is it that so many legal systems find it relatively easy to license the termination of lives where patients are not in a position to give or withhold consent and yet find it so difficult to do the same when patients are able to give their consent to physician-assisted (or physician-administered) termination and they have done precisely that?

To sharpen our appreciation of how consent figures in modern legal thinking, we can begin to unbundle the issues that are gathered up in this conceptual space. In this way, even if we do not at once understand consent, at least we should have a better sense of what we would have to understand if we were to understand consent in the law.

### *(i) The Function of Consent*[19]

We can start with the way in which we understand the function of consent. In the trio of cases with which we opened our discussion, the doctrinal function of consent seems fairly clear. The removal of the marital exemption in *R v R* signals that husbands no longer have a defence to what would otherwise be rape; the denial of the parental exemption in *R v D* signals that fathers have no automatic defence to what would otherwise be kidnapping; and, in *Gillick*, the effect of recognising a competent child is that medical practitioners need consent from the child rather than the child's parent(s) in order to have a defence against what might otherwise be the commission of various torts and crimes. This reading of consent seems to chime in with the insightful analysis offered by George Fletcher, according to whom:

> When individuals consent to undergo medical operations, to engage in sexual intercourse, to open their homes to police searches, or to testify against themselves in court, they convert what otherwise would be an invasion of their person or their rights into a harmless or justified activity.[20]

In general, this seems to be on the right track. Putting the matter formally, where A has a claim-right against B that B should not do X to A, then where A consents to B doing X, the doing of X by B will not violate A's claim right against B. Or, one might say, the doing of X by B will not involve a violation of B's duty to A. To say, as Fletcher would, that A's consent converts the doing of X by B into 'a harmless or justified activity' is perhaps not the best way of putting it—because, first, 'harmless' has to be elucidated as 'involving no violation of A's claim-right against B' and, secondly, the effect of A's consent is not to cover B's act with a substantive justification *tout court* but with a procedural justification that holds good against the

[19] We discuss the principal functions of consent in ch 3.
[20] Fletcher, above n 11, at 109.

consenting party A. Nevertheless, the idea that A's consent neutralises what would otherwise be wrongful conduct by B, or provides a defence or an immunity for B—a 'legal "flak jacket" which protects [B] from claims by the litigious' as Lord Donaldson aptly put it in *Re W*[21]—captures one of the central functions of consent.

Three of the examples given by Fletcher—consent to surgery, sex and search—fit very well with the idea of consent operating as a defence (in these examples, to what would otherwise be assault and battery, rape, and trespass to property). In each of these examples, A has a straightforward claim-right against B, and A's consent provides B with a defence to what would otherwise be a breach of duty to A. However, Fletcher's fourth example—a suspect or a defendant electing to answer questions or give evidence—might be viewed rather differently. Here, A's 'right to silence' or 'right against self-incrimination' is not a claim-right as such (although it might be supported by certain claim-rights). Putting the matter in Hohfeldian terms, A's 'right to silence' or 'right against self-incrimination' looks more like a 'liberty' to refuse to answer questions put to him by his police interrogators or prosecutors.[22] On this analysis, A breaches no duty by declining to answer questions; and, correlatively, the police and prosecutors have no claim-right that A answers or testifies. If the relationship between A, on the one side, and the police and prosecutors, on the other, is symmetrical, the latter will have a Hohfeldian liberty to put questions to A. Thus, in a textbook 'no comment interview', the police will breach no duty to A by asking him questions, and A will breach no duty to the police by exercising the right of silence and declining to answer. If, at the start of or during the interview, A signals a willingness to answer questions (and, thus, not to exercise his right to silence), we might say that A is 'consenting' to give information or evidence. However, whatever proves to be the best account of A's 'consent' in such circumstances, its function does not seem to be to give the police or prosecutor a defence to what would otherwise be a violation of their duties to A.

The possibility that the function of consent might change as we move away from claim-right/duty relationships, prompts the thought that this might become more obvious when we consider legal rules and relationships that are focused on powers rather than duties (as in HLA Hart's seminal distinction between primary rules of a duty-imposing kind and secondary rules of a power-conferring kind[23]). For example, if A consents to enter into a contract with B, the function of consent is not to give B a defence against

[21] *Re W (A Minor) (Medical Treatment)* [1992] 4 All ER 627, at 635.

[22] Wesley N Hohfeld, *Fundamental Legal Conceptions* (New Haven, Yale University Press, 1964). In ch 3, we employ Hohfeld's analysis of the basic legal relationships to locate the functions of consent in authorising a change of position relative to the terms of the basic legal relationships and in authorising the creation of new relationships.

[23] HLA Hart, *The Concept of Law* (Oxford, The Clarendon Press, 1961).

what would otherwise be a violation of A's rights. On the contrary, A's consent puts him in a position where actions *by A* that would *not* otherwise be a breach of duty to B will become just that (*qua* breach of A's contractual obligation to B). This suggests that, while consent can function as a defence against a breach of right or duty, it can also function to create new rights and duties. In this latter respect, the move from private law to public law relationships might also be significant. For example, where A 'consents' to some regime of local or national governance, this creates a political mandate or authorisation which might lead to the creation of new rights and duties, powers and immunities, and so on, in the constituency of which A is a member.[24]

This is not the place to try to improve on Hohfeldian or Hartian taxonomies of legal rules and relationships. Suffice it to say that, while it might be natural to think of consent as a defence to what would otherwise be a violation of right/breach of duty, this does not seem to exhaust its functions within the law. Whether or not this might make a difference to such questions as the conditions for consent, the capacity and competence to consent, the limits of consent, and so on, is a matter to bear in mind.

### *(ii) The Conditions for Giving a Valid Consent*[25]

In both medical law and contract law (especially consumer contract law), the modern view is that there is more to consent than saying 'Yes' or signing on the dotted line. In both areas, the law requires that consent should be free and informed. This suggests that, at any rate in private relationships, the law might set the same conditions for consent irrespective of the function played by consent (whether to serve as a defence or as a condition for the assumption of new obligations). Yet, if this suggests some simplicity in the law, it is immediately obvious that specifying the conditions for 'free' and 'informed' consent is a major challenge.[26]

[24] In ch 10, we consider how far it is possible to model public governance on consent-authorised transactions, particularly consent-based private governance.

[25] We discuss the two principal conditions for the giving of a valid consent in chs 5 and 6. These conditions are that the consent should be given as a matter of unforced choice and that it should be given on an informed basis.

[26] Article 5 of the Council of Europe's Convention on Human Rights and Biomedicine (1997) provides that 'An intervention in the health field may only be carried out after the person concerned has given free and informed consent to it.' The Article further elaborates only by requiring that the person be given 'appropriate information as to the purpose and nature of the intervention as well as its consequences and risks.' To which, one might ask: 'appropriate' relative to whose viewpoint or which standards of health care? In the Explanatory Report accompanying the Convention, it is said that this Article 'makes clear patients' autonomy in their relationship with health care professionals and restrains the paternalist approaches which might ignore the wish of the patient' (para 34); and it goes on to underline the importance of the information being presented clearly in order to put the patient in a position 'through the use of terms he or she can understand, to weigh up the necessity or usefulness of the aims and methods of the intervention against its risks and the discomfort or pain it will cause' (para 36).

A great deal of legal doctrine is predicated on the idea that where there has been a 'voluntary' assumption of obligation then the party so consenting is bound. For example, this is the basis of 'freedom of contract' and 'sanctity of contract'; it supports the idea that a 'free' contract is a fair contract; and in international relations, it is enshrined in the principle of *pacta sunt servanda*. However, determination of whether 'consent' has been given 'freely' is doubly complex: first, we need a stable and defensible conception of 'free' action; and, secondly, employing this conception, we need to be able to interpret actions with some confidence as 'free' or otherwise.

With regard to the first of these puzzles, we can probably agree that the more egregious forms of coercion, undue pressure, and influence are inconsistent with any plausible conception of *free* consent. There might also be support for the view (although perhaps less clearly so) that inducements and incentives can tell against free consent. Beyond such a core of minimal agreement, however, as Duncan Kennedy has argued, the concept of voluntariness is elastic, prey to ideological manipulation, and intrinsically unstable. Thus:

> [W]ithout doing violence to the notion of voluntariness as it has been worked out in the law, [we] could adopt a hard-nosed self-reliant, individualist posture that shrinks the defenses of fraud and duress almost to nothing. At the other extreme, [we] could require the slightly stronger or slightly better-informed party to give away all his advantage . . . If we cut back the rules far enough, we would arrive at something like the state of nature—legalized theft. If we extended them far enough, we would jeopardize the enforceability of the whole range of bargains that define a mixed capitalist economy.[27]

If we accept this analysis, there seem to be two responses, neither of which is satisfactory: either we concede that free dealing is an idea that occupies no fixed point on, so to speak, the spectrum of voluntariness (which is to admit that there is some indeterminacy in the essential idea); or we give free dealing a definite location on this spectrum (but at the apparent price of arbitrariness). Kennedy spells out the implications associated with this perceived conceptual looseness:

> Confronted with a choice, [we] will have available two sets of stereotypical policy arguments. One 'altruist' set of arguments suggests that [we] should resolve the gap, conflict, or ambiguity by requiring a party who injures the other to pay compensation, and also that [we] should allow a liberal law of excuse when the injuring party claims to be somehow not really responsible. The other 'individualist' set of arguments emphasizes that the injured party should have looked out for himself, rather than demanding that the other renounce freedom of action, and

[27] Duncan Kennedy, 'Distributive and Paternalist Motives in Contract and Tort Law, with Special Reference to Compulsory Terms and Unequal Bargaining Power' (1982) 41 *Maryland Law Review* 563, at 582.

that the party seeking excuse should have avoided binding himself to obligations he couldn't fulfill.[28]

In other words, behind the concept of consent, at any rate as it operates in the area of contractual transactions, we can uncover a conflict between an ethic of individualism and an ethic of co-operativism (or partnership).[29] On this analysis, the institution of contract is not simply built upon the concept of consent; rather, different institutions of contract (and, concomitantly, different arrangements of contractual doctrine) are built on different conceptions of consent.

An equally difficult conceptual puzzle arises from the requirement that consent should be 'informed'. Famously, in *Canterbury v Spence*,[30] the Court of Appeals of the District of Columbia held that, in the context of medical treatment, '[t]rue consent to what happens to one's self is the informed exercise of a choice.'[31] It hardly needs to be said that the question of how much information one needs before one's consent is sufficiently informed is one that has been heavily litigated in many jurisdictions; and, while courts have often favoured a physician perspective (where the flow of information is regulated by physician expectations), the more 'progressive' courts have favoured a patient perspective (where the flow of information is regulated by the expectations of a representative or reasonable patient or by the expectations of the particular person who is the patient in question).[32] Although this question has not been litigated quite so densely in relation to contractual disputes, it is nonetheless one that has troubled academic commentators. And, once again, it is the underlying tension between individualistic and co-operative (or partnership) thinking that threatens to thwart attempts to stabilise this requirement for *informed* consent.

To illustrate, suppose that A is selling goods to B. To simplify, let us further suppose: (1) that neither A nor B has been careless in failing to acquire the information held by the other party; (2) that neither party has invested resources specifically designed to acquire the information in question; and (3) that the information is material in the sense that, if disclosed, it will

[28] *Ibid*, at 581.

[29] See Roger Brownsword, 'Individualism, Cooperativism and an Ethic for European Contract Law' (2001) 64 *Modern Law Review* 628. In the different context of democratising health-care provision, the ethic of partnership comes up against utilitarian, paternalistic, and even managerial ethics. See Deryck Beyleveld and Roger Brownsword, 'Ethics Committees: Public Interest, Private Interest, and the Ethics of Partnership' in Guy Lebeer (ed), *Ethical Function in Hospital Ethics Committees* (Amsterdam, IOS Press, 2002) at 135.

[30] 464 F 2d 772 (DC Cir 1972).

[31] At 780.

[32] See, eg, *Reibl v Hughes* (1980) 114 DLR (3d) 1 (Canada); and *Rogers v Whitaker* (1992) 67 ALJR 47 (Australia). In England, the leading case, *Sidaway v Board of Governors of the Bethlem Royal Hospital and the Maudsley Hospital* [1985] AC 871, takes a much more conservative view.

affect the price. Where disclosure by the party holding the information will serve the economic interests of that same party, then we can assume that disclosure will normally take place. The problem cases are those in which there is an asymmetry in relation to relevant information and in which disclosure will count against the economic interests of the party disclosing.

Suppose that A fails to disclose information which, if disclosed, would adjust the contract price downwards in favour of B. The individualist view would be that contract is a competitive exchange; that the onus of inquiry is on B; and that the law should not require A to surrender a happenstance informational bargaining advantage. On a more co-operative approach, it is tempting to argue that sellers (such as A) should at least be required to disclose the nature and suitability of the goods (for example, disclosing latent defects).[33] However, should the law also require disclosure (by A) where the information does not relate to the nature or suitability of the goods for which B is contracting, but is nevertheless price-sensitive? For example, should the law require A to disclose that identical goods could be purchased at a cheaper price elsewhere (say, at a shop around the corner), or that, if B waited a couple of days, the goods would be cheaper? Whilst a rule permitting non-disclosure here would be compatible with the facilitation of mutually beneficial deals (A and B both gaining as they expect), it is arguable that such a rule would undermine the promotion of a climate of trust that is implicit in an ethic of co-operativism.

Turning the situation round, suppose now that B (the buyer) fails to disclose information which, if disclosed, would adjust the contract price upwards in favour of A. For example, suppose that B does not disclose to A that the latter's collection of books or paintings contains some exceptionally rare and valuable items; or that, as in the classic US case of *Laidlaw v Organ*,[34] B does not disclose to A that, if he were to delay selling for a day or two, he would get a better price for the goods. Here, the principal risk created by non-disclosure is that A (the seller) loses the opportunity to realise the full value of the goods that he is selling. The individualist line with regard to such a case is uncompromising: A needs to take better care of his own financial interests and, once again, the law should not require B to surrender a bargaining advantage that has been fairly, if fortunately, gained. One might also expect co-operativism to be relatively unsympathetic to A's loss of opportunity, at least where A is a professional seller. In other contexts, however, one would expect such an ethic to be concerned at the law's indifference to B knowingly taking advantage of A's ignorance—and whichever line is taken by co-operativism this will manifest itself in a more or less stringent specification of the information requirement.

[33] Compare *Obde v Schlemeyer* 56 Wash 2d 449, 353 P 2d 672 (1960).

[34] 15 US (2 Wheat) 178 (1817).

Even if we can stabilise our conception of free and informed consent, it needs to be sufficiently robust to be applied in the myriad of cases in which it is central to the legal finding. There is much to be said about the difficulties of applying even a clear conception of consent in contexts where there are a multitude of institutional and relational forces in play. For example, even after the abolition of the marital exemption and, let us suppose, the elimination of forcible intercourse in marriage, there remains a concern that the choices made by wives continue to be driven by partner pressure albeit less tangible and visible.[35] Similarly, even after the regulation of more oppressive forms of interrogation of suspects in the criminal justice system, there remains a concern as to whether admissions or confessions made in police interview rooms are genuinely free; and, in the same way, one might question how far plea-bargains struck in the shadow of a trial,[36] or acceptance of a probation order in the face of what would otherwise be a custodial sentence, reflect a free choice.

There is one further issue about the conditions for consent: namely, are the conditions variable (in principle or in practice (overtly or covertly))? For example, where a choice touches on a person's most basic interests or where it is irreversible (such as assisted suicide), do we (or should we) set a higher threshold for free and informed consent than where lesser interests are at stake or where the original position can be recovered? *R v Jones*[37] offers an interesting example of this issue. There, the defendant, who was facing charges relating to a robbery at a post office, entered a 'not guilty' plea at the arraignment but subsequently failed to appear for the trial. Exercising a common law discretion, the trial judge ordered that the trial should proceed and, in his absence, the defendant was duly convicted and given a long custodial sentence. Some 14 months later, the defendant was apprehended. He now claimed that the trial should not have been allowed to proceed and that, insofar as the common law permitted trial in the absence of the defendant, it was incompatible with the right to a fair trial as guaranteed by Article 6 of the European Convention on Human Rights. Rejecting the defendant's argument, the House of Lords ruled that, irrespective of whether the defendant had waived the benefit of the right to appear and to offer a defence, which is an aspect of the right to a fair trial, he had had a fair trial anyway. Two matters are of particular interest, however.

First, there is the question of whether the defendant had waived his right. Lord Bingham, following the line adopted by the Court of Appeal, had little doubt that the right had been waived:

[35] See, eg, Vanessa Laird, 'Reflections on *R v R*' (1992) 55 *Modern Law Review* 386.

[36] See, eg, the discussion of advance indications of sentence in Lord Justice Auld's *Review of the Criminal Courts of England and Wales* (London, The Stationery Office, 2001) at 434–44.

[37] [2002] UKHL 5. See, further, our discussion in ch 7, where we focus not on whether the defendant's conduct constituted a free and informed consent but what kind of consent, if any, it *signalled*.

> [In] my opinion, . . . one who voluntarily chooses not to exercise a right cannot be heard to complain that he has lost the benefits which he might have expected to enjoy had he exercised it. . . . If he voluntarily chooses not to exercise his right to appear, he cannot impugn the fairness of the trial on the ground that it followed a course different from that which it would have followed had he been present and represented.[38]

Begging to differ, however, Lord Rodger (supported by Lord Hoffmann) was not satisfied that the right had been waived:

> Doubtless, the appellant would have been aware that, if eventually brought to justice, he would be punished for absconding to avoid trial. But I see no proper basis for going further and assuming that he would actually have known that he was liable to be tried and sentenced in his absence. I am accordingly unable to draw the conclusion that the appellant had unequivocally waived his right to be present at any trial.[39]

So, for Lord Rodger, where conviction of a serious criminal offence and consequent deprivation of liberty are at stake, waiver by conduct has to be unequivocal.

Secondly, in line with his tough-minded approach to the defendant's conduct, Lord Bingham takes the view that, where a trial judge is exercising a discretion as to whether or not to allow the trial to proceed in cases such as *Jones*, the seriousness of the offence is not a relevant consideration. Thus:

> The judge's overriding concern will be to ensure that the trial, if conducted in the absence of the defendant, will be as fair as circumstances permit and lead to a just outcome. These objects are equally important, whether the offence charged be serious or relatively minor.[40]

If this seems inflexible, and too ready to infer waiver, it is worth remembering that, in other contexts, a concern that persons do not make irrational choices can lead to a questionable lack of respect for their decision-making capacity. It is one thing to double-check that a waiver really has taken place; it is another thing altogether to deny waiver on paternalistic grounds.

### *(iii) The Capacity (and Competence) to Consent*[41]

If the conditions for an authentic consent are that it is given freely and on an informed basis (however these conditions are interpreted), then the logic is that the specification of a 'subject of consent'—that is, one having the relevant capacity (or competence) to consent—will reflect these conditions. This means, first, that a person with capacity to consent will be capable of forming their own judgments and making their own decisions free from the

[38] [2002] UKHL 5, para 11.
[39] *Ibid*, para 52.
[40] [2002] UKHL 5, para 14.
[41] We discuss the questions of capacity and competence in ch 4.

influence or opinion of others; and, secondly, that such a person will be able to understand and apply the information that is material to their decision.

By and large, this approach is reflected in the landmark case of *Gillick*,[42] where the mature minor's capacity to consent was put in terms of the child having 'a sufficient understanding and intelligence to be capable of making up his own mind on the matter requiring decision'[43] or as being 'capable of understanding what is proposed, and of expressing his or her own wishes'.[44] In *Re C*,[45] where a 68-year-old paranoid schizophrenic refused, against medical advice, to proceed with an operation that would involve the amputation of a limb, Thorpe J elaborated the capacity standard in terms of whether the person sufficiently understood the nature, purpose, and effects of the treatment proposed (and declined); which, in turn, hinged on whether the person had been able to comprehend and retain the relevant information, whether he believed it, and whether he weighed it before arriving at a decision. Helpful though this is, it is clear that the more extensive the elaboration of the test of capacity, the more difficult it will be to satisfy it. For instance, if the required understanding is pitched in broad and general terms it is more likely to be met than if it is set at a very specific level (particularly so if the duty to inform is not pitched at the equivalent level of specificity); and, if the process of weighing the information must be consistent with calm deliberation and rational review of the options, this is unlikely to be met by persons who are already in a state of agitation and anxiety. It follows that where courts wish to override refusals of consent (see (viii) below), it is not difficult for them to do so provided that they pitch the test of capacity at a suitably demanding standard.

Just as the actual *giving* of consent is not always a sufficient condition for lawful action (see (iv) and (v) below), having the *capacity* to consent is not always sufficient. Thus, in test cases such as *Washington v Glucksberg*,[46] or those involving Sue Rodriguez in Canada[47] and, more recently, Dianne Pretty in England,[48] the courts have had no doubt that the terminally ill applicants have the capacity to consent to an assisted suicide. Nevertheless, the law stops short of decriminalising the act of aiding and abetting suicide or of granting a bespoke immunity against prosecution. The principal reason for this caution is that there is a concern that such liberalising steps would lead to the lives of vulnerable persons (those lacking the steadfast capacity to give free and informed consent) being terminated without the

[42] *Gillick v West Norfolk and Wisbech Area Health Authority* [1985] 3 All ER 402.

[43] *Ibid*, at 422 (per Lord Scarman).

[44] *Ibid*, at 409 (per Lord Fraser).

[45] *Re C (Adult: Refusal of Medical Treatment)* [1994] 1 All ER 819.

[46] 117 S Ct 2258 (1997).

[47] *Rodriguez v Attorney General of Canada* [1994] 2 LRC 136.

[48] *R on the Application of Mrs Dianne Pretty v DPP and Secretary of State for the Home Department* [2001] UKHL 61.

law being able to distinguish between cases of genuine consent and those where consent was more apparent than real.[49]

### *(iv) Does it Matter Who Gives Consent (including by proxy) and to Whom it is Given?*

In principle, we can distinguish a number of formally distinct consent situations, and one wonders whether there are significant differences at stake here. For example, we might distinguish the following three cases:

(1) unilateral: where A consents (to some action by B);
(2) bilateral or mutual: where A and B jointly consent; and
(3) trilateral: where C consents for (or on behalf of) A (eg to some action by B or by way of joint consent with B).

On the face of it, there is no reason why unilateral consent should be treated differently from bilateral consent; in both cases, there is direct consent by the parties. By contrast, in the trilateral situation, a third party is consenting on behalf of another. This suggests that we need to be very careful to ensure that C is communicating an accurate and reliable consent on behalf of that other. Where A is capable of giving a consent but is using C as a proxy or an agent, this can give rise to a host of difficulties if C exceeds his authority. Where this happens, is the purported consent treated as effective (leaving A to settle any differences with C) or as ineffective (putting B at risk if he has acted on the apparent consent)? Where A is neither capable of giving consent nor able to ratify C's action, we might pause to satisfy ourselves that there really is clear and compelling evidence concerning A's views with regard to the particular matter at hand—hence the insistence of the majority of the US Supreme Court in the *Cruzan* case[50] that, before artifical feeding and hydration is withdrawn from a person in a persistent vegetative state, there should be a double-check as to their known wishes.[51]

Although the distinction between direct and indirect consent is important, there is also a question to be asked about the interests of the respective parties in procuring and giving the consent. In the unilateral situation, for example, is the giving of consent by A: (a) likely to be to his advantage; (b) likely to be to his disadvantage; or (c) likely to be neither to his advantage nor to his disadvantage? If the answer is (b), extra care needs to be taken to ensure that A's consent is free and informed. In line with this cautious approach, the revised Declaration of Helsinki emphasises that medical researchers have an obligation to provide special protection to particular research populations including those who will not benefit personally

[49] See, further, our discussion in ch 9.

[50] *Nancy Beth Cruzan v Director, Missouri Department of Health* 497 US 261, 110 S Ct 2841 (1990); 111 L Ed 2d 224.

[51] See, further, our discussion in ch 4.

from the research; and, in the criminal justice system, we would expect suspects to be counselled as to the consequences if they elect to dispense with the standard protections of legal advice and assistance. On the other side of the unilateral transaction, we also need to consider whether, from B's standpoint, the giving of consent by A is (a) likely to be to his (B's) advantage; (b) likely to be to his disadvantage; or (c) likely to be neither to his advantage nor to his disadvantage. If the answer is (a), we again have reason to double-check that A's consent is free and informed.

This same question is a familiar one in the bilateral contractual situation. Ideal-typically, contracts involve a mutually beneficial act of co-operation: either A and B co-operate in order to achieve some desired end that cannot be achieved by either party acting alone; or they agree to an exchange that advances their mutual interests (A having something that B wants, and vice versa).[52] In practice, however, contracts can be very one-sided and manifestly display a significant imbalance (as European consumer contract law puts it).[53] One response to such an apparently one-sided outcome is to review the processes that led to the contract: did the apparently disadvantaged party contract on a free and informed basis? Alternatively, some outcomes might be perceived to be so problematic that they are blacklisted: either because the law now sets such limits for consent (as might be the case, for instance, with surrogacy agreements or contracts for the sale of organs) or because the law is unable to differentiate between exceptional cases of authentic consent and the general run of cases where the weaker party has been compelled to 'take it or leave it.'[54]

### *(v) The Necessity, Sufficiency, and Justifying Limits of Consent*[55]

There are many nice points to be made, and confusions to be avoided, concerning the necessity and sufficiency of consent. Even where human rights are accepted, we should not assume that consent is always a *necessary* condition for lawful action. Indeed, in medical emergencies, action taken without consent might be lawful precisely because it is judged to be necessary—witness the fate of the doomed Siamese twins, Mary and Jodie, where

[52] See Lon L Fuller, 'The Forms and Limits of Adjudication' (1978–79) 92 *Harvard Law Review* 353, at 357–62.

[53] Art 3(1) of Directive 93/13/EEC (the Unfair Terms in Consumer Contracts Directive) provides that a term is unfair if 'contrary to the requirement of good faith, it causes a significant imbalance in the parties' rights and obligations arising under the contract, to the detriment of the consumer.'

[54] Compare Joel Feinberg's essay 'Legal Paternalism' in his collection, *Rights, Justice, and the Bounds of Liberty* (Princeton, Princeton University Press, 1980). At 124–25, Feinberg considers how one might reconcile a prohibition against contracts of slavery with a respect for freedom of contract. He suggests that where practical tests of voluntariness are fallible, then a general presumption of non-voluntariness and, concomitantly, a rule against enforcement might appeal as the less risky option.

[55] We discuss the necessity and sufficiency of consent in chs 8 and 9.

the life of the former had to be sacrificed if her sister was to have any chance of survival[56]—or in a person's 'best interests'; and, more generally, action in the 'public interest' might be taken without consent, albeit often controversially so.[57]

Where, other things being equal, legal systems would treat the giving of consent as a *necessary* condition for lawful action, it is not always *sufficient.* For example, whilst a patient's consent might be sufficient to *constitute a defence* to shield a doctor against a claim by the patient, it does not necessarily render the act lawful. If the act in question was, say, an abortion or a xenotransplantation (with attendant concerns about the risk of third-party infection or a public health hazard), the doctor might still have to answer to the authorities for his actions—having a defence against a claim of private wrong is one thing, having an answer to a charge of public wrong is something else. Or, again, just because consent is necessary (or suffices) to negate an alleged violation of right, it does not follow that it thereby *creates an obligation* on the doctor to provide the treatment in question. Consent as a response to an alleged breach of duty is one thing; consent as the source of obligation is another matter.

As we have seen already in relation to the enforcement of 'contracts', even if the parties concerned are consenting, this does not secure the legality of their actions. Consistency with broader public policy considerations may also be necessary. To take a rather diffferent example, in a well-known German case, the *Peep-Show Decision*,[58] the Federal Administrative Tribunal denied a licence for a mechanical peep-show on the ground that the performance would violate Article 1(1) of the Basic Law. Having

[56] *Re A (Children) (Conjoined Twins: Surgical Separation)* [2000] 4 All ER 961. For discussion, see ch 9.

[57] For example, according to s 60(1) of the Health and Social Care Act 2001, '[t]he Secretary of State may by regulations make such provision for and in connection with requiring or regulating the processing of prescribed patient information for medical purposes as he considers necessary or expedient: (a) in the interests of improving patient care, or (b) in the public interest.' The import of this controversial provision is spelt out in para 291 of the explanatory notes accompanying the legislation:

> This section enables the Secretary of State to make regulations for and in connection with requiring or regulating the processing of patient information in prescribed circumstances. This will make it possible for patients to receive more information about their clinical care and for confidential patient information to be lawfully processed *without informed consent* [our emphasis] to support prescribed activities such as cancer registries. The Government places importance on the consistent use of informed consent as the basis for handling confidential patient information. The regulation-making power in this section is therefore intended to provide for exceptional situations where essential services cannot, having regard to the present NHS systems and available technology, operate on that basis.

[58] BVerwGE 64, 274 (1981); and see Shayana Kadidal, 'Obscenity in the Age of Mechanical Reproduction' (1996) 44 *American Journal of Comparative Law* 353.

affirmed that 'respect for and protection of human dignity are constituent principles of the Basic Law,' and having said that in the peep-show 'the woman is placed in a degrading position' and 'treated like an object' the Tribunal continued:

> The consent of the women concerned can only exclude a violation of human dignity if such a violation is based only on the lack of consent to the relevant actions or omissions of the women concerned. However, this is not the situation here because in the case at issue . . . the human dignity of the women concerned is violated by the exposition typical of these performances. Here, human dignity, because its significance reaches beyond the individual, must be protected even against the wishes of the woman concerned whose own subjective ideas deviate from the objective value of human dignity.[59]

In other words, where human dignity is independently compromised, irrespective of whether the act in question is freely performed, consent is not material. Similarly, in an important decision by the Conseil d'Etat, it was held that bans on dwarf-throwing imposed by the police in Morsang-sur-Orge and Aix-en-Provence were lawful notwithstanding that the participants were consenting adults.[60] Faced with a challenge to the legality of the bans by, among others, one of the dwarfs, the Conseil d'Etat responded that the dwarf compromised his own dignity by allowing himself to be used as a mere thing, that ordre public allowed for no such concession, and that consent could not redeem the public wrong that was perpetrated.[61]

Unlike the law in France and Germany, English law (both public and private) is less *explicitly* committed to a public policy organised around the value of human dignity.[62] Nevertheless, the much-debated case of *R v Brown*[63] provides an equally telling illustration of the limits placed upon consent. There, the question was whether the consent of participating adult sado-masochists provided a defence to what would otherwise be criminal acts of assault and wounding. In a split three-to-two decision, the majority of the House of Lords held that consent was no defence. Although each of the opinions given in *Brown* adopts its own distinctive approach, the

[59] BVerwGE 64, 274 (1981), at 277–79.

[60] Conseil d'Etat (27 October 1995) req nos 136–727 (Commune de Morsang-sur-Orge) and 143–578 (Ville d'Aix-en-Provence).

[61] See Marie-Christine Roualt's note on the two decisions, *Les Petites Affiches* (24 January 1996: No 11) 30, at 32. And, for reflections on the case, with dignity being interpreted as the essence of humanity, see Bernard Edelman, 'La Dignité de la Personne Humaine, un Concept Nouveau', Recueil Dalloz 1997, 23e Cahier, Chronique, 185, at 187–88.

[62] In a well-known paper, Dawn Oliver has contended that dignity, together with autonomy, respect, status, and security, is a key value underlying both public and private law. In this analysis, however, dignity relates quite closely to autonomy and respect. See Dawn Oliver, 'The Underlying Values of Public and Private Law' in Michael Taggart (ed), *The Province of Administrative Law* (Oxford, Hart Publishing, 1997) at 217–42.

[63] [1993] 2 All ER 75.

underlying question of principle is most clearly an issue for Lords Templeman (majority) and Mustill (minority). Put shortly, Lord Templeman's view (echoing that of many others including Justice Byron White in *Bowers v Hardwick*[64] and the minority in the more recent case of *Lawrence v Texas*[65]) is that the criminal law is for the protection of society, including the protection of society's basic values. So regarded, sado-masochism, even fully consensual sado-masochism, might be an appropriate case for regulation. As Lord Templeman evocatively put it:

> Society is entitled and bound to protect itself against a cult of violence. Pleasure derived from the infliction of pain is an evil thing. Cruelty is uncivilised.[66]

However, for Lord Mustill (echoing the viewpoint of many others including Justice Harry Blackmun in *Bowers v Hardwick* and the majority in *Lawrence v Texas*), a key consideration is that, in a free society, 'the state should interfere with the rights of an individual to live his or her life as he or she may choose no more than is necessary to ensure a proper balance between the special interests of the individual and the general interests of the individuals who together comprise the populace at large.'[67]

If not quite a wholehearted endorsement of autonomy, Lord Mustill's dissenting opinion at least gave encouragement to the defendants to appeal to the European Court of Human Rights—which they duly did, arguing principally that the decision of the House of Lords violated Article 8(1) of the Convention (the right to respect for private and family life).[68] At Strasbourg, as at Westminster, the court was divided but the majority again ruled against the appellants. For present purposes, the most striking opinion was given by Judge Pettiti, who took the view that Article 8 was not applicable, saying that the concept of 'private life' was not to be stretched indefinitely. According to the judge:

> Not every aspect of private life automatically qualifies for protection under the Convention. The fact that the behaviour concerned takes place on private premises does not suffice to ensure complete immunity and impunity. . . . The protection of private life means the protection of a person's intimacy and dignity, not the protection of his baseness or the promotion of criminal immoralism.[69]

In one sense, this is uncontroversial. Each human right has a recognised scope and application. The right to one's private life (understood as the right to respect for one's intimacy and dignity) is no different. It follows

64 478 US 186 (1986).

65 123 S Ct 2472 (2003), which we discuss at length in ch 9.

66 At 84.

67 At 116.

68 *Laskey, Jaggard and Brown v United Kingdom* (1997) 24 EHRR 39. Art 8(1) of the European Convention on Human Rights provides: 'Everyone has the right to respect for his private and family life, his home and his correspondence.'

69 (1997) 24 EHRR 39, at 61.

that, unless the conduct or interest in question falls within the scope of the right, it does not apply. Reading between the lines of Judge Pettiti's opinion, however, we might sense that human dignity here represents a preferred version of the good life, in opposition to a life of baseness and immoralism, which version is then used to constrain individual autonomy and, at the same time, *diminish the significance of consent.*

Clearly, the limits set on consent are an important clue to the kind of politico-legal order in which we are operating—and, with that, to the underlying political and cultural morality. As Glanville Williams, writing some years ago about 'the extent to which consent is vitiated in such crimes as murder, manslaughter, and assault,' rightly remarks:

> The law on this subject is not altogether clear, and its interpretation depends very much upon the prevailing political philosophy—even though that philosophy may not be made explicit in the judgment.[70]

Broadly speaking, where the cultural background has paternalistic elements, consent will not be a sufficient condition for lawful action if the conduct in question is perceived to be harmful to the actor[71] (or if it is seen as involving a breach of duty to oneself); and, even where the cultural background is free of paternalism, the consent of actors will not suffice if the rights or interests of third parties are at stake or if the conduct in question is seen as threatening the values which are basic to, or constitutive of, that particular community.

### *(vi) The Signalling of Consent*[72]

For every case in which we give our consent explicitly (for instance, by signing a contract or a consent form, by saying 'I do' during a marriage ceremony, and so on), there are cases where our consent is implicit (as, for instance, where we simply select goods and tender cash to the shopkeeper or roll up our sleeve in readiness for an injection).[73] Sometimes, even if we

[70] Glanville Williams, 'Consent and Public Policy' [1962] *Criminal Law Review* 74, at 74.

[71] We might, thus, account for the general principle that a person cannot contract out of protective legislation passed for such a person's (or class of persons') benefit: *Day v Davies* [1938] 2 KB 74. Although the factual situation in *Day v Davies* itself is not concerned with the conditions of employment, legislation designed to secure health and safety at work is an obvious example.

[72] We discuss questions of signalling in ch 7.

[73] Some may wish to draw a threefold distinction between express, implied, and written signalling of consent (see McLean, n 16 above). Or, one might have a fourfold categorisation based on express/implied, written/non-written signalling of consent. For our immediate purposes, nothing hinges on this. However, in ch 7, we distinguish between explicit and implicit signalling in relation to an ideal-typical requirement of distinct and definite signalling, the former (explicit) referring to formal and structured contexts for giving consent, the latter (implicit) to less formal and less structured contexts. Generally, we might associate written consents with more formal (explicit) contexts; but we do not treat the distinction between written and non-written consent as being significant in itself.

do not explicitly agree to the terms of engagement, we will have to take very definite steps that signal our consent by implication—for example, where we freely participate in contact sports (although how far our consent reaches beyond the rules of the game is a moot point). At other times, our consent might be implicit in a course of dealing that we have with another person—for example, one might infer from a prior sequence of explicit consents given by that person that consent would again be forthcoming, or one might infer from prior acquiescence that consent is implicit. At other times, it might be simply understood that, in a certain setting, consent to what would otherwise be plainly wrongful acts is implicit—for example, that one consents to so-called 'horseplay'.[74]

The more seriously that we take free choice and control on the part of individuals, the less comfortable we will be with implicit consent. Contract lawyers have long been suspicious of consent by silence, and inertia selling techniques tend to be specifically regulated. Similarly, proposals to adopt a 'contracting out' (or 'opt out') regime for organ donation are resisted by those who assert that 'contracting in' (or 'opt in') is the only way that we can be confident that organs are being retrieved on a consent basis. Or again, by the twentieth century, it was obvious that the notorious common employment rule (under which each employee was taken to consent to the risk of injury by a fellow employee, thereby negating the employer's liability) was a fiction and it was no longer socially unacceptable. Despite such reservations about implicit consent, English contract law deems parties to consent to terms that are incorporated by notice (on tickets and the like) provided that reasonable steps have been taken to draw attention to these terms and provided that the party who introduces the terms is not aware that the other party is not consenting.[75] Moreover, the English courts have been prepared to hold that, where a man genuinely believes that a woman is consenting to sexual intercourse, this negates the mens rea for rape even if the woman is not consenting and irrespective of the reasonableness of the man's belief that she is consenting.[76]

[74] In the extraordinary case of *Aitken* [1992] 1 WLR 1006, it was apparently practice at mess celebrations in the Royal Air Force to set light to colleagues.

[75] In England, the root authority is *Parker v South Eastern Rly Co* (1877) 2 CPD 416.

[76] In *DPP v Morgan* [1976] AC 182, the question for the House of Lords was whether an honest but unreasonable belief that a woman is consenting to sexual intercourse suffices to negative a charge of rape. In answering that the charge was negatived in such a case, Lord Hailsham, for example, said (at 215):

> [It] is my opinion that the prohibited act is and always has been intercourse without the consent of the victim and the mental element is and always has been the intention to commit that act, or the equivalent intention of having intercourse willy-nilly not caring whether the victim consents or no [sic]. A failure to prove this involves an acquittal because the intent, an essential ingredient, is lacking. It matters not why it is lacking if only it is not there, and in particular it matters not that the intention is lacking only because of a belief not based on reasonable grounds.

Where a person gives their explicit consent, this 'objectively' signals a consent. Does it follow, therefore, that we are not interested in whether they are also 'subjectively' consenting? As we have seen, we need to be satisfied that the apparent consent has been given on a free and informed basis and by one who has the relevant capacity to consent. We will also pause where there is evidence that the party to whom the consent is given is aware that the consent is problematic (particularly where the former has practised some deception on the latter or is aware that the latter is making a mistake). For instance, where on-line sellers obviously mistakenly under-price their goods, their apparent consent might be vitiated by the purchaser's appreciation that a mistake has been made. The difference between this and the rape case (in both of which the apparent consent of one party does not reflect that party's subjective state) is that, in the former, the purchaser is knowingly trying to take advantage of the latter while, in the rape case, because of an honest misreading of the situation, no advantage-taking is intended.

When we turn to implicit consent, do we operate with an objective or a subjective approach? Participation in contact sports is an interesting test case.[77] By participating, players must be taken to consent to a general risk of injury while the sport is being played according to the governing rules. At this level, there is surely no room for a 'subjective' approach. For example, it would not be plausible for a soccer player to argue that he subjectively consented to the risk of leg injury but not to that of arm injury (where the game was being played in accordance with the rules). Moreover, players must also be taken to consent to the risk of injury caused by routine 'foul play'. The question is whether consent has any role beyond this point and, if so, how it is determined. At this stage, one might wish to pursue a subjective approach, allowing each player to testify to his or her personal understanding of where, so far as he or she is concerned, the line is drawn. This would allow for a range of attitudes including and going beyond, so to speak, 'zero-tolerance'. In the well-known Canadian case of *Ciccarelli*,[78] the court tried to set the parameters of consent in a more 'objective' fashion. In the context of a team sport, such as ice hockey, the objective criteria would include the nature of the game (amateur or professional), the nature of the act, the degree of force, the degree of risk of injury, and the state of mind of the accused. Following this lead, the English Law Commission has tended towards objectivism by ruling out consent to intentional injury and by considering whether the injury occurs during actual play, during a break

[77] See the Law Commission's discussion (n 14 above) at paras 10.1–10.23; and Williams, n 70 above, at 80–81.

[78] (1989) 54 CCC (3d) 121, where the defendant was accused of common assault under s 244 of the Criminal Code, which prohibits the intentional application of force 'without the consent of another person'.

in play, or 'off the ball'.[79] Once we think in these terms, however, the nature of the exercise has seemingly changed; for we are now drawing lines (on public policy grounds) beyond which, possible subjective consent notwithstanding, violent play is off-limits (as is the case with regard to, say, duelling and prize-fighting).

### *(vii) The Scope and Interpretation of Consent*[80]

There are several questions to be pursued with regard to the way in which consent, whether explicit or implicit, is to be interpreted. For example, where consent is equivocal or uncertain, do we take a precautionary approach or do we treat the consent as given? Where consent is clearly given for X, how far can we assume that it is also given for Y and Z? And, where consent is clearly given by A, how far can we take it that it is also given for B (for example, where a parent takes a child to watch a sporting event)?[81]

A couple of well-known Canadian cases, again in the context of medical law, point to an important underlying question here. In the first case, *Marshall v Curry*,[82] a surgeon removed a diseased testicle which he discovered during the course of carrying out an operation to repair a hernia. Of course, the patient, being under general anaesthetic at the time, was not offered the opportunity to consent. In the second case, *Murray v McMurchy*,[83] a surgeon carrying out a Caesarean section found fibroid tumours in the patient's uterine wall and, fearing the risks associated with a further pregnancy, tied the woman's Fallopian tubes. Again, this secondary operation was carried out without obtaining the consent of the woman. In the former case, the additional surgery was held to be justified; in the latter case it was not; and, in both cases, in the absence of an explicit consent to this additional surgical treatment, there are a number of possible doctrinal responses. For instance, one might treat the case as an emergency (as seems to have been the view in *Marshall*); or one might treat the surgeon as a proxy for the patient, authorised to give consent on the patient's behalf in such circumstances; or one might stretch the explicit consent to cover (by implication or extension) such an eventuality; or one might argue, hypothetically, that if the patient had been asked to consent then they would (or would not) have done so. Whichever way one plays it doctrinally, however, cases such as these present a tension between the obvious convenience of carrying out the additional surgery and waiting until one has a proper explicit and specific consent.

[79] Law Commission, n 14 above, at paras 10.7–10.18.

[80] We discuss questions of scope and interpretation in ch 7.

[81] See eg *Murray v Haringay Arena Ltd* [1951] 2 KB 529 (raising an issue about the defence of *volenti non fit injuria* in relation to a child spectator at an ice hockey match).

[82] [1933] 3 DLR 260.

[83] [1949] 2 DLR 442 (BCSC).

The lesson to be taken from this is that the more a culture of human rights embeds itself, the more insistent the law will become that, in the absence of countervailing rights or public interest derogations, consent rather than convenience is the key to restricting the benefit of rights.[84] Thus, even though a specific human rights basis for the requirement is not explicitly declared, it is not surprising to find that Article 22 of the Council of Europe's Convention on Human Rights and Biomedicine provides that where, following a medical intervention, 'any part of a human body is removed, it may be stored and used for a purpose other than that for which it was removed, only if this is done in conformity with appropriate information and consent procedures.'

### *(viii) Withdrawal of Consent*

Once given, may consent be withdrawn? What if the consenting party has a change of mind? In a famous law review article, Lon Fuller sketches the hypothetical case of the speluncean explorers (a group whose hobby is to explore caverns, and the like).[85] Trapped underground, the group know that they are likely to perish before the rescue team can reach them. Having considered their options, the members of the group agree that they will throw a dice to decide which one of them will sacrifice himself for the sake of the others. The leader of the group, one Roger Whetmore, having reluctantly consented to this procedure, has a change of mind declaring that he is withdrawing his consent. Although he purports to withdraw before the cast of the dice—which we might think to be a stronger claim than if the dice had been thrown—does Whetmore have the right to do this? In some contexts—for example, breaking off an engagement to be married, or pulling out of a property deal that has been agreed 'subject to contract'—it is understood that consent is revocable; but what would we say about a consent given in the exceptional circumstances in which the hypothetical explorers find themselves? At all levels, this is an extremely difficult case because, even if we decide that Whetmore has no right to withdraw his consent, we still have to determine whether, in such adverse circumstances, his consent is effective and whether we recognise, in any circumstances (let alone those of the cave), consent as a defence to an intentional killing. We need to start with something easier.

[84] In this regard, the case of *R v Department of Health, ex parte Source Informatics Ltd* [1999] 4 All ER 185 (Latham J), [2000] 1 All ER 786 (CA), which we will treat in some detail in ch 8, is of particular interest. For Latham J, the anonymisation of confidential information did not entail that the confidant was now free to transmit the information to a third party without obtaining the consent of the confider. This was perceived to be an inconvenient result and it was reversed by the Court of Appeal.

[85] Lon L Fuller, 'The Case of the Speluncean Explorers' (1948–49) 62 *Harvard Law Review* 616.

Turning from hypothetical to actual withdrawal of consent, and from the exploration of caves to experimentation on humans, the Nuremberg Code (1949), having declared that the free and informed consent of those humans who participate in research experiments is 'absolutely essential', goes on to provide (in paragraph 9) that 'the human subject should be at liberty to bring the experiment to an end.' Nowadays, the settled consensus within the bioethical community is that, at any rate in the context of participation in scientific or medical research as well as in medical diagnosis or treatment, consent may be withdrawn. Accordingly, Article 6(1) of the UNESCO *Universal Declaration on Bioethics and Human Rights*[86], having provided that any 'preventive, diagnostic and therapeutic medical intervention' should be carried out with 'the prior, free and informed consent of the person concerned', then states that such consent 'may be withdrawn by [that person] at any time and for any reason without disadvantage or prejudice'; and Article 6(2) provides in almost identical terms for the withdrawal of consent by participants in scientific research studies or trials[87]. Where consent is withdrawn before the recipient has acted on it, this seems reasonably straightforward as a matter of both principle and practice. However, if the recipient has already acted on the consent—if the surgery is already under way or the research trial has commenced—matters look much less straightforward. What then?

First, a return to the position prior to the consent being given might not be possible. Many surgical procedures, for example, will simply not be reversible. Even if we think that it is right that withdrawal of consent should involve restoration of position, this might not be possible.

Secondly, withdrawal might put the *consenting party* at risk—again, think about withdrawing from a surgical procedure that has already commenced. If we take a paternalistic view, we will not permit consent to be withdrawn when it is manifestly to the prejudice of the consenting (but now withdrawing) party. However, if we respect the autonomy of the consenting party, then even self-harming withdrawals must be permitted.

Thirdly, withdrawal might be prejudicial to the interests of the *recipient* of the consent who has already acted in reliance on the consent (or who, as in the case of an engaged party, has an emotional investment in the relationship). The success of a research project, for example, might be jeopardised if participants withdraw. Or, consider the situation where A, who

[86] The Declaration was adopted by acclamation on 19 October 2005 by the 33rd session of the General Conference of UNESCO.

[87] Whereas Article 6(1) provides for withdrawal 'without disadvantage or prejudice', Article 6(2) provides for withdrawal 'without *any* disadvantage or prejudice' (emphasis added). We take it that the use of 'any' simply underlines that the immunity against disadvantage or prejudice is comprehensive—that is, rather than signalling a material contrast between the immunities provided for by, respectively, Article 6(1) and Article 6(2).

does not have a car, allows B (free of charge)[88] to store his car in A's garage. Relying on A's consent, B stores his car in A's garage and passes over any opportunities to store the car elsewhere. What if A now tells B that the consent is withdrawn and the car must be removed at once? As a matter of principle, is A entitled to do this?

If we take a one-sided view in favour of A, we will say that the consent may be withdrawn at any time and that this is simply tough luck for B; or, conversely, if we take a one-sided view in favour of B, we will say that A has lost whatever right to withdraw he might once have had. Neither view appeals, however, precisely because each is so obviously one-sided. If we are to take account of the legitimate interests of A and the reasonable expectation of B, we need a more complex analysis. We need to return to the terms on which the consent was given by A. Was it understood that A's consent was revocable or irrevocable? If it was understood to be revocable (which, presumably, would be the usual case) was the consent understood to be revocable at will or revocable only for certain reasons (such as A requiring the garage space for a car of his own); and was it understood that A's consent could be withdrawn without notice or only with reasonable notice to B?

In practice, of course, A and B might not have fine-tuned their understanding to the point where these questions have clear answers. Where this is so, and in the event that the parties are unable to settle their differences, their dispute will have to be resolved either by second-guessing their intentions or by relying on a default rule that applies to this kind of case. Where such resolving strategies offer no convincing answer, we are back, alas, with the speluncean explorers; we are in deep difficulty; and, this time, the difficulty is real rather than hypothetical.

### *(ix) Refusal of Consent*

There are many contexts in which consent may be refused. Patients may refuse treatment—we have already mentioned *Re C* in which a 68-year-old man refused to have an amputation—but this is by no means the only kind of case. For instance, local authorities may refuse to issue a planning consent for a development; if Dianne Pretty's husband had assisted with her suicide, the DPP might have refused to consent to a prosecution (which would still have been a matter for his discretion following the court proceedings); a contractor or a landlord might refuse to consent to an assignment or a sub-lease, and so on. In some cases of refusal, particularly licensing decisions and their cognates made by public bodies, a challenge

[88] Even without a charge, this arrangment might be regarded as contractual; but the example in the text does not assume a contractual relationship between A and B. See, further, James Gordley (ed), *The Enforceability of Promises in European Contract Law* (Cambridge, Cambridge University Press, 2001), at 118–50.

based on a reasonableness standard might be appropriate. However, in other cases, especially perhaps refusals of consent in relation to the exercise of rights relating to one's physical integrity and one's property, a reasonableness standard seems to be singularly inappropriate.[89] Indeed, some English judges would say that, where a refusal of this latter type comes from a competent adult, it matters not whether 'the reasons for making the choice are rational, irrational, unknown or even non-existent.'[90]

In principle, in the context of consent operating as a defence, a refusal should seemingly carry as much weight as a consent, a 'no' should mean as much as a 'yes'. Nevertheless, where a court finds a refusal of medical treatment to be unreasonable or irrational, there is a real temptation to intervene (to protect the patient against himself or herself); and the standard way to avoid confessing to paternalism is either to doubt the competence of the patient or to query the conditions for making a free and informed refusal (which, in principle, should be identical to the conditions for a free and informed consent). The first of these strategies is evident in a run of recent English cases involving refusals of treatment (often Caesarean sections) by women in the late stages of pregnancy;[91] and, in cases where Jehovah's Witnesses have refused blood transfusions, courts are prone to finding that the patient's decision was not free (being subject to the undue influence of others) or not fully informed (even where it is the doctors who are withholding the relevant information)[92]—and, in the English case of *Re T*,[93] the court relied on both strategies in order to justify a forced blood transfusion.

Clearly, the interaction between judicial paternalism, however well intentioned, and the recognition of individual rights will cause some friction. In the context of medical law, refusals of treatment set the values of the patient (the patient's judgment of his or her own best interests) against the judgment made by the medical profession of where the patient's best interests lie. Inevitably, as the legal profession takes sides with its medical counterparts, the capacity of patients is reduced and the significance of their consent or refusal is diminished.

[89] See further, Deryck Beyleveld and Roger Brownsword, *Human Dignity in Bioethics and Biolaw* (Oxford, Oxford University Press, 2001), ch 8 (for our 'rule-preclusionary' analysis of property rights).

[90] *Re T (Adult) (Refusal of Medical Treatment)* [1992] 4 All ER 649, at 653 (per Lord Donaldson, MR).

[91] For discussion, focusing in particular on *Re MB (An Adult: Medical Treatment)* [1997] 2 FCR 541, see Sabine Michalowski, 'Court-Authorised Caesarean Sections—The End of a Trend?' (1999) 62 *Modern Law Review* 115.

[92] See *Re L (Medical Treatment: Gillick Competency)* [1998] 2 FLR 810. On which, see Caroline Bridge, 'Religious Beliefs and Teenage Refusal of Medical Treatment' (1999) 62 *Modern Law Review* 585.

[93] [1992] 4 All ER 649.

## III Mapping the Ethics of Consent

It will be apparent from our preliminary survey of the legal landscape that there are a number of ethics competing to control the focal idea of consent. If, as our first sweep suggests, consent is most at home in an ethic that prioritises human rights and individual freedom, then there are potentially tensions *internal* to that ethic as well as *against it* from *external* competing ethics. For example, within a rights ethic, there might be disagreement about the balance between individualism and co-operativism (which might turn on whether both negative and positive rights are recognised) as well as about the freedom to waive the benefit of particular rights (which might hinge on whether the ethic views rights under a will theory or an interest theory). Against the rights ethic, we have an array of rival (external) ethics. Residual paternalistic ethics impinge on individual self-determination (limiting the significance of consent) as do communitarian or moral authoritarian ethics; and a utilitarian ethics will be ready to dispense with consent where it is inconvenient or, conversely, to imply it (or rely on it as a fiction) where it is convenient to do so. Reading what is going on in the law is not always straightforward because these rival ethics sometimes might be employed covertly—in the case of refusal of medical treatment, for instance, lip service might be paid by judges to an ethic of rights and consent while, at the same time, paternalistic protection is achieved by doubting that decisions have been made on a free and informed basis or by disputing the competence of the decision-maker.

While, in any particular case, there might be more than one plausible reading of the way that consent is handled in the law (whether by the legislators who lay down the rules or by the judges who interpret and apply such rules), we can offer some simplifying general guidance with regard to the relationship between consent in the law and background ethical perspectives. For this purpose, we can isolate three kinds of influential ethical approaches: utilitarian; rights-led (under a will theory of rights); and duty-led. In each case, the form of our question is as follows: if we were to take such-and-such an ethical approach (utilitarian, rights-led, or duty-led), how would this tend to shape our thinking about consent?

### *(i) A Utilitarian Approach and Consent*

Utilitarianism, popularised through the Benthamite epithet that we should always strive to maximise the greatest happiness of the greatest number, needs little introduction. Following such an approach, judgments as to the ethical quality of an action are governed by the utilitarian calculus, by the tendency of an action (or rule) to promote utility and/or to minimise disutility. Utilitarians count the consequences of their actions, giving credit for anticipated (or actual) utility (understood as pleasure, happiness, preference satisfaction, welfare, benefit, or the like) and debiting disutility (understood as pain, misery, preference dissatisfaction, distress, cost, inconvenience, and the like). On this view, actions are not intrinsically right or wrong; there are neither 'natural rights' (famously dismissed by Bentham as 'nonsense on stilts') nor rational duties or obligations (as Bentham signalled in his opposition to Kantian deontological ethics).

Given that, for utilitarians, utility and disutility is all that counts, it follows that this approach sees nothing special about consent or the lack of it. For an act utilitarian, the question is whether the reasonably foreseeable consequences of requiring (or obtaining) consent in this instant case are such that it is the option that promises to maximise utility (or minimise disutility). For a rule utilitarian, the question is whether the reasonably foreseeable consequences of prescribing a rule requiring consent in the specified class(es) of case(s) are such that it is a better option than any alternatives in the sense that, provided that the rule is generally followed (or applied), utility should be maximised (or disutility minimised).

In general, utilitarians will not have to look hard to see the negatives in relation to consent collection. Obtaining consent might not always be practicable; where it is, it nevertheless incurs transaction costs; and, on some occasions, it might be downright distressful. Waiting for consents to be cleared might involve opportunity costs. Moreover, policies might be frustrated if, instead of saying 'yes', those who are asked to consent say 'no'. On the other hand, dealing on the basis of consent might ease matters ex ante, it might allay concern and weaken opposition, and it might be a convenient justificatory response ex post. But, of course, for utilitarians, there is no golden rule requiring that the consent of those upon whom an action or decision impacts should be obtained. For example, requiring researchers or doctors to deal on an informed consent basis with research participants or others is not necessarily an improvement on compulsion, ignorance, or paternalism. The calculation always depends on context, convenience, contingency, and circumstance. Having said this, in a culture where preferences strongly favour the currency of consent, even if there is no golden rule requiring consent, utilitarians might well accept the sense of a general rule to this effect.

If utilitarians have no general commitment to (or predisposition towards) requiring consent, does it follow that, where utilitarians are in favour of consent, they have no commitment to any particular specification of what will qualify as an adequate consent? Indeed, it does. Utilitarians will not argue for consent through thick and thin; and, if they do argue for consent, their specification of the conditions of adequacy will be thick or thin as circumstances and consequences dictate. Let us suppose, for example, that utilitarians judge that a particular research project—a modern biobank, bringing together biological samples with medical and lifestyle information, would be a case in point[94]—promises to deliver products that will advance

[94] See, eg, JV McHale, 'Regulating Genetic Databases: Some Legal and Ethical Issues' (2004) 12 *Medical Law Review* 70; and Roger Brownsword, 'Biobank Governance: Business

public welfare. Let us also suppose that utilitarians judge that the recruitment of participants will be problematic unless the process is presented as (and perceived to be) a voluntary one. Given such suppositions, utilitarian logic indicates that no one should be recruited without their consent but that the consent requirement should be specified in a way that is no thicker than necessary for the viability of the project. This might mean, for instance, that the information sheets supplied to participants are somewhat economical with the truth (saying only that the project is for research that is of potential public benefit and not mentioning the possibility of commercial exploitation of the research); that the terms of the consent will be broadly drawn (so that researchers do not need to keep returning to participants to vary and extend their consent); and that any opportunity to withdraw will not be highlighted.

Finally, when we turn to the question of whose consent counts, the utilitarian approach again presents a 'that depends' kind of response. In general, even for utilitarians, the working assumption is that consent will be at its most convincing where it is given by the person who is directly affected by the action at issue. For example, we would expect consent given by those who are participating in a research project (such as the biobank example above) to be more effective in assuaging concerns about the voluntary nature of the exercise than consent given by third parties. Yet, if for some reason this were not the case, utilitarians would have no commitment to securing the consent of the participants themselves rather than some other token consenting party. And, in cases where the party that is directly affected is not able to consent (for example, because the party is still a child or, although an adult, has a child-like mentality), the utilitarian will take a flexible view as to whose consent will serve instead.

On all questions of consent, then, the utilitarian approach is relentlessly consequentialist and sensitive to context. Regardless of whether the question is about the need for consent, about what will count as consent, or about whose consent will count, the utilitarian will say that it depends—and what it depends on in each case is the standard utilitarian computation conducted in the light of local contingencies.

### *(ii) A Rights-led Approach (under a Will Theory of Rights) and Consent*

Against the utilitarians, theorists who argue for a rights-led approach hold that what counts is respect for the interests of each individual rather than promotion of the collective interest (general utility). Notoriously, utilitarians are able to justify acts, practices, rules, and social patterns (a slave-owning society is the extreme example) in which goods and opportunities are distributed very unevenly, and where the interests of some individuals

as Usual?' (paper given at conference on 'Property in Human Tissue' held at the University of Tübingen, 21–22 January 2005).

are neglected for the sake of the larger good. One of the principal objectives of a rights-led approach is to resist just such (unjust) utilitarian initiatives.[95]

Where a rights-led approach reflects a 'will' or 'choice' theory of rights, it is not simply respect for individual interests that is required. Rather, it is respect for the (protected) interests of an individual *so long as this is the will of that individual*. Or, to put this in the language of choice theory, the respect that is required is such as is commensurate with the degree of protection that the rights-holder chooses (within the range of choice that is offered by the set of protected interests). On this approach, the protected interests of an individual are designed to establish the conditions for individuals to act autonomously as authors of their own lives. However, the effect of the will theory is not simply to put individuals in a position where they are able to make their own life-choices in a context that assures the integrity of their person, their property, and their privacy; rather, the distinctive effect of the will theory is that it is individuals who decide whether to say 'yes' or to say 'no' where the proposed actions of others will impinge on their protected interests. Taking individuals seriously, taking rights seriously, means taking consents and refusals seriously.

By analogy, if we think of the way that a telescope extends, section by interconnected section, so it is with rights theory and consent. Unlike the utilitarian approach, the rights-led approach treats consent as an integrated part of its ethical equipment. It follows that, whatever question we are asking about consent, the rights-led approach draws down a response that fits with the basic design of the ethic rather than with the contingencies of the particular setting in which the question arises.

For consent to operate as any kind of justification it must be 'adequate'. In the rights community, it has become a mantra to insist that consent must be free and informed. However, unforced choice and informed choice are just two elements—granted, very important elements—in a larger theory setting the criteria for an adequate consent. Given that consent operates to effect a significant lowering of the rights-holder's shield (by authorising the duty-bearer to act in a way that would otherwise involve a violation of right)[96], rights theorists will be much influenced by the importance of ensuring that the party who appears to be consenting really intends to do just that. This tends towards the adoption of thick conditions of adequacy including, in particular, the requirement of a clear and distinct signal that consent is being given. For example, it would not do for a rights theorist that participants in the biobank research project (outlined above) were taken to have consented by failing to opt out rather than by unequivocally opting in.

[95] See, eg, John Rawls, *A Theory of Justice* (London, Oxford University Press, 1972).

[96] Consent also functions to bring into effect a new relationship that, potentially, will burden the consenting party with additional obligations. However, in order to simplify the discussion at this point, we can pass over this possibility.

Recalling the image of an extending telescope, rights theory extends consent through the choices available to a rights-holder. Treating the rights-holder as the one whose consent counts is not a matter of assuring others that we are not returning to the days of the press-gang; to consent or not is an entitlement that is personal to the rights-holder. Where the rights-holder is not in a position to consent (perhaps being unconscious at the relevant time), the consent of others is not a second best; it is no kind of justifying consent. To consent or not is the personal prerogative of the relevant rights-holder. Where the person affected by the proposed action does not have the capacity to consent, a surrogate consent might have some justifying relevance but not as a consent as such.[97]

Of course, even if there is a degree of constancy in the relationship between a rights-led ethical approach and consent, the details of what we see through the lens of such an ethic will depend to a considerable extent on the substance of the rights recognised by the particular version of rights theory adopted. As the discussion in this book unfolds, it will become clear that, while the form of ethic that we are presupposing is that of a will theory of rights, the particular will theory that we are relying on is Gewirthian.[98] It follows that the substantive rights recognised by this theory inform our particular vantage point. There is more than one reason why we believe that it is appropriate to start from this particular point on the ethical map; however, our reasons for starting where we do must wait until chapter two.

### *(iii) A Duty-led Approach and Consent*

Although modern rights theorists claim to oppose utilitarian thinking in a way that is consistent with the spirit of Kantianism, a strictly Kantian approach is duty-led. In modern bioethics, in particular, the emphasis on duty has given rise to the so-called 'dignitarian alliance',[99] whose fundamental axiom is that human dignity must not be compromised. It is an 'alliance' because there is more than one pathway to this ethic—Kantian and communitarian as well as religious. So, for example, if we were to express the dignitarian perspective in communitarian terms, we would say that human dignity is a good which must not be compromised by our actions or practices and that any action or practice that compromises this good is unethical irrespective of welfare-maximising consequences (against the utilitarians) and regardless of the informed consent of the participants (against the rights-led approach).

For the dignitarians, it is the duty to respect human dignity that is fundamental. Because it takes such a duty-led approach, rights are in effect a

[97] See further ch 4.

[98] See n 13 above.

[99] See Roger Brownsword, 'Bioethics Today, Bioethics Tomorrow: Stem Cell Research and the "Dignitarian Alliance"' (2003) 17 *Notre Dame Journal of Law, Ethics and Public Policy* 15.

reflex of the prior duties; and transactions with rights-holders are governed by the duty side of the relationship not by the rights side. So, for example, if dignitarians hold that there is a duty not to engage in prostitution, because the commodification of the body compromises human dignity, it follows that humans have both a right not to be pressed into prostitution as well as a duty not to engage in the trade. The fact that a person consents to participate in the trade does not release them from the duty. As we have seen already, in the examples of the German *Peep-Show Decision* and the French dwarf-throwing case, consent does not cure the compromising of human dignity. For, whatever the effect of consent in relation to the rights that are held, persons remain duty-bound not to compromise human dignity; and this is something that is simply not negotiable or waivable.

The force of the dignitarian position can be drawn out in another way. When dignitarians complain about a person being 'instrumentalised', or (as it might be expressed in Kantian language) 'used merely as a means', it is sometimes responded that the person has not been so instrumentalised or used because consent was given. From a rights-led perspective, this signals that the (consenting) party is also being treated as an end, and all is well.[100] However, from a dignitarian duty-driven perspective, all is not well. Far from it—if instrumentalisation is involved, this is use as a mere means; where human dignity is compromised, it cannot be squared by consent.

In the light of these remarks, it will be apparent that the giving of consent, the withdrawing of consent, and, indeed, the capacity to consent are simply not focal ideas for dignitarians. The giving or withdrawing of consent (whether by the principal or by a representative) makes no difference to the duty not to compromise human dignity; the duty is not switched off by the obligee's consent or switched on again by the obligee's withdrawal of consent. In the same way, the duties do not vary according to whether the duty-holder is dealing with one who has the capacity to consent or with one who does not. The duties are owed to members of the human species (or, in a communitarian account, to members of the community) and it is the interests of all members that count, not merely those of the consenting community.

## IV The Purpose and Plan of the Book

How should we relate to this plurality of ethical perspectives in and around consent in the law? Our starting point, and the perspective from which we approach our topic of consent in the law, is the moral theory of Alan Gewirth.[101] According to this theory, the supreme principle of morality is the so-called Principle of Generic Consistency (PGC), which provides that

[100] Compare the *Relaxin Opposition* [1995] EPOR 541; on which, see Roger Brownsword, 'The *Relaxin Opposition* Revisited' (2001) 9 *Jahrbuch für Recht und Ethik* 3.

[101] Seminally, see Alan Gewirth, n 13 above.

all prospective purposive agents have a right that other agents respect their generic conditions (the conditions that they must have if they are to have any prospect of successful action, irrespective of their particular purposes). Yet, how is the PGC to be justified? The principal Gewirthian claim is that the logic of rational and reflective agency requires acceptance of the PGC as categorically binding, which is to say that Gewirthian moral theory purports to show the PGC as the supreme principle within moral reason but also as the supreme principle within practical reason generally.

Now, it should be said that Gewirthian thinking runs against the current of much modern philosophical opinion which is inclined towards various degrees of moral relativism or scepticism, coupled with the need to find workable strategies for handling moral pluralism. It also has major implications for the way that we conceive of law. For, if law is an affair of practical reason (in the sense that laws claim to give reasons for action), and if the PGC is the supreme principle of both practical and moral reason, then not only is legal reason conceptually connected to moral reason, it is connected specifically to the PGC. The PGC is, as it were, the supreme constitutive principle of legal order. We have set out and defended this radical view of law elsewhere.[102] However, it is not an issue that we need debate further here. For present purposes, it suffices to understand that we take a Gewirthian approach because we think it offers the most defensible approach within moral and ethical reason; and this is where our key thoughts about consent are located.

Stated shortly, our strategy in this book is to identify the way in which consent functions in Gewirthian moral theory before employing that analysis to describe how consent should operate in a legal regime committed to Gewirthian principles. Because, we contend, consent functions distinctively as a procedural justification,[103] the focus of our analysis tends to be on the nature and effect of a consenting party's authorisation rather than on the details of the substantive rights that flow from the PGC. There is an important sense, then, in which our analysis does not tell the whole story.

We present our analysis and argument in four parts. In Part One, our Gewirthian approach is explained and defended; and the nature of consent as a procedural justification is elaborated relative to that approach. In Part Two, we discuss the prerequisites for a consent to be adequate (or valid and effective). Unless a purported consent is given by the right kind of person (a subject of consent), unless it is given in the right conditions (conditions

[102] See Deryck Beyleveld and Roger Brownsword, *Law as a Moral Judgment* (London, Sweet and Maxwell, 1986; reprinted Sheffield, Sheffield Academic Press, 1994).

[103] A procedural justification contrasts with a substantive justification in the following way. Whereas a substantive justification refers to some set of background standards characterising (in the justificatory argument) particular acts as permitted (including required), a procedural justification refers to an authorising act or decision (namely, the giving of consent). See, further, ch 3.

of unforced and informed choice), unless it is reliably signalled, and unless its terms authorise the act in question, it will not be valid and effective. In Part Three, we consider the necessity and sufficiency of consent as a justificatory reason, highlighting two key fallacies: namely, the Fallacy of Necessity (the belief that, where there is no consent, there must be a wrong, coupled with the belief that consent offers the only justificatory response to a prima facie wrong); and the Fallacy of Sufficiency (the belief that where there is consent to an act there cannot be any justification for regulating against it). Finally, in Part Four, we discuss the extent to which the authority of law (that is, the authority of the scheme of governance which sets the normative context for the operation of consent *in* the law), itself rests on consent. Without doubt, agents[104] may authorise private governance by consent but how well does consent-based authorisation copy across to public governance of the kind associated with modern politico-legal regimes?

In a culture of human rights, we conclude, it is natural for consent to become a powerful and attractive procedural justification; but such is its power and attraction that its integrity is difficult to maintain. On the one hand, procedural justification is appealed to in such inappropriate or attenuated circumstances, that it is a fiction or a fraud to claim that the act in question is authorised by a 'consent'. On the other hand, we can become so fixated with the ethic of consent that we claim too much for its justificatory significance, in particular claiming that, without consent, actions must be wrong while, with consent, actions must be right. Alas, there is no copper-bottomed guarantee against abuse and opportunism, any more than we can immunise ourselves against fallacy or fallibility. However, if we have a clear appreciation of how consent fits in a defensible ethical scheme, if we understand why and when it has justificatory significance, if we have a template against which to check the practices of legal systems, then at least we reduce the level of risk. With these opening thoughts, our inquiry begins with Gewirthian rights theory, the most defensible framework of moral thinking—so we would argue—within which to locate consent.

## *Coda*

In this introductory chapter, the dramatis personae have often appeared simply as 'A' or 'B'. However, as the story of consent unfolds, we will often refer to our characters as 'agents', as 'agent A' or 'agent B', and so on. When we so refer to an 'agent', we do so to indicate that this is a being having the capacity to act freely and to make its own choices with regard to the intended purposes of its actions as well as the means (such as giving consent) to achieve those purposes.[105] Our reasons for using this terminol-

[104] For our use of the term 'agent', see the Coda at the end of this chapter.

[105] In principle, beings with such a capacity might be human or non-human; what matters is whether the being in question has the relevant capacity, not whether it is human.

ogy will become apparent in the next chapter; and we will have occasion to fine-tune this vocabulary of agency in chapter four when we discuss questions concerning the capacity to consent.

The main purpose of this Coda is to alert readers to this usage and, at the same time, to caution against any confusion with the term 'agent' as used in legal discourse, particularly where the law of agency is in play. According to the law of agency, one party (the principal) may authorise another party (the agent) to act on his behalf. Where the agent acts within the terms of his authority (for example, to make a contract on behalf of the principal), the principal is bound by the agent's acts. Now, in our usage, the word 'agent' is not so restricted. 'Agent', as we use the term, is of much broader application, applying to those beings who have the capacity for free and purposive action. In this broader application, we would say that all the characters typically regulated under the law of agency—whether the principal, the agent (in the strictly legal sense) acting on behalf of the principal, or third parties who deal with the agent (in the strictly legal sense)—are agents (in our broad sense). It follows that, where the word 'agent' appears in our discussion, as it frequently will, this cautionary note should be borne in mind. This is not a book about consent, the law of agency, and the special class of agents who populate that sphere; rather, it is about consent, the law in its entire sweep, and the general class of agents who populate the communities that the law aspires to regulate.

Part One

# A GEWIRTHIAN APPROACH TO CONSENT IN THE LAW

# 2

# The Principle of Generic Consistency: Its Justification and Application

## I Introduction

This chapter has three sections. In the first section, we expound Alan Gewirth's 'Principle of Generic Consistency' ('PGC'), which requires all 'agents' to act in accordance with the 'rights' of all agents to the 'generic conditions of agency'. We have chosen to apply the PGC in the chapters that follow because we believe it to be the supreme principle of morality (indeed, the supreme principle of all practical rationality). In the second section, we explain why we consider the PGC to have this status, and we also provide some alternative arguments for the PGC or its contents, which, while they do not render the PGC as the supreme principle of practical rationality, nevertheless have important implications for moral and legal theory and practical rationality generally. In the third and final section, we discuss the general methodology of applying the PGC.

## II The PGC

The PGC grants rights to the generic conditions of agency, so-called 'generic rights', to all agents. Agents are beings that take voluntary steps in pursuit of their freely chosen purposes, which they treat as reasons for their actions.[1] The generic conditions of agency consist of what vulnerable agents[2] need, *irrespective of what their purposes might be*, in order to be able to act at all or in order to be able to act with general chances of success. Needs in the former category are 'basic' generic needs, termed 'basic goods' by Gewirth. Needs in the latter category are divided into non-subtractive and additive generic needs. Whereas lack of or interference with a basic

[1] We use to term 'agent' to cover also those, strictly 'prospective agents', who, while not actually pursuing purposes voluntarily, have the developed capacity to do so. This characterisation of agency is not based on the empirical features of human or any other beings. It is based on the characteristics that any beings that are intelligible subjects of practical precepts (those who issue practical precepts) and objects of practical precepts (those to whom practical precepts are directed) must be supposed to have.

[2] As we have explained in Deryck Beyleveld and Roger Brownsword, *Human Dignity in Bioethics and Biolaw* (Oxford, Oxford University Press, 2001) ch 6, morality only applies to vulnerable agents. Invulnerable agents have no need for rights.

generic need will preclude action altogether (or at least diminish an agent's chances of being able to act at all), lack of a non-subtractive generic need will adversely affect the agent's ability to maintain his/her/its[3] capacity to act, whereas interference with an additive generic good will affect the agent's capacity to increase its capacity to act—in all three cases, *regardless of the purposes involved.*

Gewirth also divides the generic conditions of agency into generic freedom (representing procedural needs) and generic well-being (representing substantive needs). Consequently, there is basic, non-subtractive, and additive generic freedom, and basic, non-subtractive, and additive generic well-being.

The generic conditions of agency (and consequently the generic rights) are hierarchically ordered according to a criterion of needfulness for agency. According to this criterion, if agent A's right to right R1 comes into conflict with agent B's right to R2, then R1 takes precedence over R2 if and only if the effect on A's capacity to act of not having R1 is greater than the effect on B's capacity to act of not having R2. According to this criterion, basic rights override non-subtractive rights, which, in turn, trump additive rights in cases of conflict.[4]

For reasons that will become clear when we present Gewirth's argument, the generic rights granted by the PGC are rights under the 'will' or 'choice' theory or conception of rights. According to this conception, agents may always waive the benefits they are granted by the rights they have (although, when we are dealing with the generic rights, not the rights themselves, because Gewirth's argument for the PGC renders the generic rights inalienable).

The generic rights are essentially claim-rights, which are rights that impose perfect duties on others.[5] This has three important consequences. First, coupled with the fact that the generic rights are rights under the will conception, this implies that there can be no perfect duties to oneself under the PGC. To suppose that there might be such duties incurs the contradiction that the rights-holder (say, oneself) may both release and not release the correlative duty-bearer (oneself) from the duties imposed on it by the PGC.[6]

[3] Because there is no reason to assume *a priori* that agents *must* be human or even gendered beings, we will henceforth use the impersonal, non-gendered pronoun.

[4] As the generic conditions of agency figure in Gewirth's argument for the PGC, they are essentially abstract categories. We comment on the material conditions that instantiate them under our presentation of the methodology of application of the PGC below.

[5] Perfect duties are duties that are only discharged if the outcomes they demand are fully achieved.

[6] While Gewirth (see *Reason and Morality* (Chicago, University of Chicago Press, 1978) at 334) appreciates the problem, he considers that there are various ways in which agents can have perfect duties to themselves. We discuss and reject these in Deryck Beyleveld and Roger Brownsword, *Human Dignity in Bioethics and Biolaw* (Oxford, Oxford University Press, 2001) at 106–8.

Secondly, the PGC cannot generate any imperfect duties[7] that there is no perfect duty to try to achieve the object of. Thirdly, putting these two ideas together, the PGC cannot generate any imperfect duties to oneself or to others that do not derive, directly or indirectly, from perfect duties to others.

The generic rights are also, in principle, positive as well as negative. That the rights are positive means that agents have rights to be assisted (by those able to do so without comparable cost to themselves) to secure/protect their having the generic conditions of agency when they are unable to do so by their own unaided efforts. That they are negative means that agents have rights to non-interference by other agents with their having the generic conditions of agency. That the generic rights are rights under the will conception, however, means that duties imposed on other agents by the positive rights are subject to the rights-holder wishing assistance, while duties imposed by negative rights are subject to interference being against the rights-holder's will.

## III Why Employ the PGC?

### *(i) The Dialectically Necessary Argument*

According to Gewirth, agents must accept and act in accordance with the PGC on pain of contradicting that they are agents. In consequence, the PGC is, as Gewirth expresses it, 'dialectically necessary' for all agents: any and every agent must accept it because it follows with necessity (purely logically or conceptually) from a premise that no agent can coherently deny, namely that it is an agent. Gewirth's reasoning may be presented as follows.[8]

If an agent has a goal (E) that it is motivated to pursue, and it is necessary for the agent to have something (X) in order to achieve E, then E gives the agent a reason to pursue X. If there are generic conditions of agency, then the agent categorically (that is, simply by virtue of being an agent) has an instrumental reason (a reason conditioned by being a means to an end) to pursue/defend having the generic conditions *whatever E might be.* In short, for an agent to have the generic conditions is categorically in the agent's interests *as an agent*, and it follows that agents, *within the context of their agency,* must recognise that they categorically ought to pursue/defend having the generic conditions or contradict that they are agents.

[7] Imperfect duties are ones directed at outcomes that cannot be guaranteed by action directed to achieve them.

[8] No attempt is made here to provide a full analysis or defence of the argument. This has been done in Deryck Beyleveld, *The Dialectical Necessity of Morality: An Analysis and Defense of Alan Gewirth's Argument to the Principle of Generic Consistency.* (Chicago, University of Chicago Press, 1991). For a shorter presentation that takes account of some later objections, see Deryck Beyleveld and Roger Brownsword, *Human Dignity in Bioethics and Biolaw* (Oxford, Oxford University Press, 2001) ch 4.

It is equally clear that, because it is categorically in the agent's interests as an agent to have the generic conditions, it is categorically in its interests as an agent that others not interfere with its having the generic conditions and, indeed, that others assist it to secure or defend having them when it is unable to do so by itself. Thus, any agent must (on pain of contradicting that it is an agent) consider that others categorically ought not to interfere with its having the generic conditions *against its will* (and, indeed, that others who can categorically ought to assist it to secure the generic conditions when this assistance is needed *and wished for*).[9] These other-referring ought-judgements must be upheld by the agent simply because this non-interference or assistance is required to satisfy the criterion of the agent's interests as an agent to which *it* is necessarily committed by being an agent. Since the argument is trying to justify a moral principle *to the agent* rather than *to the others*, it is wholly irrelevant whether or not these other-referring ought-judgements are accepted by those to whom they are addressed.

To uphold these other-referring ought-judgements is, however, to say that the agent has both negative and positive rights to the generic conditions under the will conception of rights. Thus, all agents must (as agents) consider that they themselves have both positive and negative rights (under the will conception) to the generic conditions.

But why must agents consider that other agents have these generic rights? The answer is not that other agents have as good a justification for asserting their rights as I (any particular agent) have for asserting my rights, and this is because their justification is *their* agency interests (their need for the generic conditions of agency), whereas my justification is *my* agency interests (my need for the generic conditions of agency), and the argument has not yet shown (as it must eventually) that agents must (on pain of contradicting that they are agents) guide their own actions by the interests of others in addition to their own. However, it is also not true, as some critics have alleged,[10] that it does not follow purely logically (but requires the impermissible, and, indeed, false, assumption that agents necessarily take favourable account of each others' interests) that agents who contradict that they are agents by not considering that they have the generic rights also contradict that they are agents if they do not consider that all other agents have the generic rights. This is because, if I contradict that I am an agent by not considering that I have the generic rights then I must (in order to

[9] It is because the agent must value the generic needs only instrumentally (albeit categorically so) that the agent cannot be prohibited categorically from waiving the benefits that exercise of the rights would confer. The objects of the rights are claimed for the possibility of action and successful action. As such, the value that an agent must attach to them is relative to the agent's will to achieve its purposes. The argument does not rest on the premise (hidden or otherwise) that agents must value their agency as such. Such a premise is an evaluation that would require independent justification that cannot be secured by the mere claim to be an agent.

[10] Most notably, Richard B Brandt, 'The Future of Ethics' (1981) 15 *Nous* 31–40, at 39–40.

avoid contradicting that I am an agent) accept that I cannot uphold any position that implies that I can be an agent but not have the generic rights. However, it follows from this, purely logically, that I must not merely hold that I have the generic rights; I must also hold that I have the generic rights for the self-sufficient reason that I am an agent.[11] But it follows purely logically from 'the fact that I am an agent is by itself sufficient for me to have the generic rights' that 'the fact that X is an agent is by itself sufficient for X to have the generic rights.' Consequently, I contradict that I am an agent if I do not consider that all agents have the generic rights. Since the reasoning I must accept in relation to myself all other agents must accept in relation to themselves, it follows that all agents contradict that they are agents if they do not accept that all agents have the generic rights, which is to say that the PGC is dialectically necessary.

### *(ii) An Alternative Presentation of this Argument*

This argument may also be presented as a *reductio ad absurdum*[12] of an agent's espousal of criteria for determining the permissibility of its actions that are incompatible with the PGC,[13] which one commentator has designated the 'indirect' (as against the 'direct') version of the argument for the PGC.[14]

Agents have their own personal viewpoints about what it is permissible for them to do, and these are characteristically based on various beliefs, both normative and non-normative. These beliefs of an agent might be said to constitute the agent's subjective viewpoint on practical reasonableness (SPR).

Gewirth's dialectically necessary method operates with the premise that an agent rationally may not espouse or act upon any normative principle, and consequently may not have any SPR, that involves it contradicting that it is an agent. Conversely, agents are rationally required to accept and act upon any normative principle or SPR that they are required to espouse so as not to contradict that they are agents. Consequently, each stage of the direct argument places restrictions on the normative principles/SPRs that agents rationally may adopt.

[11] See Gewirth's 'Argument from the Sufficiency of Agency' (ASA) in *Reason and Morality* (Chicago: University of Chicago Press, 1978) at 109–10. See also, Deryck Beyleveld and Roger Brownsword, *Human Dignity in Bioethics and Biolaw* (Oxford: Oxford University Press, 2001) at 75.

[12] In a *reductio ad absurdum*, a conclusion is proved by showing either that its denial contradicts a proposition that has already been established or which is, otherwise, not open to question, or, conversely, a proposition is disproved by showing that its affirmation contradicts a proposition that must be accepted.

[13] This is done fully in Deryck Beyleveld, *The Dialectical Necessity of Morality: An Analysis and Defense of Alan Gewirth's Argument to the Principle of Generic Consistency*. (Chicago: University of Chicago Press, 1991) at 47–56.

[14] See Michael Boylan, *Basic Ethics* (Upper Saddle River, NJ, Prentice-Hall, 2000) at 199.

Thus, as the direct argument proceeds, any agent's SPR is, progressively, required to be consistent, first, with the principle that the agent has a self-referring instrumental duty to pursue/defend its having the generic conditions of agency; then with the principle that other agents have duties not to interfere with the agent's having the generic conditions of agency against its will, etc; hence with the principle that the agent has both negative and positive rights to the generic conditions of agency; and, finally, with the principle that all agents have both negative and positive rights to the generic conditions of agency.

### *(iii) Deriving Acceptance of the PGC from the Acceptance of Morality*

Gewirth relies entirely on the dialectically necessary argument for the PGC. The reason why he does so is that, like Kant before him,[15] he correctly appreciates that a moral principle can only be established *as* categorically binding by showing that it is connected entirely *a priori* with the concept of being an agent (with the consequence that conformity with the principle is revealed as a necessary condition of all rational action).

It is possible, however, to construct dialectically *contingent* arguments for the PGC, which are contingent in that (unless the dialectically necessary argument is sound) their premises can be denied by agents without self-contradiction. While such arguments, if sound, should have compelling force for those who accept the premises, they cannot establish the PGC as categorically binding, simply because, *ex hypothesi*, the conclusion of the argument can be evaded by giving up the premises that compel it without any categorical irrationality. Nevertheless, because the premises in question are widely accepted, these arguments are worth presenting, bearing in mind that almost all arguments for competing moral principles are presented on the basis of contingencies of this kind.

One such argument may be directed at agents who accept the idea that there are morally binding requirements on action, defined as categorically binding *impartial* ones (that is, categorically binding requirements that require the agents to take equal account of the interests of all agents in determining what they themselves may do).[16]

By virtue of accepting that there are categorically binding requirements on action, I (any agent) must accept that there are requirements that are binding on my actions simply because I am an agent, which entails that I must accept that there are ends that I ought to pursue or contradict that I am an agent (or as Kant would have said, I must accept that pure reason is practical). However, because there are generic needs, it follows that I must

[15] Immanuel Kant, *Groundwork of the Metaphysic of Morals* (originally published in 1785), trs with an Introduction by HJ Paton as *The Moral Law* (London, Hutchinson, 1948) at 89.

[16] See Deryck Beyleveld and Roger Brownsword, *Human Dignity in Bioethics and Biolaw* (Oxford, Oxford University Press, 2001) at 91–92, for a fuller version of this argument

accept, regardless of what ends I might think are categorically binding on me, that I ought to possess the generic needs as means to my pursuit of these ends. Similarly, other agents must consider that they ought to possess the generic needs as means to their pursuit of any ends that they might consider to be categorically binding. In this sense, I must accept that it is in the interests of all agents for them to possess the generic needs. From this it follows, given my commitment to the idea that I must take impartial account of the interests of all agents, that I must accept that all agents ought to have the generic needs as means to whatever they consider to be categorically binding ends. But this is equivalent to my having to accept that all agents have claim-rights to the generic needs under the will conception of rights (which means that I must accept the PGC).

This argument is very much facilitated by, and is relative to, my acceptance of the requirement of impartiality, on which we have more to say below. However, it can also be demonstrated that anyone who accepts that there are categorically binding requirements on action must accept the PGC on pain of contradicting this acceptance, even when this acceptance does not at the outset include acceptance of the requirement of impartiality.[17]

As we have just seen, the acceptance that there are categorically binding requirements on action requires me to consider that I ought to pursue my having the generic needs as means to whatever ends I consider to be categorically binding on me. However, because the idea that an agent is categorically bound to do X is the idea that it is simply by virtue of being an agent that the agent is bound to do X, I must, on pain of *contradicting the claim that there are categorically binding requirements on my action,* hold that I contradict that I am an agent if I do not hold that I ought to pursue my having the generic needs as means to whatever I claim to be ends categorically binding on me, whatever these might be. However, as we saw in the dialectically necessary argument for the PGC, it follows *purely logically* from the proposition that I deny that I am an agent if I do not consider that I have the generic rights that I deny that I am an agent if I do not consider that the self-sufficient reason why I have the generic rights is that I am an agent. Since this inference is purely logical, it must follow *purely logically* from the premise that I deny that I am an agent if I deny that I have Q (where Q is any property), that I deny that I am an agent if I deny that the self-sufficient reason why I have Q is that I am an agent. Consequently, I must, on pain of contradicting my acceptance of categorically binding requirements on my actions, consider that I deny that I am an agent if I do not consider that my being an agent is the self-sufficient reason why I categorically ought to possess the generic needs as means to my pursuit of whatever ends I claim to be categorically binding on me. But, from this, it follows purely logically that I must (on pain of contradicting my acceptance

[17] *Ibid.*

of categorically binding requirements on my actions) consider that all other agents categorically ought to possess the generic needs as means to their pursuit of whatever they consider to be categorically binding on their actions (hence that all other agents have the generic rights under the will conception of rights).

### *(iv) The Dialectically Contingent Argument from the Acceptance of Human Rights*

Human rights are increasingly becoming central to legal thinking throughout the world. Conceived as fundamental, indeed, as overriding, categories, what they require has a regulatory impact on all law. For this reason, any argument that links acceptance of the PGC to acceptance of human rights has special significance in a book that wishes to apply the PGC to legal doctrines. For, to the extent that this link can be forged, the PGC is revealed as an internal standard that laws must meet even if the dialectically necessary argument for the PGC is not sound.

Suppose then that I (any agent) claim that I have a right to do X. It is clear that I must also claim a right to the necessary means to do X, and hence to the generic conditions of agency *whatever X might be.* Consequently, anyone who recognises that there are human rights to do anything at all must recognise that there are human rights to the generic conditions of agency. Thus, it is clear that human rights (to do things) must be structured in line with the generic conditions of agency.

This, however, does not, by itself, entail that it is necessary for any legal system that recognises any human rights to hold that these rights must be interpreted in accordance with the PGC *as such*, and that the PGC is the supreme principle of all legal reasoning. For this to be the case, human rights must be thought of as having a number of features. First, human rights must be thought of as overriding all competing considerations in the case of conflict. Secondly, being human must be regarded, at least centrally, as being an agent. Thirdly, human rights must be held to be rights under the will conception. Fourthly, human rights must impose duties not only on the State and its arms, but on all individuals who are capable of acting so as to affect rights-holders' abilities to enjoy the benefits of their human rights. Finally, human rights must be considered (where agents are capable of obeying the correlative duties) to be positive as well as negative.

First, as regards the fundamental nature of human rights, the concept of a human right contained in modern human rights instruments is of a right held for the sufficient reason that one is 'human'. As Scott Davidson says, the modern human rights instruments have their roots in the American Declaration of Independence of 1776, and in the French Declaration of the Rights of Man and the Citizen of 1789, and it is a central feature of human rights instruments with this pedigree that human rights are conceived of as:

> by nature inherent, universal and inalienable: they belong to individuals simply because they are human beings and not because they are the subjects of a state's law.[18]

This is apparent, for example, from Article 14 of the European Convention on Human Rights, according to which,

> [t]he enjoyment of the rights and freedoms set forth in this Convention shall be secured without discrimination on any ground such as sex, race, colour, language, religion, political or other opinion, national or social origin, association with a national minority, property, birth or other status.

Secondly, as regards the concept of 'being human', the claim that being human is conceived by the human rights instruments, at least centrally, as being an agent, is plausible. Basically these instruments, at least initially, were based on ideas of liberty, equality, *and fraternity*. They were conceived as civil and political rights, and later as social, economic, and cultural rights, concerned with the rights of *citizens* within a democratic order. Consequently, those who were thought of as having rights were also thought of as having reciprocal duties to rights-bearers. Insofar as this is so, rights-bearers must be held to be agents, for only agents can have duties.

Certainly, insofar as very young children, fetuses, the dead, and members of the human biological species that are apparently not agents are granted rights under the human rights instruments, this claim is open to challenge. However, it is fairly clear that most of the rights in the human rights instruments are inapplicable to any but agents, that the extension of human rights to these special groups is controversial and a fairly recent event,[19] and that the fetus is granted only a 'proportional' status by the human rights instruments if they grant it any status at all.[20] In any event, as we will explain in the next section, when we discuss how agency is to be judged in practice, it is possible for 'special' groups to fall under the protection of the human rights instruments without actually being granted rights in the central sense that the instruments employ. Consequently, we suggest that it is altogether more plausible to regard the status granted to the special groups by the human rights instruments as, in some way, derivative from or secondary to the status of agents to whom the protections of the human rights instruments centrally apply.

Thirdly, whether or not the human rights instruments operate with the will conception of rights is central to the role that consent actually plays in

[18] Scott Davidson, *Human Rights* (Buckingham, Open University Press, 1993) 5.

[19] For example, the Convention on the Rights of the Child, which grants children some independent rights (which was adopted by the General Assembly of the United Nations on 20 November 1989) and the Convention on Human Rights and Biomedicine of the Council of Europe of 1997, which grants protections to human embryos and others unable to give consent.

[20] Otherwise they would have to prohibit abortion, which they do not do.

the law. For this reason it is a question that will receive detailed attention when we come to apply the PGC. Here, we will confine ourselves to some schematic remarks.

The fact that the human rights instruments do not outlaw boxing, mountain climbing, and other dangerous activities, and do not require persons to vote, etc, suggests that the will conception (which is applicable only to agents) is to be applied to at least some of the rights. But, against the idea that the will conception is to be applied universally, it is to be pointed out that, for example, the European Court of Human Rights has, on occasion, ruled that consent to harm does not necessarily absolve a person from wrongdoing.[21] However, this is by no means conclusive, as there can be good reasons grounded in protection of the rights *of others* why persons should not be permitted, in particular circumstances at least, to waive the benefits of their rights. Furthermore, from a conceptual point of view, it must be borne in mind that the will and interest conceptions of rights are conceptions of rights as such. They cannot be applied to some rights and not to others. Thus, if it is clear that, in the main, human rights are considered to confer waivable benefits, then when agents are denied the right to waive these benefits, or 'rights' are apparently conferred on what seem to be non-agents, then coherence of approach requires that such 'exceptions' not be regarded as cases in which the interest conception applies, but as special cases where rights of other agents under the will conception require the waiver-rights of the agents in question to be overridden, or duties to or in relation to[22] apparent non-agents to be recognised.[23]

Fourthly, regarding the idea that human rights are held against individuals ('apply horizontally') as well as against States ('apply vertically'), that this is so is clear, at least in the European Convention on Human Rights, from Articles 8(2), 9(2), 10(2), and 11(2) of the Convention, which provide that the rights or freedoms of Articles 8(1), 9(1), 10(1), and 11(1) are subject to limitation or restriction for (inter alia) the protection of the rights or freedoms of others.[24] Furthermore, this entails that *all* the rights of the Convention are horizontally applicable. The reason why this is so is that confinement of such clauses to Articles 8–11 does not mean that only the

[21] *Laskey, Jaggard and Brown v United Kingdom* (1997) 24 EHRR 39.

[22] Any duty not to harm or to protect X is a duty *in relation to* X. A duty *to* X is a duty owed solely by virtue of properties possessed by X. Thus, the category of duties in relation to X includes duties that the properties of X are not sufficient to generate. Such duties will characteristically be duties owed as a result of the need to protect the rights of others (or duties to others) than X.

[23] For a discussion of some kinds of mere duties in relation to non-agents/apparent non-agents, see Deryck Beyleveld, 'The Moral Status of the Human Embryo and Fetus', in Hille Haker and Deryck Beyleveld (eds), *The Ethics of Genetics in Human Procreation* (Aldershot, Ashgate, 2000) 59–85, at 62–64 and 75–77.

[24] This interpretation is confirmed explicitly in relation to Art 10 by the Strasbourg Court in *Groppera Radio AG and Others v Switzerland* (1990) 12 EHRR 321, at 342, para 70.

provisions of Articles 8–11 apply horizontally. This is because the rights and freedoms that apply horizontally (set limits) in the exception clauses are those of the Convention that are capable of conflicting with the paragraph (1) right in question. So, for example, in Article 8(2), the rights and freedoms that limit B's Article 8(1) right to respect for family and private life are any of A's rights and freedoms (namely, A's rights under Articles 2, 3, 4, 5, 6, 7, etc—including A's right under Article 8(1)) that are capable of conflicting with B's Article 8(1) right. The fact that Articles 2, 3, 4, 5, 6, 7, etc, do not have limitation clauses comparable to Articles 8(2) to 11(2) signifies only that the former Articles have (to varying degrees) more limited restrictions than the latter.

The fact that international human rights enforcement agencies, such as the European Court of Human Rights, generally (indeed, characteristically), have no authority to enforce human rights directly against individuals, should not be allowed to obscure this. That this is so is purely a function of the fact that human rights instruments are international treaties, and bodies like the European Court of Human Rights are international courts. Horizontal effectiveness must be distinguished from horizontal applicability.[25]

Finally, are human rights, like the generic rights, positive as well as negative? Certainly, it is clear from, for example, the jurisprudence of the European Court of Human Rights, that States not only have duties not to interfere with the rights of their subjects but also have duties to protect individuals from actions of other individuals that might interfere with their enjoyment of their rights. But, even if, as we have just claimed, human rights are held against individuals as well as the State, it is another matter to suggest that individuals have positive duties in relation to human rights. However, according to the Preamble of the Universal Declaration on Human Rights 1948, that instrument (upon which all the other modern human rights instruments are based) is

> a common standard for all peoples and nations, to the end that every individual and every organ of society . . . shall strive . . . to promote respect for these rights and freedoms and . . . to secure their universal and effective recognition and observance. . . . among the peoples of the Member States themselves

and Article 1 of the Declaration asserts:

> All human beings are born free and equal in dignity and rights. They are endowed with reason and conscience and *should act towards one another* in a spirit of brotherhood.[26]

[25] Deryck Beyleveld and Shaun Pattinson, 'Horizontal Applicability and Horizontal Effect' (2002) 118 *Law Quarterly Review* 623–46.

[26] Our emphasis. This Article and the Preamble also provide further support for the claim that human rights apply horizontally. In addition, the Article, by attributing reason and conscience to all human beings, implies that being human is to be thought of, at least centrally, as being an agent.

All in all, then, we suggest that the human rights instruments do operate centrally with a conception of human rights that entails that the PGC is, implicitly, the supreme principle of human rights instruments.[27]

If we are wrong about this, then this will not affect our ability to criticise the law from the perspective of the PGC. The consequence will be that such a critique will have to be viewed as external to the human rights instruments themselves rather than as fully internal to them. In addition, the implication would be, on the basis of the dialectically necessary argument (and to the extent that human rights are viewed as fundamental, on the basis of either of the dialectically contingent arguments from the acceptance of morality that we have outlined) that the human rights instruments are defective to the extent that they depart from the PGC.

### *(v) The Dialectically Contingent Argument from Impartial Rationality*

Some moral philosophers[28] treat practical rationality as impartial, holding that it requires agents not to preference their own interests over those of others. When they try to justify particular moral principles, their project, therefore, is not one that tries to establish morally binding requirements from morally neutral premises; instead, it tries to derive morally binding requirements as constraints on action that agents who are rational (in a morally neutral way) must accept if they are to constrain their actions by the impartiality that is often taken to characterise morality as such.

Since the step in Gewirth's argument from an agent having to accept that it has the generic rights (or contradict that it is an agent) to the conclusion that it must accept that other agents have the generic rights (or contradict that it is an agent) is probably the most difficult hurdle for the majority of those who do not accept Gewirth's argument, it is worth pointing out that anyone who accepts that it is dialectically necessary for agents to consider that they themselves have the generic rights must accept the PGC as such (that is, as a principle of positive as well as negative rights under the will conception) *if* they operate with the idea that practical rationality is impartial.

While such a starting point sidesteps what Gewirth takes to be the most important task for moral epistemology, to establish the rationality (circumscribed in a morally neutral way) of reasonableness (circumscribed by impartiality),[29] it is a starting point that many regard as unproblematic.[30]

[27] See Deryck Beyleveld and Roger Brownsword, *Human Dignity in Bioethics and Biolaw* (Oxford, Oxford University Press, 2001) at 79–86, for further reflections on the PGC and human rights.

[28] For example RM Hare, *Moral Thinking: Its Levels, Method and Point* (Oxford, Clarendon Press, 1981), especially chs 5–6.

[29] Alan Gewirth, 'The Rationality of Reasonableness' (1983) 57 *Synthese* 225–47.

[30] Neil MacCormick, 'Gewirth's Fallacy' (1984) 9/2 *Queen's Law Journal* 351 goes so far as to claim that the burden of proof does not lie with those who claim that agents must take favourable account of the interests of others but with those who claim that they only have reason to take account of the interests of others if this is in their own interests.

In similar vein, it should be pointed out that those who accept that it is dialectically necessary for agents to pursue and defend their possession of the generic conditions of agency, and only contest the argument thereafter, must accept that Gewirth has uncovered what, in Kantian terms, might be described as what rational agents must will if they will anything at all, and any *moral* theory they espouse must be consistent with the generic conditions of agency being things that all agents must regard as categorically instrumentally good.

Thus, all in all, it should be appreciated that even if, contrary to our conviction, the full argument to the PGC has flaws, there are nonetheless powerful reasons to espouse the PGC as such, or in modified form, and also powerful reasons for accepting what are interim conclusions in the full argument that have important implications for rationally acceptable moral beliefs.

## IV Applying the PGC

### *(i) Empirical Specification of the Generic Conditions*

To apply the PGC, flesh must be given to the generic conditions of agency. The arguments we have presented for the PGC treat the generic conditions of agency as abstract categories. They are simply whatever is/might be necessary for action as such or successful action in general, structured according to the criterion of needfulness for action. Gewirth is a bit more expansive. Thus, for example, he specifies that the basic generic conditions comprise

> the proximate necessary preconditions of the performance of any and all of [an agent's] actions [, namely] certain physical and psychological dispositions ranging from life and physical integrity (including such of their means as food, clothing, and shelter) to mental equilibrium and a feeling of confidence as to the general possibility of attaining one's goals.[31]

Gewirth gives as an example of non-subtractive generic conditions the possession of accurate information about the context of one's actions, and increased knowledge about this context is an additive generic condition.

There is danger in this. To be sure, there is no problem with identifying, for example, life, mental equilibrium, and a feeling of confidence as to the general possibility of attaining one's goals as basic generic conditions. However, to consider physical integrity to be a (basic) generic condition of agency presupposes that agents are necessarily physical beings when there is nothing in the concept of an agent that justifies this. Physical integrity is only a generic condition of agency for embodied agents (such as human

[31] Alan Gewirth, *Reason and Morality* (Chicago, University of Chicago Press, 1978) at 53–54.

agents are), and there is nothing in the concept of an agent that entails that agents must be embodied. Furthermore, while food, clothing, and shelter are generic conditions for human agents, is it necessarily true that these are generic conditions for all possible physical agents? For example, even if it is true that all physical agents necessarily need to replenish their sources of energy (food), what will constitute food for them might vary considerably, so that what is food for one species might be a deadly poison for another.

The lesson here is that what materially instantiates the generic conditions is, to an extent, an empirical matter, being contingent upon the species of the agent. Thus, for example, while life is clearly (and purely conceptually) a basic generic condition of agency, having air to breathe is only a basic generic condition of agency for agents who need air to live. For this reason, the content of the PGC itself is the structure of the abstract categories of the generic conditions of agency, and the question of what material things actually constitute generic conditions of agency must be dealt with as empirical matters when applying the PGC rather than as contents to be specified in arguments for the PGC. This is particularly important in connection with Gewirth's claim that no agent can deny the PGC without contradicting that it is an agent, because there is no case for saying that an agent would contradict that it is an agent by not considering that it categorically instrumentally ought to pursue and defend conditions that would not be required for its purpose pursuit/achievement if it were a different species of agent.

Recognition of this also has implications for how the PGC is to be applied. Thus, suppose that there are methane breathing agents on Neptune for whom air is poisonous, as methane is poisonous to human agents. If the dialectically necessary argument to the PGC is run in the minds of human agents on the basis that air is a basic generic condition of agency, the implication would be that the PGC does not grant a generic right to breathe methane to the Neptunian agents, but only a generic right to breathe air, which would kill them. Conversely, the argument to the PGC would be run in the minds of Neptunian agents so that methane is a basic generic condition of agency, with the implication that Neptunians would not have to recognise that human agents have a generic right to breathe air, only a generic right to breathe methane. In truth, however, the PGC grants agents generic rights to life and to the necessary means to this, which for Neptunians includes methane to breathe and for human agents includes air to breathe. Thus, under the PGC, human agents must recognise a generic right of Neptunian agents to breathe methane while Neptunian agents must recognise a generic right of human agents to breathe air.

### *(ii) Judging Agency (Precaution under a Categorical Imperative)*

Perhaps the most basic issue when applying the PGC is that of how agents are to be identified in practice. This is a more complex matter than it might at first appear to be. I (any agent) only know directly that I myself am an agent, because being an agent is, in part, but still essentially, a matter of having particular mental capacities. The attribution of agency to anything else is an inference from the observable behaviour of this other being. But, unless we hold that, for example, to be in pain is simply to exhibit certain behaviour (whether or not anything is experienced), or that a being (which might be a programmed automaton without any self-awareness) reasons simply because it can calculate solutions to mathematical problems and the like), there is no guarantee that the behaviour reflects relevant mental capacities; for it is surely only if beings have particular mental capacities in the sense of an inner subjectivity or phenomenological awareness that they can be a matter of concern to themselves in a way the argument to the PGC supposes.

It is, therefore, possible for me to accept the dialectically necessary argument for the PGC (or indeed any of the other arguments), but then claim that there are no agents other than myself. To this, there are a number of reasonable responses. First, such a position is virtually impossible to sustain in practice. To sustain it, I must refrain from prescribing anything to any other being. I cannot impose duties on others, or think that there are any beings against whom I can claim the generic rights that I must claim for myself. Indeed, I cannot engage in any discourse of reasons with any being other than myself.

Secondly, while it might not be dialectically necessary for me to consider that there are any agents other than myself, it would certainly be irrational for me to deny that there are any agents other than myself on the criteria that govern everyday life. Recourse to solipsism is a high price to pay to be able to deny that the PGC has *any* force in its practical application.

Thirdly, the lack of a dialectically necessary application of the PGC would not place the PGC at any disadvantage compared with any other practical principle or moral theory, simply because the denial that there are any other agents will affect any scheme of practical prescriptions equally.

However, none of these responses is good enough to counter the central thrust of this scepticism, which is to suggest that arguments to the effect that I am categorically required to grant the generic rights to all other agents (even if successful) do not show that I am categorically required to grant the generic rights to any creatures other than myself.

Nevertheless, this scepticism is not sustainable. On the assumption that I am categorically bound by the PGC, I categorically must assume that beings that behave as though they are agents are in fact agents. This is simply because if I assume that a being is not an agent when it is an agent then I deny an agent the protection of the PGC, which I categorically may not do. On the other hand, if I assume that a being is an agent when it is not an agent then I do not thereby deprive any agent of the protection of the PGC. Thus, precaution must be exercised to the effect that beings that might possibly be agents must be treated as agents to the extent that it is possible to do so. Where a being behaves like an agent (is, as we will say, 'ostensibly an agent' or 'an ostensible agent'[32]) then the being can be treated fully as an agent, and hence must (under precaution) be assumed to be an agent and treated fully as such.

This argument, which is an application of Pascal's Wager[33] under the constraints of a categorical imperative, amounts to a moral argument for other minds. It also has implications for how agents may treat beings that might *possibly* be agents but which do not behave as though they are agents. Such beings incur the protection of the PGC in proportion to the degree to which they approach being ostensible agents. However, contrary to what Gewirth has maintained, to say this is not to say that they have the generic rights in proportion to the degree to which they approach being agents.[34] The PGC itself grants the generic rights to agents alone, because the generic rights are rights under the will conception and only agents can waive the benefits of their rights. Thus, while agents incur duties to these beings in proportion to the extent to which these beings can be treated as agents, these duties are not based on the assumption that these beings have any generic rights but to guard for the possibility that they might be agents who cannot be treated fully as such.

The basic effect of precautionary reasoning under a categorical imperative is to shift the burden of proof in relation to possession of what the categorical imperative protects. So, under the PGC, it is not necessary to show that a being is an agent in order to have the protection of the PGC. It is necessary to show that it is not an agent (or, for practical purposes, that it is impossible to treat it to any extent like an agent) for it to lose all protection of the PGC. Correlatively, such precaution does not permit beings to be treated as non-agents on the basis that the best evidence we have points to them not being agents. Instead, it requires agents to grant beings a moral status according to a principle of proportionality, which states that agents have duties to possible agents in proportion to the strength of the evidence that they might possibly be agents, where capacities to behave like agents are to be counted as evidence for agency.

32 British and US usage might have slightly different nuances here. We use 'ostensible' to mean 'putative' or 'apparent (and possibly actual)' rather than 'apparent but not actual'.

33 The seventeenth-century French philosopher, Blaise Pascal, in his *Pensées* (trs AJ Krailsheimer) (London, Penguin, 1966) at 151 argued that, given the choice between believing in God and not doing so (or at least of acting in accordance with belief or non-belief), one ought to choose to believe in God because if one chooses to believe one gains everything if God exists and loses nothing if God does not exist, but if one chooses not to believe and God exists, one loses everything. While there are problems with the idea that God might set up such a conundrum, and we consider that any being who would do so could not be God, we think that the general principle is sound that where there is a choice between two equally likely (or equally unknowable) outcomes, one only of which is infinitely disastrous, one must choose the course that avoids that disaster.

34 See Alan Gewirth, *Reason and Morality* (Chicago, University of Chicago Press, 1978) at 121–22; 142–45.

In principle, precautionary reasoning may be used to resolve certain conflicts of duties. For example, most adult human beings behave like agents and so, under precaution, must be treated as such. Dogs, cats, and other mammals, fetuses and very young children, on the other hand, do not behave (fully) like agents. On the basis of precautionary reasoning they have a lesser status, from which it may be inferred that, all other things being equal, if there is a choice between inflicting a particular generic harm on an ostensible agent and inflicting this harm on a being that is not an ostensible agent, then the harm must be inflicted on the being that is not an ostensible agent.

This said, precautionary reasoning does not by itself specify what weight is to be given to various factors that are evidence for agency. In other words, it does not determine how close to agency a particular behavioural factor brings a being that is not yet an ostensible agent. Consequently, it can only ever be sufficient to resolve conflicts that involve one variable. By itself, it cannot resolve conflicts where the choice is between, for example, harm Y to ostensible agent A, and harm X to B where the latter is not an ostensible agent. Such a resolution requires: (i) quantification of how close to agency B is; (ii) quantification of the relative weights to be attached to X and Y; (iii) commensurability between the scale of moral status under precaution (degree of approach to agency) and the scale of generic harms and needs. Furthermore, agents may incur duties in relation to beings that are not ostensibly agents that are based on the relationship between these beings and ostensible agents (so that the duties agents owe in relation to these beings might not be duties owed to these beings but duties owed to other ostensible agents).[35]

### *(iii) Direct and Indirect Applications*

The PGC is capable of justifying prescriptions directly or indirectly. Prescriptions are justified directly if they can be deduced from the PGC itself in the circumstances of its application. Essentially, the PGC permits agents to do anything that is not contrary to the generic rights of other agents. Circumstances can, of course, arise where the generic rights of A come into conflict with the generic rights of B. In such circumstances, direct application of the PGC involves use of the criterion of needfulness for agency to resolve the conflict. Conflicts between the generic rights of agents and duties of agents to beings that are not ostensibly agents additionally

[35] For further and more detailed reflections on proportionality under precaution, see Deryck Beyleveld and Shaun Pattinson, 'Precautionary Reason as the Link to Moral Action', in Michael Boylan (ed), *Medical Ethics* (Upper Saddle River, NJ, Prentice-Hall, 2000) at 39–53, Deryck Beyleveld, 'The Moral Status of the Human Embryo and Fetus', in Hille Haker and Deryck Beyleveld (eds), *The Ethics of Genetics in Human Procreation.* (Aldershot, Ashgate, 2000) at 59–85, and Deryck Beyleveld and Roger Brownsword, *Human Dignity in Bioethics and Biolaw* (Oxford, Oxford University Press, 2001) ch 6.

involve the principle of proportionality operating under precaution. Direct applications of the PGC might be described as deontological consequentialism.[36] Its procedures are consequentialist in that actions are to be judged according to their consequences for the generic rights of agents. However, despite being consequentialist, it is still deontological because the generic rights (in terms of which the consequences are assessed) are not themselves determined by any values that they serve but simply by being necessary for agents' pursuit of any values by their own actions. Thus, despite being consequentialist, the procedure is neither teleological nor utilitarian. To further distinguish the procedure from utilitarianism, the consequences are to be assessed in a strictly distributive manner rather than in an aggregative one. This is to say that lesser harms to many agents cannot be aggregated to outweigh a greater harm to one agent.[37]

Prescriptions are justified indirectly by the PGC if they are: (i) outcomes of decision-making procedures that are justified directly by the PGC; and (ii) not contrary to what the PGC justifies directly. There are three main situations in which the PGC must be applied indirectly:

(1) where the PGC cannot directly determine what ought to be done;
(2) where the PGC can, in principle, determine directly what ought to be done (in other words, there is a right answer under the PGC), but complexities involved in direct application of the PGC (particularly with judging empirical instantiation of the generic conditions and with use of the criterion of needfulness for agency) mean that rational, well-intentioned, expert assessors will regularly disagree about what the PGC requires directly;[38]
(3) where the PGC neither requires nor prohibits certain actions or policies, but some agents have preferences for such actions or policies and these are not compatible with competing actions or policies favoured by other agents.[39]

[36] See Alan Gewirth, *Reason and Morality* (Chicago, University of Chicago Press, 1978) at 216.

[37] In our view, application of the PGC is so strictly distributive that there is no sound justification for holding that one agent may be harmed to avoid this harm to many agents. However, bearing in mind the problem of other minds, there is a justification for holding that one *ostensible* agent may be putatively harmed to avoid this same putative harm to many *ostensible* agents, and this is that (because ostensible agents might not be agents) putative harm to one creates a lower risk of harming an agent than does putative harm to many ostensible agents.

[38] Ronald Dworkin, *Taking Rights Seriously,* revised edn (London, Duckworth, 1978) ch 13 argues cogently that the idea of there being a right answer to a question is compatible with the notion that what that right answer is is inherently and irreducibly controversial.

[39] It should be clear, however, that the PGC does not permit rules to be made that prohibit otherwise permissible actions if the actions/policies to be permitted and those to be prohibited are compatible with each other.

In all three scenarios, failure to come to a determination acceptable to all sides can threaten the generic rights of agents directly or indirectly (as a consequence of agents pursuing their side of the dispute). This, by itself, entails that the PGC will justify, indeed require, that there be procedures by which such disputes be settled. However, all three cases share the feature that a determination is likely to (case (1)) or will intrinsically (cases (2) and (3)) require one side to accept a decision to which it is opposed (which, in case (2) at least, will be a matter of moral principle).

For this reason, Gewirth argues that indirect applications of the PGC are grounded in the consent of agents.[40] However, the 'method of consent' does not require the actual consent of agents. Because agents may always waive the benefits of their generic rights, actual consent of all the agents affected will, of course, be sufficient to justify a dispute resolution procedure to be used in indirect applications of the PGC. However, actual consent might not be forthcoming, and is not required, because were it necessary but not forthcoming this would constitute an unacceptable threat or violation of the generic rights of various agents. Instead, it is sufficient that all agents able to give their consent be involved equitably in the process by which decisions are made or authority is delegated to make decisions.

The method of consent quite clearly bears directly on what are legitimate processes and structures for legislation, as well as for dispute resolution (including the activities of courts). For this reason, we will not attempt a detailed analysis of its particular features, but will defer an in-depth examination of such matters for chapter ten of this book.

[40] Alan Gewirth, (Chicago, University of Chicago Press, 1978) at 320.

# 3

# The Functions of Consent in the Law

## I Introduction

In practical discourse, whether ethical (moral) or legal, consent functions as a justificatory reason. Other things being equal, the fact that agent[1] A has consented to the doing of X by agent B provides B, the recipient of A's consent, with justificatory cover in relation to the doing of X. We will recall some of the instances cited by George Fletcher:[2] namely, those cases where A has consented to surgery, sex, or search by, or with, B. In such examples, A's consent to X (whether it be consent to surgery, sex, or search) provides B with an answer to what would otherwise be a violation of A's rights.

The X to which A consents will often be a particular act—a particular act of surgery, sex, or search, as the case may be. However, X might also refer to the application of a particular rule-set. For example, if A consents to play a game of chess with B, A's consent functions to bring the rules of the game into operation and it entails that B is now justified in holding A to the rules of the game (and vice versa). In mature legal systems, agents[3] are offered a broad range of institutional rule-sets to which they may consensually submit. As in the simpler case of the game, if A consents to be bound by the rules of a particular institutional set (the law of contract, the law of marriage, the law of partnership, or whatever), then B, the recipient of A's consent, has justificatory reason for holding A to the rules of the set.[4] Moreover, as agents increasingly operate in cyberspace, there is a view that regulation is best articulated in the form of optional (competing) rule-sets to be engaged by cybercitizens.[5] Whatever the merits of this view, the essential point is that, whether such rule-sets are engaged in real space or in cyberspace, their binding force arises not from imposition but from selection and self-authored consent.

[1] For our use of the term 'agent', refer to our Coda to ch 1.

[2] See ch 1.

[3] Again, refer to the Coda to ch 1.

[4] For institutional rule-sets, see DN MacCormick, 'Law as Institutional Fact' (1974) 90 *Law Quarterly Review* 102; and for the way in which the invocation of such sets is not only permitted but specifically recognised by the law as having certain legal effects, see HLA Hart, 'Bentham on Legal Rights', in AWB Simpson (ed), *Oxford Essays in Jurisprudence* (Second Series) (Oxford, Clarendon Press, 1973) at 171–201, especially at 179.

[5] Famously, see David R Johnson and David Post, 'Law and Borders: The Rise of Law in Cyberspace' (1996) 48 *Stanford Law Review* 1367; and, for comment, see Lawrence Lessig, *Code and Other Laws of Cyberspace* (New York, Basic Books, 1999) ch 14.

If consent functions to justify an agent acting in a particular way, or insisting that another acts in a particular way, the *failure* of a claimed consent defeats such a justification. For instance, consider the case of the Sohrab family from Glasgow who 'arranged' a marriage for their daughter Aneeka, a 16-year-old schoolgirl. Aneeka's chosen husband was a 19-year-old student from Pakistan who arrived in the United Kingdom just three months before the wedding took place in a Glasgow mosque. Three years later, on Aneeka's application, a Scottish court annulled the marriage. According to the court, although the families were unquestionably acting in what they took to be the best interests of their children, the fact was that the children had been put under intolerable pressure at a time when they were unable to make informed decisions about their future or act independently.[6] In short, although the parties had gone through the marriage ceremony, they had not genuinely consented; the conditions for a valid consent were not satisfied.[7]

Broadly speaking, then, the function of consent seems to be twofold: in one kind of case, the consenting agent, A, is precluded from raising a complaint about the conduct of the recipient agent B (B's 'wrongdoing' as it otherwise would be); and, in the other kind of case, A is precluded from denying that he or she is bound by the rules (the rights and obligations) to which he or she has consented.[8] In the former case, A's consent functions to release B from some part of his or her usual obligations to A; in the latter case, A's consent functions to increase A's own obligations to B. In the former case, the recipient agent, B, appeals to A's consent by way of a defence; in the latter case, B appeals to A's consent in order to advance claims. In one case, consent functions as a shield, in the other as a sword. However, if, as in Aneeka's case, the consent is not authentic it will serve no justificatory purpose of any description.

In the present chapter, our discussion is in five parts. First, we sketch the distinctive sense in which consent functions as a procedural justification, that is, as a justification that draws on the process of authorisation rather than as a substantive (or, 'on the merits') justification. In the second and third parts of our discussion, we employ Wesley Newcomb Hohfeld's[9] seminal analysis of fundamental legal relationships to identify the primary

[6] See Kirsty Scott, 'Court annuls arranged marriage' (2002) *The Guardian*, April 24, p 9.

[7] See further chs 5 and 6 below.

[8] This is 'broadly speaking'. Recall Fletcher's further example of a suspect or a defendant in the criminal justice system who elects to answer questions or to give evidence. The opportunity to so elect is made available by virtue of a person's 'right to silence' or 'right against self-incrimination'. However, where such a person consents to answer questions or to give evidence, it is not obvious that consent acts either as a defence (for its function does not seem to be to give the police or prosecutor a defence to what would otherwise be a violation of their duties to the suspect or defendant) or as a threshold condition to bring into play the rules associated with some institutional set (unless we treat the rules of admissible evidence as such a set).

[9] Wesley Newcomb Hohfeld, *Fundamental Legal Conceptions* (ed Walter Wheeler Cook) (New Haven, Yale University Press, 1923).

functions of consent within these relationships. Fourthly, using the language of empowerment and limitation, we construct a working model of the functions played by consent as legal rights are adjusted and legal powers are exercised. Finally, we argue that, because legal rights must be viewed within the will (or choice) tradition (otherwise they would be incompatible with Gewirthian theory), it follows that consent (as an expression of an agent's choice) is an integral and essential element within legal relationships.

## II Consent as a Procedural Justification

Our introductory remarks suggest that consent functions as a justifying reason. In transactions between agents, where consent is relied on, B will justify the doing of X by reference to A's authorisation. However, precisely because B relies on A's authorisation for the doing of X rather than on the rightness of the doing of X itself, it becomes clear that consent operates as a distinctive form of justification. In particular, we can isolate three distinguishing features of 'consent as a justification'. First, consent functions as a 'procedural' rather than as a 'substantive' (or, 'on the merits') form of justification. Secondly, as a procedural justification, consent amounts to a limited 'in personam' (or 'agent-relative') response. Consent does not comprehensively justify the action as such; rather, the consenting agent is precluded from asserting that he or she has been wronged (or that he or she is not bound by the agreed rule-set, or the like). Thirdly, where consent is relied on as a shield, it justifies by way of negating a wrong rather than by way of overriding a right. Each of these features merits a word or two of explanation.

First, whereas a substantive (or, 'on the merits') form of justification refers to some set of background standards characterising (in the justificatory argument) particular acts as permitted (including required), a procedural justification refers to an authorising act or decision. For example, if agent B contends that he is entitled to mow his lawn on a Saturday and go to church on Sunday because background standards (relating, say, to property and conscience) provide for the permissibility of these actions, he relies on a substantive justification. Such a contention, of course, might be contested—the very idea of property rights might be at issue, or the scope of B's claimed freedom of religion and conscience might be disputed. By contrast, if agent B claims to be so entitled by reference to the consent of his wife, or his neighbour, or the local community, the justification does not rest on background standards, contested or otherwise; rather, the claimed justification is procedural in the sense that B relies on some authorising act or decision, not background standards, to assert the permissibility of the particular actions in question.

Secondly, where consent is relied on, it justifies 'in personam' (that is, only in an 'agent-relative' way). The consenting agent, but only the consenting agent, is precluded from asserting that he or she has been wronged. In other words, although agent A, who has consented to the doing of X by agent B, is precluded from asserting that the doing of X violates A's rights, this does not make the doing of X right *tout court* (that is, right as against all-comers). For example, if B's wife, A, has consented to B mowing the lawn on a Saturday, this precludes (or estops) A from complaining; but it does not justify the mowing of the lawn as such. Other agents (B's neighbour, C, perhaps, whose afternoon nap is disturbed by the noise of the lawnmower) might have grounds for complaint to which it is no answer for B to rely on A's consent. In other words, even if A's consent gives B a complete answer to A, it might give B no answer at all to C.

Thirdly, where B relies on A's consent as a justification, how should we characterise B's answer? A, we have said, is precluded from complaining about conduct that is covered by the consent. However, what is it precisely that A is barred from saying? Is it that B does a wrong to A, but A must suffer in silence; or is it that B does no wrong to A? Given that A's consent *authorises* the action in question, it must follow that B, by doing the authorised act X, does no wrong to A. A's consent to B doing X entails that, as between A and B, the doing of X by B is permissible. Consent, in other words, justifies by negating what would otherwise be a wrong. This is to be distinguished from a response of the form that the doing of X by B is justified by reference to overriding rights, or all things considered as the lesser of two wrongs. In such a case, where A has not consented to the doing of X by B, and where the doing of X violates A's rights, then the doing of X, even if justified all things considered, involves a wrong to A.[10] For instance, if B has promised his wife, A, that he will mow the lawn on a particular Saturday afternoon and A has not consented to B not doing so, B may justify breaking his promise to A if he abandons his lawn-mowing in order to respond to an emergency, such as driving his pregnantneighbour C (who is about to give birth) to the local maternity unit.

Now, if the doing of X by B is a wrong (because it violates A's rights) but (i) the wrong will be negated if A consents to B doing X or (ii) the doing of X may be justified all things considered as the lesser of two wrongs, then this suggests that A's consent is the prior justification for the doing of X by B. Of course, if the doing of X by B involves no wrong at all, B has no justificatory burden. However, where doing X does involve a wrong, the 'priority of consent', as we may term it, indicates that, wherever possible, B should first seek A's consent (with a view to negating the wrong otherwise done to A) rather than doing the wrong and then seeking to justify it by reference to overriding rights.

[10] Mutatis mutandis, these comments apply to the case in which B relies on A's consent in order to hold A to the rules of the agreed set.

Putting these three distinguishing features together we have the following. Consent functions as a procedural justification, giving the recipient of the consent (B) a complete answer to the consenting agent (A); no wrong is done to the consenting (authorising) agent (A) by the recipient agent (B); but it does not follow that the recipient agent (B) does no wrong to third-party agents (such as C). In the absence of consent, a wrong will be done to agents whose rights are violated even if, all things considered, the wrong-doing can be substantively justified as the lesser of two evils—hence the principle of the 'priority of consent'.

The attraction of consent as a justifying reason is not hard to understand. Quite simply, not only does consent provide the recipient with a complete answer to the consenting agent but it does so without the former having to engage contestable substantive justifications. As we have explained in the previous chapter, we take Gewirthian moral principles as our substantive justificatory (background) standards. However, even though we believe that these principles represent the most defensible criteria for substantively justified action, this counts for little in practice unless there is a broad consensus to this effect (which there is not). Moreover, even if Gewirthian principles were widely regarded as axiomatic, their interpretation and application leaves plenty of room for different shades of opinion. By contrast, consent seems to offer a lifeline for those who seek to justify their actions without getting bogged down in intractable substantive justificatory arguments.

Nevertheless, a recurring theme of our commentary is that the lifeline offered by consent as a justification should not be abused. If we are to take consent seriously, at a practical level, we must guard against the 'routinisation' of consent; it will not do simply to direct a would-be consenting agent 'to sign here and here' or 'just to tick the box'. Steps should be taken to ensure that the standards governing the adequacy of consent are fully articulated and stringently applied. The collection of consent, however commonplace, should not be approached in a mechanical or a perfunctory manner. Equally, we must discourage lazy or casual appeals to consent. Where substantive justification is called for, we should settle for nothing less; in particular, we should not be satisfied with artificial procedural justifications that are tendered in their place. Conversely, where substantive arguments are called for to support condemnation of a particular act or practice, they should not be suppressed in favour of a more convenient procedural objection to the effect that no adequate covering consents are in place. In every way, procedural justification should respect the ideals of transparency.

In sum, we begin to understand consent once we appreciate that it has an important role to play in justificatory arguments; and we refine that understanding once we distinguish between appeals to procedural and substantive considerations. However, we should not make the mistake of thinking that consent as a procedural justification is the whole justificatory story.

## III Hohfeldian Analysis and Consent

In modern legal systems, where relationships are constructed around rights and duties, and powers and liabilities, and so on, the functions of consent are shaped by the basic code in which legal relationships are conceived. This being so, the natural starting point for any attempt to be more precise about the functions of consent in the law is with Wesley Newcomb Hohfeld's seminal analysis of legal relationships.[11] For, although Hohfeld was concerned to provide a more rigorous account of the notion of a legal 'right', rather than to uncover the functions of consent as such, his analysis isolates four fundamental forms of legal relationship within which, in principle, consent might play a part. Accordingly, by building on Hohfeld's framework thinking, we can see more clearly how consent functions in legal relationships. Or, to put this another way, by stripping legal relationships down to their constituent forms, we can see just what the basic consent moves are, just how the cogs of consent engage with the cogs of rights and duties, and the like.

To be sure, Hohfeldian analysis has the reputation for being extremely difficult—after all, its objective was, as we have said, to counteract the sloppiness of ordinary legal discourse. Similarly, if we are to counteract sloppy thinking about consent in the law, we must get to grips with the formal characteristics of the basic legal relationships and the way that consent plays therein. Once we have this understanding, we can take our discussion into the many different substantive settings in which we find consent operating in the law without losing sight of the functional and normative significance of such operations.

As is well known, Hohfeld presents his scheme of fundamental legal relations in the form of two tables, one a table of jural opposities, the other a table of jural correlatives. Each table comprises four pairs. Expressed as opposites, we have:

| | | | |
|---|---|---|---|
| right | privilege | power | immunity |
| no-right | duty | disability | liability |

Expressed as correlatives, this table becomes:

| | | | |
|---|---|---|---|
| right | privilege | power | immunity |
| duty | no-right | liability | disability |

Although Hohfeld says relatively little about consent, his scheme expresses a number of distinguishable relationships on the basis of which we can develop an understanding of the functions of consent within the law. For our purposes, the Hohfeldian relationships are best presented as bipolar (A's relationship with B) and with reference to a particular act, X. This does not imply either that one of the four relationships is the only (or entire) legal

[11] Wesley Newcomb Hohfeld, n 9 above.

relationship between A and B (even with regard to the particular act) and nor does it imply that A's only legal relationships are with B. We can assume that A, like B, will stand in a complex network of legal relationships with one another and with third parties—to recall a previous example, when B mows his lawn on a Saturday afternoon, he might have to answer to A as well as C. Thus, when we identify a particular jural relationship between A and B with regard to a particular act, we are simply isolating one strand in a web of relationships.

Casting the Hohfeldian fundamental relationships in the form of bipolar specific act relationships between A and B, we have (at simplest and always in relation to some specific act):

(1) A has a right; B has a duty;
(2) A has a privilege; B has a no-right;
(3) A has a power; B has a liability; and
(4) A has an immunity; B has a disability.

So stated, there is plenty of room for slippage in any application of these ideas. It is crucial to specify the subject matter of the relationship—for it is not as if A has an undifferentiated right against B, and B an undifferentiated duty to A; A's right against B and B's correlative duty to A is in relation to some particular act X. To repeat, this might not exhaust the relationship between A and B, but this is at least one strand of it. Our first step, therefore, is to formulate more precise expressions for the four bipolar relationships expressed in simple form.

### *(i) A has a Right; B has a Duty*

The right/duty relationship is clearly fundamental to legal relationships. In fact, one of Hohfeld's targets was the assumption that

> all legal relations may be reduced to 'rights' and 'duties', and that these latter categories are therefore adequate for the purpose of analyzing even the most complex legal interests, such as trusts, options, escrows, 'future' interests, corporate interests, etc.[12]

In particular, Hohfeld was conscious of the tendency to employ the term 'right' too broadly. This being so, Hohfeld accentuates the duty end of the right/duty relationship, limiting a 'right' strictly speaking to those relationships in which it stands as a claim-right correlative to a duty. He gives the following illustrative example:

> [If] [A] has a right against [B] that he shall stay off the former's land, the correlative (and equivalent) is that [B] is under a duty toward [A] to stay off the place. If, as seems desirable, we should seek a synonym for the term 'right' in this limited and proper meaning, perhaps the word 'claim' would prove the best.[13]

[12] Wesley Newcomb Hohfeld, n 9 above, at 35.

[13] *Ibid*, at 38.

Stating the 'A has a right; B has a duty' relationship in longer form, then, we have: *A has a (claim) right that B should do/not do particular act X; correlatively, B has a duty to A that he should do/not do particular act X. If B does/does not do particular act X, he will be in breach of duty to A, and A's (claim) right will be violated.*

As yet, there is no sign of consent playing any function. However, once we think about the possible relevance of consent, two obvious questions that spring to mind in relation to Hohfeld's example are: (i) what is the position if A grants a permission, or 'consents', to B entering the land; and (ii) if A's permission or consent results in a change of position as between A and B, how do we understand the means by which this change is brought about? Seemingly, not thinking about the possibility of consent as an internal feature of a right/duty relationship, Hohfeld's answer to (i) is that there is now a privilege (or liberty)/no-right relationship between the parties in favour of B; and his answer to (ii) is that this change in the parties' legal relationship is brought about as a result of an exercise of a power by A (this power being one side of a power/liability relationship between A and B which co-exists alongside the initial right/duty relationship). As we have indicated in our introduction to this chapter, in this section, we will not yet incorporate an express consent proviso into the right/duty relationship; this is a move that we reserve for the next section of the chapter. This takes us to the second of Hohfeld's relationships, that of a privilege (or liberty) and a no-right.

### *(ii) A has a Privilege; B has a No-right*

Taking up his previous example, Hohfeld says 'whereas [A] has a *right* or *claim* that [B], the other man, should stay off the land, he himself has the *privilege* of entering on the land; or, in equivalent words, [A] does not have a duty to stay off.'[14] In so saying, Hohfeld slips up. For, in principle, there are two discrete strands to, and questions concerning, the relationship between A and B with regard to access to the land as follows:

(1) whether A has a right or claim against B that B should stay off the land; and
(2) whether A has a privilege against B to enter upon the land.

To repeat, these are discrete questions. Thus, whilst, where A has a *right* or *claim* against B that B should stay off the land, it might be usual in practice for A also to have a *privilege* against B to enter upon the land, there is no iron necessity about this. For instance, these agents might have agreed that, if B promised to stay off the land, A would also stay off the land—in which event, contrary to Hohfeld's assumption, A would not have a *privilege* against B to enter upon the land. Rather, B would have a *right* or *claim* against A that A should stay off the land. Such a slip, however, matters

[14] Wesley Newcomb Hohfeld, n 9 above, at 39.

little.[15] What we are after is the distinguishing nature of a privilege/no-right relationship and, on this, Hohfeld is perfectly clear:

> Thus, the correlative of [A]'s right that [B] shall not enter on the land is [B]'s duty not to enter; but the correlative of [A]'s privilege of entering himself is manifestly [B]'s 'no-right' that [A] shall not enter.[16]

So, where A exercises or enjoys a privilege against B, A breaches no duty to B. And, stating the 'A has a privilege; B has a no-right' relationship in longer form, we have: *B has no (claim) right that A should do/not do particular act X; correlatively, A has no duty to B that he should do/not do particular act Z (A, in other words, has a privilege or liberty to do X in relation to B). If A does/does not do particular act X, he will not be in breach of duty to B, and, because B has no (claim) right, there will be no rights violation with regard to B.*

Having put the idea of a privilege (or liberty)/no-right relationship in play, Hohfeld famously tries to clear up some confusion about a certain shrimp salad. What Hohfeld is seeking to demonstrate is that legal relationships cannot be reduced to one-dimensional right/duty relationships, in particular that privileges cannot be left out of the lawyer's analytical toolbox. Thus, to simplify, we are asked to suppose that A, who is the owner of a shrimp salad, invites B to eat the salad (ie grants a licence to B) in the following terms: 'Eat the salad, if you can; you have [my] license to do so, but [I] don't agree not to interfere with you.'[17] Resisting an analysis of the relationship between A and B in right/duty terms, Hohfeld says:

> In such a case the privileges exist, so that if [B] succeeds in eating the salad, he has violated no rights of [A]. But it is equally clear that if A had succeeded in holding so fast to the dish that [B] couldn't eat the contents, no right of [B] would have been violated.[18]

Although our interest is in consent rather than in the peculiarities of reciprocal privilege/no-right relationships, it is worth picking out the strands that comprise the relationship between A and B with regard to the salad. These are as follows:

(1) A, as the owner of the salad, has a bundle of proprietary rights against (among others) B, including the right that B does not attempt to eat the salad without A's permission. So, there are a number of background claim-rights that A has against B in relation to the salad.

[15] That Hohfeld should slip up in this manner is odd because, in the very same paragraph, he points out, quite correctly, that 'if, for some special reason, [A] has contracted with [B] to go on the former's own land, it is obvious that [A] has, as regards [B], both the privilege of entering and the *duty of entering*.' What we are saying in the text is that if, for some special reason, A has contracted with B not to go on the former's own land, then A does not have a privilege of entering (even though A has a claim-right against B that the latter should not go on the land).

[16] Wesley Newcomb Hohfeld, n 9 above, at 39.

[17] *Ibid*, at 41.

[18] *Ibid*.

(2) Once A gives B permission to attempt to eat the salad, there is some modification to the background right/duty relationship between A and B with regard to the eating of the salad. In Hohfeldian terms, the modification is that, with regard to the specific act of attempting to eat the salad, B now has a privilege (to try to eat the salad) rather than a duty (not to attempt to eat the salad).
(3) By way of a complication, however, the permission that A gives to B is subject to the reservation that A makes no promises about non-interference with B's attempt to eat the salad. It follows that A has a privilege to interfere with B's attempt to eat the salad.
(4) Although A reserves the privilege to interfere, it is not clear whether the permission granted by A to B (ie B's privilege) is revocable. If it is, A can reinstate the original right/duty relationship as between himself and B with regard to the salad.

When A gives B permission or a licence to attempt to eat the salad, one thought is that this is a case of A consenting to B attempting to eat the salad and inferring from this that one of the functions of consent is for a rights-holder in a right/duty relationship to modify the position (either by an internal change of position or by substituting a privilege/no-right relationship). As we have said, however, we will defer consideration of consent provisos (and internal changes within a relationship) until the next part of our discussion.

Before we move on from privilege/no-right relationships, there is one further point to be made. Where A permits B to enter his land or to attempt to eat his shrimp salad or the like, A stands in this (dominant) position because the background baseline relationship between himself (A) and B is one of claim-right and correlative duty. It follows that these privilege/no-right relationships are not *independent*; rather, they are *dependent* on A giving the necessary permission to confer the privilege on B. However, it cannot be concluded that all privilege/no-right relationships are dependent. For, in his discussion of privileges, Hohfeld also mentions special privileges such as privileged communications in the law of libel and the privilege against self-incrimination; such privileges, Hohfeld claims, can be viewed as a negation of what would otherwise be a general duty.[19] This implies that there are two classes of privilege/no-right relationships: one dependent on the permission (we still resist saying 'consent') of a claim-right holder, the other independent of the exercise of such permission. In other words, whereas one class of privilege/no-right relationships *arises* only where a rights-holder confers a privilege on the correlative duty-bearer by granting a permission (via the exercise of a power as Hohfeld would have it) in favour of the latter, another class of privilege/no-right relationships *arises* independently of a rights-holder's so permitting. On this basis, we can infer

[19] Wesley Newcomb Hohfeld, n 9, at 45–46.

that there are two baseline positions between parties: (i) a right/duty relationship (which may be modified to create a dependent privilege/no-right relationship); and (ii) an independent privilege/no-right relationship.[20]

### *(iii) A has a Power; B has a Liability*

Hohfeld opens his account of the power/liability relationship by remarking that a change in a legal relationship may result either from 'some super-added fact or group of facts not under the volitional control of a human being' or by virtue of 'some super-added fact or group of facts which are under the volitional control of one or more human beings.'[21] Then:

> As regards the second class of cases, the person (or persons) whose volitional control is paramount may be said to have the (legal) power to effect the particular change of legal relations.[22]

So, the power-holder is able through an act of will to change a given legal relationship. The party whose legal position may be changed by a power-holder has a so-called 'liability'. However, as Walter Wheeler Cook is quick to point out in his editorial introduction, a 'liability' may be a desirable thing (as well as something disadvantageous or burdensome).[23] Thus, stating the Hohfeldian 'A has a power; B has a liability' relationship in a longer form, we have: *A has the power (through an act of will) to change the legal relationship between himself and B in relation to matter X; correlatively B has the 'liability' (positive or negative) to have his legal relationship in relation to matter X changed by A.*

According to Hohfeld, many examples of legal powers are readily available:

> Thus, [A], the owner of ordinary personal property 'in a tangible object' has the power to extinguish his own legal interest (rights, powers, immunities, etc.) through that totality of operative facts known as abandonment; and—simultaneously and correlatively—to create in other persons privileges and powers relating to the abandoned object,—e.g., the power to acquire title to the latter by appropriating it. Similarly, [A] has the power to transfer his interest to [B],—that is, to extinguish his own interest and concomitantly create in [B] a new and corresponding interest. So also [A] has the power to create contractual obligations of various kinds.[24]

Having mentioned the power to create contractual obligations in this illustrative list, Hohfeld then explains how the power/liability relationship maps onto the standard offer-and-acceptance analysis of contractual formation.

[20] Of course, where this class of relationship is found (as an exception to general duties) in the background law, the background regime itself might be founded on consent.

[21] Wesley Newcomb Hohfeld, n 9 above, at 50–51.

[22] *Ibid*, at 51.

[23] *Ibid*, at 8.

[24] *Ibid*, at 51–52.

> [S]uppose A mails a letter to B offering to sell the former's land, Whiteacre, to the latter for ten thousand dollars, such letter being duly received. The operative facts thus far mentioned have created a power as regards B and a corresponding liability as regards A. B, by dropping a letter of acceptance in the box, has the power to impose a potential or inchoate obligation *ex contractu* on A and himself. . . . What has thus far been said concerning contracts completed by mail would seem to apply, *mutatis mutandis*, to every type of contract. Even where the parties are in the presence of each other, the offer creates a liability against the offerer, together with a correlative power in favor of the offeree.[25]

Strangely, although many would see contractual relations as a paradigm of legal relations based on consent, there is scarcely a mention of consent in Hohfeld's commentary on powers. What, then, should we make of the power/liability relationship?[26]

As we have already suggested, the first half of the set works around two key baseline relationships, the right/duty and the privilege/no-right relationships. Thus, when Hohfeld gives the example of the owner of personal property abandoning his interest, the implicit baseline relationship between A, the owner, and others is one of rights and duties—or, at any rate, this is the baseline unless it has already been modified in some way. However, when Hohfeld gives the example of the creation of contractual obligations, the implicit baseline relationship between the offeror and the offeree is one of privilege/no-right, the offeror having no duty to make such an offer (unless, again, the standard baseline has been modified in some way). If we are to be clear about the way in which powers and liabilities interact with the rest of the set, we must assume, first, a right/duty baseline between the parties and then a privilege/no-right baseline.

### (a) Powers with a Right/Duty Baseline

Tempting fate, let us return to the case of the shrimp salad. A is the owner of the shrimp salad; B would like to eat it. Where the baseline relationship between the parties is one of right and duty, then the position is as follows:

> *A has a (claim) right that B should not do particular act X (namely, eating or attempting to eat the particular shrimp salad); correlatively, B has a duty to A that he should not do particular act X (namely, eating or attempting to eat the particular shrimp salad). If B does do particular act X (namely, eating or attempting to eat the particular shrimp salad), he will be in breach of duty to A, and A's (claim) right will be violated.*

If, alongside this baseline right/duty relationship between A and B, there is also a power/liability relationship between the parties with regard to the eat-

[25] Wesley Newcomb Hohfeld, n 9 above, at 55–56.

[26] Cf *ibid*, at 8, where Cook asks readers to note that, where A makes a contractual offer to B, the latter's newly conferred power arises 'without his consent'. Quite why Cook should see fit to highlight this point is not clear. He does not make the same point when talking about the case of the owner of a chattel who abandons his proprietary interest and, thus, creates in others (also without their consent) a power to acquire ownership.

ing of the shrimp salad, then it means that *A has the power (through an act of will) to change the legal relationship between himself and B in relation to matter X (namely, eating or attempting to eat the particular shrimp salad); correlatively B has the 'liability' (positive or negative) to have his legal relationship in relation to matter X (namely, eating or attempting to eat the particular shrimp salad) changed by A.*

Now, as we have seen already, A may modify this baseline relationship by giving B a licence to eat the salad, thereby bringing into effect a 'privilege (for B)/no-right (for A)' relationship between the parties. To which, by giving further examples such as those of transfer of ownership and abandonment, Hohfeld adds the possibility of A bringing into effect a new (reversed) right/duty relationship (by transfer of ownership to B) or a power/liability relationship with B (by abandonment). In other words, where there is a baseline right/duty relationship between A and B, coupled with a power/liability relationship between the parties, A may exercise the power to create: (a) a new right/duty relationship with B; (b) a new privilege/no-right relationship with B; and (c) a new power/liability relationship with B.

Although we are still reserving the possibility that A's consent, as an integral element of the right/duty relationship (when fully spelt out), might be a catalyst for modifying such a relationship, we can detect that consent is implicit in the exercise of a power. Quite simply, this is because the exercise of a power, by (Hohfeldian) definition, is the exercise of will, or choice, by the power-holder who, again by (Hohfeldian) definition, is in affirmative control of the particular legal relationship; and, if one freely chooses to exercise a power, then one must consent, as it were, to one's own act.

### (b) Powers with a Privilege/No-right Baseline

When we turn from shrimp salads to contracts, the standard assumption is that the baseline relationship between the parties is one of privilege/no-right. Where contracts are made in textbook fashion, there will be three stages to the negotiation as follows: (i) B indicates an interest in contracting (by making an invitation to treat, which might be in the form of an invitation to tender, or by placing an advertisement for the supply of goods or services, or by a shop display, or the like); (ii) A makes an offer to B; and (iii) B accepts A's offer. At stage (iii), a contract is formed. Assuming that the baseline relationship between A and B is one of privilege/no-right, B is under no duty to A to signal his initial indication of an interest in contracting. Having so signalled at (i), however, B has not yet changed the legal relationship between himself and A. An indication such as B gives might have some practical consequences but it has no legal import. At (ii), A exercises a power. Unlike the situation prior to A's offer at (ii), B is now in a position to close a contract with A. In other words, A's exercise of a power at (ii) creates a power/liability relationship in favour of B. But, of course, to exercise a power at (ii), there must already have been a power/

liability relationship between A and B, namely a relationship under which A had the power to make an offer to B and B a liability to receive such an offer from A. At (iii), B exercises the newly created power to create a set of contractual rights and duties between the parties. Articulating the formative steps of this simple legal transaction in Hohfeldian terms, we have the following:

(1) The baseline relationship between A and B is one of reciprocal privilege/no-right; neither party has contractual rights against one another, nor contractual duties.
(2) Together with the privilege/no-right baseline, there are two power /liability relationships: A has the power to make a contractual offer to B who has the liability to receive it; and B has the power to make a contractual offer to A who has the liability to receive it.
(3) By making an offer, A exercises his power, creating a new power/ liability relationship between the parties under which B has the power to accept A's offer and A has the liability to have his offer accepted (and a contract concluded).
(4) B exercises the newly created power, thereby forming a contract with A.
(5) Under the contract between A and B there will be a myriad of relationships centred on the principal reciprocal right/duty relationships that form the core of the contract.

Clearly, the movement from a reciprocal privilege/no-right relationship between A and B to a reciprocal right/duty contractual relationship is of the utmost significance if we are to understand the dynamics of legal relationships. However, where does consent fit into this picture?

Contrary to the textbook model of contract formation, modern contract lawyers do not assume that deals always come together in this formulaic way. What matters is that the parties are acting on the basis of an agreement to which, explicitly or implicitly, they have given their free and informed consent. If either party can point to an absence of free and informed consent, the contract is open to challenge. But, is this requirement something that is immanent within the notion of the exercise of a power or is it a distinctive feature of the institution of contract? This is a more complex question than it seems.

First, to exercise a power is to express one's will in a particular way, whether to create new or to vary existing relationships. Paradigmatically, an ostensible exercise of power will reflect the power-holder's will; and it is part of this paradigm that the power-holder's will should be exercised on a free and informed basis. Granted, this paradigm takes some considerable unpacking. However, the idea that the exercise of power presupposes the consent of the power-holder and that consent should be free and informed is fundamental to the paradigm.

Secondly, the idea that powers should be exercised on a free and informed basis is generic. The requirement of consent is applicable whether we are dealing with the modification of a background right/duty relationship (for example, by authorising a procedure that would otherwise involve the commission of a tort), or the creation of a new relationship (for example, by making a gift of an item of property), or by engaging a particular institutional set (such as the law of contract or the law of marriage) as a consequence of which a new relationship will be created.

Thirdly, some institutional sets provide for their own specific consent requirements. These specific requirements do not replace the generic requirement but, in practice, there is often an elision between the generic and the specific. The institutional set represented by 'the law of contract', for example, involves a dual requirement of consent. As a first step, the institutional set must be engaged (just like agents must agree to play a game); and such engagement must satisfy the generic model of consent that is built into the exercise of a power. Having engaged the institutional set, however, there is no guarantee that a contract will eventuate; for negotiations might break down. Whether negotiations fail or succeed, the parties are bound by the rules of the institutional set. Crucially, according to the rules of this set (ie the rules of the 'law of contract') a deal will be recognised as binding only if it is agreed upon by the parties, only if A's offer is accepted by B, only if A and B specifically consent.

Hence, the complexity of the question: is consent immanent within the background powers of agents or within the institution of contract? The short answer is: 'Consent is immanent within both.' To spell this out, if a background reciprocal privilege/no-right relationship between A and B is to be moved to a new relationship by an exercise of their powers, this operation (the exercise of their powers) generically presupposes their consent; if the particular exercise of power is directed at engaging the 'law of contract', A and B must consent to the application of the rules of this institutional set; and, once they consent to be bound by these rules, their successful negotiation of a deal that is recognised as enforceable by the law of contract will depend on their satisfying the consent requirements that are internal to this institutional set. It follows that the formal articulation of the process of (legally enforceable) contractual formation is even more complex than the five-step analysis presented above. Additionally, at step 3, when A exercises his power by making an offer to B, A must signal that he wishes to engage the 'law of contract', that he is making an 'offer' according to the rules of the law of contract. The story from that point on might be relatively simple, as when B signals his willingness to deal according to these rules and accepts A's offer; or, it might be more complex, as when B signals his willingness to deal according to these rules but, instead of accepting A's offer, B makes a counter-offer; or it might be a story that ends in rejection, as when B declines to deal according to the rules of contract law, or rejects A's offer, or both.

### *(iv) A has an Immunity; B has a Disability*

Having outlined three of the four pairs of relationships, Hohfeld completes the set with an immunity/disability relationship. The idea of an immunity is placed in the conceptual array as follows:

> A right is one's affirmative claim against another, and a privilege is one's freedom from the right or claim of another. Similarly, a power is one's affirmative 'control' over a given legal relation as against another; whereas an immunity is one's freedom from the legal power or 'control' of another as regards some legal relation.[27]

To illustrate, Hohfeld offers the following example:

> [A], a landowner, has, as we have seen, power to alienate to [B] or to any other ordinary party. On the other hand, [A] has also various immunities as against [B], and all other ordinary parties. For [B] is under a disability (i.e., has no power) so far as shifting the legal interest to himself or to a third party is concerned; and what is true of [B] applies similarly to every one else who has not by virtue of special operative facts acquired a power to alienate [A]'s property.[28]

Thus, casting the 'A has an immunity; B has a disability' relationship in an extended form, we have: *B has no power (or a disability) to change the legal relationship between himself and A in relation to matter X; correlatively A has an immunity (positive or negative)*[29] *to have his legal relationship in relation to matter X changed by B.*

Given that the immunity/disability relationship seems to be designed to retain legal relationships just as they are, and without adding in a consent proviso, there is little more to say.

However, the symmetry of the Hohfeldian set can now be stated in the following relatively straightforward way. Essentially, as between A and B, and in relation to particular act X, there will be one of two baseline relationships: either (i) right/duty or (ii) privilege/no-right. If the baseline relationship is coupled with a power/liability relationship, the power-holder may modify that baseline relationship; and, in general, power-holders are in control by virtue of being in a position to create new relationships. If, instead, the baseline relationship is coupled with an immunity/disability relationship, the disabled party will have no power to modify the particular baseline relationship; nor will those who are disabled be in a position to create new relationships.

## IV The Consent Proviso

Throughout the previous section of our discussion, we have resisted the impulse to add in to the set of legal relationships what we are referring to as a consent proviso. Consent is implicit in the exercise of a power and it

[27] Wesley Newcomb Hohfeld, n 9 above, at 60.
[28] Wesley Newcomb Hohfeld, n 9 above, at 60.
[29] Positive, of course, where A's immunity is against unauthorised alienation by B.

has a variety of operative effects as specified by the rules of particular institutional sets (such as the law of contract), but is it not also integral to the relationships that comprise the Hohfeldian set? If it is, consent will function in two ways within the set: namely, to create new relationships (through the exercise of a power) but also to change the position within an existing relationship. Our task in this section, therefore, is to express the four fundamental relationships with a consent proviso explicitly added.

### *(i) A has a Right; B has a Duty*

Reformulating the first baseline relationship to include an explicit consent proviso is perfectly straightforward. So reformulated, the right/duty relationship runs as follows:

> *A has a (claim) right that B should do/not do particular act X* ***without A's consent;*** *correlatively, B has a duty to A that he should do/not do particular act X* ***without A's consent****. If B does/does not do particular act X* ***without A's consent****, he will be in breach of duty to A, and A's (claim) right will be violated.*

Where A gives his consent, there is quite clearly a change of position as between A and B with regard to the doing or not doing of X. However, we might characterise the change of position in two rather different ways as follows.

(1) We might treat the giving of consent by the rights-holder, A, as bringing into existence a new (privilege/no-right) relationship with B with regard to the doing or not doing of X. Hence (taking an Hohfeldian approach), in giving his consent, A is exercising a power under a linked power/liability relationship with B.
(2) Relying on the explicit consent proviso, we might treat the change of position as *internal* to the baseline right/duty relationship between A and B with regard to the doing or not doing of X. Although the change of position resulting from A's consent mimics a privilege/no-right relationship, A's consent does not create a new *relationship* as such; the relationship between A and B remains one governed by their baseline rights and duties but the operative fact of A's consent produces a change of position within that relationship. It follows that the giving of consent by A does not here amount to the exercise of a power; it is simply a change of position internal to the right/duty relationship which has the effect of negating what would otherwise be a breach of duty.

If we assume that, in principle, a change of position by A might amount to either an internal adjustment (as in (2)) or a change of legal relationship (as in (1)), for present purposes, we need not press the matter any further.[30]

[30] Suppose, however, there is a case where A, as a rights-holder, is unable to give his consent to what would otherwise be a violation of right, and where, in place of A, a third party, say Z, is legally empowered to give the consent. In such a case, would there be a problem about

Of course, this is not to suggest that, in practice, it will not be important to determine what kind of change of position A has sought to achieve, for, depending on A's intentions, the success of his attempt will fall to be judged by the particular rules of law governing such a change of position, as will the consequences of the change (for example, whether or not the change can be revoked and, if so, when and how).

### *(ii) A has a Privilege; B has a No-right*

If we reformulate the 'A has a privilege; B has a no-right' relationship to incorporate an explicit consent proviso, it runs as follows:

> *B has no (claim) right that A should do/not do particular act X* ***unless A has so consented;*** *correlatively, A has no duty to B that he should do/not do particular act X (A, in other words, has a privilege or liberty to do X in relation to B)* ***unless A has so consented. In the absence of consent by A,*** *if A does/does not do particular act X, he will not be in breach of duty to B, and, because B has no (claim) right, there will be no rights violation by A with regard to B.*

What could this possibly mean? Consider the standard Hohfeldian example of A, as the owner of a parcel of land or a plate of shrimp salad, having a privilege in relation to B (who has a no-right) with regard to access to the land or to the shrimp salad. In principle, and in practice, A might consent to a self-imposed restraint not to go on to his land or not to eat the salad. For this restraint to connect to B, A's consent must be directed to B in the way that it would be if A made the appropriate promise to B or contracted with B about these matters. Where this happens, the position has been changed between the parties. Once again, however, we have a choice about how to characterise the change of position as follows.

(1) We might treat the giving of consent by A as bringing into existence a new (right/duty) relationship with B to replace the baseline privilege/no-right relationship with regard to the doing or not doing of X. Hence (following a Hohfeldian approach), in giving his consent, A is exercising a power under a power/liability relationship with B.

(2) Relying on the explicit consent proviso, we might treat the change of position as *internal* to the baseline privilege/no-right relationship between A and B with regard to the doing or not doing of X. Although the change of position resulting from A's consent mimics a right/duty relationship, A's consent does not create a new *relationship* as such; the relationship between A and B remains one governed by their baseline privilege and no-right but the operative fact of A's consent produces a change of position within that relationship.

either of the characterisations outlined in the text? We think not. We could follow (1) by saying that there is a discrete power/liability relationship between Z and B (the duty-bearer). Alternatively, we might follow (2) by extending the consent proviso to allow for the possibility of Z consenting in place of A.

Again, we can proceed on the assumption that, in principle, and depending on the context, either characterisation might prove to be the appropriate one. For example, where the change of position involves a fresh contractual relationship between A and B—note, a 'fresh relationship'—this looks more like the exercise of a Hohfeldian power than an internal adjustment within a governing baseline relationship.

It will be recalled that one of George Fletcher's examples of consent in the law concerned a suspect consenting to answer questions. We have also seen that Hohfeld refers to special privileges such as that against self-incrimination. In the light of this, what do we now make of, say, a suspect consenting to answer questions, or a defendant consenting to give evidence? Is this a case where the privilege of silence is replaced by a duty to respond, where the function of consent is to change a baseline privilege/no-right relationship to one of rights and duties? Or, is this a case where the consent proviso is internal to the privilege/no-right relationship and we simply have a change of position within that relationship? Again, we assume that context will point to how we should classify such a purported change of position. However, there is a sense that, if the use of contracts implies the creation of new relationships (and the use of powers), the election to answer questions or give evidence implies a mere shift of position within a baseline relationship.

Although we do not need to resolve the characterisation issue, the case of 'the right to silence' in the criminal justice system prompts an important question about the location of the consent option. Is consent operating generically within the set when an agent—such as a suspect who agrees to answer questions—forgoes the benefit of a privilege, or is this a consent that takes its meaning and significance from the particular rules of the criminal justice system (concerning the admissibility of evidence), or both? This question, it will be appreciated, parallels our earlier question with regard to the location of consent when agents seek to form a contract. In the earlier case, we were dealing with an exercise of power; in the case of the consenting suspect, we are assuming that there is a modification of a privilege/no-right relationship; but, in both cases, the function of consent is obscured by the intersection of the background set of legal relationships with a particular institutional rule-set. We need to pause to get a clear sight of these moves and how consent functions at these interfaces.

Imagine a background set that has all the right moral credentials. This means that the substance of the rights, privileges, powers and immunities within the set is compliant with Gewirthian moral principles. It also means that the set is functionally compliant, consent operating (generically) within the set as a procedural justification for changes of position and exercises of power. Moreover, consent will only so operate where it meets the criteria of adequacy as dictated by Gewirthian considerations. If this is our baseline, relationships between agents governed by the set will be morally underwritten, as will any changes sanctioned by the consent of agents.

Now, let us suppose that in place of this ideal-typical background set, we have the set of a particular regime of positive law. The legal set has the same form as the moral ideal-type, the same basic relationships between agents; and the generic function of consent is carried over—that is, the function of consent is to authorise changes within relationships and to create new relationships. However, if the positive legal set is to approximate to the ideal-type, its substantive provisions must be defensible articulations of Gewirthian principles. This means that the substance of background rights, privileges, powers and immunities as recognised by the regime must be, at least arguably, consistent with the PGC; and it means that the regime's tests for adequate consents, where those consents relate to operations at the level of the background set, must also be in line with Gewirthian standards. If the positive regime passes muster, it follows that the background relationships are morally defensible and that consent-authorised changes within, or to, those relationships are morally defensible. Provided that these tests are satisfied, the 'consent' rules *within* particular institutional sets need not be *directly* compliant with Gewirthian moral principles (such rules enjoy, so to speak, 'relative autonomy'); the binding effect of such rules derives from the agents' *consensual* engagement of the set, this originating consent being the crucial one for procedural justificatory purposes.

In the light of these remarks, we can return to the location of consent in the two cases that we have raised: that of a suspect who consents to answers questions, and that of agents who consent to contract.

With regard to the first of these cases, we have assumed that the baseline relationship between the police interrogators and the suspect is one of privilege/no-right in favour of the suspect. The suspect has the privilege of refusing to answer police questions. Let us suppose that this right, which can be related to the right against self-incrimination and the values of due process, is a defensible articulation of Gewirthian principles. On this assumption, we are dealing with a morally compliant background relationship, and any consent-authorised change must also satisfy Gewirthian standards. It follows that not only must the suspect consent to forgo the benefit of the privilege, that consent must also meet Gewirthian standards of adequacy. Where this is the case, all well and good; and the scope of the consent governs the extent to which the privilege is forgone (and the effects of this course of action). However, if the provisions of the local criminal justice regime set a lower standard (for example, by taking the suspect's 'consent' at face value and failing to protect against coercion or undue influence), they will be deficient; and the consequences triggered by this deficient test of consent (such as the admissibility of the suspect's 'confession') will not be procedurally justified.

The second case is like the first to the extent that any consent-authorised change to the background set must satisfy Gewirthian standards. Hence, when the agents exercise their powers to engage the local 'law of contract', the originating consent (implicit in the exercise of power) must meet Gewirthian standards of adequacy. If the provisions of local law fall below this standard, there is no procedural justification for the application of the rules of the institutional set. However, provided the 'law of contract' is properly engaged, its internal rules concerning 'consent' and its effects need not mirror Gewirthian standards.

Why does consent have, as it were, relative autonomy within the local law of contract but not within the local criminal justice system? Quite simply, in both cases, assuming a morally compliant background regime, an originating consent will only justify changes within, or to, background relationships provided that Gewirthian standards of adequacy are met. These standards govern, equally, the purported (consensual) change of position within a privilege/no-right relationship as the (consensual) creation of a new relationship by the exercise of a power. The relative autonomy of the 'law of contract' and its internal rules concerning consent cannot override the significance of the originating consent; and it is only because the originating consent passes muster that the 'law of contract' is engaged.

To understand the functions of consent in the law, we need to bear in mind the complexities of the intersections between ideal-typical moral and positive legal background sets; and this is a matter to which we will return frequently.

### *(iii) A has a Power; B has a Liability*

As we have said, a power-holder's consent is implicit in his exercise of the power. However, is it possible to reformulate the Hohfeldian power/liability relationship so that it incorporates an *express* consent proviso? A possible reformulation would run as follows:

> ***Unless A has disabled himself by consenting not to exercise the power****, A has the power (through an act of will) to change the legal relationship between himself and B in relation to matter X; correlatively,* ***unless A has disabled himself by consent not to exercise the said power****, B has the 'liability' (positive or negative) to have his legal relationship in relation to matter X changed by A.*

Such a reformulation again invites the question: where A changes position by disabling the use of his power, has A used a power to create a new relationship with B (one of immunity and disability), or is this merely an internal change of position within the power/liability relationship, the benefit of the power being forgone for the duration of A's consent? In principle, both possibilities might be open to A and we can assume, as before, that context will assist with the appropriate classification of A's actions.[31]

[31] It is worth noting that, if A changes the relationship from power/liability to immunity/disability, he must do so by exercising a power. If this latter power is to fit the Hohfeldian scheme, it must itself be one side of a power/liability relationship. In other words, we start with a power/liability relationship between A and B with regard to X (let us call this PL1), and we

### *(iv) A has an Immunity; B has a Disability*

Reformulating the 'A has an immunity; B has a disability' relationship to incorporate an explicit consent proviso, we have:

> ***Subject to A consenting to waive the benefit of his immunity,*** *B has no power (or a disability) to change the legal relationship between himself and A in relation to matter X; correlatively,* ***unless A has so consented,*** *A has an immunity (positive or negative) to have his legal relationship in relation to matter X changed by B.*

As with the reformulation of the power/liability relationship, there is a question about whether, when A changes the position in relation to his immunity, it involves the creation of a new relationship (substituting a new power/liability relationship in place of the prior immunity/disability relationship) or merely an adjustment of position within the existing relationship. And, as before, this is not a question that need be pursued here.

### *(v) Summary*

The analysis in this part of the chapter yields two points of general importance: one highlighting the possibility of consent functioning to authorise a change of position within a baseline relationship, the other concerning the operation of 'consent' within rule-sets, legal or otherwise, that agents are permitted to engage.

Taking up the first point, we have said that in each of the Hohfeldian relationships, one side is, so to speak, dominant. In the baseline relationships, the dominant parties are the rights-holder and the privilege-holder; in the supplementary relationships, they are the power-holder and the immunity-holder. Once the consent proviso is built into the relationships, each of these parties may consent to a change of position, *internal to*, or *within* the prevailing relationship. Thus, the rights-holder may consent to waive the benefit of the right; the privilege-holder may consent to forgo the protection or shield otherwise provided by the privilege; the power-holder may consent to forgo exercise of the power; and the immunity-holder may consent to a waiver of immunity. On this analysis, one of the key functions of consent in the law is to authorise (and procedurally justify) changes of position *within* the four relationships that comprise the basic set.

With regard to the second point, where agents engage optional rule-sets (whether the rules of a game or the rules of a legal institutional set such as the 'law of contract'), they exercise a power to engage the rule-set in question. Such an exercise of power represents an originating consent and, provided that it is an adequate consent (as judged by Gewirthian stand-

now uncover an underlying power/liability relationship (PL2) which gives A the power to change PL1. But, then, if PL2 can be changed by A, this entails PL3 (referring to PL2), and so on.

ards), it procedurally justifies the application of the rule-set. Where the rule-set includes rules that turn on the 'consent' of the players or parties (such as conceding a hole to an opponent during a golf match, or accepting an offer made by a fellow contractor, or the like) such rules (and their particular version of 'consent') operate in a relatively autonomous fashion. In other words, consent within an optional rule-set functions as the rule-set provides.

We can proceed now to synthesise our discussion of the Hohfeldian relationships with a view to developing a working model of the functions of consent in the law.

## V The Functions of Consent in the Law: A Working Model

The function of consent is to operate as a procedural justification. In the light of the Hohfeldian set, we can see that consent supplies the recipient (agent B) with justificatory reason in two contexts: first, where agent A (who stands on the dominant side of the relationship with B) consents to a 'change of position' internal to the relationship; and, secondly, where agent A (who is the power-holder in a power/liability relationship with B) consents to the creation of a new relationship with B. Where agents exercise their powers to engage a particular legal institutional set, it is the agents' consent to being bound by the rules of the set that functions as the procedural justification for applying the rules. However, as we have said, the rules themselves might also provide for consent but in their own specific way. Provided that the originating consent is adequate, the fact that 'consent' within the optional rule-set does not conform to the ideal-type of consent within the background set is not problematic—for example, *provided that the originating consent is adequate*, it is no more problematic that the rule-set disallows a party from consenting any more than that it recognises a 'consent' too easily.

If we combine this analysis with the intuition that the function of consent is to limit and to empower, what model of consent might we generate? We can start by looking at changes of position internal to a relationship and then changes that create new relationships.

### *(i) Changes Internal to a Relationship*

Where a change of position is made *within* any one of the four relationships comprising the Hohfeldian set, it is in the form of an allowance made by the dominant party. Can this allowance be represented as a case of self-limitation? And, does it amount to empowerment of another?

First, is an allowance made by the dominant party a case of self-limitation? Broadly speaking, it is. Thus, where A, as a rights-holder, agrees to waive the benefit of his claim-right against B, A limits a claim that otherwise he could make against B. Where A agrees to forgo the benefit of a privilege, an act that is otherwise permissible no longer has that status: A has, by self-limitation, foregone an option. Where A agrees to forgo the exercise of a power, he again gives up an option; and, once more, we have an example of self-limitation. Finally, where A agrees to waive an immunity, he sets aside a protection that he would otherwise enjoy. In each case, the dominant party consents to give up, or not to rely on, an advantage that defines his side of the legal relationship as the dominant one. In each case, the limit or sacrifice or restraint is self-imposed.

Secondly, if internal changes of position by the dominant party involve self-limitation by that party, do they represent empowerment of another? Again, broadly speaking, they do. Thus, A's waiver of the protection of a right releases B from the correlative duty and, in effect, invests a privilege in B; A's forgoing of the benefit of a privilege invests a claim-right in B; A's forgoing of the exercise of a power invests an immunity in B; and A's waiver of the protection of an immunity invests a power in B. In each case, then, the change of position by the dominant party invests the other party with the dominant feature of the relationship; A's self-limitation, thus, empowers B—at any rate, it does so for the duration of the allowance given.

Having said this, are these representations perhaps a bit too broad-brush? Is it not the case that, where A waives the benefit of his claim-right against B, as where A waives an immunity against B, A eases a restriction on B and thus *empowers* B? Similarly, is it not the case that, where A agrees to forego the benefit of a privilege or the exercise of a power, A *limits* his options? In other words, is it not the case that the emphasis of limitation and empowerment varies from one type of change of position to another, the emphasis being on *empowerment of another* in some types of case (namely, where rights and immunities are concerned) and on *self-limitation* in others (namely, where privileges and powers are concerned)? If we adopt this distinction, we will say that, with regard to changes of position within a relationship, consent regulates two operations: (i) empowerment of another (where the dominant party waives a right or an immunity); and (ii) limitation of self (where the dominant party forgoes an option in relation to a privilege or a power).

### *(ii) Changes that Create a Legal Relationship*

Where a power-holder in a power/liability relationship exercises the particular power, the relationship between the parties is changed and a new relationship is created. On the face of it, this is empowerment writ large. By virtue of having a particular power, the power-holder is in a position to utilise the power to achieve a variety of fresh empowerments or limitations. For example, a potential offeror might exercise the relevant power to create an offer in favour of an offeree, the latter now being empowered to accept the offer. If the latter accepts the offer, the contract that has been formed will normally involve receiprocal obligations and, thus, limitations. Given that the exercise of a power presupposes that it is at the volition of the power-holder, the law must ensure that the power has been exercised freely. Where, however, does consent fit into this?

We have already said that the power-holder's own consent is generically implicated in an exercise of the power because, if the power-holder acts freely, he must consent.[32] It is through an originating consent of this kind that the power to engage particular legal institutions is exercised. To be sure, once a particular optional rule-set has been engaged, its own provisions for consent will tend to overlap with or obscure the underlying originating consent. However, it is the latter that holds the key to the procedural justification that locks the agents into the rules of the set. Needless to say, depending upon the particular legal institution engaged, and the way in which it is engaged, such an exercise of power might result in a new relationship which itself can be analysed as a mix of limitation and empowerment.

### *(iii) A Working Model of the Functions of Consent in the Law*

Drawing together these threads, we can say that the essential function of consent in the law is threefold: namely, to provide a procedural justifying reason to be relied on by the recipient of the consent, agent B, in relation to:

(1) agent A's legal empowerment of B (where A, the dominant party to a legal relationship, waives the benefit of a right or an immunity);
(2) agent A's self-limitation or denial (where A, the dominant party to a legal relationship, forgoes an option in relation to a privilege or a power); and
(3) agent A's self-limitation and/or empowerment, where A exercises a legal power whether to change the relationship with B or to engage an institutional rule-set.

We should add that, where A and B engage an institutional rule-set, consent within that rule-set will operate in various ways to limit or empower the parties.

We can illustrate how this model would work by briefly revisiting Fletcher's examples of individuals who 'consent to undergo medical operations, to engage in sexual intercourse, to open their homes to police searches, or to testify against themselves in court.' Let us suppose that these consenting individuals are, respectively, A1, A2, A3, and A4. Where A1 consents to undergo a medical operation, this is best viewed as A1 empowering another by waiving the benefit of a right (function (1) above). Where A2 consents to engage in sexual intercourse, this is again consent functioning as in (1) above; if A2 were to consent to marriage, the function would be as in (3) above. Where A3 consents to a police search, this is another example of

[32] In ch 5, we deal more fully with the conditions for free action in general and for the particular (free) action of giving one's consent.

function (1) above. Finally, where A4 consents to testifying against himself, this looks more like function (2) above, with A4 forgoing the option of not testifying which is otherwise available to him as a privilege.

Before we leave this working model, we should observe that, because the model is constructed on the foundations of the Hohfeldian relationships, it might be thought to be geared primarily for private law situations (property, torts, contracts, and the like), together with the relationship between 'offender' (qua duty-bearer) and 'victim' (qua rights-bearer) in criminal law. On this view, public law is rather left out. Moreover, such a conclusion might be encouraged by an influential account of legal rights presented by HLA Hart.[33] Having considered claim-rights, liberty-rights (privileges), and rights which are powers, Hart claims that the distinctive element of a right is that of a legally respected choice. A claim-right leaves the holder 'at liberty to waive or extinguish or to enforce or leave unenforced another's obligation.'[34] In the case of a liberty-right, such as the right to look into a neighbour's garden, the liberty-holder is at liberty to look or not look as he chooses. And, where we are dealing with rights that are powers, they are characterised by a bilateral liberty, again in the sense that the power-holder may or may not elect to exercise the power. Such an analysis explains why liberty-rights, powers, and rights correlative to obligations are all described as rights and does so by identifying as common to three superficially diverse types of case, an element which, on any theory of law or morals, is of great importance; namely an individual choice respected by the law.[35]

Nevertheless, when we consider fundamental constitutional rights, such as rights entrenched by a Bill of Rights, Hart believes that this analysis has reached its limits. Where legislative powers are limited to safeguard the freedom and essential well-being of citizens, citizens enjoy an immunity. However, on Hart's analysis, an immunity will fit the description of a right (qua immunity-right) only if there is a meaningful choice for the immunity-holder. In some immunity/disability relationships, Hart has difficulty in identifying such a choice. For instance, 'if my neighbour has no power to exempt me from my duty to pay my income-tax'[36] it is hard to see how my immunity against a potentially beneficial exemption being given contains a choice to be respected by the law. Thus:

An individual's immunity from legal change at the hands of others is spoken of and thought of as a right only when the change in question is adverse, that is, would deprive him of legal rights of other kinds (liberty-rights, powers, rights correlative to obligation) or benefits secured to him by the law.[37]

[33] See n 4 above.
[34] *Ibid*, at 197.
[35] *Ibid*, at 197.
[36] *Ibid*, at 199.
[37] *Ibid*, at 199.

However, even if we accept this analysis, why should immunities relating to legislative disabilities not count as a species of right? Here, after all, the immunity is created precisely to secure essential freedoms and well-being, and waiver of immunity would be adverse to the dominant party. For Hart, however, this is precisely the point: if the purpose of such immunities is to protect 'basic or fundamental individual needs,'[38] then it is, at best, unhelpful to associate constitutional rights with ordinary rights where (in the case of the latter) the protection of individual choice is the paramount purpose.

We need not get bogged down in a dispute about the scope of 'rights'. It is quite clear, as MacCormick has suggested, that 'there is a class of immunities which could comfortably be brought within the Hartian version of the will theory, namely, the whole class of those immunities in relation to which the immunity-holder has a power of waiver.'[39] And, there is no obvious reason why, for our purposes, we should not treat public law rights and immunities and the like as within our working model. Consent, plainly, plays an important justificatory role in both private and public law relations, and, provided that we can identify a particular legal relationship, we should be able to track the function played by consent.

## VI The Consent Proviso and the Gewirthian Will Theory of Rights

When we introduced the explicit consent proviso, we did so in a way that assumed that, in principle, the dominant party would always have the option of changing his position within the particular legal relationship. However, the rules of positive law do not always permit rights-holders to waive the benefit of their rights (particularly where the rights-holder is perceived to be a vulnerable primary party, or where permitting waivers by non-vulnerable primary parties might jeopardise the position of vulnerable secondary parties)[40]—in some instances, there simply is no bargaining around rights. Of course, the fact that, in some cases, positive law does not allow for the operation of a consent proviso does not mean that consent never functions to regulate a change of position within a relationship. Nevertheless, there is an issue here about the nature of rights (and privileges, powers, and immunities) within the Hohfeldian set; and it takes us to

[38] *Ibid*, at 201.

[39] DN MacCormick, 'Rights in Legislation' in PMS Hacker and J Raz (eds), *Law, Morality, and Society* (Oxford, Clarendon Press, 1977) 189–209, at 195. MacCormick then gives as an example the following: '*A* has a right not to be assaulted by *B*, and *B* can't take that away from *A*, unless *A* agrees—for example, in a boxing match' (*ibid*). This looks much more like A having a waivable claim-right against B, but no matter.

[40] Cf *Regina on the Application of Mrs Dianne Pretty v DPP and Secretary of State for the Home Department* [2001] UKHL 61; *Case of Pretty v The United Kingdom* (2002) ECHR 2346/02, April 29; (2002) 35 EHRR 1; and see ch 9 below.

the debate about the will (or choice) theory of rights as against the interest theory.

Neil MacCormick helpfully sets the scene for this debate by sketching the rival views in the following way:

> Legal theorists have traditionally divided into two camps on the issue of the proper explanation of rights. One line of thought, which may be called the 'will theory', asserts that an individual's having a right of some kind depends upon the legal (or, *mutatis mutandis*, moral) recognition of his will, his choice, as being pre-eminent over that of others in relation to a given subject matter and within a given relationship. The 'interest theory', by contrast, contends that what is essential to the constitution of a right is the legal (or moral) protection or promotion of one person's interests as against some other person or the world at large, by the imposition on the latter of duties, disabilities, or liabilities in respect of the party favoured.[41]

According to MacCormick, the will theory loses plausibility when confronted with cases such as that of the right against enslavement. Thus:

> *A*'s right to personal freedom involves *B* in having (a) a duty not to reduce *A* to a servile condition, e.g. by clapping him in irons; and (b) a disability to impose upon *A* the status of a slave; and (c) a disability to change the relation (a) and (b) *even with A's consent*. *A* does not himself have power to waive his immunities in these respects.

But there's the rub, there, for the 'will theory', the paradox. For it appears that this legal dispensation, be it ever so advantageous from the point of view of securing liberty, is so forceful as to thrust liberty beyond the realm of 'right' altogether. If there be no power to waive or assert the immunity, the claim, or whatever, upon some matter, upon that matter there is, by definition, no right either.[42]

Given an understandable reluctance to concede that liberty-entrenching laws of this kind do not confer 'rights' on the protected parties, MacCormick concludes that legislative rights fit better with an interest theory. What are we to make of this?

Let us suppose that a review of the positive law of some chosen legal system or sample of legal systems will produce a number of cases of *background* 'legal rights', the benefit of which may not be waived or contracted away by the rights-holder. In such cases, where it is asserted that there has been no breach of criminal or tortious duty because the rights-holder consented to the act in question, the consent will be ineffective to protect the duty-bearer;[43] and, where it is claimed that the rights-holder has contracted for a new

[41] DN MacCormick, n 39 above, at 192.

[42] *Ibid*, at 196.

[43] Similarly, if the argument is that advance immunity should be conferred on B, in relation to an act that would otherwise be a wrong against A, because A would consent to the act, the application for a declaration of immunity will be denied: see *Pretty*, n 40 above.

relationship involving the loss of the protection of the right, the contract will also be ineffective. What this means is that, if we are trying to conceptualise rights in a way that fits with the features of positive legal rights as we find them in positive legislation, cases of this kind present problems for the will theory—which is what MacCormick is saying. However, this is all that he is saying. MacCormick is not suggesting that, if you start with a will theory of rights, *which is rationally secured,* then you must abandon it because it does not fit with the conventions of legal practice. Nor could any rational person so suggest: if reason points to the necessity of conceptualising rights in the way that will theory has it, but the conventions of contingent legal practice indicate a different conceptualisation of rights, then reason dictates that the latter should yield. Reason prevails against convention, as does necessity against contingency. Given the strong claims made by Gewirthian moral theory, and given (as we explained in the previous chapter) that the rights within that theory are in the tradition of will theory, the background legal rights recognised by positive law must be regarded as out of line (and in error) to the extent that they do not conform to the (formal) specification given by the will theory. It follows that, where positive background legal rights do not allow for the rights-holder to consent to a change of position as specified by the will theory, we need to take a harder look to detect whether this is a simple case of a misshapen right or a more complex case of a right that has had to be modified for special reasons of Gewirthian principle combined with local practice.

To avoid any misunderstanding, it should be said that these remarks apply to *background* legal rights. Agents may exercise their powers to engage particular legal institutions, the optional rule-sets of which might provide for right/duty relationships that are not susceptible to modification via the dominant party's consent. As we have said, however, the provisions of such sets are relatively autonomous; provided that an adequate originating consent is in place, the rules of these sets are binding even though they do not directly conform to Gewirthian standards. Cases of this kind, therefore, would not be relevant counter-examples even if the analysis were to be driven by the empirical features of legal practice.

We are close to concluding, therefore, that Gewirthian theory is not merely consistent with consent functioning in the way that we have sketched it, but actually requires the law to allow for changes of position made by dominant parties. However, it might be objected that, provided there is the option to change a legal relationship by exercising a power to do so, this will suffice. In other words, it might be argued that, provided such a power is available, there is no need to insist upon the consent proviso, for, whether the change of position arises from the exercise of a power or a change of position within a relationship, the outcome is much the same. Against such a reductionist view, however, we suggest that there is a distinction to be made between an adjustment of position within a relationship and the creation of a new relationship; that those changes of position that are revocable, of limited duration, and in relation to a very particular matter fit much better with the idea of an agent operating a right within a right/duty relationship; and that the characterisation of each change of position as the creation of a new relationship is not only clumsy but a distortion of how rights are operated under a will theory. We do conclude, therefore, that our analysis of the function of consent is as required by Gewirthian theory.

## VII The Agenda for Discussion

If a positive legal order, with its basic legal relationships following the form of the Hohfeldian set, is to operate in a way that is compliant with Gewirthian principles, what will be the function of consent? Essentially, consent will function as a procedural justification for holding the consenting agent to (1) changes of position within the background legal relationships and (2) the terms of new relationships brought into effect by the exercise of powers. Such a working model, however, does not address the criteria that determine the adequacy of consent. In particular, the model says nothing about who has the capacity (and competence) to consent, about the conditions for authentic consent, and about how consent is to be interpreted and signalled. Nor does the model speak to the conclusiveness of consent, or its absence, as a justificatory reason. Clearly such matters cannot be simply left to positive law—even though such regimes will offer their own tests—for the adequacy of the original authorising consent is critical for legitimate adjustment to a background regime that is underwritten by Gewirthian morality. If a procedural justification is to support such adjustments (whether qua changes of position or the creation of new relationships) it must fit the Gewirthian test of adequacy—that is, it must be a consent that Gewirthian theory recognises as adequate.

We take up the first group of questions in the next part of our discussion (chapters four to seven). In one way or another, these questions (concerning capacity, authenticity or validity, and signalling and interpretation) address the adequacy of an ostensible consent. Where we reject a consent as ineffective, we might do so for more than one reason: it might be because the author of the consent lacks the required capacity or competence; or because the circumstances in which the consent is given involve coercion or deception; or because the so-called 'consent' is not clearly signalled; or because, when correctly interpreted, it does not cover the matter in question. For practical purposes, these different reasons generate a common conclusion: namely, that the 'consent' fails and cannot be relied on. However, these are different reasons, and we need to disentangle them, exploring how they would be viewed by a legal regime that aspires to regulate in a way that is compliant with Gewirthian principles.

Assuming that we have an adequate consent, is it sufficient for all justificatory purposes or only for some? Furthermore, in the absence of an adequate consent, do Gewirthian principles recognise any other avenues for justification? These are questions that we move on to in the following part of our discussion (chapters eight and nine). We start with private law relationships, considering the necessity and sufficiency of consent in relation to private wrongs (of the kind designated by tort law) and private empowerment (of the kind exercised through the use of contract law). Then, we consider public law (particularly the criminal law) where our central questions are whether a 'victim's' consent is the only legitimate defence and whether it is a sufficient answer to a State that purports to prohibit the conduct in question.

This leads on to the final part of the book, where we turn from issues relating to consent within the law to the idea of law based on consent, to the view that consent is itself the basis of justified or legitimate governance. Put simply, if agents may agree to waive the benefit of their rights in favour of another, or to change their legal relationship with another, or to authorise representative action on their behalf (by proxies and the like), this implies a model for consent-based participation in groups or larger collectivities. Yet, representative governance, even in the best of democracies, falls a long way short of each agent consenting to some change of position or to a specific authorisation. How far, then, can the model of consent as procedural justification, the model as we have it in individual transactions and private relationships, be applied to public and political governance generally?

Part Two

# CONSENT IN THE LAW I: QUESTIONS OF ADEQUACY

# 4

# Subjects of Consent: Questions of Capacity and Competence

## I Introduction

When the majority Law Lords ruled, in the famous *Gillick* case,[1] that some children below the age of 16 years might have the capacity to make their own decisions about medical treatment, that such children might have achieved (in Lord Scarman's words) 'a sufficient understanding and intelligence . . . to give consent valid in law,'[2] they offered a radical answer to a very important question. This is the question of who is to be treated in law as competent to give consent, or, as we will say, as a 'subject of consent'. By accepting that some children under the age of 16 (namely, those who are judged to be '*Gillick*-competent') might qualify as subjects of consent, the House allowed for the possibility of procedural (consent-authorised) transactions with such children. Had the House decided that no child below the age of 16 years should be treated as a subject of consent, then it would have faced a different, but no less important, question. This is the question of how transactions with those who are *not* subjects of consent are to be justified. In such cases, does the justification lie in the authorising consent of some third party (such as a young child's parents), or in a substituted judgment (second-guessing what the subject would have said if asked to consent), or in some substantive justification that appeals to the rights of other agents or to the best interests of the subject? Broadly speaking, this chapter considers these two questions: first, what are the relevant criteria to determine whether someone is a subject of consent; and, secondly, how are actions to be justified where the other party to the transaction is not a subject of consent?

If we hoped to find the answer to these questions in the practice of legal systems, we would probably be disappointed, for different legal regimes will

[1] *Gillick v West Norfolk and Wisbech Area Health Authority* [1985] 3 All ER 402.

[2] *Ibid*, at 423. Applying this general test of capacity to the more specific question of consent to advice and treatment concerning contraception, Lord Scarman said (at 424):

> When applying these conclusions to contraception advice and treatment it has to be borne in mind that there is much that has to be understood by a girl under the age of 16 if she is to have the legal capacity to consent to such treatment. It is not enough that she should understand the nature of the advice which is being given: she must also have a sufficient maturity to understand what is involved.

require or permit consent for various different purposes, setting various thresholds and conditions in relation to persons[3] from whom a valid consent may be obtained. For example, the law might specify that a person able to give a valid consent must have a specified interest in the matters affected by the consent—particularly where the effect of a valid consent is to legitimate actions of others that impact negatively on a person's interests.[4] However, in other cases, the consent of third parties might be required in addition to or instead of that of the first party. When the consent of the first party is required, the consent might be valid only if certain conditions of competence (to give consent for the particular purpose) are satisfied—for example, legal regimes might specify that the consenting party must have reached a prescribed age, have a minimum set of mental abilities, have attained particular educational or professional qualifications, and so on. Where the consent of a third party is required or permitted, a third party might only be considered competent to provide consent where, in addition to conditions of competence similar to those that apply to first parties, the third party stands in a particular relation to the first party, such as being a close relative of the latter.

Looking to the positive provisions of legal systems, however, is not the way to tackle the questions of capacity and competence with which we are concerned in this chapter—no more, we should say, than it is the way to seek a coherent view of the 'person' in law.[5] Rather, we must go back to first Gewirthian principles. As we have explained, the PGC prescribes the normative framework, the most basic ground rules, for a community of agents. Essentially, agents have generic rights; and, concomitantly, their responsibilities, negative and positive, entail respecting the generic rights of

[3] In practice, 'persons' rather than 'agents' will generally be referred to in court judgments and statutes. While, with our Gewirthian hats on, we would regard 'agents' as a subcategory of the category 'persons', agents being those persons (who are beings that have capacities to reason) who deploy reason in relation to their behaviour, this is not how the term 'person' is generally deployed. Some will distinguish persons from human beings by treating persons as, in effect, human agents. Others will treat persons simply as those human beings that have the protection of the law. Yet others will treat all human beings as persons. The usage will, in part, reflect different philosophical presumptions, but need do no more than reflect a tradition.

[4] Where an action is judged to impact *positively* on a person's interests, the willingness of the particular legal system to authorise such an action in the absence of a consent by the person in question will reflect the balance that it strikes between paternalism and autonomy. In general, the more paternalistic the legal regime, the readier it will be to authorise such action; by contrast, the greater its commitment to individual autonomy, the less willing it will be. These background considerations flow through a number of critical decisions, such as where the line is drawn between those who have the capacity to consent and those who do not, whether the law will ever override the 'irrational' decisions of autonomous persons (eg to refuse life-saving treatment), and how 'substituted judgment' and 'best interests' tests are applied (see further, section III of this chapter).

[5] For discussion, see Ngaire Naffine, 'Who are Law's Persons? From Cheshire Cats to Responsible Subjects' (2003) 66 *Modern Law Review* 346.

other agents. The argument for the PGC entails that these (generic) rights are under the will conception of rights, which is to say that, by their very nature, they are rights of an agent not to have its generic interests interfered with *against the agent's will* or to be assisted in promoting its generic interests *if the agent so wishes* (and is unable to do so by itself). It follows directly from this that to interfere with, or to fail to protect, the generic rights of agents *against their will* is to violate the PGC. To ask whether or not an agent so wills is to ask whether or not an agent consents. The will theory of rights, in other words, already contains the idea of consent.[6]

Viewing consent as immanent within a Gewirthian will theory of rights, its function (as we have seen in chapter three) is to operate as a 'procedural' rather than as a 'substantive' form of justification. In some transactions (for example, where a rights-holder agrees to a change of position with the duty-bearer), the effect of the consent is to authorise an action that would otherwise amount to a wrong. In other transactions (where a power-holder exercises a power to create a new relationship), the effect of the consent is to authorise the binding application of the terms of the new relationship. In both types of case, the consenting agent, having initiated the change, is precluded from asserting that he or she is not bound by the change so initiated; and the recipient of the consent has a justification for action (or inaction) that, prior to the consent, was not available. Those who have the capacity and competence to give consent, those who are 'subjects of consent', thus hold an important key to the justification of transactions between agents. Indeed, we can say that, *as a general principle*, consent is required from agents to legitimate any action or failure to act that impacts *negatively* on their generic interests, *unless* (whether or not it is possible to seek consent), in the particular circumstances, action without consent is required in order to protect more important generic rights of others. Furthermore, the fact that an action is in the generic interests of an agent is not necessarily sufficient for that action to be performed without the agent's consent. Unless more important generic rights of others justify not getting consent, 'paternalistic' actions also require the consent of the agent, except where it is impossible to seek this consent at the time when the action must be performed if the agent's generic interests are to be protected.

So much is clear enough in the abstract. However, the application of the general principle presupposes that the identification of subjects of consent is unproblematic. Clearly, however, even if the ideal-typical subject of consent is none other than the ostensible agent, this leaves the status of many others unsettled. For example, what do we make of ostensible agents who have incapacitated themselves through drink or drugs, or who are in what we take to be a temporary state of unconsciousness? More challengingly, as we indicated in chapter two, we interpret the PGC as requiring precaution

[6] As, indeed, it already contains the idea of a 'person'. See Naffine, n 5 above, at 363.

to be exercised proportionately in relation to those who, despite appearing not to be agents (hence not ostensible agents), might be agents. However, the positions of such possible (but not ostensible) agents are not all the same. For example, while human embryos, fetuses, neonates, and young children are potential agents who, normal development permitting, will become ostensible agents, ex-ostensible agents who are now in a persistent vegetative state have a history of agency but without any evidence of present agency and without any prospect of recovering agency. By contrast, the severely mentally handicapped seem to have ostensible agency neither in the past nor potentially in the future.

For practical purposes, there is one important difference between respecting another as an agent and respecting the will of a subject of consent. While it is possible to respect another ostensible agent as a bearer of rights without the agent having to demand that its rights be respected, it is not possible to act on the decisions of a subject of consent without the subject communicating its will (to give or to withhold consent). This means that, even if the ideal-typical or paradigmatic agent is the ideal-typical subject of consent, and vice versa, we cannot put a procedural justification into operation unless the agent (subject of consent) signals that its will is to consent. For practical purposes, therefore, even if communicative competence, the ability to communicate, is not one of the defining conditions for a subject of consent, it is a pre-condition for procedural justification. It follows that a legal system that aspires to model itself on Gewirthian principles will start with an ideal-typical case in which the capacity and competence elements for the application of procedural justification are present before formulating guidelines (using a precautionary approach to agency) for the various non-ideal-typical cases.

The ideal-typical case is fairly straightforward. The paradigm is a transaction involving an ostensible agent who is a subject of consent, and, what is more, this is a subject who has the requisite level of communicative competence and the ability to communicate consent (or refusal) in the particular-occurrent circumstances (ie the particular circumstances at hand). Other things being equal,[7] when such an agent signals consent, this amounts to a procedural justification.

The non-ideal-types deviate from this focal case in several different ways. Some involve ostensible agents who are temporarily incapacitated or who have incapacitated themselves; some involve potential ostensible agents; some involve parties who are no longer ostensible agents; and some parties who never have been and never will be ostensible agents. Each case is different; each raises its own distinctive considerations. Consider the following indicative sample:

[7] This qualifier refers to the further conditions for a valid and effective consent that we discuss in chs 5, 6 and 7.

—Where an ostensible agent is asleep or drunk, or under the influence of drugs, or the like, the ideal-type is not instantiated. However, this is only because the agent is (temporarily) disabled from communicating consent (or refusal) in the particular-occurrent circumstances.

—Children approaching adulthood are a different kind of case. They are on the cusp of ostensible agency. They are very possibly agents. They are also very possibly subjects of consent with communicative competence. In line with the thinking in the *Gillick* case, extra care needs to be taken in dealing with those who are about to enter into the consenting community.

—At the very beginning of human life, human embryos, fetuses, and neonates, even if precaution reminds us that they are possible agents and possible subjects of consent, do not have communicative competence. In their cases, there is no real possibility of procedural justification; and the fact that they are treated as possible rights-holders (under precaution) means that special justification is needed where action is taken against their generic interests. In general, the shape of such a special justification is that the action is necessary in order to protect the possible agent's own, more important, generic interests, or to protect the more important generic interests of another possible agent, or to protect the generic interests of an ostensible agent.

—Then, there are the mentally incompetent, those who are treated as being neither ostensible agents nor subjects of consent. Such persons might be able to say 'Yes, I consent' or put a tick in a box on a consent form, but they do not understand the import of their actions. Their mental capacities put them on a par with young children and, for practical purposes, they invite being treated as such.

—At the end of life, ex-ostensible agents who are now in a persistent vegetative state, or who are dead, are beyond the ambit of simple procedural justification, and no special justification is required for their treatment. However, the idea that there should be respect for their wills as one-time ostensible agents, when they were subjects of consent and did have communicative competence, merits consideration.

If a legal regime is to conform to Gewirthian principles, it must steer between two unacceptable positions. On the one side, it must avoid over-reaching legitimate paternalism. It must, thus, avoid denying to those who should be treated as ostensible agents the opportunity to operate as subjects of consent—accordingly, it must take care not to rule out the possibility of procedural justifications in relation to those who are temporarily disabled from communicating consents (or refusals) and those who are at the margins of ostensible agency. On the other side, where the transaction involves one who cannot be treated as a subject of consent, it must not fabricate or fictionalise consent—for example, the doctrine of substituted judgment must not be passed off as representing the decision of a subject of consent when it relates to one who never has been (and might never be) such a subject.

Our discussion in this chapter is in two principal sections. In section II, we deal with the ideal-typical subject of consent before speaking to precautionary reasoning and the particular problem of setting age-limits for various rights. Having put in place its qualifying standard for a subject of consent (and, concomitantly, having specified the ideal-typical capacity and competence elements for procedural justification), a legal regime faces two further sets of questions, one relating to the ideal-typical subject of consent, the other relating to the various cases that deviate from the ideal-type. So far as subjects of consent are concerned, it remains for the law to spell out the complete terms of the procedural justification. Under what conditions (over and above those relating to capacity and competence) will a subject of consent be judged to have given a valid and effective consent? We deal with this issue in chapters five, six, and seven, where we discuss the nature of an unforced and informed choice to consent, and the scope and signalling of consent. As for the principles governing transactions that do not instantiate the ideal-type, we discuss the principal candidates—substituted judgment, best interests, proxies, and the like—in section III of the present chapter.

## II Identifying Subjects of Consent

As we said in our introductory remarks, if consent is to be recognised as a procedural justification, decisions must be made about who has the capacity and competence to consent, about who is to be treated as a subject of consent. In this part of the chapter, we start by sketching the Gewirthian ideal-typical subject of consent, before viewing that ideal-type under the precautionary principle, and then addressing the hard practical question of setting thresholds to determine when, as it were, one comes of age as a subject of consent.

### *(i) The Ideal-typical Subject of Consent*

Transactions between agents in a Gewirthian community are regulated by a background scheme of rights and duties validated by the PGC. Within such a community, consent functions to enable agents to modify their relationships with one another or to put in place new relationships. Agents are *not required* to modify their relationships (they may stand on their rights) any more than they are required to exercise their powers (they may keep their powder dry). However, without these options given by consent, many agents will find that the background scheme is over-rigid and that they lack the flexibility that they need to pursue many of their individual projects and purposes. In this context, the ideal-typical subject of consent is not the agent who actually makes use of consent; rather, it is simply one who has the capacity to form a will about the giving or refusing of consent—in other words, the ideal-typical subject of consent is the ideal-typical agent.

When a simpler Gewirthian community evolves into an institutionalised legal order, the power of the community to enforce the background standards assumes a more concentrated and co-ordinated form. However, the essential features of the Gewirthian community remain the same. Agents are agents; rights are rights; consent is the vehicle for modifications to relationships and the creation of new relationships; and the ideal-typical subject of consent is the ideal-typical agent.

When we say that the ideal-typical subject of consent must have the capacity to form a will about the giving or refusing of consent, this calls for three points of clarification.

First, the capacity in question must be a *developed* capacity. It might well be correct to view a human embryo or fetus as already having the roots of a capacity for making judgements as to the giving or withholding of consent.[8] However, this is not yet a developed capacity, and the ideal-type specifies that potential is not sufficient. Of course, once the ideal-type is viewed under precaution, it might be argued that we cannot be sure whether the human embryo or fetus (1) merely has the relevant capacity in a radical or potential form or (2) has the relevant capacity in a developed form but lacks the ability to signal its will. However, so far as procedural justification is concerned, this is not critical. If the human embryo or fetus (or young child, for that matter) does not yet have the relevant capacity in a developed form, it is not a subject of consent, and procedural justification is ruled out in principle. If, on the other hand, the human embryo or fetus (or young child) has the capacity in a developed form but (as a 'locked-in agent' unable to display its agency) it is unable to communicate its will, procedural justification is ruled out in practice (we will add a caveat about communicative competence below).

Secondly, what precisely is it that the qualifying capacity of a subject of consent enables the agent to do or to understand? In chapters five and six, we will discuss the making of an unforced and informed choice as conditions of an adequate consent. This unpacks the general concept of agency as an exercise in voluntary and purposive action. It presupposes a capacity for free action and for action based on relevant knowledge and understanding. So far as the capacity to consent is concerned, one will not qualify as an ideal-typical subject of consent unless one understands the nature and significance of consenting. Accordingly, a subject of consent will understand that, in the procedural justificatory paradigm, the giving of consent is *optional* in accordance with one's will. If A, the supposed subject of

[8] See, eg, John Keown, 'Restoring Moral and Intellectual Shape to the Law after *Bland*' (1997) 113 *Law Quarterly Review* 481.

consent, is under the mistaken impression that the giving of consent is *required*, this suggests that A is not yet a subject of consent or that some improper pressure or misinformation is in play. (Of course, if the giving of consent actually is morally required, then procedural justification is redundant; the justificatory driver in such circumstances is the principle that generates the requirement to consent, not the consent itself). Assuming that A understands that consenting is optional, if A then consents to an act by B that would otherwise violate A's rights, A must also understand that he is authorising such an act. Similarly, if A consents to the exercise of a power that changes his relationship with B, A must understand that he is authorising such an act. It is not enough for A to understand that, if he signs the consent form, B will go ahead with some medical procedure or that, if he signs the contract with B, he will be indebted to a certain amount to B. Over and above this appreciation, A must understand that by so consenting he is precluded from challenging the legitimacy of B's actions in reliance on the consent. To put this another way, no one will be a subject of consent unless their moral education has taught them the significance of consent.[9]

Thirdly, not only must ideal-typical subjects of consent have the developed dispositional capacity to consent and to understand the implications of consenting, they must have this capacity at the relevant particular-occurrent moment. When an ostensible agent is under the influence of drink or drugs, and so on, there is a temporary disruption to his or her capacity to consent. The fact, for example, that a woman, when sober, can consent to sex does not mean that the consent she gives when under the influence of drink or drugs should be treated in the same way. When an ostensible agent's capacity to consent is thus impaired, this is no longer an ideal-typical subject of consent, and the recipient of the 'consent' has no reasonable basis for reliance on the 'consent'.[10]

Alongside these conditions for an ideal-typical subject of consent, procedural justification requires a subject of consent with particular-occurrent communicative competence. When ostensible agents are asleep, or unconscious, or under a general anaesthetic, or the like, the difficulty is not so much that their capacity to understand the implications of consent is impaired (as where an agent is under the influence of drink or drugs) as that they are unable to communicate their will. In practice, it probably makes little difference whether agents are so fatigued that they can no longer think straight (and, thus, no longer qualify as ideal-typical subjects of consent) or whether they are simply asleep (and, thus, lack particular-occurrent

[9] The education, experience and maturity of the subject of consent must also be commensurate with any special features of the decision once made (eg its irreversibility or wholly negative impact on the agent's generic interests). See further below at 113.

[10] If the recipient honestly and reasonably believes that the agent retains the capacity to consent, and has consented, there might be a defence based on honest mistake. Compare the discussion of the principles underlying signalling in ch 7.

communicative competence). The fact of the matter is that workable procedural justifications presuppose ideal-typical subjects of consent in settings that meet the proviso for communicative competence.

### *(ii) Subjects of Consent Viewed under the Precautionary Principle*

The precautionary principle addresses the risk that the other party to a transaction, even if not seeming to be an agent (that is, even if not an ostensible agent), nevertheless actually is an agent and, thus, has generic rights (and, of course, is entitled to be treated as a bearer of generic rights). In other words, the precautionary principle is designed to avoid the risk of treating an agent as a non-agent and to minimise any damage that might unwittingly be occasioned to an agent's generic interests.

Schematically, we can distinguish two levels of possible agency at which precaution is required. At the first level, the question is whether the other party to a transaction is an agent (and, thus, has generic rights). Because our judgements might not always correctly discriminate between parties who are agents and those who are not, precaution dictates that our practical reasoning should recognise the *possibility* of agency. In other words, where there is at least the possibility of agency, agents are required to act on the basis that they are dealing with a possible rights-holder. At the second level, the question is whether the other party to the transaction is capable of exercising its will in relation to its rights (actual or possible), which is to say, the question is whether we are dealing with a subject of consent. However, as we have said, it is one thing to respect the possibility that some being is a bearer of generic rights (qua agent), it takes rather more to be in a position to respect the specific will of that being. For, unless the other party has particular-occurrent communicative competence, consent cannot be operationalised in practice, and this is not an ideal-typical case for procedural justification.

In this section, we present some indicative remarks about precautionary reasoning as follows. First, we speak to the basis and extent of the protection afforded to those who are beneficiaries of the precautionary principle; secondly, we consider some classes of beneficiaries; thirdly, we deal with so-called 'intermittent agents'; and, finally, we introduce the general idea of task competence and, in particular, 'specific task competence' and 'societal competence'.

#### (a) Protection under Precaution

Those who benefit from the PGC under precaution achieve this status through the *possibility* that they are agents (and, concomitantly, the *possibility* that they are subjects of consent). They are to be treated on the footing that they might be agents (subjects of consent) who, for one or other reason, are not able to display the free and purposive behaviour that is characteristic of agency—including displaying a developed and demonstrable capacity for giving free and informed consent to actions that impact negatively on their generic well-being. *In theory*, the presumption is that they *might be* agents (subjects of consent), not that they *are* agents, although, in some cases, *for practical purposes*, precaution requires the probability that they might be agents to be presumed (with the effect that they are to be presumed, for practical purposes, to be agents). The concept of probability applies simply because it is of application to the category of *possible* agents. However, this raises issues as to how the degree of probability is to be assessed. This, in turn has two components, a qualitative one and a quantitative one.

Qualitatively, precautionary reasoning grants moral status to ostensible agents on the basis that they can be treated as agents, and this is so because they display the ability to behave as agents. That a being displays the ability to behave like an agent is, however, something that is subject to evidence, which admits of degrees. Proportionality is, hence applicable, and we can infer that the probability that a non-ostensible agent is an agent is proportional to the strength of the evidence that the non-ostensible agent has the capacities of ostensible agency. The *capacities* for ostensible agency, however, are not displayed in overt behaviour alone; they are usually inferred from biological structures and states that are generally associated with ostensible agency. Consequently, it is not unreasonable to presume that moral status is proportional to the degree to which a being possesses such structures and states.

This intuition is at least consistent with two other ways of approaching the idea of probability in this context. The first of these ways is that non-ostensible agents are to be presumed to be agents in proportion to how 'easy' it is to imagine that they are agents who simply cannot display ostensible agency. However, the more associated states a being has, the less fanciful will be the hypotheses (some speculative and metaphysical) that will need to be true if they really are agents. The second of these ways is that non-ostensible agents are to be presumed to be agents in proportion to the degree to which they approach being agents (which is in turn correlated with the degree to which it is possible to treat a being as an agent). For example, although to be an agent (or subject of consent) a being must have the capacity to give free and informed consent, and those who only have the capacity to give consent that is not free or informed are not agents, those who can give consent (albeit not free or informed) are closer to being agents (subjects of consent) than those that cannot give any sort of consent.[11]

From this perspective, the qualities that are relevant to a calculus of proportionality fall to be determined by empirical psychology and biology.

[11] It is on such a basis that Gewirth reasons that non-agents acquire generic rights in proportion to the degree to which they approach being agents. But it must be remembered that we are critical of this, as it lacks consideration of the issues that bring precautionary reasoning into play, and agree only that agents have duties to non-ostensible agents on the basis of such proportionality (and, with that, the possibility of their agency).

This, however, does not help with quantitative considerations, which are important because, just as respect for the generic well-being of two ostensible agents can come into conflict, so protecting the generic well-being of non-ostensible agents can sometimes come into conflict with respect for the generic well-being of ostensible agents and other non-ostensible agents. In principle, such conflicts are to be resolved on the basis that the strength of duty to a being is a product of (1) the probability that the being is an agent and (2) the severity of the generic harm that the being is threatened with suffering (severity being correlative to the degree of needfulness of the particular generic capacity that is threatened in relation to action and/or successful action in general).

Except for a special case, for such considerations to be applied to resolve conflicts, however, requires that it be possible to quantify both the degree of probability of agency and the degree of severity of harm. Moreover, assuming such scales of probability and severity to be possible, it is further required that the two scales should be commensurable (which is to say, it is necessary that the calibrations on the scales and their conversions make it possible to say that a specific degree of probability of agency is equivalent to a specific degree of severity of generic harm). The special case is that of a 'one variable only' conflict, whether that variable concerns the probability of agency or the severity of harm. Such cases arise where the choice is between imposing generic harm of equal severity on either A or B, the probability of agency differing as between A and B—for instance, where to save the life of an ostensible agent (A) requires the death of a non-ostensible agent (B); or where the choice is between imposing generic harm of different severity on either A or B, the probability of agency being the same in relation to A and B—for instance, where to save the life of an ostensible agent (A) necessitates an invasion of the privacy of another ostensible agent (B). Even here, the direct resolution of conflicts will depend on it being clear (if not quantifiable) that the one generic harm is greater than the other (or the probability of agency in one case is greater than the other).

In chapter nine, we discuss a particularly difficult multi-variable case, *Re A (Children) (Conjoined Twins: Surgical Separation)*.[12] On our analysis, in this case, two hard choices have to be made. One choice, a life and death choice, has to be made between neonates; neither is an ostensible agent but it is arguable that the probability of agency is greater in A than in B. The other choice to be made is between the generic rights of the parents, C and D (who themselves refuse to make a choice between A and B), and whichever of the neonates is favoured by the first choice. In making this second choice, the problem of commensurability is particularly acute because we have to choose between some level of harm to the generic interests of ostensible

[12] [2000] 4 All ER 961. See, too, Naffine, n 5 above, for an analysis of the court's implicit presuppositions about the status of the twins as legal persons.

agents C and D and the right to life of non-ostensible agent A. Problems of this kind, we believe, can only in part be solved on the basis of scientific evidence. To some extent, they must be left to the discretion of authorised bodies acting in good faith to make decisions that might not have determinate answers under the PGC. We will return to this general issue in chapter ten.[13]

(b) Beneficiaries of Precaution

In principle, there are agents and non-agents. If legal systems were able to differentiate cleanly and correctly between agents and non-agents, the 'in principle' distinction could be applied in practice. However, legal systems have no special detectors for agency. In practice, therefore, the operative distinction has to be that between ostensible and non-ostensible agents. In this latter category, inanimate objects and primitive lifeforms might not be candidate agents. However, what do we make of higher animals, very young children (including the unborn), severely mentally handicapped and damaged persons, and others who display the capacities of agency in part but not in full? What do we make, in other words, of those classes of beings that Gewirth terms 'marginal agents'?

According to Gewirth, marginal agents have the generic rights in proportion to the degree to which they approach being agents.[14] As we pointed out in chapter two, however, this aspect of Gewirth's analysis cannot be correct because the generic rights are rights under the will conception, and it is only agents who can have such rights. To be sure, so-called marginal agents can approach, to varying degrees, the point at which they will qualify as bearers of generic rights; but they cannot have the generic rights to varying degrees.[15] They are either agents, in which case they have the generic rights in full, or they are not agents, in which case they have no generic rights. In the latter case, however, agents may, nonetheless have both positive and negative duties in relation to the generic interests of marginal agents.

These duties can derive indirectly as a result of the relationship between marginal agents and agents that requires protection of marginal agents' generic *interests* in order to protect the generic rights of agents. There are a

[13] For extended discussion of the dilemma presented by *Re A*, see Deryck Beyleveld and Roger Brownsword, *Human Dignity in Bioethics and Biolaw* (Oxford, Oxford University Press, 2001) at 254–63; and for the idea of good faith legal judgments in the context of a polity committed to the PGC, see Deryck Beyleveld and Roger Brownsword, *Law as a Moral Judgment* (London, Sweet and Maxwell, 1986; reprinted in paperback: Sheffield, Sheffield Academic Press, 1994) chs 5 and 7–9.

[14] Alan Gewirth, *Reason and Morality* (Chicago, University of Chicago Press, 1978) at 121–22, and 142–45.

[15] Compare James F Hill, 'Are Marginal Agents "Our Recipients"?' in Edward Regis Jr (ed), *Gewirth's Ethical Rationalism: Critical Essays with a Reply by Alan Gewirth* (Chicago, IL, University of Chicago Press, 1984) at 180.

number of strands of indirect protection but they are not of immediate concern to us here.[16]

More importantly, for present purposes, the duties of ostensible agents in their dealings with marginal agents can arise under precautionary reasoning. The point, it will be recalled, is that, although marginal agents do not display the capacities of agency and thus do not appear to be agents, they might, nevertheless, be agents, and the categorical nature of the PGC requires this to be taken into account. Specifically, precaution must be exercised in proportion to the probability that marginal agents might be agents, which will be in proportion to the degree to which they approach being ostensible agents.[17] In effect, this means that Gewirth is right, *for practical purposes,* when he reasons that agents owe proportional duties to marginal agents in proportion to the degree to which they approach being agents. Nevertheless, he is wrong in contending that the reason why they owe these proportional duties is because of the proportional generic rights possessed by marginal agents (on account of the degree of their approach to agency). The proportional duties are owed to marginal agents, not as possessors of some generic rights or the generic rights in part, on account of their being partially agents, but because of the varying degrees of probability that they might be agents in full and, thus, have the generic rights in full, and the categorical duty of agents not to deny the full protection of the PGC to all agents.

While this framework applies to all marginal agents, it is important to bear in mind that different groups of marginal agents have their own distinctive features that require special analysis.

*Unconscious Adults Expected to Recover* Strictly speaking, unconscious adult persons (including those who are merely asleep), even where they possess the capacities of agency, are not agents. But they are also not, strictly speaking, 'marginal agents'. They are prospective agents (or 'prospective purposive agents' in Gewirth's own terminology). Of course, it is not wholly impossible that those who display the capacities of agents when conscious lose these capacities when they are unconscious, and regain them (albeit mysteriously) when they regain consciousness. However, whatever speculative doubts there

[16] Some grounds are: the affection that agents might have for marginal agents; brutalising effects on agents of insensitivity to the ostensible suffering of marginal agents; and marginal agents being the property of agents. For discussion of indirect protection, see Deryck Beyleveld and Roger Brownsword, *Mice, Morality and Patents* (London, Common Law Institute of Intellectual Property, 1993); and 'Legal Argumentation in Biolaw' in Peter Kemp, Jacob Rendtorff and Niels Mattson Johansen (eds) *Bioethics and Biolaw (Vol 1: Judgement of Life)* (Copenhagen, Rhodos International Science and Art Publishers and Centre for Ethics and Law, 2000) at 179.

[17] For this argument in fuller form, see Deryck Beyleveld and Shaun Pattinson, 'Precautionary Reason as the Link to Moral Action' in Michael Boylan (ed), *Medical Ethics* (Upper Saddle River, NJ, Prentice-Hall, 2000) at 39.

may be about a person's possession of the capacities of agency while they are unconscious, precautionary reasoning dictates that we treat such persons as agents—or, at any rate, it so dictates where such persons, when consciousness is regained, characteristically display ostensible agency.

How should we characterise such unconscious ostensible agents in relation to their status as subjects of consent? Should we say that they are subjects of consent in their waking hours but not while they are asleep; or that they are subjects of consent throughout, but the proviso for particular-occurrent communicative competence does not hold while they are asleep? For the same reason that we treat beings as ostensible agents even when they are asleep, we should treat subjects of consent as such even when they are asleep. Accordingly, although sleeping subjects of consent are not ideal-typical cases, they present no real difficulty. If a procedural justification is sought, such agents can be woken up and their consent requested.

More interesting issues arise in connection with those whose unconsciousness renders them what we might call 'ostensible prospective agents' who cannot simply be woken up in order to obtain a required consent. This group includes those who have suffered a concussion rendering them unconscious, or those to whom an anaesthetic has been administered, in cases where the action for which consent is required cannot be deferred until the person regains consciousness if it is to be carried out successfully or without unacceptable risk.

We will return to consideration of such persons when dealing with proxies and the justification of actions affecting persons in this group negatively later in this chapter.

*Human Embryos, Fetuses and Very Young Children* If ostensible agents who are temporarily unconscious are a relatively uncontroversial case, quite the opposite applies to human embryos and fetuses as well as to very young children (at any rate, in principle, if not generally in practice). Although these are marginal agents who are not yet ostensible agents, they are generally potential ostensible agents. Some, including Gewirth, claim that their potentiality suffices to give them a degree of moral status.[18] However, they should not be thought of as potential agents (unless this is merely shorthand for 'potential ostensible agents'). This is because they might (albeit unknowably), in fact, be agents, who, for various reasons, about which we can only speculate, cannot display their agency. Indeed, something like this must be the case under metaphysical doctrines like reincarnation or metempsychosis.[19] Furthermore, it should be clear, at least under

[18] See also Klaus Steigleder, 'The Moral Status of Potential Persons' in Elisabeth Hildt and Dietmar Mieth (eds), *In Vitro Fertilisation in the 1990s* (Aldershot, Ashgate, 1998) at 239–46.

[19] This is the doctrine that souls pre-exist in heaven before conception, when they are inserted into the zygote. Wordsworth alludes to this in his 'Ode on Intimations of Immortality from Recollection of Early Childhood'.

Gewirthian theory, that potential agency cannot confer any generic rights, simply because potential agents in not being actual agents cannot exercise rights under the will conception of rights. And, more generally, it is surely the case, as Judith Jarvis Thomson and others have claimed, that potential agency, as such, confers only potential moral status (potential generic rights in a Gewirthian context), not a degree of achieved moral status (or a degree of generic rights).[20]

Nevertheless, because it is possible that members of this group are agents, precautionary reasoning requires this to be taken into account, with the consequence that agents owe duties to members of this group in proportion to the degree to which they approach being ostensible agents. Furthermore, because having the properties that define being a potential ostensible agent makes it more likely that a being might be an actual agent, precautionary reasoning entails that potential ostensible agency is itself a factor that confers a degree of moral status (although not a degree of generic rights) on this group (ie generates duties of agents to members of this group).

When considering this group, it is important to distinguish their status as potential ostensible agents from their status as future ostensible agents. To illustrate: during gestation, it is possible for the pregnant mother to act in various ways that will impact negatively on the generic conditions of agency of her unborn child.[21] If she were to do comparable things to an ostensible agent these would be violations of the generic rights of the ostensible agent. Assuming that the damage caused to the unborn child is not such that it prevents the unborn child becoming an ostensible agent, the damage caused is to be regarded as a violation of the generic rights of the child viewed as a future ostensible agent. To this it might be objected that nothing is actually done to any existing agent and that this renders such a construction impermissible. We disagree, for two principal reasons. First, many actions with effects on existing ostensible agents have these effects in the future, meaning that there is a time-lag between the performance of the action and the effects that the action has on the ostensible agent. The difference between the time-lag in such cases and in relation to future ostensible agents is surely merely one of degree, not of kind. While this is not irrelevant, as (generally) the greater the time-lag the greater the opportunity to ameliorate the effects, it surely does not justify regarding future ostensible agents as of less concern than presently existing ostensible agents. Secondly, there

[20] See Judith Jarvis Thompson, 'A Defence of Abortion' in RM Dworkin (ed), *The Philosophy of Law* (London, Oxford University Press, 1977) at 112; and John Harris, *The Value of Life* (London, Routledge and Kegan Paul, 1985) at 11–12 (if potential agency equates to actual agency, then it seems that the potential death of an agent equates to an actual agent's death—in which case, potential agents are already as good as dead).

[21] Compare *Winnipeg Child and Family Services (Northwest Area) v G* 152 DLR (4th) 193, where a welfare agency sought an order for the detention of a pregnant woman in order to prevent her from consuming intoxicants.

is no reason to think that an action that intentionally, negligently, or otherwise culpably impacts negatively on the generic well-being of a future ostensible agent is not intentional, negligent or otherwise culpable infliction of generic damage on an ostensible agent. If, *at the time* of commission, no damage is done to any agent, it nonetheless involves a lack of respect for the generic well-being of agents, which is prohibited by the PGC.[22]

The import of these various considerations concerning potentiality and futurality is that human embryos, fetuses and very young children must be treated as possible agents, as possible bearers of rights, who are on a development track that will generally take them to ostensible agency. Their present status as possible agents enjoins present *caution*; and their future status as ostensible agents enjoins *present* caution. Potentiality is not actuality, but it does invite precaution. So far as procedural justification goes, however, there is no practical possibility of dealing directly with the members of this group as subjects of consent. Even if they might be subjects of consent, even if they probably will become subjects of consent, the proviso for particular-occurrent communicative competence is not satisfied. If we are to justify acting against their possible generic rights, some other kind of justification is required. We return to this question in the second part of the chapter where we discuss strategies for dealing with non-ideal-typical subjects of consent.

(c) Intermittent Agents

To understand the position of young children it is also necessary to consider the possibility of intermittent agency, which becomes more important the closer the child comes to being an ostensible agent.

At any particular instant in time, a child must be either an agent or a non-agent. However, it is possible for a being that has developed the capacities of agency to lose them and then regain them (and, perhaps, lose them again). Such a being will be an intermittent agent. Furthermore, whether or not we are actually dealing with an agent, that being might display the capacities of agency only intermittently, and hence be an ostensible intermittent agent.

How should we treat young children who, during their development, at times appear to be capable of rational thought, only to appear to lose this capacity temporarily?[23] As far as the moral status of intermittent agents *as such* is concerned, they have the generic rights when they are agents and lack them when they are not. However, it does not follow that if a human

[22] Compare Joel Feinberg, 'The Rights of Animals and Unborn Generations' in Joel Feinberg, *Rights, Justice, and the Bounds of Liberty* (Princeton, NJ, Princeton University Press, 1980) at 159.

[23] Intermittent agency also characterises the behaviour of persons recovering from certain kinds of stroke or other severe brain injuries, as well as the behaviour of some persons with severe mental illness.

being X is ostensibly only an intermittent agent then X is to be treated as having the generic rights only some of the time (while X displays agency).

If we are to treat an ostensible intermittent agent X as an intermittent agent (ie as having no generic rights at one time, and all the generic rights at another time) we will need to know whether, at any particular time, X is an agent or not an agent. Suppose, then, that we attempt to assess X's status vis-à-vis having the generic rights. We will find ourselves confronted with at least two serious difficulties. First, whatever the result of our test, it cannot be used to justify treating X according to that result for, by the very nature of the case, X might have altered status in the meantime. Secondly, in order to assess X's status, various procedures will have to be gone through, and the moral permissibility of such procedures will rest, to some extent, on X's status. For these reasons, we will not be able to find out what X's status is in advance of particular interactions.

Of course, while we cannot seek to ascertain X's status at any instant, we might be able to assess, over a moderate period of time, how close X is to having the capacities needed to be an agent in a standing fashion. Thus, it is tempting to say that if X, over a moderate period of time, more reliably displays the capacities needed to be an agent than does Y, then X is to be accorded more status than Y. However, while this is not incorrect, it is unclear just how X and Y are to be treated, and it is important that the idea that X and Y are to be treated as having a different status not be misunderstood.

If X is an agent, the PGC requires us to grant the generic rights to X. The first duty that agents have under the PGC is to grant its protection to agents. If X is an agent and agents do not grant X the generic rights, then they have violated the PGC. Since the requirement to obey the PGC is absolutely categorical, it might seem that the PGC requires agents to treat X as an agent to the extent that it is possible to do so, unless it is absolutely certain that X *is not* an agent.

However, matters are not quite so simple. For *if agents assume that X is an agent*, and try to treat X accordingly *and X is not in fact an agent*, then they will be attempting to impose duties on X that X is unable to discharge (in particular, the duty to abide by the PGC). Furthermore, in cases where the interests of X come into conflict with the generic rights of agents, agents might be required to restrict their exercise of the generic rights for the sake of generic rights that X is presumed to have, but does not have. Thus, it might seem that agents should not treat X as an agent unless it is absolutely certain that X *is* an agent.

However, since we cannot know (at the relevant point in time) whether X is an agent or a partial agent, we must apply precautionary reasoning. This reveals that the apparent antinomy is not real. The negative consequences of an error *in failing to grant X the generic rights* are not commensurable with the negative consequences of an error *in granting X the generic rights*. The burdens that are placed on agents by restricting their actions in relation to X, on the basis of the presumption that X is an agent when X is not, do not deny the generic rights to agents. What will be restricted are various actions that agents can perform as an exercise of the generic rights, not the generic rights themselves. Furthermore, if it is an error to grant X the generic rights, thereby placing burdens on X that X cannot discharge, then this is not something that affects X's generic rights (for if it is an error, X has no generic rights). It is, therefore, under the PGC, worse to err in assuming that X is not an agent than to err in assuming that X is an agent. Thus, *for practical purposes*, precautionary reasoning requires that X be assumed to be an agent.

(d) Task Competence

Partial agents and intermittent agents must not be confused with agents who lack competence to perform specific tasks without unintentionally harming themselves or others ('specific task-incompetent agents'). All agents lack competence to perform some specific tasks, and their task competence varies. Consequently, although all agents have all the generic rights equally, it does not follow that they all have equal rights to perform specific tasks. For example, the fact that X and Y are agents with all the generic rights equally does not give X and Y an equal right to be airline pilots, or even an equal right to train as airline pilots. This, however, does not impact on their possession of the *generic* rights. It impacts, rather, on their right to exercise the generic rights for particular purposes, which does not depend on their having the capacities needed to be agents (to be able to act at all), but on their having the capacities beyond this that are necessary for the successful performance of particular actions only.

The tasks that an agent must be able to perform without unintentionally harming itself or others vary from society to society. Thus, specific task competences that an agent must achieve to enable it to lead an independent existence without unintentionally harming itself or others will vary from society to society. We may designate as 'societally competent agents' those agents who have achieved such a level of task competence (the level of competence to be expected of a normal adult) relative to the demands of life in their particular society. The more demanding it is to function in a particular society, the higher the threshold for societal competence.

With this in mind, we can be more precise about how ostensible intermittent agents are to be treated. If X is an ostensible intermittent agent then X will sometimes not be able to exercise intentional control over its actions, and sometimes will behave in ways that cause unintended harm to itself or others because of its inherent inability at these times ostensibly to *act*. In relation to specific actions, generally ostensible intermittent agents will behave no differently from the way in which ostensible specific task-incompetent agents will act. So ostensible intermittent agents are, in practice, to be treated as societally incompetent agents—agents of restricted task competence who (as agents) possess all the generic rights, but lack the capacities of agency to the degree necessary for them to be able to cope independently with some of the 'normal' interaction-situations they are likely to encounter in their social environment without causing unintended harm to themselves or others.[24]

If we were to put these ideas into a normal developmental sequence, the staging posts would be: some signs of agency and task competence but not yet an ostensible agent; an ostensible agent with some task competence but without yet being a societally competent agent; and an ostensible agent with sufficient task competence to be treated as a societally competent agent. Beyond this point, some agents (such as the airline pilots) will acquire further specialised task competence; but the achievement of societal competence is as far as we need to go. When we consider the case of children who are maturing through ostensible agency to societal competence, this developmental progression is important for determining whether the child is a subject of consent who has competence in relation to the particular task.

### *(iii) When does one Become a Subject of Consent? The Question of Age Limits*

If the findings of developmental psychology are to be believed, then children achieve ostensible agency at around 7–11 years of age, and often much earlier. This raises two questions. First, how is the law to handle children in this age band, some of whom will be ostensible agents, others not? Is there any need, or justification, for resorting to universal qualifying age-limits? Secondly, is there any justification for setting age-limits, often in the high teens, for voting, contracting, marrying, consenting to medical treatment or research, jury service, and the like? If even slow-developing children are already ostensible agents at 11, why delay their entitlement to participate in elections, contracts, or marriages and the like for a further five or more years?

With regard to the first question, it is trite that universal age-limits favour calculability and economy rather than flexibility and investment in individualised judgment. However, there are also questions of fairness and right at stake. The deeper dilemma is nicely put by Laurence Tribe:

> To assume that *this* seven-year-old is unfit to vote, to work, to choose his or her own school, simply because *most* persons of like age have certain characteristics is to condemn by association, by statistical stereotype, by what the Supreme Court . . . has invalidated as 'conclusive presumptions.' Yet, to tailor all determinations to the individual case . . . would be to encourage arbitrary choices, choices

[24] For comparison with Gewirth's own views, see Deryck Beyleveld and Roger Brownsword, *Human Dignity in Bioethics and Biolaw* (Oxford, Oxford University Press, 2001) at 117–34.

that depart from the goal of treating similar cases similarly, and choices that could well conceal substantively impermissible grounds of decision.[25]

Employing our Gewirthian perspective, the passage from pre-ostensible agency to ostensible agency (from possible rights-holder to ostensible rights-holder) is smoothed by precautionary reasoning. Under precaution, young children, not yet ostensible agents, are protected as possible agents. Unless a choice has to be made between their generic interests and the generic interests of an ostensible agent, their generic interests will be respected as though they were covered by the rights of an ostensible agent. To this extent, there will be no sea change in the way that such children are treated when they become ostensible agents (although, of course, the basis on which their generic interests are protected changes from one of precautionary duty to one of ostensible rights entitlement). If a hard choice has to be made between the generic interests of a young child and the generic interests of an ostensible agent, the status of the young child becomes important. If the child is judged to be not yet an ostensible agent its claims are weaker than if it is already an ostensible agent. If a legal system were to rely on a general qualifying age for ostensible agency, this would not be satisfactory; rather, judgements about the status of the child should be made on a case-by-case basis. It follows that the answer to the first question is that legal systems do not, in general, need to have a rule prescribing the precise point at which a child becomes an ostensible agent; and, where a legal system needs to make a precise judgement, a general rule will not serve—in such cases, an individualised judgement is essential.

Turning to the second question, how can a legal system justify the mixed bag of age-limits set for various acts, such limits typically being well above what we take to be the normal age-range for ostensible agency?

As regards the voting age, the right to vote (which is not a generic right in and of itself) is a method of observing the generic right to participate consensually in decisions or decision-making processes affecting oneself. However, the right to vote also empowers agents to make decisions affecting the lives of others. As such, it is permissible to restrict it to those who possess a specific level of task competence. Given that the right to vote (whether as an option or as a requirement) is accorded to all who attain the stipulated voting age (which, let us suppose, is typically 18 years old), this raises two questions. First, since not all 18 year olds will have this competence, should not those who lack it be deprived of the vote? Secondly, since many agents younger than 18 will have this competence, should they not be given the right to vote earlier? *In the abstract*, the answer to both questions must be yes. However, *in practice*, attempting to individualise the voting age and deprive some human beings of the vote altogether not only

[25] Laurence H Tribe, 'Childhood, Suspect Classifications, and Conclusive Presumptions: Three Linked Riddles' (1975) 39 *Law and Contemporary Problems* 8, at 10–11.

runs into practical difficulties and the precautionary need to give the benefit of the doubt to unclear cases, it is also open to outright abuse—we need only contemplate capacity-testing at the entrance to polling stations. All three grounds (practical difficulty, precaution, and possible abuse) argue for universality. The issue, then, is whether the rule may be a *qualified universal* rule (for example, one which restricts the franchise to *all* human beings *above a certain age*). In our opinion, this is permissible provided that the restriction is not one that disqualifies any agents as such (as, for example, one based on gender, or race, religious belief, or level of education would do) but is something that all agents (barring factors beyond anyone's control) can expect to achieve automatically (such as a particular age).[26]

Where, unlike the vote, decisions do not affect others, this removes one class of (task competence) reason for limiting the exercise of the generic right to autonomy. However, autonomy might be exercised in ways that are detrimental to the agent; and, whilst legal systems have no business restricting the autonomy of societally competent agents (who must be permitted to make decisions that they regret), they need to regulate the decision-making of those teenage subjects of consent who are still maturing. Such teenage children might not have the ability to understand the nature and implications of their proposed decision, nor the maturity to appreciate that their decision is entirely prejudicial to their generic interests, or that it is irreversible, or that it has legally backed consequences, and so on. Having said this, legal systems must be careful not to deny autonomous decision-making to such younger subjects of consent as they approach societal competence.

In this light, a legal regime might be justified in setting a lower age-limit for a young person to be permitted to consent to basic dental or medical treatment than to consent to participation in a research trial (at any rate, one in which there is likely to be no benefit to the participating agent). However, if the treatment options are complex or unusual, or have other unusual features, it is important that the child has the competence to appreciate the implications of the specific intervention that is proposed. The functional bureaucratic view of 'consenting' patients or research subjects might well be to give the medical authorities some paper cover; but the child's consent is not worth the paper it is written on unless there is the capacity and competence to generate a real procedural justification.[27]

Finally, where a legal system sets age-limits to determine eligibility to enter into an optional legal transaction, such as a contract or a marriage, the argument for the restriction is not that younger children are not ostensible agents, nor that they are not yet subjects of consent, but that they do not

[26] Whether or not 18 is the right age is another matter, which we cannot go into here.

[27] For critical commentary on the 'gap' between the idealists' view of informed consent in health care settings and the realists' perception (and practice), see Peter H Schuck, 'Rethinking Informed Consent' (1994) 103 *Yale Law Journal* 899.

yet have the maturity or experience that qualifies them as societally competent. On this basis, even if it is not altogether clear why legal regimes should set different ages for marriage and contract, there is a plausible argument for delaying access to such formal institutional sets.

## III Dealing with Non-ideal-typical Subjects of Consent

Where the parties to a transaction are ostensible agents, who are societally competent, and where the proviso as to particular-occurrent communicative competence is satisfied, we have subjects of consent in the ideal-typical setting for procedural justification. As we have seen, however, there are many ways in which there can be deviations from this paradigmatic case. Some parties are on a developmental track towards the ideal-typical situation, some only a short way up the track, others much further; some are of an age where they should be ideal-typical subjects but who will never develop the capacity to consent; and some, who once were in the ideal-typical situation, are no longer so and have no prospect of return.

Legal systems addressing these non-ideal-typical cases must not foist procedural justifications on the parties; consent must be a reality not a fiction. Equally, however, in cases where there is a real possibility that a party has the relevant capacity, it is wrong to deny to such beings the opportunity to exercise their will through consent (or its refusal). In response to these considerations, legal systems resort to a variety of second-best strategies—in particular, relying on substituted judgement, judgements of best interest, and proxies. In this part of the chapter, we discuss these various strategies (and their particular appropriateness or inappropriateness) before speaking briefly to the treatment of the dead and the possibility of substantive justification.

### *(i) Substituted Judgement: The Case of Jerry Strunk*

In 1969, the Kentucky Court of Appeal upheld a lower court ruling authorising the removal of a kidney from Jerry Strunk to be transplanted to his brother Tommy.[28] Jerry was 27 years old, but, with an IQ of 35, he was mentally incompetent; Tommy was 28 years old but dying with kidney disease. On the face of it, Jerry had little to gain from undergoing surgery for the removal of a perfectly healthy kidney, but, by portraying the relationship between Jerry and Tommy in a certain way, the lower court was able to hold that the procedure was actually in Jerry's best interests. Whilst we might jib at this on the facts and hesitate to embrace the utilitarian justification that we sense to be lurking in the background, at least the lower court's reliance on Jerry's best interests makes no pretence that Jerry consented. The appeal court, however, sought to improve the justification by

[28] *Strunk v Strunk* 445 SW 2d 145 (Ky 1969).

introducing the idea of a 'substituted judgement'—that is, the idea that a court could justify the medical procedure by reference to the authorising judgement that Jerry would have made had he been mentally competent. Such an idea was not without precedent. In fact, the court was able to trace the doctrine back to Lord Eldon who, in the early nineteenth-century case of *Ex parte Whitbread*,[29] had ordered payment from a lunatic's surplus income on the ground that this is what the lunatic would have willed. Despite the pedigree of this doctrine, in a brilliant critique, Louise Harmon has highlighted problems relating to: (1) confusion concerning the classes of competence (and incompetence); (2) the distancing of the judgement from the party for whom the substituted judgement purports to speak; and (3) the fictionalising of consent,[30] which we will consider in turn.

First, at the time of *Ex parte Whitbread*, English law drew a distinction between 'lunatics' and 'idiots'. Whereas the former had, at one time, been subjects of consent, the latter had never qualified as such. In other words, whereas so-called lunatics at least had some track record of agency, from which one might detect an indicative pattern of their willed preferences, with idiots there was not even this measure of evidential assistance. In these terms, Jerry Strunk was an idiot. From this, it followed that it was not simply speculative to appeal to what Jerry would have consented to had he been competent, it was misleading to put the case in the same line as those precedents in which the speculation was supported by evidence drawn from a period when the subject of the substituted judgement was competent.

Secondly, when a court makes a substituted judgement in relation to one Jerry Strunk, there is no 'Jerry Strunk as an actual competent agent' to which the judgement can be anchored. It simply cannot be done; and, to speak as though the substituted judgement tracks the preferences of a competent agent is highly misleading. By contrast, when a court makes a substituted judgement in relation to one who once was an ostensible agent—to a Karen Quinlan,[31] a Nancy Cruzan,[32] or a Tony Bland[33]—it can seek to reconstruct the particular agent's profile and anchor its judgement in what seem to have been that agent's characteristic preferences. It *can* do this; but it does not follow that, the court's rhetoric notwithstanding, this is what it actually does. A court's exercise in substituted judgement might pay lip-service to the preferences of the party who once was an ostensible agent, while doing exactly what the court did in a case such as that of Jerry Strunk

[29] 2 Meriv 99, 35 Eng Rep 878. The doctrine was imported into the United States some years later in *In re Willoughby* 11 Paige Ch 257 (NYCh 1844).

[30] Louise Harmon, 'Falling off the Vine: Legal Fictions and the Doctrine of Substituted Judgment' (1990) 100 *Yale Law Journal* 1.

[31] *Re Quinlan* 70 NJ 10, 355 A 2d 647 (1976).

[32] *Nancy Beth Cruzan v Director, Missouri Department of Health* 497 US 261, 110 S Ct 2841 (1990); 111 L Ed 2d 224.

[33] *Airedale NHS Trust v Bland* [1993] 1 All ER 821.

(in which there was not even the possibility of reconstructing the preferences of a party who once was an ostensible agent). In these cases, there is a distance between the flesh and blood person for whom the substituted judgement purports to speak and the generically 'reasonable' reference point for which the judgement actually speaks. Hence, as Harmon pointedly observes, whereas, in *Ex parte Whitbread*, 'Lord Eldon seems to have just looked around and found a generic, reasonable lunatic—a generic, reasonable lunatic prone to give his money away,'[34] in *Strunk*, the court makes its substituted judgement on behalf of a 'generic, reasonable idiot prone to give his organs away.'[35] Small wonder, then, that Lord Eldon's doctrine 'has proved a useful mechanism.'[36]

Thirdly, where the court's substituted judgement speaks for a generic 'reasonable' agent, it fictionalises consent. In Harmon's view, it is not at all clear that this is a benign fiction:

> [T]aking organs from incompetents, terminating their life-support systems, sterilizing them, and forcing psychotropic medication upon them all raise deeply disturbing moral issues. And those deeply disturbing moral issues should be examined by the light of day, not hidden in the dark.[37]

We concur. Consent, as we have said, is an attractive procedural justification. If Jerry Strunk consented to the removal of his kidney for the benefit of his brother, then no wrong was done to Jerry by the removal of the organ. However, to rest the justification on the ground that (incompetent) Jerry would have consented to the procedure had he been a subject of consent who was minded to assist his dying brother is worse than a fiction, it is almost a fraud. If the procedure is to be justified by reference to Jerry's consent, it cannot get to first base unless either Jerry is a subject of consent who purports to consent or, although he is not a subject of consent, he once was so and his biography gives us a basis for treating him as consenting. If such a justification is not available, we need a substantive justification—for example, along the lines that Tommy has a positive right that Jerry should come to his rescue in the emergency. If there is a good substantive justification, then we should not rely on a bad procedural justification, and if neither justification will fly, then we should not allow our sympathy for Tommy to distort our justificatory thinking.

In the light of these remarks arising from the *Strunk* case, we can sketch the limits of legitimate use of substituted judgement. Clearly, where the party for whom the substituted judgement purports to speak has never been a subject of consent, there is no relevant biography for the judgement to tap into. Accordingly, it is a necessary condition for substituted judgement that

[34] Harmon, n 30 above, at 23.

[35] *Ibid*, at 35.

[36] *Ibid*, at 54.

[37] *Ibid*, at 62–63.

the party has a history of being a subject of consent—thus ruling out embryos, fetuses, and children who are not yet ostensible agents as well as incompetents such as Jerry Strunk. This, however, is not sufficient, for we cannot contemplate substituted judgement as even a second-best procedural justification unless the evidence meets a fairly high threshold of plausibility. How high a threshold should a legal system set? Given that we are not dealing with precise advance directives or testamentary dispositions that specify the wishes of a subject of consent about what she wants to happen should she become incompetent, it has to be recognised that the reconstruction of a particular party's preferences involves some degree of speculation. If the party's prior statements and past decisions, coupled with their known values and preferences, leave the issue unclear, it is tempting to supplement such direct biographical evidence by appealing to the preferences of supposedly similar persons in like situations.[38] However, if the price we pay for making the case more plausible is that we put distance between the actual party and the representative reference point, we weaken rather than strengthen the substituted judgement. At all events, it is surely beyond dispute that the minimum evidential condition for a substituted judgement is that it must be at least more likely than not that the party would have consented; and, in this context, we should be slow to criticise legal regimes that seek clear and compelling biographical evidence before acting on the basis of a substituted judgement.[39]

### *(ii) Best Interests*

In practice, so-called best interests justifications are applied in a variety of contexts (child custody, medical treatment, and so on) and to a range of beings who are not ideal-typical subjects of consent. For even the most conscientious and conscionable decision-makers, the best interests standard presents difficulties in its interpretation and application. As Robert Mnookin highlighted in an influential paper, decision-makers often face conflicting expert assessments, added to which, in modern pluralistic societies, there is rarely a 'clear-cut consensus about the values to be used in determining what is "best" '.[40] In some cases, particularly where the focus

[38] Compare *Re AC* (1990) 573 A 2d 1253 (DC CA) (emergency order to perform a Caesarean section on a terminally ill pregnant woman who was near to death).

[39] To avoid any misunderstanding, it should be emphasised that this is not to align ourselves with the defenders of the much-criticised decision in *Cruzan* (n 32 above). There is a difference between insisting upon compelling evidence for a particular substituted judgement (namely, the judgement that the ex-ostensible agent would have wanted any medical support to be withdrawn) and requiring compelling evidence for any substituted judgement, irrespective of its substance. We are taking the latter, not the former, view. See, further, Deryck Beyleveld and Roger Brownsword, *Human Dignity in Bioethics and Biolaw* (Oxford, Oxford University Press, 2001) at 248–49.

[40] Robert H Mnookin, 'Child-Custody Adjudication: Judicial Functions in the Face of Indeterminacy' (1975) 39 *Law and Contemporary Problems* 226, at 229. In the context, not of

is on potential ostensible agents, the future is as important as the present, and developmental considerations are very much to the fore; in other cases, particularly where the focus is on ex-ostensible agents, it is more difficult to place the party's interests in any meaningful time-frame, past, present, or future. As Lord Mustill bluntly put it in the *Bland* case, it is not clear what it means to ask whether the withdrawal of support would be in the young man's best interests because the 'distressing truth which must not be shirked is that . . . [Bland] has no best interests of any kind.'[41] Whatever the direction of a best interests assessment, there is a standing danger of abuse, a danger that 'best interests' justifications operate as fairly thinly disguised rationalisations for doing what is actually in the interests of a third party. In mitigation, it can be said that best interests judgements do not purport to be consent-based justifications. Even if the lower court strained the idea of best interests to order the removal of Jerry Strunk's kidney, it did not claim that this was procedurally justified by Jerry's consent. However, in the larger jurisprudential picture, a fiction of best interests is no better than a fiction of consent.

Where decisions must be made that affect the generic interests of those who are merely possible agents, and for whom substituted judgement is not appropriate, precautionary reasoning should dictate the general shape of a legal system's best interests thinking.

In the case of young children, the parents will typically bear the responsibility for making decisions concerning the child's best interests. As a fail-safe for cases where the parents' judgement is questionable, a legal regime might invest a guardian *ad litem* (ie an independent person to act for the child in court) with authority to speak to an independent assessment of the child's best interest. Where the parents or guardian judge that some transaction with the child (for example, a course of medical treatment) is in the child's best interest, they consent to the act, and a procedural justification is in play. However, *this is not a procedural justification that flows back to the child.* The recipient of the parents' or guardian's consent will be justified in relying on that consent as an answer to the parents or guardian; but, in so far as the child is concerned, the justification is that the action is judged to be in the child's best interests—and the fact that the parents or guardian have consented speaks only to the credentials of the best interests judgement, the decision-maker being able to plead in support of the decision its good faith conformity with the views of those agents whose primary responsibility it is to act as trustees for the child's best interests.

In the case of ex-ostensible agents, where the evidence does not support a substituted judgement, the justification might again be on a best interests

child custody, but medical treatment and research, see PD Skegg, 'Consent to Medical Procedures on Minors' (1973) 36 *Modern Law Review* 370.

[41] *Airedale NHS Trust v Bland* [1993] 1 All ER 821, at 894.

basis. Here, 'best interests' does not focus on developmental considerations of the kind that apply to children, but precautionary reasoning still applies. Once again, the family might be given primary responsibility for making the best interests judgement; and this might issue in a consent of some kind. However, as with children, this is not to be mistaken for a consent that flows back to the ex-ostensible agent.

These remarks lead on quite naturally to a third strategy for dealing with non-ideal-typical cases, that of reliance on proxies or proxy consents.

### *(iii) Proxies*

When persons are unable to give their consent, either because the law sets a legal age for competence, or because the person, for whatever reason, lacks the mental maturity to give a valid consent or is too mentally disturbed to do so, or because the person is unconscious, and so on, the law (and, in medical situations, sometimes medical practice alone) sometimes permits actions that affect the generic well-being of the person to be authorised by the consent (or at least the non-objection) of some third party.

At the most general level, there are two possible functions that proxy authorisation might be intended to achieve. First, it might be intended to be a way of representing the will of the person unable to consent. Alternatively, it might be intended to protect the interests of the person, quite independently of whether or not the person would have consented or would consent if in a position to do so.

To start with a relatively straightforward case: let us suppose that A, who is a subject of consent with societal competence, authorises fellow ostensible agent B to act as his proxy. Let us suppose, for example, that A is a shareholder in a company and that B is to attend the company's annual general meeting as A's proxy. B, as A's proxy, might be authorised to act only in a very specific way (for instance, to cast a vote on a particular matter in a particular way) or the terms of B's authorisation as A's proxy might give him some discretion. Provided that B operates within the terms of the authority given by A, then B's actions on behalf of A are fully procedurally justified, reliance on B's actions reaching back to A's initiating consent that B should act as his proxy.[42]

There are many ways in which there can be deviations from the straightforward case where A is a subject of consent and has designated a proxy (B) to act on her behalf. For example, B might not have been nominated by A, and, indeed, the proxy that the law will recognise might be someone

[42] Legal systems recognise (legal) agency of various kinds, which we discuss in ch 7. The essential pattern of agency is no different to that of proxy. A, a subject of consent, authorises B to act on his behalf and, provided that B acts within the scope of his authority, procedural justification is applicable. Even if the agent or proxy, B, acts in a way that he judges to be in A's best interests, there is still a straightforward procedural justification provided that A has so authorised B (B still represents the will of A).

whose interests conflict with those of A. It is also possible that the law might permit a proxy other than the person nominated by A, and that this person might make decisions that run contrary to indications given by A's nominated proxy.

There can also be deviation from the straightforward case, on account of A not ever being a subject of consent. In this case, the function of proxy authorisation is no longer straightforward. Those who purport to speak for A's best interests are exercising some responsibility but not by virtue of agency or proxy initiated by A. And, as we have seen, where substituted judgements are used, it is a necessary condition that A, if not now a subject of consent, was once so.

The UK Medicines for Human Use (Clinical Trials) Regulations 2004[43] are of interest in relation to these deviations. Schedule 1, Part 1, paragraph 2(a) of the Regulations specifies, in relation to authorisation for entry into a clinical trial on medicinal products for human use, that for an adult and minor in England and Wales and Northern Ireland, and a minor in Scotland, where the person is unable to give informed consent by virtue of physical or mental incapacity, one of the following (whose informed consent shall, in the case of an incapacitated adult, represent the incapacitated adult's presumed will (see Schedule 1, Part 5, paragraph 12, unless the incapacitated person has previously refused to participate: see Schedule 1, Part 1, paragraph 1(5)) may act as a legal representative of the person:

> [A] person, other than a person involved in the conduct of the trial, who—
>
> (aa) by virtue of their relationship with that adult or that minor, is suitable to act as their legal representative for the purposes of that trial, and
> (bb) is available and willing to so act for those purposes, or
>
> if there is no such person, a person, other than a person connected with the conduct of the clinical trial, who is—
>
> (aa) the doctor primarily responsible for the medical treatment provided to that adult, or
> (bb) a person nominated by the relevant health care provider.

There is much cause for disquiet here. Above all, the Regulations illegitimately treat such a proxy consent as providing a procedural justification given by an incapacitated adult when the conditions for this are clearly not satisfied. Furthermore, they permit persons to be designated as legal representatives who arguably are not only not in a position to represent either the will or the best interests of the incapacitated persons, but are in a position of conflicting interest (possibly, eg, a doctor employed by the health-care provider who is a researcher but not involved in the clinical trial at hand). There is also no explicit priority to be given to a proxy nominated by an incapacitated adult prior to becoming incapacitated, should there be one

[43] SI 2004/1031.

(and, indeed, such a person is not even explicitly mentioned), which opens up at least a possibility that a person other than the incapacitated person's nominee might be appealed to (even though, in principle, such a nominee would seem to be the ideal-type of a 'suitable' person to act as legal representative).[44]

Finally, there might be occasions where third parties are asked to consent (or, at least, to indicate no objection) either on their own part or as 'proxies' for some other party, but in both cases merely as a courtesy. For instance, if A authors a work but then assigns the copyright in the work to B, B has the relevant rights concerning reproduction of the work. C, who wishes to reproduce the work, must have B's consent; but C might also consult A to confirm that A has no objection. The 'consent' by A is detached from any right and is a mere courtesy.[45] Alternatively, if A has died and C consults A's family on the same matter, the family acts as a proxy for A only in this attenuated sense.

### *(iv) Dealing with the Dead*

We do not believe that we know or even that we can know what happens to us when we die (meaning, when our lives as physical beings cease). Correlatively, we do not know whether the dead (if they were agents and not merely ostensible agents when living) continue to be agents or not. The dead are to be treated as ex-ostensible agents, who nevertheless might be agents.

Even if the dead must be treated as possible agents, the proviso for communicative competence is not satisfied. Granted, some might believe in the possibility of receiving reliable signals from those 'on the other side'; but, if even Harry Houdini was unable to communicate after his demise, the odds seem to be stacked against lesser ex-ostensible agents. Moreover, when the message is transmitted by a medium (whether or not for payment), the opportunity for abuse is obvious. We suggest, therefore, that, if the dead are to be treated as subjects of consent, then this can only be in relation to wishes they have expressed while living.

At once, however, this raises the thorny issue as to why the wishes of the living (or promises made to the dead when they were living) should be

[44] The position in England, Wales and Northern Ireland, at least in relation to the latter feature, contrasts with the position in relation to incapacitated adults in Scotland, where priority is to be given to a guardian or welfare attorney with power to consent for the adult, failing which the adult's nearest relative may act, failing which (on condition that one of the latter two cannot practicably be contacted) there may now be recourse to a doctor or person nominated by the relevant health-care provider. (See the Medicines for Human Use (Clinical Trials) Regulations 2004, Sch 1, Pt 1, para 2(b)).

[45] In ch 8, we spell out fully the fallacy of supposing that, in the absence of consent, there must be a wrong. This is not so. The wrong is constituted by the violation of a right, not by the absence (or refusal) of consent as such.

respected when they have died. There are at least three good reasons for doing so, apart from considerations that attend to the wishes, expectations, and rights of living persons who might be beneficiaries of these wills.

First, people make wills, or consent (or object) to the removal of their organs after death, and so on, with the expectation that their wishes will be respected. Not to respect the wishes of such ex-ostensible agents is, hence, not to respect the living person who made the wish. In this sense, we have a mirror image of the futurality argument—to act against the interests of the now-deceased ostensible agent is to do a wrong to the ostensible agent who once was.

Secondly, to the extent that institutions and practices that secure the wishes of the deceased enhance the options available to living agents, then actions that diminish trust in such institutions are detrimental to living agents (not only to the beneficiaries that we have already mentioned, but to those agents who would otherwise make use of such institutions).

Thirdly, precautionary reasoning yet again steps in. Precisely because we do not know whether or not the dead continue as agents, we must attend to the possibility that they do continue as agents. If they do, then we violate their generic rights in all cases where not to respect their wishes as a living ostensible agent would be to violate the PGC. If they do not continue as agents then by respecting their wishes we do not violate the rights of any agent.

We can draw several threads together by considering a final illustrative case. Suppose the question is whether recently deceased agent A's organs should be made available for transplantation. First, if A has expressed his will on the matter in the recognised way (whether by advance directive or opt-in, or the like) during his lifetime of ostensible agency, then this is an easy case. We simply observe A's instructions, his giving or withholding of consent. Secondly, however, what if A has not expressed his will in this way, and what if it is argued that, by not opting out, A has implicitly signalled his consent? This is a much more controversial case and, in chapter seven, we will reject opt-out schemes as reliable indicators of an agent's will. In such a case, therefore, if transplantation is justified, it is not because A has consented. Thirdly, if it is argued that transplantation is justified because A would have consented if asked, we are employing a substituted judgement. As we have suggested, there might be a few cases where such a judgement is analogous to a procedural justification but, for the most part, this is little more than a fiction—it is just too easy for result-orientated decision-makers to lean on substituted judgement as a convenient rationalisation. Finally, if the question is not whether transplantation is justified but simply whether, as a matter of courtesy, A would have objected, various forms of evidence might be adduced. For a legal system that wishes to avoid acting out of line with A's general inclinations, it is important to get this right; but, as a matter of mere courtesy, we are not dealing here with a question of rights as such and we are outside the realm of required justification, procedural or otherwise.[46]

### *(v) Justifying Actions without Consent*

Is it possible to justify an action that infringes the generic rights of an agent if one is not the recipient of a relevant consent? Is procedural justification not only sufficient but also necessary? This is a question that we will take up at some length in chapters eight and nine. Here, it suffices to recall the general principle: namely, where one is dealing with an ostensible agent (a subject of consent), it is wrong to act against that party's generic rights without an authorising consent. However, there might sometimes be an overriding justification for the action if it is necessary in order to protect more compelling rights. As a matter of general principle, therefore, the answer to the question is that procedural justification is sufficient but not necessary.

If it is possible to justify an action that violates the rights of a subject of consent (from whom consent has not been obtained), is it also possible to justify an action that is detrimental to the generic interests of a party who is not a subject of consent? Again, the answer is that such action may be justified provided that, within a framework of precautionary reasoning, the action seeks to serve more compelling generic rights or interests. What merits special mention here is not so much that such action might be so justified but that legal regimes might be tempted to bypass such justification by resorting instead to a fictitious procedural justification.

## IV Conclusion

Where a transaction is prima facie in line with the PGC, where no rights are violated, where acts are permissible, no justification is required. However, where action runs counter to the generic interests protected by the PGC, justification is called for.

Where one is dealing with a subject of consent, reliance on a consent-based procedural justification is the first line of response. In the absence of consent, or an outright refusal, it might be possible to justify a violation of generic rights substantively, by reference to overriding rights. However, there is an obvious burden of justification in such a special case. Where one is dealing with those who are not subjects of consent, it is trite that there can be no procedural justification. Justification for transactions with such parties has to be of a substantive kind and viewed under precautionary reasoning. Whilst the detailed jurisprudence of precautionary reasoning takes some developing, the general principles are tolerably clear. In this light, legal systems need to be alert to three different kinds of error.

[46] Compare the argument in John Harris, 'Law and Regulation of Retained Organs: The Ethical Issues' (2002) 22 *Legal Studies* 527.

First, when dealing with those who are not subjects of consent, there is a temptation to fictionalise consent, to proceed as though the action is authorised by consent. The loose use of substituted judgement decision-making is a particularly egregious example of this error.

Secondly, when dealing with those who are at the cusp of ostensible agency or who are intermittently agents (subjects of consent), there is a temptation to deny the parties the opportunity to exercise the generic rights that they very possibly have. It is one thing where this arises from genuine uncertainty as to the status of the party; but it is quite another where best interest judgements are made paternalistically to allow the decision-makers to do what they, not the affected party, consider to be for the best.

Thirdly, having identified a party as a subject of consent, a legal system must resist the temptation to rush to judgment. Before a legal system pronounces that a subject of consent actually has given a valid and effective consent, there are several further questions to be asked. Procedural justification is too convenient to be licensed for perfunctory or premature use. In the following three chapters, it is to these further questions that we turn.

# 5

# The Conditions of (Valid) Consent I: Unforced and Informed Choice

## I Introduction

It is trite that consent has no meaning in the absence of a transaction[1] between agents. In chapter three, we suggested that an agent's purpose in consenting might be to make some concession in relation to the enjoyment of the benefits associated with the dominant side of a particular relationship[2] or to authorise a wholly new relationship (or the application of a particular rule-set). However, whether a purported consent concerns a change of position within an existing relationship (whereby the agent gives up something of value) or the creation of a new relationship (whereby the agent might or might not hope to gain something of value), the transaction will be authorised and defensible by reference to that ostensible consent only where the conditions for a valid consent are satisfied. Only then will there be the basis for a procedural justification.

Where the authorisation matters for the purposes of making a moral judgement, the relevant conditions are those set by the governing moral theory (which we take to be Gewirthian moral theory). Where the authorisation matters for the purposes of making a legal (legal–moral) judgement (ie as to the validity and effect of the consent underlying the particular transaction), the relevant conditions are those set by the governing legal (legal–moral) regime.[3]

[1] By a 'transaction', we simply mean an action that affects agents other than the author of the action. For the same usage, see Alan Gewirth, *Reason and Morality* (Chicago, IL, University of Chicago Press, 1978) at 129.

[2] The concession might involve waiving the benefit of a right or an immunity or accepting a limitation on a power or permission (privilege) held against another.

[3] For the move from a simple Gewirthian community of rights to a legal order committed to Gewirthian principles, see below at 338–342.

It should be noted that, under a legal idealist conceptualisation of law, legal orders are essentially legal–moral, and positive instantiations of law are posited articulations of the legal–moral. By contrast, under a realist or positivist conceptualisation of law, legal orders are not essentially legal–moral, and positive instantiations of law are simply posited regulatory articulations made by the appropriate sources in the appropriate manner relative to local criteria of recognition. For defence of the legal idealist conceptualisation of law, see Deryck Beyleveld and Roger Brownsword, *Law as a Moral Judgment* (London, Sweet and Maxwell, 1986; reprinted Sheffield, Sheffield Academic Press, 1994). Whether we view a legal order under an idealist or a positivist conception of law, we can ask whether the conditions of consent expressed in its regulatory articulations are compliant with the standards set by the governing moral theory.

It is the nature of these conditions, the conditions determining whether or not a 'consent' is valid, that is the focus for this chapter.

Our discussion is in two principal parts. In the first part, we sketch a Gewirthian account of the conditions that must obtain before we can hold that an agent has acted voluntarily. Broadly speaking, these conditions are carried through into the analysis of consent. Thus, Gewirthian moral theory will not recognise an ostensible consent as an authentic consent unless it is freely given (qua an unforced choice) as well as being made with relevant knowledge and understanding—in other words, it is only if the consent is free and informed that it is valid. Notoriously, these prerequisites are open to interpretation—where do we draw the line between forced and unforced choices; and relative to whose viewpoint is knowledge judged to be relevant? In the second part of this chapter we address these questions, developing ideal-typical conditions pertaining, first, to the idea of an *unforced* choice and, then, to that of an *informed* choice. We treat the application of external pressure, bearing *negatively* on the target agent's generic interests, as characteristic of *forced* choice. It follows that we equate unforced choice with the absence of threats rather than the presence of offers and that we do not treat an ostensible consent as invalidated simply because the agent was faced with a choice between unattractive options. On the other hand, the application of negative pressure to secure a forced choice is quite clearly incompatible with reliance on a procedural justification (even if the pressurising agent is able to justify its actions substantively).[4] As for the idea of a choice made with relevant knowledge and understanding, we treat the consenting agent's own subjective viewpoint as the test of whether a consent is materially *informed*; however, we also place a measure of responsibility for information collection on the consenting agent, as a result of which such an agent is barred from pleading lack of informed choice (to impugn an otherwise valid consent) where the particular failure lies within the agent's own field of responsibility.

One further introductory remark is in order. In principle, questions about the scope and interpretation of a consent (or a refusal)[5] are distinct from questions relating to the conditions under which a valid consent is given.

[4] In fact, we will specify the ideal-type of forced choice in such a way that the pressurising agent will not have an antecedent justification available. However, this leaves open the possibility of an overriding rights justification (in which event, of course, the pressurising agent would not need to rely on the (disqualified) procedural justification). See further 132 below.

[5] With regard to a refusal of consent, it might be thought that 'No means no' and that there is little room for interpretation. However, there might be situations in which a refusal (such as a refusal of a blood transfusion) runs through a period of time during which the circumstances change. If the refusal is expressed to hold in any circumstances, this leaves less scope for interpretation than if it is not so expressed: cf *Malette v Shulman* (1990) 72 OR (2d) 417 and *Re T (Adult: Refusal of Medical Treatment)* [1992] 4 All ER 649. But, then, we run into the question of whether the issue is to do with signalling or interpretation: see further ch 7.

The former concern the specific extent of the covering authorisation, the latter the general adequacy of the consent. In practice, however, where the information supplied is incomplete or lacks specificity, as a result of which the consenting agent and his recipient act on radically different understandings as to the nature of the consent given, it might be difficult to say whether the misunderstanding goes to matters of scope and interpretation or to the validity of the consent itself.[6] We will return to questions concerning the scope and interpretation of consent (and refusal of consent) in chapter seven.

## II A Gewirthian Approach to the Conditions of Consent

The giving (or refusal) of consent is a particular type of action. Like any action, the act of giving or refusing consent has a moral significance; for, in principle, we can ask whether such an act is morally prohibited, permissible, or required. In the light of our analysis of the distinctive function(s) played by consent in transactions between agents, we can say that, beyond the question of the permissibility of an agent giving consent, there lies a further question bearing on the validity of the particular ostensible consent. However, before we tackle the specific case of acts pertaining to consent, we need to sketch how we understand an agent's action in general.

According to Gewirth,[7] an action in the strict sense must be voluntary (or free). To meet this standard, a number of conditions must be satisfied:

> Negatively, the behaviors must not occur from one or more of the following kinds of cause: (a) direct compulsion, physical or psychological, by someone or something external to the person; (b) causes internal to the person, such as reflexes, ignorance, or disease that decisively contribute, in ways beyond his control, to the occurrence of the behavior; (c) indirect compulsion whereby the person's choice to emit the behavior is forced by someone else's coercion. Positively, the person must control his behavior by his own unforced and informed choice.[8]

[6] Suppose, for example, that a particular agent who consents to donate tissue for research believes that the research to be carried out is of type R1, but the researchers believe that they have the agent's consent in relation to research types R1, R2, and R3. In such a case, if we allow that the agent has given an informed consent to the donation of tissue for research type R1, the question in relation to research types R2 and R3 is about the scope or interpretation of this consent. However, if the agents have radically different understandings about what is covered by 'tissue', we might question whether an informed consent of any kind has been given: see, eg, some of the misunderstandings revealed by inquiries into organ retention (n 38 below and discussion in text). The question, we might say, is not so much whether the researchers have a consent for R1 that also reaches to authorising the use of the tissue for R2 or R3, but whether, given a fundamental misunderstanding, they have a valid consent for any purpose.

[7] Note 1 above.

[8] *Ibid*, at 31.

Only where such conditions obtain, only where an agent is thus in control, can we say that the agent is choosing on the basis of informed reasons, knowing 'what action he is performing, for what purpose, its proximate outcome, and his recipients.'[9]

Such a view places great emphasis on the agent's choice being unforced. Where a gunman confronts an agent with the demand 'Your money or your life,' there is a choice to be made; but it is a choice tainted by compulsion, undesirableness (in the sense that neither option is desirable) and threat.[10] As such, it is a forced choice and it takes little imagination to see how it would distort the meaning of 'consent' if it were to be suggested that the agent had, in such circumstances, 'consented' to hand over the money to the gunman. But, in a world of unequal resources and uneven needs, does it follow that most choices are forced, most ostensible consents invalid? Gewirth thinks not. Quite apart from the absence of threat, 'the economic view [that] everything short of the whole of all possible values would be "undesirable", since it regards as undesirable whatever contains less good than some other possibility one might want to have . . . assumes a fantastic exaggeration of human desire, on the model of Plato's insatiable tyrant or Freud's id.'[11]

This background account of action in the strict sense informs Gewirth's analysis of consent:

> To begin with, just as the agent's choice must not be forced if his action is to be voluntary, so the recipient's consent must not be forced if his participation in the transaction is to be voluntary. In general, the conditions of forced consent are similar to those of forced choice; in both cases these conditions may vary in degree.[12]

To this first condition, that the consent must be unforced, Gewirth adds two further requirements. These are that 'the recipient must have knowledge of relevant circumstances'[13] and that 'the recipient must be in an emotionally calm state of mind.'[14] In brief, then, provided that the agent is calm when consenting, is free in doing so (unforced), and is informed (has relevant knowledge), the consent should be accepted as valid and effective for its particular purpose.

We might pause over the inclusion of emotional calm in these conditions for consent. Gewirth does not enter the same caveat when discussing voluntariness in general—indeed, he allows that some choices might be made 'with little or no antecedent deliberation' and that '[w]ithin limits, choices

[9] Note 1 above, at 31.
[10] See *ibid*, at 32–33.
[11] *Ibid*, at 33.
[12] *Ibid*, at 257.
[13] *Ibid*.
[14] *Ibid*.

may be foolish and uninformed.'[15] In support of this requirement in relation to consent, Gewirth merely remarks that it 'is parallel to the whole set of "internal" factors, including reflexes and disease, that may operate as causes that decisively contribute, in ways beyond a person's control, to the occurrence of some behavior and that debar that behavior from being an action.'[16] Nevertheless, there are at least two reasons for thinking that emotional calm is a requirement worth listing. First, the giving of consent, as we have said, takes its meaning from a particular *transactional* setting. In many cases, participation in a consensual transaction will be detrimental to the consenting agent in the sense that the level of benefit enjoyed by that agent after the transaction will be reduced from the level enjoyed prior to the transaction taking place. Certainly this is so where the function of consent is to modify an existing relationship (the consenting agent making a concession to the recipient agent) or where consent signifies that a new relationship has been created under which there is donation from the consenting agent to another.[17] As a general rule, therefore, it makes good precautionary sense to require calm before consent (or a refusal of consent).[18] Secondly, not only might a lack of calm indicate some internal factor that renders the consent inconsistent with the requirement of unforced choice, it might also indicate a lack of knowledge or understanding. Writing in a medical context, Ruth Faden and Tom Beauchamp[19] connect patient calm to patient understanding as follows:

> Clinical experience suggests that patients . . . exhibit wide variability in their understanding of information about diagnoses, procedures, risks, prognoses, and the like. Although some patients . . . are calm and attentive, others are nervous, anxious, or distracted in ways that affect understanding. The quality of autonomous decisionmaking may therefore differ dramatically, in accordance with how well a person understands.[20]

Or, to put this explicitly in the terms of our discussion: the quality of understanding underlying an agent's purported consent might differ dramatically depending upon that agent's state of emotional calm.

[15] *Ibid*, at 31.

[16] *Ibid*, at 258.

[17] Even where the new relationship leads to an exchange, as in a contractual transaction, there is no guarantee that this will improve the consenting party's freedom or well-being.

[18] Where an agent who lacks emotional calm *refuses* to consent, it clearly makes no sense to treat this as if a consent has been given. Instead, one might judge it appropriate to treat the emotionally disturbed agent on a 'best interests' basis, in which event the practical outcome might be to authorise the very actions that would have been authorised had consent been given. Caution needs to be observed, therefore, lest the emotional calm requirement becomes a convenient way of displacing the consent paradigm where an agent's refusal is viewed negatively by the recipient agent(s). For refusals of consent, see further ch 7.

[19] Ruth Faden and Tom Beauchamp, *A History and Theory of Informed Consent* (New York, Oxford University Press, 1986).

[20] *Ibid*, at 248–49.

Putting to one side the requirement of emotional calm, we are left with the pivotal conditions of unforced choice and relevant knowledge (and, by implication, understanding). In both cases, as Gewirth explicitly states, it is assumed that these conditions might vary in degree. For their part, Faden and Beauchamp conceive of autonomy in much the same way: autonomous actions are a matter of degree; at one end of the spectrum there is the fully autonomous action characterised by full understanding and complete non-control (by others); at the other end of the spectrum, there is the fully non-autonomous action, characterised by complete ignorance and complete control (by others); and, somewhere on the spectrum, there is a point at which we can conceive of the conditions for what Faden and Beauchamp term 'substantially autonomous action'. What more can we say to sharpen this conceptual understanding of the conditions of consent?

First, each of these conditions is at least necessary: we do not have a consent that satisfies the Gewirthian standard unless it represents the unforced choice of the agent *and* is made on the basis of relevant knowledge and understanding. Where the gunman says 'Your money or your life,' the agent under threat might understand perfectly well what is at stake; but deciding to hand over the money is not making an unforced choice and the transaction is not backed by consent. Conversely, an agent who freely gives his money to what he understands to be a charitable institution does not truly consent if it turns out that the institution is essentially private and for profit.

Secondly, it is easy to agree (without a great deal of critical reflection) that the case of the gunman's threat is the paradigm of a forced choice; and this would extend readily if the threat were not directly to the agent with the cash but to a third party agent (and the former was aware of this threat). It seems to follow that the paradigm of an unforced choice must be one that is clear of such obvious coercion of the agent's will. However, it is important to observe that there are two material elements to the gunman's threat: one element is the nature (and immediacy) of what is threatened ('your money *or your life*'); the other element is the assumed lack of legitimacy (the gunman, let us assume, has no moral warrant to make such a threat). If we are looking for the paradigm of an unforced choice, what is it that really matters, the absence of threats or the absence of *illegitimate* threats? As we turn to look more carefully at the conditions of consent, this is one of the questions that we need to address.

## III Consent: The Pivotal Conditions

It is relatively uncontroversial to suggest that it is implicit in the idea of consent (or, at any rate, in the idea of an adequate consent) that it should be given on a free and informed basis. There are also some paradigms, such as the gunman's threat, where we can readily agree that consent is not truly given. However, if we try to be more precise about the specification of the 'free and informed' basis that consent presupposes, we soon run into difficulties. We could, of course, respond to these difficulties by setting a very loose standard for positive legal compliance. Following such an approach, provided that a legal system subscribed to the general principle that a so-called consent does not count unless it is given on a free and informed basis, we would treat the law as ethically compliant. Such a standard would not be so loose as to have no critical purchase—after all, in some positive legal regimes, consent might *not* be doctrinally predicated on free and informed action—but it would offer a broad band for compliance. In an attempt to narrow the margin for compliance and, at the same time, to strengthen the critical purchase of our Gewirthian approach to consent, our aim in this section is to tighten our analysis of the pivotal conditions of unforced choice and informed choice.

### *(i) Unforced Choice*

Where an agent makes an unforced choice, that choice (by definition) is free of external 'force'. The force applied to a target agent by an intervening agent might take various forms, some more open, more explicit, less relational than others, some more insidious or implicit than others, some more self-consciously applied than others,[21] and so on—a gunman demanding 'Your money or your life' is one thing, a family arranging a daughter's marriage (recall the case of Aneeka Sohrab[22]) is something else. In the light of these distinctions, we might wish to classify some forms of external force (as applied by an intervening agent) as 'coercion', others as 'pressure', and others as 'influence'. However, for present purposes, it suffices to treat 'force' as a power-play on the part of the intervening agent that is designed to elicit the consent of the target agent. Thus understood, force, when externally applied, seems to jeopardise the possibility of an unforced choice being made by the target agent and, at the same time, it raises a question mark about the validity of a 'consent' so obtained.

As we have noted already, in relation to external power-plays, our model of unforced choice might be guided by the kind of force or pressure applied (taking into account such factors as the strength of the pressure, its immediacy, and the like) or by the legitimacy of the pressure applied. If we are guided by the former, we will tend to judge matters from the standpoint of the target agent, focusing on the impact of the pressure on that agent; if we are guided by the latter, we will tend to judge matters from the standpoint of the intervening agent—or, at any rate, our essential question will be whether the intervening agent has legitimate reasons for applying the

[21] There might be cases where one agent exerts an influence over the decision-making of another agent without realising that this is so. See below, at 167–170, for discussion of the essence of undue influence (as a factor invalidating an ostensible consent).

[22] See ch 3.

pressure. Clearly, the significance of taking one approach rather than the other is not simply that each approach generates its own characterisation of external pressure; each approach goes beyond this to generate its own distinctive account of what it is to make an unforced choice. In what follows, we will suggest that external pressure militates against unforced choice where the pressure applied has a *negative* bearing on the target agent's generic interests. Ideal-typically, the intervening agent will intend that the pressure applied should have a negative bearing; and the target agent will so apprehend the pressure. To this extent, our account of external pressure is one of a simple negative power-play rather than one that inquires as to its possible legitimacy. However, this is not quite the whole story.

First, our ideal-type, by fixing on pressure that bears negatively on an agent's generic interests, focuses on action (by the intervening agent) that is prima facie illegitimate. This, after all, is an assault on the conditions of agency. Secondly, previous dealings between the agents might offer the intervening agent grounds for an antecedent justification. If the gunman is seeking to rectify a past wrong, our overall assessment of the legitimacy of this agent's conduct might need to be revised. However, even if there is (substantive) antecedent justification, the negative pressure still disqualifies the possibility of procedural justification. In other words, even if the gunman is justified in forcibly taking the money, the justification lies in the past, not in the present with the target agent's 'consent'. Accordingly, we will sharpen the focus of our ideal-type by stipulating that the agents come to the transaction with clean hands (thereby sidelining, without eliminating, the possibility that the intervening agent acts with an antecedent justification).[23] Thirdly, having set aside arguments about antecedent justification, there is still the possibility that the intervening agent might have another kind of substantive justification, such as one that appeals to overriding rights. For example, the gunman might argue that his actions are legitimate all things considered because, like Robin Hood, he robs only the rich to give to the poor. We do not exclude this possibility, as such, from our ideal-type, but, for the purposes of deciding whether the intervening agent has a procedural justification, it is not a question that we need to pursue. The point is that, if the intervening agent assaults the generic conditions of the target agent, there can be no procedural justification, no matter that the former might be able to defend the legitimacy of its actions in some other way.

We will develop this proposed account and elaborate it in the following stages: (a) by outlining a Gewirthian approach to the question of what

[23] It should be noted that this stipulation actually applies to *both* agents. The point in the text hinges on the possibility that the target agent has previously wronged the intervening agent, who now seeks rectification. But there is also the reverse antecedent possibility, namely that the intervening agent is already a wrongdoer in relation to the target agent. This possibility (as covered by our clean hands stipulation) has implications for the way that we characterise the pressure applied by the intervening agent. See nn 25 and 28 below.

counts as external force (leading to a model of unforced choice); (b) by considering whether a forced choice equates to an agent acting against its will; and (c) by filling out our proposed model of unforced choice to deal with the case in which a limited number of options are offered.

(a) What Counts as External Force?

In what sense might one agent seek to apply force or pressure to another agent with a view to procuring the latter's consent? From a Gewirthian agency perspective, the idea of force or pressure presupposes some intended engagement with the target consenting agent's generic interests in freedom and well-being. Such engagement might be intended to have a negative impingement on the interests of the target agent (as in the case of some kind of threat) or it might be intended to impinge in a positive way (as in the case of some incentive or inducement). Generally, it will be fairly clear whether the orientation of the pressure is negative or positive—it will be fairly clear, in the terminology of much rights-discourse, whether it is a 'threat' or an 'offer'.[24] For example, in the absence of some exceptional context, when the gunman commands 'Your money or your life,' the impingement is negative just as the impingement is positive if a philanthropist offers to put up the money for a hospital to be built or for a life-saving operation to be carried out. Some cases, however, might be less clear. For example, what would we make of a charity that solicits for financial support? Is the intention to offer the target agent an opportunity to enhance its well-being by making a donation (a positive impingement) or to burden the agent with guilt if no donation is made (a negative impingement)? If we treat all impingements on an agent's interests, whether negative or positive, as instances of external force or pressure, then this is not a question that need detain us. However, our proposed position is that external force (as relevant to the condition of unforced choice) should be confined to cases of negative impingement. So, the case of charitable solicitation is one to which we must return shortly.

First things first, however: why should we restrict the concept of external force or pressure to those instances in which the intention is to engage *negatively* with the target consenting agent's generic interests? Quite simply, as we have said, pressure brought to bear negatively on an agent's generic interests is an assault on agency; positive pressure is not. Let us turn the

[24] Seminally, see Robert Nozick, 'Coercion', in Peter Laslett, WG Runciman and Quentin Skinner (eds), *Philosophy, Politics and Society* (4th Series) (Oxford, Basil Blackwell, 1972) 101, at 112–20. The distinction between a threat and an offer is not merely terminological. As Nozick suggests, one begins to sense what is at stake if we recognise that 'the Rational Man would normally (be willing to) choose to make the choice among the alternatives facing him in the offer situation, whereas normally he would not (be willing to) choose to make the choice among the alternatives facing him in the threat situation' (at 133). For an insightful overview, see Michael J Trebilcock, *The Limits of Freedom of Contract* (Cambridge, MA, Harvard University Press, 1993), ch 4.

question round. Let us ask instead whether it is plausible to treat a target agent as being subject to external pressure—and, potentially, as being denied the opportunity to make an unforced choice (which, it must be remembered, is for the purpose of procedural justification)—where the intention of the intervening agent is to present an option having a positive impingement on the agent's interests? In some such contexts, particularly those of gift and exchange, it would be extraordinary if we did not treat the target agent's choice as unforced—or, to be more precise, it would be extraordinary if we dismissed the claim that the agent made an unforced choice simply on the ground that the choice was 'tainted' by some external factor having a positive bearing on the agent's interests. Unless we are ready to dismiss the very idea of a valid consent being given in settings of gift or exchange (including contract), plausibility demands that we allow for the possibility of unforced choices being made here. And, more generally, where an agent is presented with an externally generated option that is designed to promote its generic interests and which it would not otherwise have, it runs counter to the additive dimension of agency to suggest that, for this very reason, the agent cannot make an unforced choice and cannot give a valid consent. Surely, agents are not required to look all gift horses in the mouth (for fear of participating in a transaction tainted by forced acceptance).

Before we go any further, we should restate that it is a baseline premise (or stipulation) in our account of unforced choice that the ex ante (ie prior) relationship between the intervening agent and the target agent is not distorted by any relevant violation of Gewirthian moral principles. For example, it is not as though there is some background issue of corrective justice to be straightened out. Thus, at the point at which the pressure (whether with a positive or a negative bearing) is applied, neither the intervening nor the target agent is morally indebted to the other.[25] They come to the transaction with clean hands. This is not to suggest that pressure is only ever applied in cases of such moral equilibrium; however, to identify the ideal-typical case of unforced choice, it is helpful to assume such an ex ante relationship between the parties. Accordingly, our position, stated more formally and more fully with regard to positive interventions, is as follows: where (i) the ex ante relationship between agents, A and B, is one of moral equilibrium; and (ii) B presents A with an option that A otherwise would not have; and (iii) B intends that the option, if taken up, would advance A's interests, then this does not constitute external force applied by B to A.

[25] This premise also governs whether we treat external pressure as having a negative or positive bearing (whether it is a threat or an offer; see n 24 above). For example, consider the case of a gunman who says, initially, 'I am going to shoot you,' but then says, 'No, on second thoughts, I will spare you if you hand over your money.' Assuming that the ex ante relationship between the parties involves no breach of Gewirthian moral principles, the gunman's initial intervention is negative and it precludes reading the gunman's subsequent, more generous 'offer' as a free-standing positive intervention.

Hence, if A (the target agent) takes up the option, the choice made cannot be impugned as 'forced' by dint of being made under external pressure. Of course, this is a long way from saying that the target agent's consent is valid. It must be borne in mind that, even if the absence of external force or pressure eases concerns about a choice being forced, unforced choice itself is just one element of giving a valid consent. Thus, we can say only that, other things being equal, a consent given in such a context is valid.

Even with the caveats that we have entered, our position invites some rather obvious objections. In particular, what do we say about those all-too-familiar cases where agents who are in extreme or necessitous circumstances are tempted by financial inducements or other forms of incentive to enter into deals which they would not seriously contemplate were it not for their indigent or exiguous circumstances? Are we seriously suggesting that such agents—say, organ sellers in the Third World or surrogate mothers or plea-bargaining defendants in the First World—thereby make unforced choices and give valid consents to the bargains into which they enter? Of course, we are not suggesting any such thing. The most that we are saying is that such transactions cannot be impugned simply because the choice made by the needy agent was given in response to an external element having a positive bearing on the agent's interests. Whatever other reservations we might have about such transactions, such a positive alone does not entail a negative (at any rate, not so in relation to the possibility of unforced choice).

Yet, do these remarks shake off the sense that transactions that are facilitated by positive inducements are suspect, that offers that cannot be refused are likely to be as problematic as threats that cannot be resisted? Quite probably, they do not. However, there is more than one possible source of our discontent; and our point is simply that positive pressure does not invalidate consent, not that transactions induced by such pressure are never morally or legally suspect. For even if we are satisfied that an agent, having the capacity to consent, has given a consent that fully meets the conditions of adequacy (including being an unforced choice), we might still believe that there are grounds for impugning the transaction—for instance, where a public official accepts a bribe, or where a financial inducement interferes with altruistic giving (as with blood donation), or where the conduct of the agent who offers the inducement raises concerns about unfair advantage-taking, or the like.[26] In other words, there are reasons aplenty to

[26] It might be argued, for instance, that inducements 'distort' the marketplace judgements of consumers as well as the casting of political votes; or that offers to impoverished agents take unfair advantage of the needy circumstances in which the latter find themselves. To some extent, such arguments might reduce back to questions concerning the adequacy of the apparent consent, such as whether the choice was made calmly or whether the ex ante relationship between the parties was clean. However, they might also draw on considerations of equity and fair dealing, democracy, and welfare that reach beyond matters of consent (some of which would be more easily squared with Gewirthian morality than others).

take a hard look at transactions of this kind, including reasons that are consent-related; however, the mere fact that the consent was induced by positive pressure does not equate to a forced choice.

There is also a more general point to be made. One of the recurring themes of our commentary is that it is too easy to resort to consent by way of lazy procedural justification; and the less stringent the conditions for an adequate consent, the easier it is to indulge this temptation. However, there is a danger that runs in the opposite direction. This is that, where the conditions for an adequate consent are very stringent (such as a specification of unforced choice that demands a choice insulated against both foreground and background pressure), then it is too easy to present all objections to a transaction as a matter of failed consent. Consider, for example, the extraordinary case of Bernd Brandes, a 43-year-old computer specialist from Berlin, who answered an internet advertisement placed by Armin Meiwes, in which the latter sought out 'a young well-built man who wants to be eaten.'[27] The bizarre story that unfolded at Meiwes' trial, including Meiwes recounting how he had cooked Brandes in olive oil and garlic before consuming him along with a bottle of red wine, became international headlines. What possible defence could Meiwes have for such acts of cannibalism? Quite simply, his defence was that Brandes had consented. Now, on one view, provided that the evidence bore out Meiwes' account, Brandes' consent was a sufficient defence. However, if we recoil from such a view, we might want to say bluntly that consent is simply no answer in such circumstances (that is, that there are limits to the justificatory force of consent). There is a temptation, however, to fudge the matter by arguing that Brandes' supposed consent must have been defective—in which case, for example, we might be drawn by the prosecutor's view that Brandes was suffering from a serious personality disorder which disabled him from thinking rationally; or we might insist that Brandes simply could not have made an unforced choice to offer himself up in this way, or that he was not properly informed, or the like. Had Meiwes' advertisement offered a financial inducement to those who put themselves forward for consumption, we might be tempted to hide our real 'on the merits' objection behind the argument that Brandes had not truly consented because the positive pressure of the financial inducement precluded his making an unforced choice. If we are to maintain the integrity of consent, the lesson is this: where we are in favour of a transaction, it is tempting to assert that it is authorised by consent, but where we are opposed to a transaction, it is equally tempting to deny that it is authorised by consent. In both cases, there is an element of disingenuousness that should be discouraged.

[27] See, eg, Theodore Dalrymple, 'The Case for Cannibalism' *City Journal* (5 January 2004); http://www.city-jopurnal.org/html/eon-01-05-04td.html (last visited 15 February 2005).

To return to the main track of our discussion, if we discount external factors that have a positive bearing on an agent's interests, we are equating external force or pressure with those external interventions that have a negative bearing on an agent's generic interests. However, is the critical reference point, for the purpose of identifying external pressure, the intention of the intervening agent who applies the pressure or the apprehension of the target agent? As we have seen already, it is not altogether clear how we should classify charitable solicitation; and, whichever reference point we adopt, our difficulties are not obviously eased. For, if we focus on the intentions of the charity, they might be equivocal; and, if we focus on the perceptions or apprehension of the target agent, these might vary from one agent to another. So, what are we to take as our reference point for making a judgment in a particular case that external force has been applied? We suggest that where we judge solely by reference to the intentions of the agent applying the pressure, we are dealing with an *attempted* application of external force and, concomitantly, an *attempt* to generate a forced choice on the part of the target agent. Where, by contrast, we judge solely by reference to the apprehension of the target agent, we are ignoring whether there is an *attempted* application of external force and judging only whether an agent apprehends a choice as forced by virtue of external pressure. And, where, by further contrast, we judge by reference to both the intentions of the agent applying the pressure and the apprehensions of the target agent, we seem to have the apparatus to formulate the ideal-typical case of forced choice by virtue of external pressure. This ideal-typical case is instantiated where there is, on the one side, an *attempted* application of external (negative) pressure and, on the other side, an *apprehension* of external pressure bearing negatively on one's interests. Assuming that the external force or pressure is a causative factor in the choice made, this is the ideal-typical case of forced choice by reason of external pressure.

Given this ideal-typical case, we can say that there are two ways in which charitable solicitation might fail to qualify as external (negative) pressure. If the intention of the charity is not to apply negative pressure, this will fail to be a complete case of external pressure (even if the agent solicited perceives the solicitation in a negative light). Similarly, even if the intention of the charity is to apply negative pressure, this will again fail to be a complete case of external force if the target agent does not perceive the solicitation in the same negative light. This still leaves room for argument in any particular instance as to whether we are dealing with external force or pressure (as relevant for consent) but we cannot derive any more conceptual assistance.

If an intervening agent attempts to apply external pressure and the target agent apprehends this as pressure with a negative bearing, there is still the possibility that a robust target agent might resist the pressure. If this results in a refusal to give consent, the question of the validity of a consent does not arise. However, there is the possibility, too, that the robust agent might resist the pressure and yet, independently, decide to consent. Where the chain of causation between the pressure applied by the intervening agent and the consent given by the target agent is broken by the latter's independent judgement, this is not an ideal-typical case. In practice, however, where the other elements of the ideal-typical case are present, we should raise a very strong presumption that causation is also present. For we certainly do not want to burden the target consenting agent (now wishing to disavow the consent) with the responsibility for showing either (a) that it was reasonable in the circumstances to succumb to the pressure (by consenting) or (b) that the consent was caused by the pressure rather than being freely given for independent reasons.

(b) Unforced Choice, Involuntary Action, and Acting against one's Will

To recapitulate, our model of unforced (forced) choice focuses on external force or pressure that bears negatively on an agent's generic interests, this application of pressure being predicated on an ex ante relationship between the parties that violates no relevant moral principles. Hence, in our ideal-type of forced choice, the following three conditions are satisfied:

(i) the baseline relationship between the intervening agent and the target agent is compliant with Gewirthian moral principles (the agents come to the transaction with clean hands; there is no record of previous wrongdoing (or, at any rate, no previous uncorrected wrongdoing) between the parties);
(ii) the intervening agent intends its power-play (the force or pressure applied) to have a negative bearing on the generic interests of the target agent, and the target agent so apprehends the intervention; and
(iii) the force or pressure applied is a causative factor in eliciting the consent of the target agent.

Where these conditions are met, the consent ostensibly given by the target agent does not meet the requirement of being an unforced choice, and, thus, such a so-called 'consent' does not satisfy the ideal-typical conditions for a valid consent.

Operating with this model, the application of negative pressure is taken to be sufficiently illegitimate to disable the intervening agent from reliance on a procedural justification based on the forced 'consent'. Whether or not the intervening agent is able to justify its actions substantively is another matter. In the ideal-typical case, as we have specified it, the intervening agent will not have an antecedent justification; but where the facts fall outside the ideal-type because of previous wrongdoing, such a justification might be available.[28] There is also the possibility of overriding rights

[28] It should be added that, so far as the question of unforced choice is concerned, the moral baseline, distinguishing between the ideal-typical and non ideal-typical ex ante relationship, is relevant, too, for the purpose of determining whether the pressure applied is to be treated as

justification, but, as we have said, this is not pertinent to the question of procedural justification. In short, if the intervening agent has applied negative pressure, there can be no procedural justification; and, if it turns out that the intervening agent has a substantive justification, procedural justification is not required anyway.

If we wish to differentiate between various kinds of negative pressure, and concomitantly various gradations of forced choice, our model allows for this. At one end of a spectrum, the pressure applied may be characterised as 'strong' while, at the other end, the pressure applied may be characterised as 'weak'. Operating with such a construct, we might characterise the gunman's threat to life as 'strong', threats to property (unless life-threatening) as less strong, and threats of a purely economic nature as relatively 'weak'. Indeed, from a Gewirthian perspective, we might calibrate the force of the pressure by reference to the hierarchy of an agent's generic needs. So measured, threats to the target agent's basic interests would be judged to be 'stronger' than threats to the agent's non-subtractive or additive interests. However, precisely where we locate such instances of external pressure is much less important than the fact that pressure with a negative bearing (strong or weak) has been applied. It follows that, although the pressure to which the target agent is subjected is a matter of degree, the making of an unforced choice is *not* itself a matter of degree.

Wherever a target agent's ostensible consent is not the product of an unforced choice, should we say that the agent has acted against its will? According to Michael Philips, we can distinguish two senses of 'acting against one's will'.[29] In a narrow sense, one acts against one's will where one's will is overborne; this is a case of involuntary action in the strict sense. Thus:

> In the strict sense, an agent acts involuntarily if he fails to satisfy some necessary condition of free agency. Where this is so, his act cannot be construed as an authentic expression of his will in his situation. We say this, for example, when someone is so mentally deranged that he literally cannot choose rationally, for he does not know what he is doing. We also say this when he is subjected to such severe physical or emotional pressure that he is either incapable of making a rational choice or of acting on it.[30]

By contrast, Philips suggests, one acts against one's will in a broader sense where one has a choice, albeit a choice between a rock and a hard place. According to Philips, where an agent so exercises a choice, this is *not* a case of involuntary action even if there is pressure or coercion. Thus, Philips is

having a negative or a positive bearing on the interests of the target agent. So, for example, if A, knowing that B is desperate for money, offers B $50 in full and final settlement of a $100 debt, this so-called 'offer' by A is to be characterised as negative pressure on B (and B's 'consent' should be read accordingly).

[29] Michael Philips, 'Are Coerced Agreements Involuntary?' (1984) 3 *Law and Philosophy* 133–45.

[30] *Ibid*, at 133.

critical of the view that the paradigm of involuntary action is to be found in the case of highway robbery or submission to the gunman's demand.[31] For Philips, involuntary action is one thing, coercion (or external force as we would say) quite another.

In advancing this analysis, Philips has a dual aim. First, because conceptual order is important for its own sake, he wants to ensure that the idea of involuntary action is confined to those cases where the agent has lost internal control. Secondly, because conceptual sloppiness can lead to confused policy, Philips is concerned that lawmakers should not be led astray. In particular, he wishes to resist conceptual sloppiness that encourages muddled reasoning along the following lines:

(i) where an agent acts involuntarily, it acts against its will [in the narrow sense] and the law rightly disregards any 'choice' so made;
(ii) where an agent makes a choice between two unpleasant alternatives or under external pressure, the agent also acts against its will [in the broad sense]; thus,
(iii) if the law disregards a choice made where an agent acts against its will [in the narrow sense], then it should do so where an agent makes a choice between two unpleasant alternatives or under external pressure [ie where the agent acts against its will in the broad sense].

If we lose sight of the equivocation over an agent 'acting against its will', then we are liable to fall into the trap set by step (iii); and, in consequence, legal policy will be deficient either (a) because it refuses to enforce choices too readily or (b) because it identifies the wrong reason for such a refusal (thinking that involuntariness is the appropriate reason for refusal when the appropriate reason is actually that the kind of coercion or pressure applied is independently problematic). On this basis, Philips approves of the approach in *North Carolina v Alford*,[32] where an accused (still protesting his innocence) pleaded guilty to second-degree murder in an attempt to try to avoid being tried and convicted of first-degree murder (a capital offence). The majority of the Supreme Court ruled that, while Alford faced unpleasant alternatives, this did 'not necessarily demonstrate that the plea of guilty was not the product of a free and rational choice'[33] in the circumstances.

[31] In particular, Philips directs this criticism at the analysis offered by Kenneth Kipnis, 'Criminal Justice and the Negotiated Plea' (1976) 86 *Ethics* 93–106.

[32] 400 US 25 (1970), 27 L Ed 2d 162.

[33] 27 L Ed 2d 162, at 168. White J, for the majority, continued (at 171–72):

> Here the State had a strong case of first-degree murder against Alford. Whether he realized or disbelieved his guilt, he insisted on his plea because in his view he had absolutely nothing to gain by a trial and much to gain by pleading. Because of the overwhelming evidence against him, a trial was precisely what neither Alford nor his attorney desired. Confronted with the choice between a trial for first-degree murder, on the one hand, and a plea of guilty to second-degree murder, on the other, Alford quite reasonably chose

As for the law becoming too willing to refuse to recognise ostensible choices, Philips points to coercive situations where employers yield to strike threats made by their workers. Whilst such threats place the employer in a coercive choice situation, submission by the employer does not (per Philips) equate to involuntariness; thus, if we are looking for a legal ground for non-enforcement or invalidation, involuntariness is not the answer. Moreover, Philips cautions against finding an easy exit for an employer who has chosen to go along with the workers' demands. Thus:

> To be sure, there is a sense in which one party to such agreements enters into them involuntarily. But this is not a sense of 'involuntary' relevant to assessing the legality of agreements. Nor ought it to become relevant. Indeed, it is difficult to imagine what a society would be like in which a person could invalidate a contract simply by showing that she was placed in a position of having to choose between unattractive alternatives.[34]

What do we make of this relatively uncompromising approach advocated by Philips?

First, we agree with Philips that there is a distinction between involuntary action in the strict sense (where the will is overborne) and those cases where the action is voluntary but made under pressure. In the former case, there is some condition *internal* to the agent (such as mental derangement) that leads us to characterise the action as involuntary. Indeed, in a case of this kind, it would be more accurate to say that the agent failed altogether to form a will rather than acted against its will. In the latter case, where the action is not involuntary but nevertheless made under external pressure, we can say that, in a broad sense, the agent has acted against its will. However, if we do say this, we are hinting that the agent's act is suspect and that we need to consider whether a consent given against an agent's will (in this broad sense) is compatible with the requirement of unforced choice or, more generally, whether the law should enforce the choice made by the agent. In other words, if we say that an agent acted against its will (in the broad sense), this points to a set of questions that need to be asked rather than to any particular answer.[35]

> the latter and thereby limited the maximum penalty to a 30-year term. When his plea is viewed in light of the evidence against him, which substantially negated his claim of innocence and which further provided a means by which the judge could test whether the plea was being intelligently entered . . . its validity cannot be seriously questioned.

The minority (Brennan, Douglas, and Marshall JJ), however, did question the validity of the plea. Having concerns about the constitutionality of the threat of the death penalty, they felt that this cast a shadow over the validity of the plea. As Brennan J put it (at 173), Alford's 'decision to plead guilty was not voluntary but "was the product of duress as much so as choice reflecting physical constraint".'

34 See n 29 above, at 140.

35 At any rate, this is so unless our point is simply to emphasise that the agent did not act involuntarily.

Secondly, where we are dealing with the case of an agent who has not acted involuntarily, but against its will in the broad sense, one question is whether the agent has made an unforced choice. If Philips' discussion implies that, provided the action is not involuntary, then it is not against the agent's will in the critical narrow sense, and it is not, therefore, a forced choice, we disagree. If the intervening agent applies pressure with a positive bearing, then, on our analysis, force is not being applied. However, where the pressure bears negatively on the target agent's generic interests, the choice made is not unforced.

Thirdly, in the light of what we have just said, it might be possible to maintain the position that the defendant made an unforced choice to plead guilty in *North Carolina v Alford*. Certainly, if the ex ante relationship between the parties was one of moral equilibrium, the deal offered to the defendant was an option not otherwise available. On the other hand, if the State was in moral deficit in relation to the defendant (who protested his innocence), the deal it offered arose in a context of pressure bearing negatively on the defendant's interests and so the choice made by the latter should not be treated as unforced.[36]

Fourthly, whilst Philips is right to say that contractual agreements should not be lightly set aside simply because one party had to choose between unattractive alternatives, the employer who succumbs to a strike threat seems to be making a forced choice. If the ex ante relationship between the parties is one of moral equilibrium, the employer's argument that the ostensible consent was not genuine seems persuasive. Equally, even if the employer is in moral deficit to his workers, the point that the consent was not the product of an unforced choice is well taken—although, here, the employees might well be able to justify their demands all things considered. At all events, in both situations, any attempt to hold the employer to the agreement on the ground that the employer consented to it is open to the objection that the consent was not freely given (was not an unforced choice) and that it should not, therefore, bear its usual (procedural) justificatory weight.

Finally, it should be said that once we broaden the focus of the inquiry from apparent consent to action more generally, the distinction between voluntariness and involuntariness raises a host of questions about where a legal regime will draw the lines in excusing agents or holding them to account for their actions, and where it will allow that, although an agent is accountable, there are mitigating circumstances to be taken into account (thereby, for instance, permitting some downward departure from the standard penalties set for a particular criminal offence). Mapping on to Philips' concern that agents, in general, should be held to account, regimes

[36] Compare the position taken by the minority judges in *Alford*, n 33 above.

of criminal law will tend to be nervous about allowing for exemption or mitigation on the ground that the act was involuntary (in the narrow sense) or against an agent's will. For example, a defendant might plead that, because of dependency on alcohol or drugs, he did not appreciate what he was doing; or defendants of the future might plead (as some have done already) that, because of their genetic make-up, they are predisposed to act in certain (criminal) ways. To counteract the first kind of argument, the criminal code can simply take the defendant's argument back to the time when he was in control; and to counteract the second, it is enough to insist upon a residual element of control by distinguishing between genetic predisposition and genetic determinism.[37] Where a defendant admits responsibility, he might argue in mitigation that the act was against his will in that he made a choice between unattractive alternatives. To hold the line here, a legal regime might treat it as irrelevant that the defendant faced personal financial difficulties or economic pressure upon his trade or business. On the other hand, if the defendant has been subjected to severe physical pressure or duress, this is likely to be viewed more sympathetically. To be sure, a great deal more could be said about such matters,[38] but we must not get diverted from our particular inquiry, the immediate focus of which is the requirement of unforced choice as a prerequisite for an adequate consent.

### (c) Limited Choice

Where an agent is presented with a limited number of options, is there any room for arguing that the choice of one of the options presented is forced (with the corollary that the law should decline to enforce the choice made)? In the light of the ideal-typical model of forced choice that we have formulated, the answer to this question largely turns on whether the options presented represent force or pressure having a negative bearing on the target agent's generic interests. If the intervening agent presents the target agent with one or more options having a negative loading (as in the paradigmatic highwayman situation, or that of a ransom payment), the latter makes a forced choice; and, if the target agent subsequently wishes to be released from the choice, the obvious way of arguing the point is by saying, quite simply, that the choice was made under the influence of external force. To add that the options presented to the target agent were limited would do nothing to improve the argument for release. If, by contrast, the intervening agent presents the target agent with one or more options having a positive loading (as in a plea-bargaining situation where there is moral

[37] Compare Celia Wells, '"I Blame the Parents": Fitting New Genes in Old Criminal Laws' in Roger Brownsword, WR Cornish, and Margaret Llewelyn (eds), *Law and Human Genetics: Regulating a Revolution* (Oxford, Hart Publishing, 1998) at 132.

[38] We offer a few more schematic remarks in ch 9.

equilibrium between the parties), no relevant external force is applied and the choice made is unforced. For such a target agent to suggest that the choice was actually forced (and that there should be a release from the choice made) because further options were not presented is absurd—contracts would again unravel if a party could escape simply by pleading that some further option, a more attractive offer, was not made (or that, in different circumstances, the offer actually made would not seem sufficiently attractive to accept).[39]

Does it follow, then, that contract lawyers have been misdirecting themselves in supposing that there is something suspect about so-called 'Bad Samaritan'[40] agreements? In these scenarios, an agreement to salvage a stricken vessel being typical, the premium price extracted by the Samaritan for performance of the rescuing act is portrayed as 'exorbitant' or 'unconscionable'. Once the act has been effected, the stock move is to advance one or both of two lines of argument against enforcing the agreed price. One argument maintains that there was no real consent to the price (this was a forced choice); the other contends that the price is unfair (relative to some benchmark price, actual or hypothetical). Our interest is in the first of these lines of argument. In the light of our ideal-type, is it plausible to suggest that this was a forced choice? Clearly, the key to this is whether the ex ante relationship between the parties involves any disturbance of Gewirthian moral principles. Given that these principles incorporate a relatively strong set of positive obligations in relation to other agents, one of the paradigms being the duty to rescue, it is quite likely that the Samaritan will already be under an obligation to attempt to effect a rescue.[41] In such circumstances, when an agent with such an obligation proposes to pass on by unless a certain price is paid, this is a threat, not an offer. Once again, to complain that the Bad Samaritan did not come up with a more reasonable offer is rather to miss the point. Occasionally, however, it might be that making a rescue attempt would be beyond the scope of an agent's positive obligations. In such a case, any price named by the agent (who would then attempt the rescue) would be an option not otherwise available and it would be inap-

[39] Compare, eg, Michael H Shapiro, 'Is Bioethics Broken? On the Idea of Ethics and Law "Catching Up" with Technology' (1999) 33 *Indiana Law Review* 17, at 75 (in the context of surrogacy agreements):

> 'Your money or your life' is one thing. 'Would you like to make some money having a child for me?' is something else. Concerns about the social, economic and environmental conditions that limit choice and move people to do things that they would not do if they were better off do not justify disregarding their choices within that prevailing adverse situation.

[40] See, eg, Trebilcock, n 24 above, at 85–90.

[41] Gewirth, n 1 above, at 217 et seq.

propriate, after the event, to seek to avoid the agreement by complaining that the consent was forced by dint of limited choice.[42]

None of this is to say, however, that the holding back of an option is never relevant to the validity of a consent. If what is being held back is information about a further option (as in the context of medical treatment), then this is quite another matter. But it is a case of an agent who has a duty to perform failing to do so rather than the case that we have just been considering of an intervening agent offering only a limited range of inducements to the target agent.

### *(ii) Knowledge and Understanding*

If we assume that an agent has made an unforced choice, the consent given may be relied on unless there is a problem with the other pivotal condition, namely that the consent must be based on relevant knowledge and understanding. How are we to interpret this condition of consent, each element of which—the nature of 'knowledge' and 'understanding', the relationship between the two, and the criterion of 'relevance'—invites a treatise in its own right?

We suggest the following as a working model. An agent who gives its consent does so in the context of a transaction informed by certain operative beliefs (beliefs that 'X is the case', and so on). The beliefs with which we are concerned are not free-standing or plucked from the air; rather, they are justified by reference to the information that lies, so to speak, within the agent's particular field of awareness (let us call this 'the agent's informational field') and the significance attached by the agent to data within that informational field (that is to say, the understanding that the agent has of such data). If this is our model, we will conceive of an agent's 'understanding' as 'the meaning attached by an agent to data within its informational field'; and we will conceive of an agent's 'knowledge' as 'the beliefs formed by an agent by reference to the data within its informational field and the understanding that it has of such data.'

Adopting this model, to say that an agent has consented without having relevant knowledge or understanding is to flag up a problem that relates in

[42] Compare Nozick, n 24 above. At 115, he gives as a hypothetical the case of a promise by a drowning man to pay $10,000 to his rescuer within three days of reaching shore with the rescuer's aid. The question of whether the promise is to be characterised as being in response to a threat (not to rescue) or an offer (to rescue) hinges, for Nozick, on whether a gratuitous rescue would be seen as being in the normal or expected course of events. If it would, the rescuer is making a threat; if it would not, the rescuer's proposition is an offer. According to Nozick, this baseline (normal or expected course of events) allows one to straddle or shift between what is '*predicted* and [what is] *morally required*' (at 112). Whilst a test of what is (reasonably) expected might be helpful in linking the question to more than one source of moral requirement (namely, the PGC applied both directly and indirectly), Nozick's test is not helpful if its reliance on the normal course of events weakens the moral baseline of positive obligation.

some way to the agent's informational field, or to the agent's interpretation of data within that field, or to the beliefs formed by the agent by reference to the data within the informational field and the way in which such data is understood. For example, relevant data might be missing from the agent's particular informational field (in which event, the agent's consent is based on ignorance or a certain lack of awareness), or, where fraud or deception is involved, some of the data within the agent's informational field might be distorted (in which event, the agent's consent is based on misinformation). Or, where data is open to more than one interpretation, the particular way in which the data is interpreted might lead to a consent based on a 'misunderstanding'—for example, such a misunderstanding might be pleaded by parents of recently deceased children who consent to a request from the hospital for retention of 'tissue' without appreciating that this term, as the hospital understands it, includes whole organs.[43] Or, again, where an agent, unaware that there are other options, consents to a particular treatment, T1, its consent is based on the erroneous belief that T1 is the only option.

In all of these scenarios, because consent presupposes a transaction between agents, there will be a consenting agent and at least one other agent. In some of these scenarios, this latter agent will be responsible for the consenting agent acting without relevant knowledge and understanding—for instance, where there is fraud, or misrepresentation, or non-disclosure on the part of the latter. However, it will be clear from what we have said already that the agent's lack of relevant knowledge and understanding might arise independently of the actions of the other party to the transaction (or, indeed, of the actions of any other agent). In other words, the particular items of data that lie within the consenting agent's informational field, and the operative interpretation thereof, might or might not be traced to the other agent to the transaction (or any other agent). Because the literature on 'informed consent' (especially in the context of medical treatment) takes us so quickly to transactions in which there is an informational asymmetry, we need to pause over this distinction between those cases in which the consenting agent's lack of relevant knowledge and understanding is independent of the (blameworthy) actions of some other agent and those in which another agent is responsible for this shortcoming.[44] Thus, where the

[43] See Margaret Brazier, 'Retained Organs: Ethics and Humanity' (2002) 22 *Legal Studies* 550, responding to John Harris, 'Law and Regulation of Retained Organs: The Ethical Issues' (2002) 22 *Legal Studies* 527.

[44] Because the transmission of information from one agent to another is not a mechanical process (akin to sending a packet of data from one point to another), there is always the possibility that the receiving agent will interpret the information that is transmitted in a way that deviates from the sender's interpretation. However, provided that the sending agent has acted in accordance with whatever informational obligations are in play, then although the receiving agent's informational field has been served by the sender, any deficiency in the consenting (receiving) agent's knowledge and understanding is now independent of any blameworthy action on the part of the sending agent.

consenting agent to the transaction is A, the other agent to the transaction is B (the recipient of A's consent), and C is a third party agent, we should distinguish the following three cases:

(i) A gives a consent (to B) that does not satisfy the requirement of relevant knowledge and understanding; but A's lack of knowledge and understanding is not attributable to any blameworthy act or omission by B or C;
(ii) because of fraud or non-disclosure, or the like by B, A gives a consent (to B) that does not satisfy the requirement of relevant knowledge and understanding; and
(iii) because of fraud or non-disclosure, or the like by C, A gives a consent (to B) that does not satisfy the requirement of relevant knowledge and understanding.

In the first of these cases, where A's consent is (broadly speaking) under-informed or misinformed, but not because of any blameworthy act or omission by B or C, the question of informed consent arises in a pure form: that is to say, the issue is simply about the informational prerequisites for an adequate consent. Before we consider how far the logic of our working model holds in such a case, however, we must comment briefly on the second and third cases, where the emphasis is on a violation of informational obligation by B or C, and its consequential impact on the consent apparently given by (misinformed) A.

To take the second case, suppose that B, who is HIV-positive, does not disclose this fact to his female partner A (similarly, if B lies to A about his condition). Unaware of the risk that she is running, A has unprotected sex with B. B does not intend to cause A harm but, in due course, A also tests positive for HIV. Let us suppose that B's failure to disclose to A that he is HIV-positive is a breach of a background informational obligation that B has to A. The law now has to decide what effect this breach has on A's consent which, other things being equal, provides B with a defence to various criminal offences. It might be argued that B's breach invalidates A's consent in relation to having sexual intercourse with B. However, if A's response to being told by B that he was HIV-positive would not have been to refuse to have sexual intercourse with B but to refuse to have *unprotected* sex with B, then the legal response needs to shadow the subtlety of A's response. In other words, notwithstanding his breach of the informational obligation, B would be able to rely on A's consent in response to an allegation of rape; however, he would not be permitted to rely on A's consent to respond to a charge of knowingly exposing A to risk of HIV infection (in whichever way a legal system formulates such a charge).[45]

[45] Compare *R v Mohammed Dica* [2004] EWCA Crim 1103.

Or, consider another example of the second kind of case. Suppose that B, a surgeon, fails to disclose to A that a particular medical procedure carries with it a tiny, and wholly unpredictable, risk. Unaware of the risk, A consents to the procedure. The risk eventuates and A is seriously disabled. Let us suppose that the legal system in which this issue arises has adopted a patient-driven approach to the informational obligations of physicians and that, relative to this standard, B is in breach of his informational obligations. Now, if A were to testify that she would not have undergone the procedure if she had been advised of the risk, arguably B should not be able to rely on A's consent to respond either to a charge of battery or to a claim for compensation for the disability suffered. Needless to say, although the medical profession would be able to live with the compensatory implications of this view, it would resist the removal of consent as a routine response to allegations of assault or battery.[46] Suppose, however, it is not clear how A would have responded had she been told that the procedure carried with it the risk in question; she testifies that, had she been fully informed, she would certainly have thought harder about undergoing the procedure but even she is uncertain whether she would have proceeded in these different circumstances. In such a speculative scenario, the one thing that we can be certain about is that (ex hypothesi) there has been a breach of informational obligation, but what this implies in relation to consent or compensatory liability is a moot point.[47]

When we turn to the third type of case, it is B who seeks to rely on A's consent but it is C who is in breach of an informational obligation relative to A. For example, let us suppose that C is the surgeon in the hypothetical we have just sketched. Accordingly, C, in breach of his informational obligations, fails to disclose the risk of the procedure to A. A decides to proceed with the treatment but she asks B (not C) to undertake it. B, in good faith, assumes that A is already fully informed, and, for the purposes of this example, we can assume that B is not in breach of any obligations to A. When B carries out the procedure, the undisclosed risk materialises. Two questions arise: first, given that C is in breach of his informational obligations to A, what compensatory responsibilities does he have towards A; and, secondly, is A's apparent consent available to B as a procedural justification if B is charged with battery against A? So far as the first question is concerned, the answer depends on the kind of considerations already indicated, particularly whether A would have consented had she been told of the risk. As to the second question, this is analogous to the first kind of case, which we can now move on to consider.

46 See, further, our discussion in ch 6.

47 Compare *Chester v Afshar* [2004] UKHL 41, and its Australian counterpart, *Chappel v Hart* (1998) 195 CLR 232.

Although the law must take a position on the responsibility of an agent in B's or C's situation, where there are breaches of informational obligations, the single issue raised by the first case gives us a clear sight of the fundamental question. That question is how far we go with the logic of our working model to hold that an agent has consented without relevant knowledge and understanding.

Each consenting agent, as we have said, will act on the basis of certain operative beliefs which, in turn, draw on the agent's own particular informational field. However, each agent will have its own distinctive informational field. Some agents will have more extensive informational fields than others; some agents will have informational fields that are relatively intense at the site of the particular transaction, other will not; and so on. But no agent is omniscient; no agent will have a comprehensive and completely accurate informational field. In principle, therefore, any consenting agent might plead after the event that its informational field lacked some relevant item of data or that it included inaccurate data. How readily does such a plea translate into the proposition that the agent gave a consent without relevant knowledge and understanding: that this was not a properly informed consent? Such a question prompts two angles of inquiry: first, there is more to settle about the *materiality* of the missing or inaccurate data; and, secondly, there is more to settle about who bears the *responsibility* for inaccurate data or for the omission of material data from the consenting agent's informational field.

In principle, the item of data in question might have been *material* to the agent's decision to consent at more than one level. At weakest, the data might simply have raised a consideration that the agent would have wished to address, but it would not have changed the agent's mind about consenting. At strongest, the data might have caused a reversal of the agent's decision: instead of consenting, the agent would have refused. And, in between these extremes, the data might not have caused the agent to withhold consent but it would have led to some qualifying condition (or reservation) being placed on the consent. Which of these senses of materiality should we adopt for our condition of relevant knowledge and understanding, and whose standpoint should we be guided by (that of the consenting agent, or a reasonable agent, or some other representative agent)?

It seems to us that a strong line in subjectivism is consistent with a Gewirthian approach to this question. Accordingly, the standpoint that matters is that of the agent who has ostensibly consented; for it is the consent that has been ostensibly given by this agent (not some other agent, real or representative) that is at issue. In practice, the agent is unlikely to plead a lack of informed consent unless, once aware of the data item, the agent would not have consented or would have given only a conditional consent. Nevertheless, we suggest that the ideal-typical case here treats materiality in the weakest sense as sufficient. In other words (and now the strong subjectivism becomes apparent), in the ideal-typical case, a consenting agent acts without relevant knowledge or understanding if that agent's informational field lacks an item of data that the agent would judge (sincerely) to be material in the sense that it at least raises a consideration that it would have wished to consider before making a decision as to consent.

This is not quite a licence to avoid the consequences of consents that one regrets, for we must also bring into the reckoning the question of who bears *responsibility* for the omitted (or incorrect) item. Two sets of considerations are relevant to this question. First, there are the informational obligations, background and special, that agents owe to one another.[48] Secondly, there are the responsibilities that agents have for the accuracy of their own informational fields.

To address the first of these considerations: in a Gewirthian community, the background regime of rights and duties will include negative obligations against fraud and misinformation as well as positive obligations to inform, such as the obligation of one (informed) agent to warn another (ignorant) agent of a hidden danger (paradigmatically, a life-threatening danger). The extent of such positive obligations will be guided by the twin principles that: (a) agents should not be encouraged to free-ride on the information-seeking activities of others; and (b) that no agent should be required to inform where this would represent a disproportionate burden relative to its own generic interests. These background informational obligations (both negative and positive), it will be understood, arise quite independently of consent—that is, the reason why these obligations are owed is not to increase the possibility that the act of consenting in particular will be informed but to increase the possibility that action in general will be taken on an informed basis. For example, the reason why there is a background duty to inform an agent that there is a fire ahead is not so that the agent, once warned, can give an informed *consent* to a transaction of some kind but simply so that the agent in question is equipped to act on an informed basis. It follows that these are obligations that agents owe to one another irrespective of whether the immediate context is one in which an agent is considering giving consent and irrespective of whether the information bears directly on an agent's decision whether or not to consent.

Having said this, the nature and extent of an agent's background positive informational obligations does vary from one context to another (as well as from one kind of relationship to another). Even in the case of the most general obligations, there is always a particular context that accounts for the agent having the positive obligation in question. In the next chapter, we will discuss information-giving in medical and contractual contexts. In both

[48] Such considerations taking us back to the second and third scenarios above, where A's lack of knowledge or understanding was attributable to misinformation or non-disclosure by B or C that, we assumed, constituted a breach of informational obligation.

cases, we can say that, potentially, these contexts bring into play a second layer of positive informational obligations. For example, it is arguable that, in modern complex societies with high divisions of labour, suppliers of specialised goods or services have positive obligations to disclose the specialist features of those goods or services. Within these distinctive contexts, the features of particular transactions might bring into play a third layer of positive obligations—for example, obligations to ensure that vulnerable agents are as informed as non-vulnerable agents would be expected to be. Accordingly, when we refer to an agent's background informational responsibilities, we are including all such responsibilities as are imposed on the agent, in the particular context, by the background rule regime.

Assuming that the background (and any special) informational obligations are being discharged, we turn to the second consideration: namely, the responsibility to be borne by each agent for its own informational field. The question is: precisely how much responsibility is this to be, bearing in mind that, by holding the agent to its consent, we will be holding it to an act of will that is (subjectively) under-informed? What is to be the extent of the consenting agent's responsibility under the default position that is now being contemplated?

First, it is easy to hold that the consenting agent must bear the responsibility if it acts recklessly in relation to its own informational field. For example, if agent A is put on notice that, before consenting, it would be prudent to check out that 'X actually is the case' (as A assumes), then this surely must be A's risk if A proceeds to consent without double-checking that X is the case.[49]

Secondly, it must also be the consenting agent who bears the risk if it fails to take reasonable care. Remember, we are hypothesising a situation where the recipient of the consent has clean hands; where the background negative and positive informational obligations have been discharged; and where, to the extent that the informational responsibility may be transferred in special cases—for example, where one agent assumes the responsibility, explicitly or by implication, to inform the other—this is not such a case.

Thirdly, we come to a genuinely hard case, one in which both agents to the transaction have acted reasonably and responsibly, yet the consent has been given in ignorance of material (present) information.[50] Let us suppose that, for one reason or another, there was no real possibility of the agents having access to the information in question at the time of the transaction; or the hard case might be a tripartite situation such as the one we discussed

[49] Of course, those with informational obligations to A are not permitted to shift the responsibility to A by advising A that he should make his own checks. Compare the famous case of *Redgrave v Hurd* (1881) 20 Ch D 1.

[50] We take it that the consenting agent must bear the risk in relation to unknown future facts. If procedural justifications were vulnerable to the consenting agent changing its mind in the light of future facts, the recipient could not rely on the consent with any confidence at all.

earlier (where C fails to disclose material facts to A who then gives a consent to B). Which side, the consenting agent or the recipient, should bear the risk and responsibility?

Such a case sets up a tension between two regulative principles that we will meet recurrently. On the one hand, it is fundamental to Gewirthian thinking that we should strive to give effect to the agent's will; in other words, it is fundamental that we give due weight to a principle of fidelity to the consenting agent's will. On the other hand, agents cannot function without a degree of transactional security and it is important for practical purposes that the reasonable expectations of the recipient agent are given due weight—otherwise, in practice, there will be no reliance on what seem to be perfectly valid consents. We cannot give unqualified effect to subjectivism in relation to an informed consent without undermining the recipient's reasonable expectation. In this light, to hold the reckless or careless consenting agent to the (albeit informationally deficient) consent is the better accommodation of these principles. However, where the consenting agent is neither reckless nor careless, there is reason to think that the fidelity principle reasserts itself. In such a hard case, where neither agent is the obvious risk-bearer, each legal regime will have to make its own good faith judgement as to the respective weights to be accorded to fidelity (for the sake of the consenting agent) and reasonable expectation (for the sake of the recipient of the consent). If we set aside future information (treating this as the consenting agent's risk),[51] then the focus for any division of responsibility is information that is 'in' but inaccurately so or information that, although available, is 'not in' (for example, the under-informed patient who, in ignorance of T2, thinks that T1 is the only treatment). It seems to us that a plausible default position for the hard case is to hold: (a) that the consent does not meet the condition of an informed choice; but (b) because the recipient has acted in good faith, reliance on the consent is excused although not procedurally justified.[52] Taking this view, we would say in the tripartite situation that, while A has a claim against C for C's breach of an informational obligation, B (who has acted in reliance on A's apparent consent) is excused any wrong done to A that would otherwise be covered by the consent. Having said this, it is worth repeating that this *is* a hard case, and that, faced with such powerful but competing regulative principles, we feel the force of Learned Hand's view that the spirit of free-thinking militates against being too sure that you are right.

To recap, then, a consenting agent might plead that the consent was under-informed in the following ways. First, the agent might argue that the

[51] See n 50 above.

[52] In some cases, where there has been reliance, there might be no practical difference between treating the recipient's acts as excused rather than procedurally justified. However, where there has been no reliance, there will be the possibility of reversing the transaction.

recipient agent was in breach of background informational obligations, saying that, although these obligations arise independently, the particular breach has a bearing on the informational field that is relevant for the purposes of the consent (and, let us recall, it is the consenting agent's subjective view of relevance that governs). Secondly, the agent might argue that this is a special case where (exceptionally) the responsibility is transferred to the recipient agent and where there has been a failure to inform that is relevant for the purposes of the consent. Thirdly, the agent might argue that, although there is no failure of informational obligation, background or special, nevertheless the consent was not informed. We have (tentatively) suggested that a plausible default position here is that the consenting agent bears responsibility for informational failures that are referable to its own recklessness or carelessness. However, if the consenting agent has not been reckless or careless, the consent fails to qualify as informed.

Finally, how far is it correct to treat informed choice (consent based on relevant knowledge and understanding) as a matter of degree? First, it is clearly correct to say that individual informational fields vary from one agent to another. Secondly, it is also correct to say that, in relation to a particular choice involving the giving of consent, some informational fields will be fuller than others. Thirdly, where an agent consents on the basis of an informational field that is deficient or defective in a respect that the agent sincerely judges to be material, then the consent fails to satisfy the ideal-typical condition of relevant knowledge and understanding—and, although informational deficits can be of different kinds and depth, we are no longer dealing with a question of degree: quite simply, this is not an informed consent.[53] Fourthly, however, the practical risk of such an uninformed consent depends upon whether the failure falls within the agent's own sphere of informational responsibility. If the failure does so fall, then the consenting agent may not plead a lack of relevant knowledge and understanding; but if it does not so fall, the lack of informed consent may be pleaded. Once again, however, at this practical level, it is not informed consent that is a matter of degree so much as the informational deficit that characterises the absence of an informed consent.

## IV Conclusion

In this chapter, we have drawn on Gewirthian thinking to formulate ideal-types of both unforced choice and informed choice, and with that, an

[53] Compare Faden and Beauchamp, n 19 above, at 252:

> A person has a full or complete understanding of an action if there is a fully adequate apprehension of all the relevant propositions or statements (those that contribute in any way to obtaining an appreciation of the situation) that correctly describe (1) the nature of the action, and (2) the foreseeable consequences and possible outcomes that might follow as a result of performing and not performing the action.

account of the pivotal conditions for a valid consent. Our position is that an ostensible consent is invalid if it is given as the result of a negative power-play (directed at the target agent's generic interests) by an intervening agent—such is the essence of a forced choice; or if the agent's informational field lacks an item of data, or includes an inaccuracy, that the agent would judge (sincerely) to be material (here, there is a lack of informed choice). However, the consenting agent is estopped from pleading failure of informed choice where the deficiency in the agent's informational field lies within the sphere of its own default responsibility.

It will be recalled that, according to Faden and Beauchamp, 'no sharp line can be drawn purely on conceptual grounds to distinguish autonomous from nonautonomous action,' and the decision as to where to draw the dividing line 'is invariably based on moral and policy considerations.'[54] So far as the pivotal conditions associated with a free and informed consent are concerned, we would want to restate this in the following way. The conceptual lines are to be drawn in the light of a Gewirthian moral theory. So drawn, there is a clear line between an unforced choice and a forced choice as there is between an informed choice and an uninformed choice. It is once we cross from unforced choice to various degrees of forced choice and from informed choice to various degrees of uninformed choice that we find some shading in the idea of (non-)autonomous action. Whether or not, as a matter of policy, regulatory orders will take consent so seriously that these bright line conditions are insisted upon is another story. In the next chapter, we will review some aspects of modern medical law and contract law to see how well they fare relative to this standard.

[54] Compare Faden and Beauchamp, n 19 above, at 240.

# 6

# The Conditions of (Valid) Consent II: Duress, Undue Influence, and Disclosure

## I Introduction

Having developed our ideal-typical conception of free and informed consent, our next step is to apply this model to some positive regulatory articulations of what are commonly assumed to be modern legal systems.[1] Necessarily, this involves some selectivity. In relation to the condition of unforced choice, we will discuss the doctrines of economic duress and undue influence; in relation to the condition of informed consent, we will discuss some leading doctrines (including the so-called doctrine of 'informed consent') concerning disclosure of information. In both cases, our discussion, which is in two parts, ranges across contract law and medical law.

In the first part of the chapter, we examine the doctrines of duress and undue influence, mainly in relation to contract law but also with regard to influence exerted in medical settings. Although consent is central to the very idea of contract, the context in which contractors meet to deal is one of a marketplace in which bargaining positions are in a constant state of flux. It follows that, while regimes of contract law have little difficulty in regulating duress applied to person or property, they have much more difficulty in dealing with economic pressure or necessity. The question for these regimes is whether there is a point at which the application of economic pressure, or the impact of economic necessity, is no longer compatible with the idea of an agent making an unforced choice (as required by a consent-based theory of contract).[2] If so, where is this point; and, in practice, can unforced choice be ring-fenced without eliminating those inequalities of bargaining position that are integral to a marketplace? Despite these difficulties, we believe that modern regimes of contract law are fully justified in seeking to protect the integrity of consent by developing doctrines of economic duress.

[1] Here, as conceived in legal positivist terms: see ch 5, n 3.

[2] For three different senses in which contract can be treated as 'consent-based', see below at 157.

One of the reasons why a party may have a bargaining advantage is because it has material information that the other lacks—for example, a seller who obtains a premium price today knowing (unlike the buyer) that the shortfall in supply (which accounts for premium prices) will end tomorrow. In such situations, no one suggests that a forced choice has been made by the buyer; but, where there are asymmetries in information of this kind, there is a question about whether the contractor's choice is sufficiently informed. This leads into the second part of the chapter where, alongside the question of disclosure in contract law, we focus on the doctrine of 'informed consent' as it has been developed in the context of medical law. Here, the most patient-centred of modern legal regimes insist not only that patients should freely consent to undertake the prescribed treatment and that they should understand the nature of that treatment but that physicians should inform them as to the risks associated with the treatment in question and advise as to alternatives. On the face of it, this takes consent far more seriously than either physician-centred (and paternalistic) regimes of medical law (where consent is obtained in a routine and perfunctory fashion) or classical regimes of contract law in which a duty to disclose is regarded as the exception rather than the rule.[3]

Following up on the analysis of the previous chapter, we will suggest that there are two drivers legitimately operating to move doctrine towards greater disclosure and co-operative relationships. One is that background informational responsibilities are taken more seriously; and the other is that 'transfers over' of informational responsibility may be increasingly seen as appropriate. In both cases, even if these doctrinal developments are not straightforward articulations of the view that consent must be informed, relative to Gewirthian morality, they are quite clearly progressive in nature.

## II Free Choice, Economic Duress, and Undue Influence

That contract is predicated on consent might seem too obvious to warrant extended comment. Yet, this predicate, while obvious and taken for granted, has more than one reference point and more than one articulation. To maintain our bearings, the following three matters should be borne in mind.

First, in our analysis, the key reference point is that of the originating consent by which the parties engage the local 'law of contract' for the purposes of their transaction. By so consenting, the parties agree to submit themselves to the governance of the rule-set represented by the particular 'law of contract'. The 'law of contract' so engaged, however, is also a possible reference point for the predicate. For, when the parties reach agreement on their particular deal, negotiated under the terms of the local 'law of contract'

[3] Seminally, see Lord Cockburn CJ in *Smith v Hughes* (1871) LR 6 QB 597, at 603–4.

that their prior consent has engaged, the rules of this set might prescribe their own consent requirements. If so, consent is double-banked: contract is predicated not only on an originating consent (to engage the rules of the 'law of contract') but also on consensual dealing (as provided for by the rules of the 'law of contract'). Contract is, thus, predicated on consent twice over.

Secondly, where dealings that are to be regulated by the 'law of contract' are preceded by a distinct process of consensual engagement—in other words, where originating consents have to be decisively signalled—the detailed provisions of the rule-set so engaged can be treated as enjoying, so to speak, 'relative autonomy'. That is to say, where originating consents are in place, it is not essential that the 'law of contract' so engaged seeks to mimic Gewirthian principles. Of course, if a rule-set that mimics Gewirthian principles of consent is judged to be functional (economically or culturally) for a particular community, then there is good reason for the 'law of contract' to track Gewirthian thinking in requiring that agreements are made on the basis of free and informed consent. However, in principle, under relative autonomy, a rule-set may or may not incorporate consent requirements and, to the extent that consent requirements are incorporated, they may or may not mimic Gewirthian standards of adequacy.

Thirdly, where dealings that are to be regulated by the 'law of contract' are *not* preceded by a distinct process of consensual engagement, or by a process that can be properly monitored, it is unsafe to grant relative autonomy to the rule-set. There is not yet a procedural justification in place. As a corrective measure, the 'law of contract' might make its own provision for consent. Even if the 'law of contract' has difficulty in providing a surrogate test for an originating consent, it might at least take steps to ensure that no contract made by the parties is enforced unless it is the product of a free and informed consent (subject to Gewirthian standards of adequacy). In other words, even if there is no procedural justification for holding agents bound by the 'law of contract', the law might check that to hold agents to the contract that they have made is procedurally justified.

In the light of these remarks, it will be apparent that, when we say that contract is consent-based, we might be referring to any one or more of three different interpretations of this predicate. We might mean that contract is based on an originating consent (the paradigmatic case of empowerment); or that consent is functional for the rule-set; or that consent plays a corrective role within the rule-set (to compensate for a deficiency at the point where originating consents would operate in the paradigmatic case).

Having unpacked some of the complexities that hide behind the innocent suggestion that contract is consent-based, it is perhaps not altogether surprising that, while most standard accounts of contract include consent as part of the picture, commentaries tend to give greater prominence to ideas such as promise or agreement, expectation or reliance, welfare or efficiency, and so on. In opposition to such theories, Randy Barnett is unusual in arguing for the primacy of consent.[4] According to Barnett:

> A consent theory posits that contractual obligation cannot be completely understood unless it is viewed as part of a broader system of legal entitlements. Such a system, based in morality, specifies the substance of the rights individuals may acquire and transfer, and the means by which they may do so. Properly understood, contract law is that part of a system of entitlements that identifies those circumstances in which entitlements are validly transferred from person to person by their consent. Consent is the moral component that distinguishes valid from invalid transfers of alienable rights.[5]

Clearly, on this account, the setting for contract is a background theory of entitlements (and rights). Thus:

> According to an entitlements approach, rights may be unconditionally granted to another (a gift), or their transfer may be conditioned upon some act or reciprocal transfer by the transferee (an exchange). Contract law concerns ways in which rights are transferred or alienated.[6]

Hence, '[r]equiring the consent of the rights holder as a condition of a valid transfer of rights is absolutely vital to a regime of entitlements';[7] and '[t]raditional contract defenses can be understood as describing circumstances that, if proved to have existed, deprive the manifestation of assent of its normal moral, and therefore legal, significance.'[8] In fact, Barnett proposes three groups of defences:

(1) where the manifestation of consent is obtained improperly: eg duress, misrepresentation, and possibly unconscionability;
(2) where the party purporting to consent lacks ability to do so: eg incapacity, infancy, and intoxication; and
(3) where the consent does not fully express agreement as to contingencies that affect performance: eg mistake, impracticability, and frustration.

Broadly speaking, the first group of defences relates to the conditions of free and informed consent, the second to the capacity to consent, and the third to the scope of consent. For our present purposes, it is the first category that matters and, in particular, the defences of duress and undue influence.[9]

[4] Randy E Barnett, 'A Consent Theory of Contract' (1986) 86 *Columbia Law Review* 269–321. If we wished to join the debate between Barnett and his critics, it would be important to establish whether the basis of contract is the parties' prior originating consent or a functional consent requirement within the rule-set. This is not critical for our purposes, but we do touch again on this matter in ch 7 below at 201–202.

[5] *Ibid*, at 270.

[6] *Ibid*, at 292.

[7] *Ibid*, at 303.

[8] *Ibid*, at 318.

[9] Barnett does not cite undue influence as a defence.

*(i) Duress*

In the common law jurisprudence, instances of duress against the person and duress against property are regarded as relatively easy cases; the party to whom the duress has been applied should not be bound by the transaction. These are instances where the law readily recognises that consent has been obtained improperly. However, there are two ways of theorising the legal response as follows:

(1) because the party who has applied the duress has committed an independent wrong, the law should not assist this party to take advantage of the wrongfully procured transaction; or
(2) because the party to whom the duress was applied did not freely consent, the law should not enforce the transaction if consent is the ground for enforcement.

Where the second account is given, it has often been set alongside the view that duress implies an 'overborne will' and that an 'overborne will' entails a lack of consent. However, the overborne will theory has largely gone out of fashion because commentators are not convinced that a consent under duress presupposes an overborne will. Far from it: indeed, as John Dawson famously argued, the more extreme the pressure, the more real the consent because 'the more unpleasant the alternative, the more real the consent to a course which would avoid it.'[10] As we saw in the previous chapter, there is considerable scope for confusion where we say that an agent acted against its will. And, whilst we can agree with Dawson that external pressure does not always signify that the target agent's will has been overborne (that the agent has acted against its will in the narrow sense), it does not follow that the agent has made an unforced choice. Given that unforced choice, on our analysis, is one of the conditions for a valid consent, we should not, therefore, rush to conclude that, in the absence of overborne will, we have a valid consent. On our view, where there is negative pressure in the form of threats to person or property, the target agent's consent is unlikely to be valid. In other words, even if the overborne will theory has been rightly rejected, it is a serious mistake to reject with it the question of whether the ostensible consent was an unforced choice.

In practice, even if the law was losing its grip on the consent perspective, it made little difference to the outcome; for, so long as the pressure was applied to person or property, the fact that the duress represented an independent wrong sufficed as a ground for relief. (We need not here pursue the question of whether an ostensible consent, obtained by duress of this

[10] John P Dawson, 'Economic Duress—An Essay in Perspective' (1947) 45 *Michigan Law Review* 253, at 267.

kind, should be treated as void or (a)voidable.)[11] However, once the law started to recognise that economic pressure might qualify as a form of duress, and was no longer taking its bearings from the requirements of consent (consent being assumed in the absence of an overborne will), a notoriously problematic chapter in the development of the law was opened. This has given rise to a host of contested questions concerning such matters as: whether the focus should be on the (improper) pressure applied or on the impact of the pressure on the other party (and the options open to that party) or on the extent of any resulting imbalance (or all three factors);[12] whether there is a non-arbitrary line to be drawn between (acceptable) commercial pressure and (unacceptable) economic duress; whether there is economic duress only if the will of the target consenting party is overborne;[13] whether pressure for renegotiation of a contract is distinguishable from pressure applied ab initio; and so on.

Let us start with what most would agree to be a relatively easy case, *Alaska Packers Association v Domenico*.[14] There, the defendant had hired seamen to fish for salmon. However, once in Alaskan waters, the seamen threatened not to work unless higher wages (than those originally agreed) were paid. Given the short fishing season and the unavailability of other seamen, the defendant had little choice but to accede to the seamen's demand. Subsequently, when the legal effect of the defendant's promise to pay higher wages was put to the test, the court ruled that it was unenforceable.[15] Intuitively, this looks like the right answer, but how do the situation and the result align with our model of consent and, in particular, our ideal-type of unforced choice?

The seamen's case for payment of the higher wages rested on the defendant's agreement to pay such wages. In the language of consent, the case was that the defendant had consented to pay such sums. The counter-argument was that the ostensible consent did not satisfy the conditions for a valid consent (and transfer) because the defendant's choice was forced. Assuming that the ex ante (ie prior) relationship between the parties involved no disruption of Gewirthian moral principles, the seamen applied

[11] If the law treats the consent as void, the transaction will be of no legal effect; if the law treats the consent as voidable, the party who has given the invalid consent may take steps to avoid what would otherwise be the legal effects of the transaction (but, usually, this will be subject to time-limits and the protection of innocent third parties).

[12] Cf Clare Dalton, 'An Essay in the Deconstruction of Contract Doctrine' (1985) 94 *Yale Law Journal* 997.

[13] Cf, eg, Patrick S Atiyah, 'Economic Duress and the "Overborne Will"' (1982) 98 *Law Quarterly Review* 197.

[14] 117 F 99 (9th Cir 1902).

[15] The doctrinal ground at this time was 'want of consideration', but it is obvious why, nowadays, this is seen as a paradigm of economic duress.

external (negative) force against the defendant;[16] the defendant assuredly would have apprehended the pressure as having a negative bearing; and we can assume that it was this pressure that elicited the defendant's consent to the seamen's demand for higher wages. On these premises, the defendant would have been right to have directly pleaded invalid consent, and the court was, anyway, right to rule that the agreement was unenforceable.[17]

In England, the courts did not explicitly recognise a doctrine of economic duress until the 1970s and the context in which they did so was, as in *Alaska Packers*, one of contractual renegotiation or modification. The landmark case in England was *The Atlantic Baron*,[18] where the dispute was between a shipyard in the Far East and a client. The contract provided for a price to be measured in US dollars. It followed that, when the dollar was devalued, the value of the contract to the shipyard also fell. With a view to covering such loss of value, the shipyard indicated to the client that the order would not be fulfilled unless the price was adjusted upwards. Reluctantly, the client agreed to pay the higher price. The court ruled that the demand made by the shipyard was an instance of economic duress and that the client, provided action was taken promptly, was entitled to avoid (or disclaim) the agreement to pay more than the original contractual price. If the ruling in *Alaska Packers* was correct, was the court also correct in *The Atlantic Baron*?

The situation in *The Atlantic Baron* is not quite four-square with that in *Alaska Packers*. In the latter, the seamen (so we assume) attempted opportunistically to put themselves in a better financial position than they would have been in had the contract been carried out as originally agreed; in *The Atlantic Baron*, by contrast, it is arguable that the shipyard sought only to maintain the financial benefit that it would have obtained if the contract had been carried out as originally agreed and if the dollar had not been devalued. We must be careful, however, not to allow the possible mitigation that the shipyard might plead to cloud the question of whether the client's consent was given as a matter of unforced choice. In effect, there are two issues threaded together. First, there is the question of whether the client should be held to the higher price because, *and sufficiently because*, it ostensibly consented to pay such sums. In other words, did the shipyard have a procedural justification for holding the client to its agreement to increase the price? Secondly, there is the question of whether the client should be required to cover (or, at any rate, contribute towards) the shipyard's loss occasioned by the devaluation of the dollar, whether because this was the

[16] If the ex ante relationship revealed prior exploitation of the seamen by the defendant, the seamen might be (substantively) justified in applying pressure for additional wages. However, the defendant's ostensible consent would not provide a procedural justification for holding the defendant to account.

[17] Cf n 15 above.

[18] *North Ocean Shipping Co Ltd v Hyundai Construction Co Ltd: The Atlantic Baron* [1979] QB 705.

parties' original agreement about where this risk (of devaluation) would lie or because the law imposes (or ought to impose) such risk-sharing rules on contractors. Because, on our analysis, the ex ante relationship between the parties is material to the question of whether the pressure applied is negative or positive, these two questions cannot be treated as entirely independent of one another, the answer to the second bearing on the answer to the first. Essentially, the relationship between the two questions works as follows:

(1) If the answer to the second question shows that the shipyard is entitled to a covering or contributory payment from the client, then the ex ante relationship between the parties is one of the client being indebted to the shipyard; from which, it follows that the first question does not arise in an ideal-typical context and that the shipyard's demand cannot be characterised at once as negative pressure bearing on the client's generic interests. If the shipyard is entitled to a covering increase, its demand should be characterised as nothing more than a reminder to the client of its obligations. Even the shipyard's indication that delivery of the tanker would be withheld might be construed not as a threat, but as a legitimate suspension of performance mandated by the contract. On this reading of the transaction, the significance of the client's consent is little more than a practical indication of a willingness to pay—what grounds the claim to payment is not so much the expression of consent as the terms of the parties' ex ante relationship.[19]

(2) If the answer to the second question shows that the shipyard is *not* entitled to a covering or contributory payment from the client, then the ex ante relationship between the parties is such that the client is not indebted to the shipyard; from which, it follows that, relative to this moral baseline, the answer to the first question is that the shipyard's demand represents the application of negative pressure. On this hypothesis, the client's consent is the basis of the claim to payment and the question of whether the consent is freely given is critical.

Assuming that the facts in the *Atlantic Baron* fit with (2), then it is plain that the court was right to treat the pressure applied by the shipyard as an instance of economic duress entailing that the client had not given a valid consent.

[19] In this light, what would we say about the widespread practice of compromising claims by consent, (a) where the claim is clearly well founded, and (b) where the validity of the claim, or the extent of the liability, is uncertain? In (a), consent does no real work in founding the claim; the claim is well founded and there is liability irrespective of consent. But, of course, the effect of a valid consensual compromise is to preclude the consenting claimant from reopening the claim (or, at any rate, this is the usual form of a compromised claim). In (b), consent is fundamental, grounding a contract of compromise. Provided that the claimant is not indebted to the claimee, the latter's consent seems to be in response to an offer (ie positive rather than negative pressure).

If this seems relatively straightforward, why is economic duress regarded as such a difficult and possibly subversive idea in contract law? We should recall the nature of the contested issues. First, there is disagreement as to the focus of the doctrine. This is best expressed as a dispute about the necessary and sufficient conditions for a court to hold that there has been economic duress. The most stringent standard sets three conditions along the following lines: (i) improper (economic) pressure has been applied; (ii) in the face of the pressure, the consenting party had no reasonable option but to accede; and (iii) the effect of going along with the pressure was to the manifest economic disadvantage of the consenting party. Each of these conditions invites interpretation and argument on the facts (was the pressure *improper*?; was there no *reasonable* alternative option?; was the disadvantage *manifest*?), but our question is whether, relative to our model of unforced choice, they are appropriate. The first condition starts in the right place because economic duress, on our analysis, arises only where there is external negative pressure. Once such pressure is applied, our ideal-type of forced choice requires a causative effect. However, we suggested that, in practice, there should be a strong presumption in favour of causation once external force is applied. If the second condition allows for the agent who applies the pressure to rebut the presumption of causation, this is in line with our model—but there is an obvious danger that the second condition, as drafted, puts the burden on the wrong party (namely, the consenting agent) to prove the wrong thing (namely, that it was reasonable in the circumstances to submit to the pressure). As for the third condition, while it might explain the ostensibly consenting agent's practical interest in avoiding the transaction, as a doctrinal requirement for duress, it seems irrelevant and inappropriate.

Secondly, having correctly identified the first condition as critical, many contract commentators have doubted that it is feasible to draw a clean line between (acceptable) commercial pressure and (unacceptable) economic duress. One thought is that we might draw the line by reference to the standards of fair dealing accepted within each particular business community. However, if our interest is in unforced choice (as it is), we must be guided by whether the intervening agent applies negative pressure to the target agent's generic interests in order to procure the consent. In this light, compare these three variations on the facts of the *Alaska Packers* case: (i) the seamen, when first approached about fishing in Alaska, refuse to work except for wages that are higher than the employer wishes to pay; (ii) the seamen, having agreed to do the work, threaten not to perform their contractual obligations unless the employer agrees to pay a higher wage; and (iii) the seamen, having agreed to do the work in the current season, threaten not to work for the employer in future unless he agrees to pay a higher wage for the current season than that agreed. Let us suppose that, in each case, the employer reluctantly agrees to pay the higher wage demanded by the seamen. We have already said that the negative pressure applied in a case such as (ii) amounts to economic duress. What do we make, however, of the pressure in (i) and (iii)? In (i), assuming that there is moral equilibrium between the parties, the seamen are under no obligation to work for the prospective employer, let alone work for him at the wage he offers. When they put forward their own terms, the seamen do so with clean hands; they make an offer, not a threat. Similarly, in (iii), although the seamen are under an obligation to carry out their obligations for the current season, they are not threatening not to do so. Their proposal is that they will commit to the employer in future if he improves their current wages. Unless the seamen are morally obligated to work for the employer in future, this is again an offer not a threat.

To put the point just made in slightly different terms, although the employer has a negative attitude towards the bargaining position taken by the seamen in (i) and (iii), the latter does not amount to external force with a negative bearing. To be sure, the employer's specific purposes are not assisted by the position taken by the seamen; but the critical point is that the employer's generic interests are not engaged because the relevant (non-subtractive) interests are not vested—it is not as though the seamen are depriving the employer of goods that are already his. Case (ii), however, is different because the position taken by the seamen bears directly, and negatively, on the employer's vested contractual interests.[20] The employer is entitled to have the benefit of the performance promised by the seamen; notionally, this performance already, as it were, is an asset belonging to the employer; it is one of the employer's legitimate holdings; and, by threatening to withhold performance, the seamen are exerting a negative pressure on the employer's legitimate assets. What this suggests is that economic duress is more likely to be found in situations of pressurised renegotiation rather than hard bargaining ab initio (ie from the outset). There is no iron rule about this, however: as case (iii) indicates, renegotiation might not always add up to economic duress; and, if there is moral indebtedness, ab initio dealing might reveal economic duress.

Finally, although some equate economic duress with overborne will (that is, the consenting agent's will being overborne), it is clear that this is not what we are looking for. Where the agent's will is overborne, this is a case of involuntary action (in the strict sense) rather than a forced choice arising from external negative pressure. Neither, however, are we looking

[20] The same would apply if we were to turn the situation round. Suppose that the agreement was that the seamen should be paid at the end of the fishing season. However, when the time for payment came, the employer, knowing that the seaman were desperate to be paid and knowing that they would have serious difficulty in pursuing a claim for non-payment, 'offered' a reduced payment in full and final settlement. Given the vested rights of the seamen, this would be external force with a negative bearing; the seamen would not validly consent to underpayment; and the transaction would be rightly reviewable for economic duress. Cf *Headley v Hackley* 45 Mich 569, 8 NW 511 (1881).

for hard bargaining simpliciter. The argument for economic duress requires the application of external economic force (pressure with a negative bearing) but it does not presuppose the capitulation of the target agent in the sense of the latter's will being overborne.

We conclude, therefore, that, whilst many doubt the wisdom of developing a doctrine of economic duress within the rules of the 'law of contract' (because it seems to lack focus, it defies non-arbitrary line-drawing, it jeopardises certainty, and so on), there is no reason why a perfectly coherent jurisprudence of economic duress cannot be developed. Moreover, such a development is entirely appropriate *if we wish to defend the possibility of contractors giving consent as a matter of unforced choice.* And, as we have explained, this is something that we might wish to do because we think that such a consent-based rule-set is functional (whether for economic or cultural reasons) or because we need to take corrective steps to compensate for a deficient process of originating consent.

### *(ii) Undue Influence*

In a number of legal systems, the courts have been called upon to deal with a dispute of the following kind. Agent A, whose business is in difficulty, seeks a loan from a bank. The bank will make the loan provided that agent B acts as a surety (or guarantor), typically this requiring B to put up the family home (shared by A and B) as security for the loan to A. *Agent B consents to this arrangement*, and the loan is advanced. However, the loan fails to save the business; A is unable to repay the money; and the bank now calls on B as surety. B argues that the consent was invalid because it was obtained in circumstances of undue influence (A having undue influence over B). Two questions arise for decision: (i) was there undue influence as between A and B; and (ii) if so, does this preclude the bank, a third party, from enforcing the arrangement to which B has ostensibly consented? In practice, it is the second question that causes most of the problems, as the law tries to set fair and workable ground rules determining whether the bank will be treated as having notice of the possibility of undue influence between A and B and, concomitantly, what procedures (eg for giving independent advice) the bank might put in place to enable it to take the security from B (and, subsequently, to enforce it) with a clear conscience. As a matter of principle, however, the first question is at least as troublesome, because the conceptual focus of undue influence is less clear than it should be. As a result, the precise relationship between the doctrine of undue influence and other relieving doctrines, particularly duress and unconscionability, is left unresolved by the jurisprudence.

One of the best-known examples of the kind of dispute sketched above is the Australian case of *Commercial Bank of Australia v Amadio*.[21] There,

[21] (1983) 151 CLR 447.

Deane J began the task of disentangling the various relieving doctrines in the following terms:

> The equitable principles relating to relief against unconscionable dealing and the principles relating to undue influence are closely related. The two doctrines are, however, distinct. Undue influence, like common law duress, looks to the quality of the consent or assent of the weaker party . . . Unconscionable dealing looks to the conduct of the stronger party in attempting to enforce, or retain the benefit of, a dealing with a person under a special disability in circumstances where it is not consistent with equity or good conscience that he should do so.[22]

More recently, in an attempt to focus theorisation of the doctrine of undue influence, Peter Birks and Chin Nyuk Yin echoed the distinction drawn by Deane J by submitting that relieving doctrines can be broadly characterised either as defendant-sided or plaintiff-sided.[23] According to Birks and Yen, if we equate undue influence with bad, wicked, or exploitative, or similar such conduct on the part of the agent who exerts influence (the conduct of the stronger party in Deane J's terms), then we treat undue influence as a defendant-sided doctrine. By contrast, if we equate the idea with a loss of autonomy on the part of the agent who consents under the influence of another (looking to the quality of the consent of the weaker party in Deane J's terms), then we treat undue influence as a plaintiff-sided doctrine. Also echoing Deane J, Birks and Yin's position is that we should treat undue influence as a plaintiff-sided doctrine. What do we make of this?

The distinction between defendant-sided and plaintiff-sided doctrines might well be a helpful way of bringing relieving doctrines more clearly into focus. Moreover, it might well be possible to find support for a plaintiff-sided analysis in the case-law. For example, in *Royal Bank of Scotland v Etridge (No 2)*,[24] the most recent and now leading English case on the matter, Lord Nicholls said that influence becomes undue and, hence, unacceptable 'whenever the consent thus procured ought not fairly to be treated as the expression of a person's free will.'[25] However, for our particular purposes, this distinction is of limited assistance—indeed, it could be a diversion, raising classificatory puzzles that do not advance our analysis.[26] Our particular interest, it will be appreciated, is in relieving doctrines that are triggered by a failure in the conditions of consent. On our analysis of

[22] (1983) 151 CLR, at 474.

[23] Peter Birks and Chin Nyuk Yin, 'On the Nature of Undue Influence' in Jack Beatson and Daniel Friedmann (eds), *Good Faith and Fault in Contract Law* (Oxford, Clarendon Press, 1995) at 57.

[24] [2001] 4 All ER 449.

[25] At 457.

[26] For example, should we treat duress as a defendant-sided doctrine (because it only gets to first base where the defendant agent applies external (negative) force to the consenting agent) or as a plaintiff-sided doctrine (because it touches and concerns the quality of the consent)?

these conditions, some relieving doctrines should respond to failure of unforced choice, others to failure of informed choice, some will monitor factors internal to the agent, others external factors, and so on. Duress is a doctrine that responds to a failure of unforced choice; and undue influence looks as though it might respond to another similar failure concerning this condition of consent. Of course, the particular way in which the choice of the consenting agent is affected, and is then picked up by each of these doctrines, bears careful analysis; but the question of whether the doctrines are best viewed as defendant-sided or plaintiff-sided seems to be, in more than one sense, something of a side-issue.

What is the paradigm of undue influence? Although some of the precedents intersect with duress as we would view it, the focal cases involve a special relationship between agent B, who ostensibly consents, and agent A, who is in a position to influence B's decision. In some of the leading cases, the context is one of affective decision-making, the consenting agent being emotionally driven. Here, it is arguable that subsequent appeals to undue influence amount to claims that the agent lacked emotional calm at the time of giving the ostensible consent. However, many of the cases arise in less emotionally charged relationships, for the law presumes undue influence where the relationship between the agents is one that involves B having trust and confidence in the advice offered by A (for example, common relationships such as those between doctors and patients, priests and their devotees, parents and children, and the like, but also one-off special relationships having this feature). How do cases of this kind fit with our model of an unforced choice?

It is implicit in the Gewirthian model of consent that the choice made by the agent (to give or to withhold consent) is the agent's own choice. So, for instance, if an agent indicates consent under hypnosis, this quite clearly fails as a valid consent. Nevertheless, it is in the nature of relationships of trust and confidence that an agent advisee attaches special weight and significance to the advice of the adviser agent. In such relationships, there might well be opportunities for advisers to abuse their position by giving self-serving advice—and some would argue that the essence of undue influence is precisely that agents who are in a fiduciary position abuse the trust reposed in them.[27] However, whilst this undoubtedly exposes wrongdoing, it strays from our focus on the conditions of unforced choice. This is something that we need to hold on to, because undue influence, qua undue reliance on the opinion and advice of another, is relevant to any giving of consent, whether the context is commercial or medical.

In principle, in a special relationship, can we draw a line between the following two cases: (i) where agent B gives a consent that mirrors the advice

[27] Cf Rick Bigwood, 'Undue Influence in the House of Lords: Principle and Proof' (2002) 65 *Modern Law Review* 435.

given by agent A but where B's decision to consent is independent of A's advice; and (ii) where agent B gives a consent that both tracks the advice given by agent A and lacks independence from that advice? Case (i), it should be said, allows for a number of ways in which there might be distance between B's consent and A's advice, which ensures that the former is independent of the latter. For example, B reflects on the substance of A's advice and judges, all things considered, that it is sound; or, while B does not subject the substance of A's advice to independent scrutiny, B independently judges that A is a person whose advice (whatever it is) is to be respected and acted on. In cases of this kind, we can say that, although B follows A's advice, B retains not only the sense that he has the final word but also the capacity to reject A's advice, or A as an adviser, should the occasion so warrant. As we elaborate this 'in principle' question, it seems that we already have an affirmative answer—in principle, there is a distinction between those cases where B's decision, albeit mirroring A's advice, reflects an independent judgement by B and those cases where it does not, that is, those cases where B's consent is invalid because of undue influence. Whether or not, *as a matter of practice*, we can operate a doctrine of undue influence that accurately identifies those cases in which agent B has not exercised independent judgement is quite another question.

Where there is a possibility of relational undue influence, we might put the burden on the subordinate agent, B, to prove that he had no sense of having the final word nor the capacity to reject A's advice; or the burden might be placed on the dominant agent, A, to prove that B understood that the final decision was his and that he had the opportunity to act against A's advice; or the burden might be shared by the parties. The common law preference is to put the burden on the dominant agent, this being expressed doctrinally as A having the burden of rebutting the presumption of undue influence. With the burden set this way, there is an obvious incentive for dominant agents to put in place procedures that improve the chances of the subordinate agent, B, making an independent judgement. For instance, in commercial contexts, it is common practice to insist on B obtaining independent advice from a third party; and other practical safeguards include reminders that B has responsibility for making the final decision and building in a time-break between A's advice being given and B making the decision. None of this guarantees that B will make an independent judgement but it can be said in support of legal regimes that place the burden on the dominant agent that they at least aspire in the right direction.

Turning to medical contexts, there is a real danger that patients will uncritically follow the advice of their doctors. Where the medical information does not point clearly to a particular medical judgement, relatively few agents will have the confidence to make an independent judgement on the merits; and there might be a temptation to go along with the doctor's advice without making an independent (strategic) judgement that the best rule of thumb is, normally, to follow the advice given by health care professionals, or some such (independent) judgement. In such a context, where there is a predisposition to go along with the professional advice given, it is not going to be easy in practice to distinguish between those judgements that are genuinely independent and those that are not (and which, in other contexts, would readily attract the complaint that the consent was defective because of undue influence).[28]

Occasionally, in a medical context, a case will arise in which the subordinate agent is not predisposed to accept the advice given by the dominant agent. Such a case was *Re T (Adult: Refusal of Medical Treatment)*,[29] where a pregnant woman signed a form of refusal of consent to a blood transfusion. There was a suspicion that she did this under the influence of her mother, who was a Jehovah's Witness. Subsequently, the question arose whether, notwithstanding the refusal of consent, it would be lawful to administer a blood transfusion to the woman. On the point concerning undue influence, the trial judge ruled that, although the woman was under the influence of her mother, her decision was her own; however, the Court of Appeal disagreed. According to Lord Donaldson MR:

> A special problem may arise if at the time the decision is made the patient has been subjected to the influence of some third party. This is by no means to say that the patient is not entitled to receive and indeed invite advice and assistance from others in reaching a decision, particularly from members of the family. But the doctors have to consider whether the decision is really that of the patient. It is wholly acceptable that the patient should have been persuaded by others of the merits of such a decision and have decided accordingly. It matters not how strong the persuasion was, so long as it did not overbear the independence of the patient's decision. The real question in each such case is: does the patient really mean what he says or is he merely saying it for a quiet life, to satisfy someone else or because the advice and persuasion to which he has been subjected is such that he can no longer think and decide for himself?[30]

In concurring judgments, Butler-Sloss LJ said that, on the facts, she found it difficult to accept the trial judge's view that the mother's influence had not sapped the woman's will or destroyed her volition;[31] and Staughton LJ said that 'for an apparent consent or refusal of consent to be less than a true consent or refusal, there must be such a degree of external influence as to persuade the patient to depart from her own wishes.'[32] In some respects, these statements might be criticised as giving undue influence too broad a

[28] Cf Carl E Schneider and Michael H Farrell, 'Information, Decisions, and the Limits of Informed Consent' in Michael Freeman and Andrew Lewis (eds), *Law and Medicine* (*Current Legal Issues 2000, Vol 3*) (Oxford, Oxford University Press, 2000) at 107.

[29] [1992] 4 All ER 649.

[30] *Ibid*, at 662.

[31] *Ibid*, at 667.

[32] *Ibid*, at 669.

compass—for instance, bullying or intimidating external influence belongs with duress; and the agent who settles for a quiet life or who chooses to make a decision that will please another might well be exercising an independent judgement—but they are close to the focal question, namely whether the agent understood its own responsibility for making the final decision and was sufficiently able to hold the influence at arm's length to exercise control over that decision.

These remarks point to a fairly straightforward conclusion. So long as the doctrinal role of undue influence is understood to be the monitoring of the independence of the choice made by the agent who ostensibly consents (or refuses to consent), it has an important and distinctive function. Even in the absence of negative pressure of the kind that might trigger the doctrine of duress, the law should assure that an agent's apparent consent reflects that agent's own choice. Within an array of relieving doctrines, it falls to the principle of undue influence to perform just this task, to defend the requirement that unforced choice presupposes a choice that is, so to speak, the agent's own work.

## III Informed Consent and Disclosure

In the landmark decision of *Canterbury v Spence*,[33] the Court of Appeals of the District of Columbia observed that '[t]rue consent to what happens to one's self is the informed exercise of a choice, and that entails an opportunity to evaluate knowledgeably the options available and the risks attendant upon each.'[34] It was, thus, that the modern doctrine of informed consent was born. And, on this basis, it was held that it was no longer sufficient for physicians to follow their own lights, or the general practice of the profession, in deciding what information to give to patients about their treatment options and, in particular, the risks associated with a proposed course of treatment. Patients (subject to limited exceptions for emergency and for 'therapeutic privilege')[35] have a right to know. The lead given by *Canterbury* was followed in other common law jurisdictions, notably by the Supreme Court of Canada in *Reibl v Hughes*,[36] and by the High Court of Australia

[33] 464 F 2d 772 (DC Cir 1972).

[34] At 780.

[35] In ch 5, we noted that Gewirth includes emotional calm as a pre-condition for an agent giving a valid consent. We also noted that, in medical contexts, some patients are calmer than others, and that the calmer the patient the better the chance of information being understood and evaluated. Arguably, this suggests that it may be legitimate for physicians to hold back anxiety-inducing information in order that patients are able to stay calm and assimilate what information they are given. However, any such move to allow 'therapeutic privilege' to qualify physicians' informational obligations needs to be watched very carefully lest it paves the way for a return to paternalistic medical practice.

[36] (1980) 114 DLR (3d) 1.

in *Rogers v Whitaker*,[37] as the common law world moved towards rejecting physician paternalism in favour of a patient-centred approach to the disclosure of medical options and risks.

Ruth Faden and Tom Beauchamp have famously told the story of how, in the US case-law, consent as a defence to an action for battery evolved into an informed consent (notice of risk) requirement of negligence law.[38] However, even those who are sympathetic to this doctrinal evolution may wonder whether, for the purposes of informed consent, it is being informed or giving one's consent that is the vital factor. For example, in *Rogers v Whitaker*, the majority distanced themselves from the US terminology as follows:

> In this context, nothing is to be gained by reiterating the expressions used in American authorities, such as 'the patient's right of self-determination' or even the oft-used and somewhat amorphous phrase 'informed consent'. The right of self-determination is an expression which is, perhaps, suitable to cases where the issue is whether a person has agreed to the general surgical procedure or treatment, but [it] is of little assistance in the balancing process that is involved in the determination of whether there has been a breach of the duty of disclosure. Likewise, the phrase 'informed consent' is apt to mislead as it suggests a test of the validity of a patient's consent.[39]

Similarly, the English courts, having declined to embrace either the language or the substance of the doctrine of informed consent in *Sidaway v Board of Governors of the Bethlem Royal Hospital and the Maudsley Hospital*,[40] have signalled their doubts about the smoothness of this evolution.[41] What these judicial reservations alert us to is the possibility that, whilst the language of consent has been carried forward from the settled understanding that consent is a defence to battery, the doctrine of informed consent might not actually be grounded in the idea of the patient giving a consent that complies with the information conditions that (in our analysis) govern a valid consent. In our view, these reservations are correct. To see how this detachment has occurred, we can review Lord Scarman's well-known dissenting judgment in *Sidaway*, this being the strongest support that English law gives to a modern informed consent regime.

In *Sidaway*, the claimant contended that she had not been told by the neurosurgeon who operated on her that there was a small (1%–2%) risk of

[37] (1992) 67 ALJR 47.

[38] Ruth Faden and Tom Beauchamp, *A History and Theory of Informed Consent* (New York, Oxford University Press, 1986).

[39] (1992) 67 AJLR 47, at 52 (Mason CJ, Brennan, Dawson, Toohey and McHugh JJ).

[40] [1985] 1 AC 871. Most recently, however, compare *Chester v Afshar* [2004] UKHL 41.

[41] For example, see Lord Diplock in *Sidaway* itself, [1985] 1 AC 871, at 894; and in *Re T (Adult: Refusal of Medical Treatment)* [1992] 4 All ER 649, at 663, Lord Donaldson MR says, very pointedly, that a doctor's failure to give such information as the law requires is a breach of duty that sounds in negligence and 'does not, as such, vitiate a consent or refusal.'

damage to nerve roots and damage to her spinal cord. In the event, although the operation was carried out with due care and skill, damage to the spinal cord occurred, leaving the claimant severely disabled and partially paralysed. Because key parts of the claim were not sufficiently supported by the evidence, the claim was doomed; but, as a matter of principle, the majority of the House of Lords ruled that the traditional 'reasonable doctor' standard governed the information that the doctor was required to disclose to the patient. Dissenting on this question of principle, Lord Scarman alone favoured a different approach. For Lord Scarman, the patient's right of self-determination—'the right of a patient to determine for himself whether he will or will not accept the doctor's advice'[42]—is axiomatic. Thus:

> A doctor who operates without the consent of his patient is, save in cases of emergency or mental disability, guilty of the civil wrong of trespass to the person; he is also guilty of the criminal offence of assault. The existence of the patient's right to make his own decision, which may be seen as a basic human right protected by the common law, is the reason why a doctrine embodying a right of the patient to be informed of the risks of surgical treatment has been developed in some jurisdictions . . . [qua, in the US, the doctrine of informed consent].[43]

So, for Lord Scarman, we have consent as a defence to assault and battery; and we have the right to informed consent, which is an articulation of the right to make our own decisions. This split comes through dramatically in *Sidaway* when Lord Scarman says that, despite the lack of information, Mrs Sidaway would *not* have an action for trespass because she 'did consent to the operation'[44]—in other words, even if Mrs Sidaway was under-informed as to the risks of the procedure, she had still sufficiently consented to the operation to give the defendants an answer to an action in trespass. Approaching the matter from a consent perspective, we can detect three strands in Lord Scarman's thinking as follows: (i) each agent has a right to make its own decisions; to consent to treatment must be the agent's own choice; (ii) consent operates as a defence to what would otherwise be a trespass; and (iii) flowing from an agent's right to make its own decisions, in the doctor/patient relationship, a patient has a right to be informed as to the material risks associated with a treatment or procedure. These ideas, however, simply do not hang together, and they reveal, ironically, a relatively casual approach to the conditions of consent.

On the first point, the right of (competent) agents to make their own decisions entails that decisions as to whether or not to submit to treatment, or to a particular course or type of treatment, must be made by (competent) patients, not by their physicians. In a culture of paternalism, physicians will determine what is in the patient's best interests and then act on their judge-

[42] [1985] 1 AC 871, at 882.
[43] *Ibid*, at 882.
[44] *Ibid*, at 885.

ment. To accept that patients have a right of self-determination is to say that this paternalistic approach will not do. It is for physicians to advise and assist; but, in the final analysis, it is for patients to decide. Such, as we have seen already, is the essence of a consent given free of undue influence.

If patients have the right to decide, then physicians need the authorisation of patients before they can legitimately proceed with treatment. Where a patient consents to treatment, thereby signalling his or her authorisation for that treatment, it is common ground that the physician has a defence to a subsequent complaint made by the patient that there was no right to administer the treatment. However, there is room for argument about the conditions for a valid consent. If the need for consent is premised on an agent's right to self-determination, it is clear that an ostensible consent will be valid only where it is the agent's own unforced choice; but it remains to be settled to what extent the agent's decision must represent an *informed* choice. In our Gewirthian account, an informed choice is one of the pivotal conditions for a valid consent; by contrast, Lord Scarman's judgment that a valid consent was given by Mrs Sidaway seems to be made independent of whether she consented on an informed basis. On the face of it, this sets a relatively weak informational standard for a valid consent—indeed, the impression here and elsewhere is that, because physicians need to have a routine response to allegations of trespass, the law will accept a routine defence of consent.

If Lord Scarman allows for an ostensible consent to be valid even where the agent acts on an uninformed basis, he compensates for this by placing physicians under a demanding informational responsibility with regard to their patients. In Lord Scarman's thinking, this responsibility also stems from an agent's right to self-determination, and it issues in a test of a markedly subjective nature. Thus:

> Ideally, the court should ask itself whether in the particular circumstances the risk was such that this particular patient would think it significant if he was told it existed. I would think that, as a matter of ethics, this is the test of the doctor's duty. The law, however, operates not in Utopia but in the world as it is: and such an inquiry would prove in practice to be frustrated by the subjectivity of its aim and purpose. The law can, however, do the next best thing and require the court to answer the question, what would the reasonably prudent patient think significant if in the situation of this patient. The 'prudent patient' cannot, however, always provide the answer for the obvious reason that he is a norm . . ., not a real person: and certainly not the patient himself.[45]

The upshot of this, therefore, is that Lord Scarman requires physicians not only to ensure that the patient's informational field is not deficient but (so

[45] *Ibid*, at 888–89. Lord Scarman also rightly remarks that, whilst the doctor's concern is with a medical judgement, the patient's judgement may turn on a range of considerations (purely medical matters being just one factor), at 885–86.

far as this is possible in 'the world as it is') to do so in a way that is sensitive to the particular patient's criteria of relevance. Where physicians fail to do this, they have to answer for a failure of informed consent—but not so much because the conditions for a valid consent are not satisfied but because there has been a failure to discharge an informational responsibility.

One way of characterising Lord Scarman's version of informed consent is to say that it is strong on *information* and relatively weak on *consent*. It is strong on information in two respects: first, it adopts an account of materiality that tries to get as close as is practically possible to subjectivism; and, secondly, the doctor's duty to inform seems to be a matter of background positive obligation (the patient's right to self-determination placing doctors under this responsibility). Consent, by contrast, routinely gives a defence to trespass pretty much regardless of the information supporting the consent. So stated, however, it is clear that Lord Scarman's version of informed consent comprises not just two elements but two doctrines: one a doctrine of informational obligation which, contingently, bears on consensual decision-making; the other a defence of consent to an intentional tort. For those who support a patient-centred approach, it is perhaps enough that Lord Scarman places doctors under a background duty to disclose. However, for those who see the patient's informed *consent* as critical to the justificatory process, Lord Scarman's view invites further analysis with regard to the patient's informational responsibilities and their possible transfer to doctors.

Before we take this any further, however, we should recall that the majority in *Sidaway* declined to place physicians under the kind of informational responsibility contemplated by Lord Scarman and that, in so resisting the tide of modern patient-centred thinking, they expressed two rather different views. One view, the ruling orthodoxy in English law, is that the medical profession should be left to set its own guidance, explicit or implicit, as to the information to be given to patients.[46] In some situations, the profession might think it appropriate to present patients with a full account of the options and risks; in others, it might be thought right to give only sketchy information unless asked directly by a patient. At all events, provided that a physician acts within the band of acceptable professional practice—which will be a shifting standard contingent on local practice—the doctor's informational obligation will be satisfied. The other view, evident in Lord Templeman's thinking, is that we should recall the contractual origins of medical obligation. The assumption in contract law, at any rate of the classical ilk, is that contractors do not lightly assume obligations. Thus, if doctors reason like contractors, they will not wish to assume extensive informational responsibilities; and the law should not impose obligations beyond the bounds that would be agreed by contract.

[46] The leading case is *Bolam v Friern Hospital Management Committee* [1957] 2 All ER 118, as qualified by *Bolitho v City and Hackney Health Authority* [1997] 3 WLR 1151.

It is interesting that Lord Templeman should introduce hard-nosed contractual thinking into the medical equation. For, disclosure of information, by one party to the other, is one of the most hotly contested questions in contract law. As in the informed consent debates in medical law, protagonists find themselves drawn to one of three general standpoints. Those who favour an ethic of self-reliance in contract place the informational responsibility on each party and do not require disclosure. Those who favour a co-operative ethic require contractors to disclose to one another facts that the other would treat as material to the transaction (this being analogous to the modern informed consent approach in medical law). And those who think that the standards for disclosure should be set by the particular contracting community require the parties to disclose to the point demanded by local custom and practice (which again gives us a shifting and contingent standard). Any attempt to try to work round these positions by introducing notions of reasonable expectation or good faith inevitably takes the inquiry back to one of the three basic positions: self-reliance, co-operativism, or contingent custom and practice.[47] And so it is in medical law.

What, then, is the answer to this informational conundrum? As we have said, background Gewirthian moral principles place agents under a responsibility to assist other agents whose generic conditions are at risk (for example, if A can rescue B who will otherwise drown, he has a duty to do so). Such background principles include positive informational obligations. For example, if A knows that a bridge is unsafe or that a building is on fire, he is under a duty to warn B who will otherwise be unaware of this risk. Such positive obligations, informational and non-informational alike, have their limits. First, Gewirthian principles do not require A to undertake heroic acts or to make disproportionate sacrifices in relation to A's own generic conditions. Thus, A is only required to act if he can do so without suffering comparable cost to his own generic conditions. Secondly, neither do Gewirthian principles encourage others to free-ride on A's good will: positive obligations kick in only where the other agent cannot meet his generic requirements through his own unaided efforts. If no positive obligations are in play, agents must rely on their own resources. In the case of information that is material to the giving of consent, it follows that, if no positive informational obligations are applicable, and if there has been no special case transfer of responsibility (ie by voluntary assumption of informational obligation on the part of the transferee), we are left with the personal responsibility of the consenting agent. This responsibility, we suggested in chapter five, is such as to put the risk on the consenting agent unless that agent has exercised reasonable care in regard to gathering and tending the data in its own

[47] See Roger Brownsword, 'Individualism, Co-operativism, and an Ethic for European Contract Law' (2001) 64 *Modern Law Review* 628.

informational field. Granted, there is a treatise to be written on the application of these guideline principles. Nevertheless, we can see how they push towards the following general principle: *subject to the applicability of background informational obligations, and the transfer of responsibility in special cases, a consenting agent has the responsibility for gathering and tending the consent-relevant data in its own informational field; this responsibility entails that the consent will be treated as valid, albeit not properly informed, if the agent has been reckless or has failed to take reasonable care with regard to its personal informational responsibilities; but, where (in the hard case)*[48] *the under-informed consenting agent has taken reasonable care, there is no valid consent and the recipient, even if excused, cannot rely on a procedural justification.*[49]

In this light, consider, first, the medical case. Is it plausible to treat doctors as having a positive obligation to inform patients so that they might have a better understanding of the medical options available and the risks associated with particular interventions or courses of treatment? Although some positive informational obligations are of very general application (an agent does not need to be a structural engineer to warn about an unsafe bridge, or a fireman to warn about a fire hazard), the specification of obligations always depends on the context of who knows (or ought to know) what, when, and where (the obligation to warn has no purchase unless the context involves an agent with the relevant information concerning the hazard). It follows that, when we elaborate the positive informational obligations in the medical case, we do so in a particular health-care context. One thing that is striking about this context is that the information in question will usually have an important bearing on the physical well-being of the patient; for one agent to the transaction, important generic interests are at stake. In *Rogers v Whitaker*, for example, the physician omitted to inform the patient that the procedure carried with it a very slight risk that she might lose her sight. The risk might have been slight but this was highly material information from the patient's standpoint and, to require the physician to disclose the risk, would impose no comparable cost on the doctor. More importantly, perhaps, the context is one of highly specialised knowledge and training. Doctors are experts relative to a particular kind of information—information that is not readily available or, at any rate, that is not readily comprehensible. In this light, it is unrealistic and unreasonable to argue that patients free-ride on doctors by looking to them for informed advice. It is true that patients might have trained as physicians and obtained the relevant information through their own unaided efforts. However, in societies that are organised around divisions of labour, specialisation, and various kinds of personal expertise, this seems inefficient in the extreme.

48 As discussed in ch 5.

49 We have suggested, it will be recalled, that the recipient's risk in a hard case should be restricted to present information.

Accordingly, while patients might be expected to be self-reliant in gathering general information about the risks of surgery and the like, when the information lies deep in a particular field of medical expertise, there is no invitation to free-ride in requiring disclosure. Indeed, reflecting this approach, the law does not normally require doctors to disclose what are assumed to be generally available medical facts; rather, informed consent focuses on disclosure of specialised information, not readily accessible to lay agents.

We should not understate the scope and importance of background positive obligations. Agents have general informational obligations; doctors have more specialised informational obligations (tailored to the informational needs and capacities of a standard agent—akin perhaps to a prudent patient standard); and the particular medical context might make it appropriate to extend the doctor's informational obligations beyond the usual health-care informational responsibilities (tailored to the special needs of vulnerable agents and the like). For example, it might be clear that a patient needs to be alerted to quite minor risks or that he or she needs to be aware of the full range of treatment options, in both cases the information in question going beyond the usual information to be supplied to patients. There comes a point, however, when background positive informational obligations are exhausted. At that point, unless this is a special case where the doctor has personally assumed responsibility for ensuring that the consent is informed, there is no transfer of responsibility, and patients must rely on their own informational resources.

Following Lord Templeman's approach in *Sidaway*, what happens if we treat the medical case as a commercial (contractual) transaction? Everything that we have just said about positive informational obligation, context, and special case transfer continues to apply. So far as information about medical risk is concerned, nothing changes (unless the medical context itself changes). However, there are two ways in which the introduction of commerce (contract) is significant. First, the context is now not simply medical but medical-commercial. In this changed context, *economic* information assumes a relevance that it did not previously have. Information about the fee to be charged by the physician, the availability of less expensive options elsewhere, and so on, is material to the patient. Hence, it needs to be determined where the background obligations lie in relation to such information. Doctors might have background obligations to disclose *medical* risks, but do they also have background obligations to disclose *economic* risks? Secondly, where the agents engage 'the law of contract', the rules of the institutional set will include provisions about disclosure during the negotiation of a contract. These might or might not assist the patient. Accordingly, unless the background rules (including special case transfer) or the rules of contract law put the informational burden on the doctor, the risk in relation to economic information will lie with the patient.

Turning to contracts generally, the marketplace has become a densely regulated area, with a tendency towards regulation that is tailored to particular kinds of contracts (for example, insurance contracts, credit agreements, contracts made at a distance, and so on) and particular kinds of contractors (with a regulatory line dividing business-to-business contracts from business-to-consumer contracts). Trying to capture the development of the modern law in a sentence or two is not easy. However, in relation to consumer contracting, the trend is away from caveat emptor, whether by requiring suppliers to get more information into the marketplace or by immunising consumers against unfair trading terms and practices.[50] And, in relation to commercial contracting, it is arguable that the modern law is more sensitive to the co-operative 'relational' principles to which much business practice is geared.[51] To some extent, the regulation of the marketplace is a matter of background obligation but, to a great extent, it derives from the modern rules of the law of contract. It follows that a full assessment of the provisions for disclosure made by any legal regime would need to review the appropriateness of the background positive informational obligations, the handling of special case arguments for the transfer of the default responsibility, and whether the disclosure provisions within the law of contract itself are optimal.

If we were to review the disclosure rules bearing on contracting, and particularly within 'the law of contract' itself, we should bear in mind the pattern that we have outlined already in relation to the regulation of duress and (un)forced choice. Essentially, we would start with the point at which the rules of the 'law of contract' are consensually engaged. Just as an originating consent must be an act of unforced choice, so too it must be an informed choice. The background informational obligations must be discharged, and so on. Provided that an originating consent is in place, relative autonomy takes over and the design of disclosure rules within the 'law of contract' depends upon judgements as to the perceived functionality of particular institutional sets. In some areas of contract law, notably that of insurance contracts, disclosure has long been treated as functional.[52] However, to the extent that the modern law requires disclosure, this has been a story of the resistance of the classical law being gradually broken down; for whatever reasons, the classical model of adversarial dealing is no longer seen as a func-

[50] Generally, see Roger Brownsword, *Contract Law: Themes for the Twenty-First Century* (London, Butterworths, 2000).

[51] Seminally, see Stewart Macaulay, 'Non-Contractual Relations in Business' (1963) 28 *American Sociological Review* 55; Ian R Macneil, 'The Many Futures of Contract' (1974) 47 *Southern California Law Review* 691 and 'Contracts: Adjustments of Long-Term Economic Relations under Classical, Neo-Classical and Relational Contract Law' (1978) 72 *Northwestern University Law Review* 854; and, for a complementary philosophical account, see David Gauthier, *Morals by Agreement* (Oxford, Clarendon Press, 1986).

[52] Seminally, see *Carter v Boehm* (1766) 3 Burr 1905.

tional default position for contracts in general. If, however, the proviso for originating consent is not satisfied, if the process for securing and screening originating consents is deficient, then the rules for informed consent within the 'law of contract' should be viewed in a corrective role—their function is to ground procedural justification in relation to the agreement reached (if not in relation to the rules of the 'law of contract' itself).

In this context, consider the vexed question of good faith in contracts, or, at any rate, good faith as it bears on questions of disclosure.[53] Where agents enter into contractual negotiations, it is a moot point whether the law should require those negotiations to be conducted in good faith. Even in legal regimes where it is firmly established that contracts should be performed and enforced in good faith, there has been hesitation about extending good faith to cover negotiation. Moreover, where good faith does cover negotiation, there is some ambivalence about whether this should be treated as a tort principle or a contract principle. This question (is it tort or is it contract?) bears on the measure of compensation that will be awarded for breach of good faith. However, for our purposes, the question raises another issue—namely, are we treating the requirement for good faith negotiation under background and contextual informational principles (in the way that we have dealt with informed consent in medical law) or is it a requirement internal to a particular optional institutional set, the 'law of contract'? Let us suppose that we start by viewing good faith in negotiation as a matter of background (tort law) obligation, mindful that where agents have engaged the 'law of contract' the particular provisions within the rule-set will apply to their dealings from the point of the originating consent onwards.

Good faith in negotiation clearly implies that agents do not string one another along or break off negotiations without giving any thought to the interests of the other party. However, what does this requirement imply about disclosure? In particular, the following two situations are seen as especially problematic: (i) where A (the seller or supplier) fails to disclose information which, if disclosed, would adjust the contract price downwards in favour of B (the buyer); and (ii) where B (the buyer) fails to disclose information which, if disclosed, would adjust the contract price upwards in favour of A (the seller or supplier).[54] In the first kind of case, why should we say that B's consent is invalid if A does not disclose (to B) that identical

[53] The line between (passive) non-disclosure and (active) misrepresentation is not altogether clear. Where the default position of a legal regime (such as the English law of contract) is set so as to limit liability to the latter, the line is important but, as ideas of good faith negotation gain currency, even in restrictive regimes, there is pressure to extend the idea of an active misrepresentation. For a nice example, see *Spice Girls Ltd v Aprilia World Service BV* [2002] EWCA Civ 15.

[54] Here we pass over cases in which one party obstructs access to, or conceals, information that is material to the other: see, eg, *Obde v Schlemeyer* 56 Wash 2d 449, 353 P 2d 672 (1960) (concealment by vendors of termite infestation).

goods can be purchased at a cheaper price elsewhere (say, at a shop around the corner), or that, if B waited a couple of days, the price of the goods would fall and a cheaper price would be paid? Why, in the second kind of case—for example, where, as in the classic US case of *Laidlaw v Organ*,[55] B does not disclose to A that, if he were to delay selling for a day or two, he would get a better price for the goods—should B's non-disclosure invalidate A's consent? When and why is there a consent-affecting responsibility to add to the informational field of the other contracting party?

We can assume that, in a Gewirthian moral order, contractors would embark on negotiations with the support of various background *positive* informational rights. However, in general, it is difficult to see why agents who meet in a commercial marketplace should have positive rights to be assisted in garnering information that works to their economic advantage but to the economic disadvantage of the agent who is required to disclose. Granted, there might be cases where mutual disclosure increases the shared pool of information in such a way that the resulting contract is to the economic advantage of both contracting agents. However, in the standard example of asymmetric economic information, the agent who assists by disclosing will do so at a disproportionate cost to its own interests (in other words, disclosure violates the comparable cost limitation on positive rights). Moreover, a positive rights requirement for economic disclosure encourages free-riding (and, thus, violates the other limitation on positive rights). Why should A be required to disclose to B that identical goods can be purchased at a cheaper price elsewhere? Is B not capable of obtaining this information without A's assistance? Further, in any case where A has made a special investment to obtain the information, the background argument in favour of disclosure looks unappealing.[56]

If disclosure is not required by the more general background positive obligations, the law of contract should nevertheless be sensitive to positive obligations in particular contexts, as well as allowing that the default informational responsibility may be transferred in special cases. Consider the following hypothetical test case framed by Reinhard Zimmermann and Simon Whittaker in their major study of good faith in European contract law.[57] Agent O, a retired physics professor, invites agent D, a dealer in fine art, to look at some items with a view to purchase. Acting on this invitation, D buys a picture from O for which she pays £1,200. The picture (as D suspects *but does not disclose to O*) turns out to be a rare and valuable drawing by Degas which D subsequently sells for £85,000. In the Zimmermann and

[55] 15 US (2 Wheat) 178 (1817).

[56] See, further, Anthony Kronman, 'Mistake, Disclosure, Information, and the Law of Contracts' (1978) 7 *Journal of Legal Studies* 1, and 'Contract Law and Distributive Justice' (1980) 89 *Yale Law Journal* 472.

[57] Reinhard Zimmermann and Simon Whittaker (eds), *Good Faith in European Contract Law* (Cambridge, Cambridge University Press, 2000).

Whittaker study, reporters from 15 European countries were invited to comment on this hypothetical. Almost all indicated that their local law of contract would give some relief to O. However, the facts of the hypothetical invite a variety of reasons for relief, some of which are not relevant for our purposes—for instance, in some legal orders, the huge difference between the price paid by D for the painting and the real value is recognised as an independent ground for relief (as violating a principle of rough equality of exchange). What we are interested in is whether O's ostensible consent to a sale at £1,200 is invalidated by his lack of information as to the real value of the painting (and, concomitantly, by D's non-disclosure).

Our starting point, to repeat, is that agents, in the absence of general background positive informational duties or particular contextual obligations, or special transfers, have a degree of personal responsibility for their own informational fields. The general principle, we have suggested, is that the consenting agent must bear the risk of its own informational recklessness or carelessness. However, where agents engage rule-sets such as the 'law of contract', they subject themselves to the informational risks prescribed by those rules. Some rule-sets prescribe strong principles of self-reliance; others are more protective. Thus, speaking as to the hypothetical (of the Degas drawing), the English reporter says quite correctly that, aside from a handful of exceptional cases, English law recognises 'no general duty of disclosure of information or opinion by one would-be party to a contract to another, even where the first party knows that the information would affect the latter's decision to contract or the price at which he would contract.'[58] However, the facts as sketched in the hypothetical allow for D's role to be interpreted as a buyer *simpliciter* or as an 'adviser-cum-buyer'; and, as the German report suggests, the more that we cast D in the role of an adviser, the more reasonable it is to expect D to pass on the benefit of her expertise (and, with that, a measure of economic benefit).[59] Following up this suggestion, we might see this as a case in which general *background* positive informational rights and responsibilities are qualified by the particular context (or possibly that this is a case of transferred responsibility); or this might be a situation that the 'law of contract' itself recognises as distinguishable from the general run of cases and where it is judged to be functional to require disclosure by the adviser. If so, O, who has ostensibly consented, will have an arguable case that his consent is invalid for informational deficiency.

In both medical and *informal* contractual settings, therefore, we see that an agent who has ostensibly consented may appeal to: (i) background positive obligations (general or particular); or (ii) special case transfer; or (iii) an unknown material fact that could not reasonably be detected, in

[58] *Ibid*, at 226.
[59] *Ibid*, at 210.

order to argue that the consent was invalid as an uninformed choice. And, in each case, the reference point for the materiality of the information is the subjective viewpoint of the ostensibly consenting agent. Where agents (*formally*) engage the 'law of contract', they may make exactly the same appeals in relation to their ostensible originating consents; and the 'law of contract' so engaged will make provision (judged functionally) for what, within the set, counts as an informed consent.[60]

Finally, it is worth saying that whilst, in both medical and contractual settings, the problem is often one of informational asymmetry, this is not invariably the case. In particular, contract regimes may make provision for those cases where *both* contracting agents are unaware of some material fact.[61] From a consent perspective, each agent might be barred from pleading a failure of informed consent because no other agent has responsibility for correcting their ignorance (and the failure lies within the area of their own personal informational responsibility). Where the parties' ignorance (their 'common mistake', as it would show up in common law regimes) means that neither party wants the contract, it is pointless for the law to recognise the agreement as enforceable. However, there will be cases where one agent sees advantage in enforcing the contract. For example, if the facts of the Degas hypothetical were varied so that neither O nor D had any idea that the painting was worth more than £1,200, D would have overwhelming economic reasons for wanting to enforce the contract (or to resist avoidance). According to our *general* principle, the consent should only be set aside as uninformed if the consenting agent has discharged its personal informational responsibility (hence the question: was O careless in failing to identify the drawing as a Degas?). However, this is not to say that, under relative autonomy, the 'law of contract' might not treat this as a failure of consent,[62] and

[60] Bearing in mind that the rules of institutional sets enjoy relative autonomy, the standard that they adopt might be that of Gewirthian adequacy, or it might be less stringent, or even more stringent. If it is more stringent (admittedly, an unlikely scenario), non-disclosure that does not invalidate the originating consent might invalidate a supposed consent under the rules.

[61] *Sherwood v Walker* 66 Mich 568, 33 NW 919 (Mich SC 1887) is perhaps the best-known textbook example. There, the parties contracted for the sale of a cow, 'Rose 2d of Aberlone', on the assumption that it was a barren beef cow worth $80. However, Rose turned out to be with calf and worth some $750 as a breeding cow. The majority held that the contract should be set aside for common mistake.

[62] Compare James Gordley, 'Contract' in Peter Cane and Mark Tushnet (eds), *The Oxford Handbook of Legal Studies* (Oxford, Oxford University Press, 2003) at 3. Commenting on the puzzle presented by common mistake cases such as *Sherwood v Walker* (n 60 above), Gordley remarks (at 13):

> It seems, then, that we are inevitably forced to confront a question that we do not know how to answer: when is it meaningful to say that the parties did agree? We are not likely to answer it until we have a considerably more sophisticated theory of consent.

In our view, the first step towards articulating such a theory is to distinguish between the conditions for an originating consent and those for consent as prescribed by the rules of an

nor is it to suggest there are not other reasons for placing checks within the body of the 'law of contract' against the institution becoming a vehicle for unintended gift rather than planned exchange.

Thus, we arrive at a slightly surprising conclusion. This is that the doctrine of informed consent as pioneered in medical law is not quite what we might assume it to be; it is not a simple and straightforward, pure and progressive, articulation of what it is for a consent to be authentic. Of the three key strands in this doctrinal development, only one—the subjective test of materiality—reflects a *simple* fidelity to consent. For, to the extent that the doctrine draws on a background positive obligation to provide information, it is not consent-focused at all; and, to the extent that it is (contingently) consent-focused, we have argued that its operation should be read as depending upon the default principle of personal responsibility in conjunction with the possibility of transfer in special cases. We could say something similar, too, about the modern doctrinal trend towards disclosure in contract law. Once again, it is not the sentiment, pure and simple, that consent needs to be taken more seriously that has generated a doctrinal move away from self-reliance. Rather, it is developments such as the specialised provision of goods and services (encouraging purchasers to become more reliant on the expertise of suppliers) and the recognition of co-operative trading cultures in the business community that have been the drivers of legal change. All in all, the modern legal phenomenon that we have uncovered in this part of the chapter is not so much the development of informed *consent*; rather it is the development of positive *informational* obligations (and responsibilities) of various kinds that provide the context for consent-based transactions.

## IV Conclusion

Assuming that we are dealing with agents who are societally competent, legal orders will adopt thicker (ie more stringent) or thinner (ie less stringent) conditions for a valid consent. Where thinner conditions prevail, the law will require an unforced choice (which itself can be given a more or less stringent reading); where thicker conditions prevail, the law will require both unforced choice and informed choice (again with varying degrees of stringency applied to these conditions). Where legal orders adopt thicker conditions of consent, they seem to take consent more seriously; however, it should not be assumed that modern doctrines of informed consent, and the like, are straightforwardly 'informed by consent'.

institutional set enjoying relative autonomy. The acid test for the meaningfulness of consent is whether what passes for an originating consent passes muster. If it does, consent within the institutional set can take on its own particular functional meaning.

In relation to the doctrinal features that we have considered, the particular Gewirthian consent perspective that we have elaborated suggests the following conclusions.

First, although many doubt the wisdom of developing a doctrine of economic duress in contract law, on our analysis, there will be no procedural justification for enforcing contracts unless the contracting agents have made an unforced choice either to engage the rule-set (informal or formal) under which enforcement takes place or to do the particular deal that they have done. If one of the agents has applied negative pressure to the generic interests of the other (including generic interests of an economic nature), the choice will not be unforced, the consent will not be adequate. It follows that, for contracting to be procedurally justified, there must be a safety-check to ensure that there has been no negative pressure of an economic nature—if not in relation to originating consents, then in relation to the particular contract supposedly agreed upon. Of course, if adequate originating consents are in place, under the umbrella of relative autonomy it might be judged that the 'law of contract' itself would be more functional if it dispensed with a doctrine of economic duress. This might be judged to be so for all sorts of reasons, some more plausible than others—for example, because the community wishes to encourage more aggressive dealing, or to discourage agents from submitting themselves to this rule-set, or to make less use of the courts, and so on. However, if the reason for dispensing with the doctrine is its perceived uncertainty, this is a poor call: for, provided that the law focuses on the application of external force bearing negatively on the target agent's generic economic interests, it should be perfectly possible to build a coherent jurisprudence of economic duress.

Secondly, the desire to defend the possibility of unforced choice also supports the development of a doctrine of undue influence. What needs to be emphasised here is that the giving (or refusal) of consent must represent the independent choice of the agent making that decision. Provided that the doctrinal role of undue influence is understood to be the monitoring of the independence of the choice made, there should be no danger of losing sight of the distinctive focus of undue influence alongside duress and, more generally, as one of a number of relieving doctrines.

Thirdly, even though the modern doctrine of informed consent (as developed in medical law and copied across to areas such as consumer law) sounds as though it is an articulation of a consent requirement, it is not quite as simple as this. There are duties to inform that arise as a matter of background positive obligation (general, contextual, and transaction-specific) and which might, on occasion, impinge on an agent's decision whether or not to consent. Where this is so, the materiality of the information that has not been disclosed is to be judged relative to the consenting agent's subjective viewpoint. Beyond the background regime, which protects (negatively) against misinformation and assists (positively) by requiring disclosure, and aside from any special case transfer, the default position is that agents must bear a degree of personal informational responsibility. Accordingly, in the context of consent being given, we have suggested that agents should bear the default responsibility for exercising due diligence with regard to the accuracy and completeness of the informational field that relates to the transaction in question.

Fourthly, there might seem to be some concurrence between the position adopted by the classical version of contract law (in which disclosure of economic information is treated as the exception rather than the rule) and the view that we have taken that agents bear some personal responsibility for their own informational fields. However, the view that we are taking is nested within a background regime that includes positive obligations, informational and otherwise, as well as allowing for the transfer of informational responsibility in special cases. Moreover, the standard of personal responsibility is fault-based rather than strict. In contrast with the classical view, we have suggested that a jurisprudence of good faith disclosure should be elaborated, starting with the Gewirthian principles governing positive informational obligations.

Finally, we might put these last two points together to underline that the development of informed consent in medical law and good faith disclosure in contract law are steps in the right direction. These progressive developments deserve better than the accusation that they betray a lack of respect for doctors or the virtues of adversarial dealing. Equally, they deserve better than the intuitive sense that they take consent more seriously. To do justice to informed consent, there are two frames of reference that we need to keep in mind. One is the general context of Gewirthian moral theory, with its background scheme of negative and *positive* informational obligations, as well as the possibility, in the context of particular transactions, that there might be an extension (or a transfer) of informational responsibility. The other frame (which applies to contract rather than to medical law) is the idea of originating consent and, concomitantly, relative autonomy for the institutional sets that agents have engaged under conditions of free and informed consent. This is a frame, as we have said, that applies to the regulation of both unforced and informed choice in relation to optional sets such as the 'law of contract'. For a legal regime to take this analysis on board, it is true, a degree of sophistication is required—but the doctrinal refinement involved is by no means so complex as to be unworkable and this is a challenge to which the law can and should rise.

# 7

# Questions of Signalling and Scope, Withdrawal, and Refusal

## I Introduction

In this chapter, we discuss two further questions that bear on the adequacy of consent. One concerns the signalling of consent; the other concerns the scope and interpretation of consent, this becoming an issue where consent has been signalled but where there is now a dispute about whether the terms of the consent that has been signalled cover some proposed conduct (or, indeed, action that has already been taken). We also discuss briefly the negation of consent, whether ab initio in the form of a refusal or, at a later stage, when a consenting party purports to withdraw its prior authorisation.

In addressing these matters, we will be reminded once again that, for legal regimes that aspire to be PGC-compliant, it is important to respect the principle of fidelity to an agent's will but without neglecting the principle that justified transactional expectations are to be protected.[1]

The principle of fidelity to an agent's will is fundamental to Gewirthian thinking; for it is axiomatic that, other things being equal, the enforcement of consent-based rights and duties should be in alignment with the will of the relevant agent. To act as though agent A has consented to X when this is not agent A's will, is to act against the will of agent A. Other things being equal, such compulsion (or coercion of A's will) should be avoided. It follows that, in relation to signalling, it is important that we do not proceed without having reliable evidence that an agent has actually consented. Similarly, in relation to questions of scope and interpretation, it is important that we act only on those readings of the agent's consent that we can confidently judge to be an expression of the agent's will. To avoid the risk of unjustifiable compulsion or coercion of an agent's will (masquerading as a consensual expression of the agent's will), our ideal-type of signalling together with our approach to the scope and interpretation of consent should be designed to render accurate readings of the agent's intention. In the case of signalling, this invites an orientation towards the agent's subjective state of mind; it underlines the need for a personal, distinct and unequivocal indication of consent on the part of the authorising agent; and it suggests that the standard vehicle for signalling consent should be by way

[1] See chs 5 and 6 (particularly in relation to the hard case of an under-informed consent).

of 'opting in' rather than 'opting out'. In the case of questions concerning the scope and interpretation of consent, this again invites an orientation towards the agent's subjective understanding of the consent that has been given; it does not, as such, favour a 'literal' or a 'purposive' approach (sometimes agents will say what they mean, but sometimes they will not); the paramount consideration (dictated by the principle of fidelity to an agent's will) is that interpreters should avoid going beyond the reach of the agent's will (or, at any rate, they should avoid overreaching an agent's will where the agent's consent is their only justificatory platform).

Because, as we have frequently repeated, consent assumes significance in the context of a transaction between agents, our quest for reliable evidence of an agent's will cannot fairly be pursued in a one-eyed way. Alongside the principle of fidelity, the law also has a responsibility to protect the interests of the other (the recipient) agent to the transaction. If we are to protect justifiable transactional expectations, we must also view the transaction (generated by the signals sent by the allegedly consenting agent) from the perspective of the recipient agent. From this perspective, however, it is not so much the subjective intentions of the allegedly consenting agent that are focal as the subjective perceptions of the recipient agent. Fairly obviously, we run into problems where there is a lack of concordance between the subjective will of one agent and the subjective perceptions of the other; and, if we are to resolve this potential impasse of conflicting subjective understandings, we need to introduce standards of honesty and reasonableness on both sides of the transaction—as lawyers would put it, we need to introduce an element of objectivity.[2] It follows that, when the principle of justifiable transactional expectations is brought into play, the emphasis on fidelity and reliability is qualified by considerations of good faith and reasonableness that guide the development of a practical framework of responsibilities, excuses, and entitlements.

Our discussion of these issues is in three sections. In section II of the chapter, we tackle the questions surrounding the signalling of consent; in section III, we discuss the scope and interpretation of consent; and, in section IV, we consider the issues raised by withdrawal and refusal of consent.

## II The Signalling of Consent

Consent (as the basis for a procedural justification) assumes significance in the context of a transaction between agents. In such a context, by consenting, agent A essentially signals one of two things: either a willingness on the

[2] Cf Randy Barnett, 'A Consent Theory of Contract' (1986) 86 *Columbia Law Review* 269, at 306: contract law must protect 'the rights and liberty interests *of others*, whose plans and expectations would be severely limited if they were not entitled to rely on things as they appear to be and to take the assertive conduct of [the ostensibly consenting agent] at face value.'

part of A to modify its position in relation to the particular background scheme of rights and duties, permissions and immunities, and the like, that regulates the relationship between A and fellow agent B (the recipient of the consent); or a willingness on the part of A to put in place a new relationship with B. Where A signals consent to the creation of a new relationship with B, this might be by virtue of some simple dynamic (such as the giving of a promise or agreement to an exchange of goods) or it might be by virtue of some more complex institutional set (as is the case, for example, if A invokes the law of contract or the law of marriage) or regulated scheme (such as those licensing assisted conception or physician-assisted suicide). Where A thus signals consent, and where that consent satisfies the criteria of validity, then A is precluded from asserting that B may not justifiably rely on, or hold A to, the agreed change of position or the terms of the new relationship. None of this, however, gets to first base unless A has actually *signalled* consent.

Because consent is signalled in the context of a transaction between agents, and because the effect of a valid consent is to bar certain sorts of argument by the consenting agent (or to shield the recipient agent against certain sorts of claims), we can sense at once a potential tension between a signalling theory that prioritises the interests of the (allegedly) consenting agent and one that prioritises the interests of the recipient agent. If we were to construct an ideal-typical working model of signalling, designed to keep faith with the intentions and interests of the (allegedly) consenting agent, then we suggest that it would run along the following lines:

> *Agent A, subjectively intending to consent to X, personally, distinctly and definitely, and unequivocally, signals ex ante (ie prior) consent to X; and, where there is a delay between A consenting to X and X being done, then A subjectively maintains the intention to consent to X.*

Applying this model, we are looking for A's *subjective* (not objective) intention; we are looking for this intention to be given *personally* by A, to be *distinct and definite*, and to be *unequivocal*; we are also looking for the signal to be given ex ante rather than ex post—that is, before the authorised act rather than after it; and, if there is a delay, as with an advance directive for instance, we are requiring the signal to be *maintained* right through to the relevant time.

Such a one-sided model, however, fails to protect the interests of agent B who, in good faith, believes that he or she is the recipient of a consent signalled by agent A. If B interprets A's actions (whether A's words or conduct) as indicating consent, or if B's understanding is that C is signalling consent on behalf of A, *and if B's interpretation or understanding would be shared by most agents*, then how far can we justifiably hold to the ideal-typical model of signalling? In other words, where B is relying on a reading of the situation that is not only in good faith but also (as most agents would affirm) 'reasonable', there seems to be at least an arguable case for qualifying the ideal-type, for balancing the principle of fidelity against the principle of justifiable transactional expectations.

In the light of these preliminary remarks, we can examine more carefully each of the defining features of our provisional ideal-typical case of signalling.[3]

### *(i) The Subjective Test*

In several areas of law, notably in the fields of contract law and criminal law, we find the jurisprudence divided between 'subjectivist' and 'objectivist' approaches to the intention of agents. Looking at the 'sending' side of a transaction, should the law be guided by what a party *subjectively* intends or by what a party so situated would reasonably (i.e *objectively*) expect others to make of its words or actions? Looking at the 'receiving' side of the transaction, should the law be guided by what the recipient agent *subjectively* takes to be the sending agent's intention or by what a reasonable agent (*objectively*) would make of the other's words or actions? Our ideal-typical model of consent incorporates a subjectivist approach to signalling (that is, a subjectivist approach viewed from the side of the allegedly consenting agent). Does it follow that objectivism, which has quite a hold on the law—

[3] Two other thoughts invite consideration. First, is there a case for setting a different standard for signalling where the function of consent is to modify an agent's position within an existing relationship (characteristically involving some *reduction* of the benefit of the agent's entitlement) as opposed to where the function of consent is to put in place a new relationship (characteristically involving the assumption of *additional* obligations)? Secondly, is there a case for distinguishing between signalling requirements depending upon the class of agency interests (basic, non-subtractive, and additive) involved? For example, should we set a more demanding standard where the transaction bears on an agent's basic interests than would be the case if it bore only on non-subtractive or additive interests? With regard to the first question, thus far, we have resisted setting different standards for different categories of transaction (that is, for categories of transaction that are distinguished by the particular function played by consent). So, for example, when (in chs 5 and 6) we discussed the standard of a valid consent, we did not suggest that a consent that qualifies as free and informed for the purposes of modification of position should not also qualify as free and informed for the purposes of creating a new relationship, or vice versa. A priori, there seems no good reason to depart from this approach in relation to the question of whether a consent has been signalled. A priori, the ideal-type of what constitutes a signalled consent, no less than what constitutes a valid consent, should be constant irrespective of the category of transaction. The idea behind the second question looks more plausible. However, there is more than one way of responding. Rather than departing from our a priori instinct that the ideal-type is constant, we might, in practice, vary our evidential standards in a way that reflects the importance of the generic interests at stake. So, for example, we might set our most demanding evidential standards before we accept that an agent has signalled consent to a procedure for physician-assisted suicide, with rather less demanding standards being set before we accept that an agent has signalled consent to having his hair cut or nails clipped.

for example, an objectivist approach to the interpretation of intention in contracts was settled back in the nineteenth century[4]—is misconceived?

The choice between subjectivist and objectivist approaches presents a formidable thicket of questions. We can break into it by supposing that, contrary to the ideal-type, agent A does *not* subjectively intend to signal consent. In other words, viewed from A's perspective, there is no intention to signal consent; hence, if the recipient agent B argues that A has signalled consent, from A's perspective, B is in error. Where such a situation obtains, the ideal-type indicates that A has not consented; and, so far as the fidelity principle is concerned, that is that. However, if we are to take into account the protection of B's interests (under the principle of justifiable transactional expectations), then we need to consider how A's signal looks from B's standpoint. Generally, legal regimes will concern themselves with either the honesty or the reasonableness (or both) of B's beliefs, yielding in principle the following six descriptions of B's beliefs:

B(i): B does not honestly believe that A has signalled consent;
B(ii): B honestly believes that A has signalled consent;
B(iii): B does not reasonably believe that A has signalled consent;
B(iv): B reasonably believes that A has signalled consent;
B(v): B does not honestly and reasonably believe that A has signalled consent; and
B(vi): B honestly and reasonably believes that A has signalled consent.

Because there is more than one possible reference point for the reasonableness of B's belief, this list could be extended but, for our purposes, these six descriptions suffice.

The first case, B(i), is an easy one. The ideal-type is not instantiated; B does not honestly believe that it is instantiated; so there is no reason to deviate from the ideal-typical case. So, for example, if a patient's subjective intention is to refuse treatment, and if a physician administers the treatment knowing full well that the patient is not consenting, there is no reason to hold that the patient has signalled consent. Again, if in a criminal case, such as a prosecution for rape, the victim has not subjectively consented and the defendant subjectively knows this, there is no reason to hold anything other than that consent has not been signalled.

In each of these examples, we assume that there is a symmetry between agent A's subjective intention and recipient agent B's subjective understanding of A's position. Suppose, however, agent A (subjectively intending not to consent) acts in a way that might lead some (but not B) to believe

[4] Famously, in *Smith v Hughes* (1871) LR 6 QB 597, at 607, Lord Blackburn said:

> If, whatever a man's real intention may be, he so conducts himself that a reasonable man would believe that he was assenting to the terms proposed by the other party, and that other party upon that belief enters into a contract with him, the man thus conducting himself would be equally bound as if he had intended to agree to the other party's terms.

that a consent is being signalled. For example, suppose that manufacturing agent A places an advertisement making rash claims about its product and apparently promising a large reward if the product disappoints purchasers.[5] B, unlike most agents who read the advertisement, has inside information alerting him to the fact that A does not mean what it seems to be saying. If B were then to put it to the court that, even though he did not take the advertisement at face value, it would be reasonable to read it as signalling that A was consenting, would this be a reason for departing from the ideal-typical model? Clearly, it would not. From a Gewirthian perspective, there is no reason to deviate from the ideal-type when the recipient agent has correctly understood that the subjective intent of the 'sender' is not to signal consent. It follows that, where the particular permutation in description B(v) is that of a recipient agent who does not honestly believe that a consent has been signalled, even though other agents might reasonably believe that a consent has been signalled, there is no reason to weaken on the ideal-type (although this is not to say that steps should not be taken to regulate misleading advertising).[6] More generally, we can say that, if there is to be any deviation from the ideal-type in favour of the recipient agent, it is a *necessary* condition of such deviation that the recipient agent honestly believes that a consent has been signalled.

If the recipient agent honestly believes that a consent has been signalled, this satisfies a necessary condition for deviation from the ideal-type, but is it *sufficient*? Would deviation be justifiable on the grounds of honest belief alone, as in description B(ii), or is it only when the recipient agent can satisfy the dual requirement of honesty and reasonableness as in description B(vi) that deviation is legitimate?

If we treat B's honest belief, as in description B(ii), as sufficient, we are saying that where agent A subjectively intends not to signal consent, and agent B honestly believes that agent A does intend to signal consent, then agent B's subjective perception of the situation governs—consent is taken to be signalled. This, however, inverts the ideal-type, no longer treating agent A's subjective will as dominant but, instead, treating agent B's subjective perception as dominant. Without more, there is no reason to subordinate the fidelity principle in this way. Having said this, we might detect in some legal regimes a degree of willingness to make allowances for B's subjective view. Whereas regimes of contract law are unlikely to treat B's

[5] Readers might like to compare the facts of the famous case of *Carlill v Carbolic Smoke Ball Co Ltd* [1893] 1 QB 256, which we discuss in the next chapter.

[6] The other permutation in B(v) is that of B having an honest belief that A has signalled consent, but without having reasonable grounds for the belief. If A intends to mislead B, or is reckless in this regard, B's honest belief will suffice to treat A as having signalled consent. However, if A is merely careless in misleading B, the agents' mutual carelessness cancels things out, and we are left with the fidelity principle concluding that A has not signalled consent. See below at 194.

subjective perception without more as sufficient to treat A as signalling agreement, a defendant in a criminal or a tort case might materially plead a subjective belief that the other party was consenting. If we judge that such honest mistakes should constitute an excuse, then that is one thing—although care must be taken not to allow the excuse to be pleaded in a way that privileges certain classes of defendants (such as males in rape trials or physicians in malpractice actions); however, to hold in such cases that the other party has consented is to add insult to injury.[7]

If we need more than B's honest belief, then perhaps description B(vi) supplies the additional ingredient to justify qualifying the ideal-type. If B not only believes in good faith that A has signalled consent but also has reasonable grounds for this belief, then B's case is improved in two ways. First, if there is any lingering doubt about the honesty of B's belief, the fact that it is based on reasonable grounds at least eases such concerns. Secondly, and more importantly, the context in which B interprets A's words or conduct lends credence to B's belief that A is signalling consent. Since it is implicit in Gewirthian theory that the PGC both protects and promotes the agency of purposive actors, B has cause for complaint if the normative context in which he is acting leaves him unprotected against signals given by A that reasonably seem to indicate consent. This suggests that, if we are to deviate from the ideal-typical case, B's beliefs must fit the description in B(vi); that is, the necessary and sufficient conditions for treating A as having signalled consent, notwithstanding a lack of matching subjective intent, are that B honestly believes that A is consenting and that B has reasonable grounds for so believing.

Before we endorse such a proposition, however, we need to draw out A's possible state of mind. All that we have supposed thus far is that A does not subjectively intend to signal consent. There are, however, any number of ways in which it might happen that A lacks the subjective intent but nevertheless sends out a misleading signal. For example, there might be a slip of the tongue on A's part, or A might be unaware of local conventions (where 'no' means 'yes'), or A might fail to advert to the signals sent out by his conduct, and so on. If these remarks prompt us to think in terms of A's responsibility for his actions then, broadly speaking, A's state of mind might fit any one of the following three descriptions:

A(i): A intends that others should think (incorrectly) that he intends to consent; or A is reckless in the sense that he is indifferent whether other agents form the correct or incorrect impression;

A(ii) A fails to take reasonable care to avoid other agents forming the incorrect impression as to his intention to consent; and

[7] Provided that the belief in case B(ii) is treated as a potential excusing condition and not as a basis for asserting consent as a defence, the ideal-type remains constant between cases in which consent is presented as a defence and those in which it is the basis of empowerment.

A(iii) A takes reasonable care to avoid other agents forming the incorrect impression as to his intention to consent.

In the first of these cases, where A intentionally or recklessly misleads B, then if B honestly and reasonably forms the impression that A is signalling consent, it seems appropriate that the law should proceed as though A has signalled consent.[8] In fact, A's conduct here is so reprehensible that there is a powerful argument for treating A as having signalled consent if B merely honestly forms the impression that A is signalling consent (ie irrespective of whether B's belief is reasonable). Granted, the streetwise Bs will not be misled by A's signals and they will take care of themselves. But this leaves the less streetwise Bs, and it is not clear why such vulnerable agents should be left to count the cost of having trusted A.

In the second case, A is careless. If, as a result, B honestly and reasonably forms the impression that A is signalling consent, it seems appropriate that A should bear the responsibility and that the law should proceed as though A has signalled consent. It follows that, in such a case, A will be precluded from claiming that B has acted in a way that, A's consent apart, would constitute a wrong; and, similarly, A will be precluded from pleading lack of consent where B seeks to hold A to a new relationship, the formation of which presupposes that A has consented. If, however, B is also careless (although honest) in misinterpreting A's careless signal, it seems appropriate to treat the carelessness on the one side as cancelled out by the carelessness on the other. On this analysis, A would be taken not to have consented. Here, B will need to plead an honest mistake (not consent) to answer A's claim that a wrong has been done; and, similarly, B's argument for the formation of a new relationship will rest on mistake rather than consent.

Finally, in the third case, we have a classic hard case of two innocent agents: A in good faith does not intend to consent and takes reasonable care not to signal otherwise; nevertheless, B in good faith forms the reasonable impression that A is signalling consent.[9] No legal regime will find an entirely comfortable solution to this puzzle in which the interests of the agents seem to be evenly balanced. However, we suggest that, while it is tough on B, fidelity demands that we should stick with the ideal-type and hold that A has not signalled consent. In such a case, B will need to plead honest and reasonable mistake (not consent) to answer A's claim that a wrong has been done; and, similarly, B's argument for the formation of a new relationship will rest on mistake rather than consent. Whilst legal regimes are likely to look favourably on B's plea in response to an alleged crime or tort, they are

[8] Compare the case of undisclosed agency. A does not wish B to realise that he, A, is acting as an agent for P. In the event of a dispute, A will not be permitted to disown the transaction with B. B reasonably believes that A is acting in his known capacity.

[9] Compare the hard case of under-informed consent discussed in chs 5 and 6.

much less likely to accept that a contract can be constructed on the basis of a one-party mistake to which the other party has not contributed (and remembering that the latter is not consenting to the agreement).

Putting these pieces together, we arrive at the conclusion that the law may justifiably deviate from the subjectivity of the ideal-type in the following two cases: first, where we have A(i) in conjunction with B(ii) (or, a fortiori, B(vi)); or, secondly, where we have A(ii) in conjunction with B(vi). In the light of this, we can see that it is a mistake to suggest that the law should be orientated to either 'pure subjectivism' or 'pure objectivism'. To do justice to the subtlety of signalling issues, a PGC-compliant regime must look to both subjective and objective considerations.

The complexity of this prescription should not be underrated. Recent English legislation, for example, authorises the interception of private communications where 'the communication is one which, or which [the interceptor] has reasonable grounds for believing, is both (a) a communication sent by a person who has consented to the interception; and (b) a communication the intended recipient of which has so consented.'[10] This is ugly drafting; but it might be thought to reflect the right approach. Essentially, what the law provides is *either* (i) that the parties to the communication (the sender and the recipient) must have actually consented *or* (ii) that the interceptor must have reasonable grounds for believing that they have so consented. However, following our analysis, it will be apparent that this is not quite enough: even if we assume that authorisation by actual consent is unproblematic, authorisation simply by reference to the interceptor's reasonable beliefs will not do—in addition, we must check whether, and how, the other parties have contributed to the interceptor's (mis)understanding of the position. In a sense, it is not enough first to look right and then look left, we also need to look right again.

Putting the point more generally, we can say that objectivists are in error if they claim that the law should not be interested in either (a) the subjective beliefs of agent A (this is where the ideal-type is centred) or (b) the subjective beliefs of agent B (the honesty of agent B is an essential condition for any departure from the ideal-type). Equally, however, subjectivists are in error if they claim that the law should not be interested in either (a) the reasonableness of A's conduct (this is a critical factor in determining where the risk of a misunderstanding lies) or (b) in the reasonableness of B's beliefs.[11]

We started with the problematic case of an agent, A, who subjectively does *not* intend to signal consent. However, can we assume that where agent

[10] Section 3(1) of the Regulation of Investigatory Powers Act 2000.

[11] To be sure, there is one case, A(i) in conjunction with B(ii), where the reasonableness or not of B's beliefs is not critical, but, this one case apart, it will only be where B's beliefs are reasonable (and honest) that there is a case for departing from the ideal-type.

A subjectively intends to signal consent there is no problem? Certainly, if agent A subjectively intends to signal consent and the recipient agent B interprets A's signal correctly, there is no problem. But, what if agent B misinterprets or misunderstands A's signal?

In practice, for the most part at any rate, if B (mistakenly) thinks that A is not signalling consent, B will proceed on the basis that A is refusing. Moreover, if B, in consequence, does not go ahead and act in the way that A really wants (remember, A subjectively intends to signal consent), then A will soon correct B's misapprehension and all will be well. However, the fact that B acts in reliance on a perceived refusal by A will not always be unproblematic; and this is particularly so where A subsequently tries to hold B to account by reference to A's subjective intention to signal consent—in other words, where A purports to hold B to account in the way that would be appropriate if it was accepted that A had signalled consent. For example, suppose that A subjectively intends to authorise surgery encompassing X and Y, but as the surgeon, B, understands the situation, A is signalling consent only to X, and B duly carries out surgery X. What if A, now facing a fresh round of surgery for Y, complains about B's performance? Or, consider one of the classic contract puzzles generated by the nineteenth-century common law rule that a letter of acceptance is binding from the time that it is posted.[12] Suppose that A, wishing to hedge his bets, posts a letter of acceptance to B agreeing to buy shares from B but, while the letter is in the post, A sends a second (speedier) communication (by express mail, telegram, telephone, e-mail, or similar) indicating to B that he does not wish to accept. B, relying on the first communication received, the apparent non-acceptance, sells the shares to C. Will the law now permit A to base a claim against B for breach of contract by reference to the first posted letter of acceptance, subjectively signalling A's consent?

We can probably make short work of the postal rule hypothetical. A is plainly acting in bad faith, abusing the postal rule, and merits no assistance from the court. Moreover, why should we accept that the first letter of acceptance accurately reflects A's subjective signalling intentions? We only have A's word for this and, given A's duplicity, his word does not count for much. The case of the under-performed surgery, however, is less straightforward. The obvious question is: why did B misunderstand A's signal (relative to A's subjective intention)? Was A in some way responsible for this? As before, we can identify three states of mind on A's part as follows:

AA(i): A intends that B should think (incorrectly) that he does not intend to consent to Y; or A is reckless in the sense that he is indifferent whether B forms the correct or incorrect impression;

AA(ii): A fails to take reasonable care to avoid B forming the incorrect impression as to his intention to consent to Y; and

[12] See, eg, *Adams v Lindsell* (1818) 1 B & Ald 681.

AA(iii): A takes reasonable care to avoid B forming the incorrect impression as to his intention to consent to Y.

If AA(i) applies, this is an easy case; there is no merit in A's claim and, provided that B honestly believes that A is not consenting to Y, B cannot be held responsible for failing to do Y.

Where AA(ii) applies—for example, because A has ticked X on the consent form but carelessly put a cross against Y—A has contributed to his own problems. Provided that B honestly and reasonably believes that A is not signalling consent to Y, there is no reason why B should take any share of the responsibility for not undertaking Y.

Finally, if AA(iii) applies, we have the makings of a genuine, but unfortunate, misunderstanding. Signals and wires sometimes do get crossed; such is life; and there is no easy solution. On the one side, A has subjectively signalled consent to Y and has taken reasonable care to ensure that the signal is understood by B; on the other side, let us assume that B in good faith and reasonably believes that A has not signalled consent to Y. On the one side, we cannot deny that A has signalled consent to Y; on the other side, B has good reason for not acting on A's subjective signal. The best that we can do, it seems, is hold that B is excused from not acting on A's signalled consent.

To sum up, the same pattern of principle applies whether A subjectively intends *not* to signal consent (or, more pointedly, A intends to signal a refusal) or whether A's subjective intention is to signal a consent. In both kinds of case, the ideal-type of signalling entrenches A's subjective intention. The law, we have suggested, may justifiably depart from the subjectivity of the ideal-type in just two types of case as follows: first, where A intentionally or recklessly misleads B (that is, where we have A(i) or AA(i) in conjunction with B(ii) (or, a fortiori, B(vi))); or, secondly, where A fails to take reasonable care with his signalling and where B honestly and reasonably misreads A's intention (that is, where we have A(ii) or AA(ii) in conjunction with B(vi)).

### *(ii) Signalling in Person*

Our ideal-type stipulates that agent A *personally* signals consent. If we are to allow for anything other than personal signalling, the spirit of the ideal-type demands that the signalling party is the alter ego of the authorising agent (or principal) whose consent is being signalled.[13] And, indeed, this is

[13] This also presupposes that the principal is an ostensible agent with capacity. The argument that parents may signal consent or refusal on behalf of their children should not be viewed as a case of the children signalling their consent or refusal through parents who act as their agents for this purpose (see ch 4). Where a spouse or partner purports to speak for the other, there is no special problem about signalling. However, legal regimes need to take a hard look at the authorising relationship itself to ensure that it meets the conditions for a valid (authorising) consent.

precisely how many legal regimes view an 'agent'[14] who acts on behalf of a 'principal'—in French law, for instance, the agent is seen as an extension or instrument of the principal.[15] Even if the relationship between authorising principal and agent[16] is not viewed in quite these terms, the ideal-type demands that the agency should be set up in a way that clearly defines the extent of the agent's authority. This is important for two reasons: first, so that the consent signalled by the agent accurately reflects the will of the principal; and, secondly, so that the other agent to the transaction is able to rely on the agent's signals. All this points to the need for express and unequivocal agreement as between the principal, A, and B, who is to act as A's agent, in setting up the agency.[17]

In practice, legal regimes recognise agency in many instances other than that of express authorisation. We encounter agents whose authority is said to be 'implied' or 'apparent' as well as 'agency of necessity'. We can put to one side so-called 'agency of necessity', which is a rather special and exceptional case arising in the context of jettisoning of cargo and the like.[18] However, what do we make of the other forms of agency?

If it is argued that an agency is implied, this turns on how we interpret the scope of the express authorisation. Characteristically, the principal will contend that the agent has exceeded his authority, going beyond the reach of the express terms. In response, the agent, or a third party who has dealt with and relied on the agent, will argue that the terms of the agent's express authority impliedly extend to the circumstances in question. The resolution of this kind of dispute turns less on signalling than on how we interpret the principal's express consent to the agency. As we will see in the next part of this chapter, questions of interpretation, like questions of signalling, implicate both the fidelity principle and the principle of reasonable transactional expectation; and the general approach in both cases is to treat the allegedly consenting (or authorising) agent's subjective will as determinative unless that agent has intentionally, recklessly, or unreasonably misled the other.

[14] Here, we mean 'agent', and 'principal', as used in the technical legal sense associated with the 'law of agency'. (Note our Coda at the end of ch 1.)

[15] See Code Civil, para 1119.

[16] Likewise proxies. For present purposes, we need draw no distinction between agents and proxies, in each case acting on behalf of an authorising principal.

[17] In *R v Human Fertilisation and Embryology Authority, ex parte Blood* [1997] 2 All ER 687, Mrs Blood testified that she and her now-deceased husband had discussed starting a family and that he would have wanted her to have his children. On this basis, Mrs Blood argued, in effect, that she was authorised to act as her husband's agent in consenting to the taking and posthumous use of his sperm. Even though Mrs Blood's compelling testimony struck a chord with the majority of public opinion, the distance between the facts of her case and the ideal-type indicates that caution is appropriate. This is not to say that the taking and use of the sperm might not be justified, all things considered but, in the absence of a signal from the husband or an express agency agreement, a consent-based procedural justification looks problematic.

[18] See ch 8, at 254.

Hence, if the principal's subjective will is not to authorise the agency in the implied way contended for, and provided that the principal bears no responsibility for creating a misunderstanding as to the scope of the authority, the agency will be limited to its express terms.

Where it is argued that an agent has apparent authority, a third party contends that the principal has either created this impression and must now bear the responsibility; or that the principal has failed to correct the ordinary assumption (in the particular context) that the agent has authority, and again must bear the responsibility.[19] This is a signalling issue. On the one side, the fidelity principle demands that we do not recognise the agent as having an authority that the alleged principal subjectively did not intend. On the other side, the principle of reasonable transactional expectation demands that the third party should be able to rely, honestly and reasonably, on the signals apparently given by the principal (or the principal's acquiescence). This form of dispute is one that we have discussed at length already and the guidelines elaborated already are applicable.

### *(iii) Distinct and Definite Signalling*

The ideal-type specifies that consent should be signalled distinctly and definitely, meaning that it should be positively indicated. Provided that the signal stands out, in its particular context, as a distinct indication of assent, it does not matter whether it is given in writing or by word of mouth or electronically (by the click of a mouse or by hitting the 'enter' key), by some symbolic act such as a shake of hands or a nod of the head, or even implicitly by conduct (such as the tendering of money).[20] No doubt, these various modes of signalling could be classified in various ways. For our purposes, however, it suffices to say that a distinct and definite signal might be given 'explicitly' or 'implicitly' in the following stipulative senses:

- Where a distinct and definite signal is given in a formally structured context, in response to a clear prompt for consent, we can treat this as an 'explicitly signalled consent'.
- Where a distinct and definite signal is given informally, in a less structured context, we can treat this as an 'implicitly signalled consent'.

[19] In the famous case of *Watteau v Fenwick* [1893] 1 QB 346, the principal had expressly limited the scope of the agent landlord's authority. However, without bringing this limitation of authority to the attention of third parties, the principal had not taken steps to correct the ordinary assumption as to the authority of landlords on the basis of which third parties supplied the landlord and extended credit to him. For discussion, see Randy Barnett, 'Squaring Undisclosed Agency Law with Contract Theory' (1987) 75 Cal LR 1969.

[20] Clearly, legal systems need to be vigilant in accepting that consent has been implicitly signalled. For example, the popular press is ready to argue that celebrities, who have previously courted publicity, or who appear in public places, implicitly consent thereby to intrusive (and unwelcome) press coverage that would otherwise violate their right to privacy. See, eg, Gavin Phillipson, 'Transforming Breach of Confidence? Towards a Common Law Right of Privacy under the Human Rights Act' (2003) 66 *Modern Law Review* 726, especially at 740–42.

These stipulations (or similar stipulations concerning 'express' and 'implied' consent)[21] do not, of course, ease our problems of interpretation of conduct. Whether or not a signal is to be classified as explicit or implicit is not fundamental; provided that it is distinct and definite, the signal fits with the ideal-type. However, where an agent's conduct is arguably *consistent* with giving an implicitly signalled consent, but no more than that, this falls short of the ideal-type. The fact that an agent has not distinctly and definitely signalled a *refusal* of consent is, after all, weak evidence of an intention to consent and no substitute for a consent that is distinctly and definitely signalled.

Legal regimes (rightly) tend to be nervous about treating inaction as a signal of assent and, in this section, we can concentrate on the controversial question of 'presumed' consent under so-called 'opt-out' schemes. For, where procedural justification rests on presumed consent, there is a clear and present danger that a convenient fiction is in play.[22]

There is one sense in which legal regimes make widespread use of what are, in effect, opt-out provisions (even though not usually described in such terms). As we have said, the framework for each legal regime will be set by a scheme of background rights and duties. Some of these background provisions will be non-negotiable (mandatory or imposed obligations) but others will operate as default provisions, applicable unless agents agree otherwise (for example, agents may be permitted to bargain around some liability rules). To be PGC-compliant, these background provisions must be consistent with the PGC under either its direct or indirect application. Where such provisions apply (whether because they are mandatory or because agents have not agreed otherwise), the principal justification is that the measures are PGC-compliant, not that agents have signalled consent. It follows that any element of opt-out detected in such default provisions is not problematic relative to the idea of procedural justification.

Within the framework formed by the background provisions, a legal regime will offer agents the option of invoking various institutional sets. Typically, these sets will be loaded with default provisions of one kind or another—for example, a default table of articles of association for an off-the-shelf company, a default set of implied terms for contracts of sale, and so on. To invoke the set, agents need to opt in; and, having opted in, they will need to take opt-out steps if they wish to disapply the default provisions. If the application of such default provisions in the absence of opting out occasions some concern, we need to go back one step to the point at which the set is invoked. In the ideal-typical case, the agents will invoke the particular set by self-consciously opting in. In the case of the institutional

[21] Later in this chapter, we will return to 'express' and 'implied' consent, which we treat as categories arising under an explicitly signalled consent but concerning interpretation rather than signalling. See below at 212–221.

[22] Compare our comments about substituted judgement in ch 4.

set represented by the law of contract, for example, the paradigm is one of agents invoking the framework rules of the law of contract, signalling that they consent to their relationship being governed by this particular set (including the default rules that go with the set). Having signalled that they wish to be bound by these framework rules, the agents do not yet have a contract; they have merely put themselves in a position where their attempts to reach an agreement and where the effect of any such agreement is governed by the law of contract that they have consensually invoked.[23] In other words, they have signalled that this is the 'law game' that they are now playing; they are playing according to the rules given by the law of contract. To the extent that the rules of the game are default provisions, applicable unless the players agree to modify them, and to the extent that the agents do not modify the rules, in the ideal-typical case we can say that the initial originating consent authorises the application of the rules of the game.

In practice, the ideal-typical case might not be readily instantiated—the sheer informality and regularity of contracting means that, on many occasions, agents will not self-consciously invoke this particular institutional set (or, at any rate, they will only indicate that this is the game they are playing much later when things go wrong and they look to the law for a remedy). Doctrinally, too, there seems to be some confusion concerning the requirement that the parties intend to be legally bound. This is understood to be one of the law of contract's own requirements for the formation of a binding contract, a requirement, that is to say, that is internal to the institutional set. However, if the correct analysis is that agents must first invoke the institutional set by signalling that they intend to be bound by the rules of that set, this act of invoking the set looks very much like the agents signalling that they intend to be legally bound (or more accurately, that they intend to be bound by the law of contract). In other words, the doctrinal requirement of an intention to create legal relations is redundant once the parties have invoked the set; and, on this analysis, the requirement should be seen, not as *internal* to the contract rule-book, but as an *external* threshold requirement to be satisfied by agents who wish to invoke the set. Once we have this threshold requirement in focus, it must bear the full weight of a consent-reliant procedural justification. In other words, the initial opt-in must be both free and informed. Accordingly, unless the agents know not merely that there are default rules, but know what those default rules are, there are problems about arguing that their initial consent justifies the application of the default provisions. However, in the ideal-typical case, it seems perfectly correct to treat the initial opt-in as a complete answer to concerns about the opt-out nature of default provisions within the particular set.[24]

[23] Recall our account in ch 3, at 73.

[24] See Randy Barnett, 'The Sound of Silence: Default Rules and Contractual Consent' (1992) 78 *Virginia Law Review* 821.

It is worth pausing to remark that a consent theory of contract might be understood in both a minimal and a maximal sense. In both senses, the agents' originating consent is the threshold condition. Without meeting this condition, the agents simply do not engage the law of contract. In a minimal version of consent theory, this is as far as consent need be taken. For, under relative autonomy, the institutional set (the 'law of contract') engaged by the agents' consent need not itself have any doctrinal commitment to dealings that are consensual: in principle at least, the rules of the institutional set may permit all manner of one-sided, under-informed and coercive dealing. In practice, such a set would be at odds with our conventional understanding that contract is fundamentally about consensual exchanges, an understanding that reflects the maximal version of consent theory—it might also, of course, be dysfunctional as an institutional set. Given the maximal version, consent is not only the threshold condition, it is also the guiding ideal that informs the particular institutional set. Consent in this version is double-banked. So far as default provisions are concerned, the distinction between the minimal and the maximal version is significant. If we assume the minimal version, the default rules may be geared for efficiency or fairness, they may be designed to reflect some hypothetical bargain or a common sense expectation, or indeed some other value.[25] If we assume a maximal version, however, default rules should be designed in such a way that they have the best chance of reflecting the parties' tacit consent. For instance, if the default rule is in line with commonly held expectations, this will be least likely to surprise the parties and most likely to accord with their tacit expectations.[26]

From default rules in contract law, we can turn to opt-out schemes in the sense that they are more commonly understood. When the State prescribes its background scheme of rights and duties, this will lay down the regulatory framework for both private relationships between agents and public relationships between the State and agents. In specifying the latter, the State might rely on opt-out provisions as a means, so it judges, of advancing its conception of the public interest (or for reasons of the general good). For example, the State might judge that the public interest requires young

[25] Cf Jules L Coleman, Douglas D Heckathorn, and Steven M Maser, 'A Bargaining Theory Approach to Default Provisions and Disclosure Rules in Contract Law' (1989) 12 *Harvard Journal of Law and Public Policy* 639, and Richard Craswell, 'Contract Law, Default Rules, and the Philosophy of Promising' (1989) 88 *Michigan Law Review* 489.

[26] See Barnett, n 24 above, at 874–97. Barnett points out that, where one agent has knowledge of the (common expectation) default rules but the other does not, and if the former wishes to modify the default position, this will lead to express bargaining on the matter. Where both agents are repeat-players who regularly modify the default rules, it is less important that the default position reflects tacit expectations because consent will be forged around the modification.

men to undertake national service, all adults to give blood periodically, all citizens to carry identity cards, to supply tissue for a national data bank, to donate their organs post-mortem, and so on. If the State straightforwardly decrees that these requirements are obligatory, then there is no issue about the signalling of consent; for the State's justification is that it can demonstrate the legitimacy of its public interest measures by reference to the PGC rather than by relying on its citizens' consent. However, where the State presents its public interest requirements as optional, but subject to an opt-out scheme, we face a real issue about signalling.

Legal regimes, like moral regimes, will draw a fundamental distinction between actions that are required as obligatory and actions that are optional. However, there are ways in which the distinction is qualified. For instance, the obligation to perform military service might make some allowance for conscientious objection; and the option to serve as an organ donor might be subject to an 'opt-out' scheme. When the distinction is so qualified, there might be some blurring of the line between what, for justificatory purposes, is to be characterised as non-consensual and what as consensual. Where the State makes action X obligatory, its justification is not the procedural one that agents consent to do X; some agents might do X perfectly willingly, but the State's general justification for requiring X is not that those who do X do so consensually. Where, by contrast, the State treats action X as optional, the State's general justification is that agents who elect to do X, opt in and thereby signal their consent—no one who does X is forced to do it. Now, for our purposes, where the State declares that X is optional but employs an opt-out scheme, this not only places a practical question-mark against the extent to which those who do X do so as a matter of free choice, but it also deviates significantly from the ideal-type under which consent is to be distinctly and definitely signalled.

Understandably, opt-out schemes have attracted their fair share of criticism. However, it is important to distinguish between those criticisms that doubt the instrumental rationality of opt-out schemes, and those that question the adequacy of the opt-out signal relative to consent theory.

Dealing, first, with instrumental rationality, it might be that opt-outs sometimes contribute less effectively to the desired end than is the case with opt-ins. Paradoxically, when contributing to the general good is unreservedly optional (on an opt-in basis), agents might contribute more effectively than when contribution is taken for granted unless agents opt out. Agents have the option under opt-out as under opt-in, but the psychology of giving might be affected by the regulatory tilt. Where this is the case, States might be disappointed to find that where they move from opt-in to opt-out in an effort to close the gap between supply and demand for, say, human organs (for transplantation), there is no increase in the stock of organs made available (or, even if supply increases, there is an off-setting decrease in quality). Where the culture of giving for the public good is sensitive to any move in the direction of quasi-conscription, the signals sent out by the State are important.[27]

Where the adoption of an opt-out scheme would prove counter-productive relative to the State's public interest objectives then it would be irrational for the State to adopt it. However, where opt-out would be productive, there remains the objection that such a scheme is wrong in principle. From a utilitarian perspective, the benefits generated by opt-out will have to be set against whatever costs or disbenefits it produces. Such a calculation might or might not come out in favour of opt-out; but whatever the outcome, it fails to address the fundamental Gewirthian objection that opt-out relies on a signal that is simply too unreliable if the State is to rest its justification on the consent of its (non-opting-out) citizens. Here, then, we have the crucial objection: if the State cannot justify its actions in the absence of consent, then opt-out does not satisfy the signalling requirement presupposed by a consent-based justification. It should never be forgotten: consent is easily claimed (as a public procedural justification) but adequate consents are much less readily attained.

We can put this objection to the test by reference to the important, but controversial, national gene data bank project being undertaken in Iceland. The commendable idea of this project (operated by a private company, DeCode Genetics) is to improve our understanding of how genes and environment interact to generate serious diseases. Potentially, the fruit of this project could be of real benefit to the relatively closed community that comprises the Icelandic public; and, indeed, there might be a public benefit that extends well beyond the shores of Iceland. However, participation in the data bank scheme is on an opt-out basis and this invites the objection that consent is not being taken sufficiently seriously.[28] However, first things first: before we inquire as to the adequacy of opt-out relative to consent, we must establish whether the Icelandic State needs a consent-based justification in order to defend the legitimacy of its project.

As we have said, where the State is able to justify its policy by drawing on the PGC in its direct or indirect applications, it has no need to resort to a particular procedural justification of the kind that we currently have in contemplation. Accordingly, if the State may legitimately require participation in a data bank project, seeking the consent of participants is a local courtesy rather than a moral requirement. However, a moment's reflection

[27] Compare Richard M Titmuss, *The Gift Relationship: From Human Blood to Social Policy* (London, Allen and Unwin, 1970). Granted, Titmuss was contrasting simple voluntarism with incentivisation via a market. However, the general point holds: we should not assume that attempts to improve on simple opt-in donation (whether by making it financially attractive to supply or practically unattractive and inconvenient not to supply) will, all things considered, prove effective. All that we can say is: it just depends.

[28] Compare Vilhjálmur Árnason, 'Coding and Consent: Moral Challenges of the Database Project in Iceland' (2004) 18 *Bioethics* 27.

on the rights of agents that might be implicated in such a project suggests that, if the State may justifiably require participation, it is not an issue that is free of rights complications.

On the one side, there are rights that argue against unwilled participation. In particular, agents will plead such rights as those relating to bodily integrity, privacy, property, and conscience. On the other side, insofar as agents have a positive right that others assist in promoting their health and well-being, this will argue in favour of participation (as a matter of positive obligation). To some extent, the arguments against participation might be met: for example, if the data in the bank is anonymised, this might suffice to respond to the privacy objection, and if those whose conscience prevents them from participating are permitted to be exempted, this might answer the objection based on freedom of belief. If it is accepted that this leaves a conflict between the physical and property interests of agents whose preference is not to participate and the physical interests of agents whose preference is to participate, it is not implausible to treat the latter as more compelling—but the issue is far from clear-cut. What conclusion is to be drawn?

If the PGC supports a State in requiring participation, subject to anonymisation and a conscience clause, then the State's opt-out scheme needs no justification based on consent. Conscientious objectors, it is true, must put forward their case for exemption but this seems reasonable enough—and, in any event, their failure to come forward with their case for exemption does not signal consent. If, by contrast, the PGC does not support a State in requiring participation *unless agents consent*, then an opt-out scheme is quite unacceptable. Where this is the situation, we should not allow a State to get away with an easy justification based on 'presumed' consent; we should put it to the more difficult challenge set by a non consent-based substantive justification.[29] Indeed, there is a double danger presented by opt-outs: first, that the presumed consent is a fiction; and, secondly, that by relying on a (presumed) procedural justification, the State avoids the need to engage with a substantive justification. States, quite simply, should not be allowed to so presume.

### *(iv) Unequivocal Signal*

Our ideal-type requires the signal to be unequivocal. To avoid any misunderstanding about this, it should be said that there is a distinction between requiring that what we treat as an agent's signalling of consent should be unequivocally a signal of consent and requiring that the terms of the consent that is signalled should be unequivocal. If the terms are not unequivocal, we have a problem about the scope and interpretation of the consent

[29] See, further, chs 8 and 9.

given; and this is a matter to which we will return in the next section of the chapter. Our present concern is with the former requirement.

When we have the requirement of an unequivocal signal focused in this way, it is not immediately obvious that it adds to the requirement that we already have for a distinct and definite signal.[30] For a signal to be distinct and definite, we said that it must stand out from the background. To say that the signal must be unequivocal might seem to be saying much the same thing. Such a view is encouraged by *R v Jones*[31] where, it will be recalled, the defendant, who was facing charges relating to a robbery at a post office, entered a not guilty plea at the arraignment but then subsequently failed to appear for the trial. The trial having gone ahead in his absence, the question subsequently arose whether this was compatible with the right to a fair trial as guaranteed by Article 6 of the European Convention on Human Rights. One of the issues to be decided was whether the defendant, by absconding, had waived his right—or, to put this more precisely, whether the defendant, by absconding, had signalled his consent not to stand on the right to a hearing. On one side, Lord Bingham took the view that, by absconding, the defendant had sufficiently signalled his intent; but Lord Rodger (supported by Lord Hoffmann) took a different view:

> Doubtless, the appellant would have been aware that, if eventually brought to justice, he would be punished for absconding to avoid trial. But I see no proper basis for going further and assuming that he would actually have known that he was liable to be tried and sentenced in his absence. I am accordingly unable to draw the conclusion that the appellant had unequivocally waived his right to be present at any trial.[32]

Having been sensitised to the many dimensions of consent, this could be read in more than one way. Lord Rodger might be thought to be doubting that this was an *informed* consent, rather than doubting that the consent had been unequivocally signalled. However, if *Jones* is thought to illustrate a signalling question, we might wonder whether the relevant question is whether the signal is distinct and definite rather than that it should be unequivocal.

In fact, while both requirements (for a distinct and definite and for an unequivocal signal) underline the need for something more than inaction or

[30] Compare the following three provisions of the European Union Directive on Data Protection, Directive 95/46/EC. In Art 2(h) 'the data subject's consent' is defined as meaning 'any freely given specific and informed indication of his wishes by which the data subject signifies his agreement . . .'; Art 7(a) provides that data may be lawfully processed if 'the data subject has unambiguously given his consent'; and Art 8(2)(a) creates an exception for processing especially sensitive data where 'the data subject has given his explicit consent.' Arguably, whereas the first of these provisions seems to relate to non-signalling matters of adequacy, the latter two are concerned with signalling issues (relating, broadly speaking, to what we are calling a distinct and definite signal and an unequivocal signal).

[31] [2002] UKHL 5.

[32] *Ibid*, para 52.

conduct that does not stand out from the background, it is possible that a distinct signal is not unequivocal. For example, if on-line purchasers are to indicate their consent by striking the enter key, we have a signal that satisfies the distinct and definite requirement—indeed, in a structured situation of this kind, the signal is explicit. However, there is the possibility that the enter key is struck accidentally and, so long as there is a real doubt about this, the act is not an unequivocal signal. Similarly, in some contexts, a nod of the head or the holding up of a hand is treated as a signal of consent.[33] However, if there is some cultural uncertainty about this or if the acts in question might have been involuntary, they are equivocal and less than wholly reliable indicators of consent. The requirement of an unequivocal signal, therefore, tackles a further layer of doubt that might arise even where the signal is distinct and definite. It follows that where the law anticipates such doubts by, for example, requiring the double-click of a key or the like, it is responding to the need for an unequivocal signal of consent.

In the light of this, if the concern in *Jones* is as to the reliability of the signal given by the defendant's absence, then the concern might be whether absence stands out sufficiently from the usual background to be treated as a distinct signal or whether, if it is a *distinct and definite* signal, it is nevertheless *equivocal*. In practice, it is difficult to imagine how the law might sensibly remove any equivocation (the defendant is hardly likely to affirm in such circumstances); but, in principle, one's doubt about the signal might be that, although distinct and definite, it is equivocal.

### *(v) Ex Ante*

Arguably, there are several ways in which an ex ante authorisation of action X is materially different to an ex post ratification or release in relation to action X. For example, one might argue that, whereas in the former case no wrong is done, in the latter a wrong is done; that the former serves the principle of reasonable transactional expectation more effectively than the latter; and that, in the latter scenario, the consenting agent might be under a pressure to consent that is absent from the former, and so on. However, these distinguishing features do not speak to the signalling requirement that is our present concern. Are we correct in assuming that ex ante expression of consent is an ideal-typical signalling requirement?

If the focal case is one of agent A consenting to agent B doing act X, or of A consenting to the creation of a new relationship Y with B, then because act X and relationship Y are in the future it is analytically true that the authorising or empowering consent must be given ex ante. However, if we

[33] For example, compare *O'Brien v Cunard SS Co* 154 Mass 272, 28 NE 266 (1891), where the plaintiff, who was in a line of immigrants on board a ship, held up her arm to receive the vaccination that was a pre-condition for landing. In this context, the defendant was entitled to rely on the consent that was apparently signalled; but, in a different context, the raised arm might have been a signal of protest rather than consent.

allow that a 'consent' to act X or to relationship Y may be given ex post, is there any reason to think that an ex post signal of consent is less reliable than an ex ante signal? In both cases, ex ante and ex post, we assume that the signal meets the other ideal-typical requirements—in other words, we assume that the consent is signalled personally, distinctly, and definitely by A. From a signalling perspective then, does it matter whether A so signals his consent ex ante or ex post?

Our guiding principle in setting the signalling ideal-type is that of fidelity to the consenting agent's will. Accordingly, we want to avoid reading A as signalling consent unless A's will is to consent. However, provided that we require that A's signal should be personal, distinct, and definite, it perhaps does not matter whether that signal is given ex ante or ex post. On the face of it, a signal meeting these common requirements is as reliable ex post as ex ante.

Contrary to our working model, therefore, we suggest that ex ante indication is not, as such, an ideal-typical signalling requirement. Whilst there might well be significant differences between authorisation given ex ante and authorisation given ex post, these do not seem to bear on signalling as such, and our ideal-type needs to be revised accordingly.

### *(vi) The Timing of Consent and the Proviso re Delay*

In the light of what we have just argued, it seems that, other things being equal, the principle of fidelity is neutral as between ex ante and ex post signalling (even if the principle of reasonable transactional expectation favours the former). However, in all cases of ex ante authorisation, there will necessarily be some delay between agent A giving the consent and agent B acting on it. Potentially, delay raises issues in relation to both guiding principles. With regard to the principle of fidelity, delay places a question mark against the continuing will of the consenting agent: does A still consent to X? And, with regard to the principle of transactional expectation, delay might raise a doubt in the recipient agent's mind: is it still prudent to rely on A's consent to X? It is the first of these questions that is our immediate concern.

Philosophers have long agonised about the question of the 'heroic agent' who declares that his (primary) will is to do X (typically, at great personal risk or involving sacrifice) and that it is also his will (his secondary will) that others should not release A (the heroic agent) from doing X even if A requests release. When A duly requests release the puzzle is whether we respect A's agency by holding him to X or by releasing him (contrary to his secondary will) for the sake of his well-being (and in the expectation that A will ratify release ex post). Lawyers are likely to be no more successful than ethicists in resolving this riddle—although the law might put in place procedures that make it exceptionally difficult for agents to put themselves in such a bind or, at any rate, to give clear guidance to others faced with the classic dilemma. At all events, for our purposes, what we can draw from this puzzle is the background assumption that a change of will is permissible; for, if A is not permitted to change his mind about doing X, his self-denying ordinance makes no sense. It follows that our thinking about the signalling of consent, where there is a significant delay in acting on the consent, must start with the distinction between cases (i) where A is permitted to change his mind (that is, A may withdraw or modify his consent) and (ii) where A is not permitted to change his mind.

### (a) Where a Change of Mind is Permitted

The puzzle concerning the heroic agent arises, as we have said, against a background that permits agent A to change his mind. In some contexts, it is understood that a consent may be withdrawn or a change of mind permitted. Let us be clear: this is not a context in which agent A consents to X, and then is invited to consent to Y, and then Z, and so on; it is a context in which, if agent A consents to X, the consent may nevertheless be withdrawn before X has been done. For example, where agents become engaged to be married it is understood that unilateral withdrawal, even during the marriage ceremony, is permissible (albeit emotionally devastating to the other agent); and where an agent invokes the law of succession to make a 'final' will and testament it is nevertheless the rule that the will may be revoked or modified at any time before death. If agents do not withdraw in such cases, their consent is signalled: in the case of marriage, the acts of the agents during the marriage ceremony supersede any previous consents; and, if the testator does not change his will, the rules of the institutional set to which the agent has consensually submitted govern.

Later in this chapter, we will discuss a number of cases in which there are questions about the scope and interpretation of consents to medical treatment given by patients. Generally, it is understood that such consents may be withdrawn at any time before it is no longer medically feasible for the procedure to be halted. Whether or not, in practice, patients understand that they retain the option of withdrawal and have the opportunity to do use it, might well be an issue. However, in principle, provided that these conditions are satisfied, there is no real problem about signalling. On the other hand, if we turn the situation around and imagine an agent declaring by way of an 'advance directive' that, in certain circumstances (eg where they are comatose and brain-damaged following an accident), they do not wish to be ventilated or intubated or the like, then we have the makings of a very difficult problem.

Advance directives are capable of giving rise to at least two kinds of problems. One set of problems arises from the scope and interpretation of the particular directive (it might be vague, ambiguous, or incomplete; or the circumstances in which its application is under review might not have been contemplated by the agent who issued the directive). The other problem—

the one with which we are immediately concerned—relates to signalling. Quite simply, how confident can we be that the agent's prior expressed will—not to be treated, or to decline feeding and hydration—remains that agent's will?[34]

Understandably, legal regimes often display some nervousness about recognising and enforcing advance directives. In some cases, this might result in a legal paralysis, leaving the effect of particular advance directives to be determined informally by particular doctors in each particular case. Or, the case-by-case approach might be slightly more structured with it being recognised that, where there is an advance directive, doctors rightly give it *some* weight in forming a judgement as to what is in the patient's best interests or for the purposes of making a substituted judgement as to what the patient would have willed in the circumstances. For agents seeking clarity and calculability, however, these legal positions are unhelpful. Such agents are deprived of the opportunity to exercise control over their futures—or, at any rate, the state of legal uncertainty means that such agents cannot be confident that they have their future under control. Of course, if the legal regime repairs the uncertainty by declaring that advance directives shall be of no legal effect in any circumstances, agents know where they stand but those agents who would wish to assert their will by giving an advance directive are now altogether deprived of this option. It follows that such agents will not be assisted unless the legal regime repairs the uncertainty by putting in place a scheme under which advance directives will be recognised.[35] Where an agent invokes such a scheme, the process should be seen as analogous to invoking the law of succession to write a will. In both cases, the agents who give the directives understand that their directives will be acted upon when the time comes unless they have withdrawn the directives in the meantime; they know that they cannot be sure when precisely (if ever, in the case of an advance directive) the directives will become operative; and they know that there is a risk that, at the operative time, the

[34] Compare Allen Buchanan, 'Advance Directives and the Personal Identity Problem' (1988) 17 *Philosophy and Public Affairs* 277. Buchanan points to various asymmetries between contemporaneous choice in favour of X and choice purporting to favour X at some future time. Some such asymmetries (eg a changing environment or a different context for choice) bear on questions of interpretation; other asymmetries (especially the extent of counselling where choice is contemporaneous) bear on questions of signalling. Buchanan also discusses whether there is a continuity of personal identity, linking the agent who issues an advance directive to the agent who is subsequently treated (or not) in accordance with that directive. If there is a discontinuity, what are the implications? May the advance directive of the previous agent legitimately bind the present agent? And what weight does an advance directive have if, at the time of its proposed application, the previous agent is no longer an agent (such as where the party is in a persistent vegetative state)?

[35] Where an advance directive is fully recognised, those who act in accordance with the directive will be exempt from claims for private (and public) wrongdoing, and those who act against the terms of the directive will be open to claims for private wrong.

directive might not accurately reflect their last subjective will. So be it; this is the risk involved in this particular option; and the initial consent invoking the option must bear the justificatory weight of applying an institutional set in which the risk of the original signal becoming unreliable over time rests with the agent whose decision it is to invoke the set in the first place. If this seems to be too casual about possible changes of will, a legal regime might fine-tune its schemes so that long-term directives have to be renewed periodically. Given that periodic renewal might make more sense for some directives than others, as for some agents more so than others, a sophisticated legal regime might be able to offer agents the option of entering their directives in a scheme that requires regular renewal of their directives.

(b) Where a Change of Mind is not Permitted

In some contexts, the default position is that a change of mind is not permitted; unilateral withdrawal is not an option unless it is expressly reserved. Normally, this is the position with promises and contracts. As Steven Burton[36] has pointed out, the essence of contract is that each party forgoes taking advantage of market opportunities that would otherwise be available. Fairly obviously, where the market moves after the contract has been struck, this will be to the advantage of one of the contractors and to the disadvantage of the other. However, having made their contract, the parties are stuck with the agreed contract price (unless they agree to revise the terms of the contract) and the fact that, the contract aside, the parties would now be guided by different market prices is immaterial. When an agent invokes contract law, he does so on the understanding that the will reflected in the contract will bind even though, by the time that performance is required, that will might be quite different.

Currently, there is considerable debate about whether pre-nuptial agreements should be recognised as legally enforceable. For various reasons—particularly reasons to do with the 'contractualisation' of relationships of love and affection, and the respective jurisdictions of family law and contract law—there is a reluctance to encourage the use of such agreements. This reluctance does not amount to a prohibition on the making of pre-nuptial agreements but legal regimes will not lend their assistance to the enforcement of such agreements. If it is argued that such reluctance is justifiable because agents who signal their consent to a pre-nuptial agreement might come to have very different wills, regretting the terms of the agreement when they kick-in many years later, this is unconvincing. As we have said, the institution of contract law is designed to be proof against such changes of will as circumstances change, whether the circumstances be of an economic or emotional nature; for the purposes of contract law, present

[36] Steven J Burton, 'Breach of Contract and the Common Law Duty to Perform in Good Faith' (1980–81) 94 *Harvard Law Review* 369.

will (at the time of agreement) is deemed to be future will (at the time of performance or enforcement). Of course, if circumstances change in a totally unforeseen and dramatic way, it might be arguable that the terms of the agreement no longer apply;[37] but this raises a question of scope and interpretation (to which we will turn very shortly) rather than one of signalling.

### *(vii) Taking Stock*

In the ideal-typical case, agent A will be taken to have signalled consent to X where consenting to X is A's subjective will and where the consent is distinct and definite, unequivocal, and personal. These criteria apply irrespective of whether A signals consent ex ante or ex post. Guided by the principles of fidelity and transactional expectation, the law will prioritise A's subjective will provided that A has taken reasonable care with signalling; but where A fails in his signalling responsibilities, B's honest and reasonable reliance will be protected.

## III The Scope and Interpretation of Consent

In a broad sense, questions of interpretation arise whenever we ask whether a consent given by an agent covers a particular matter. The reasons prompting such a question are various. For example, it might be that the language of the authorising consent is vague or ambiguous; or it might be that the particular circumstance (although foreseen or foreseeable) was not provided for; or it might be that the situation arising was simply not foreseeable.[38] The well-known case of *Mohr v Williams*[39] illustrates some of these difficulties. There, the plaintiff consented to an operation on the right ear. However, the defendant surgeon, detecting a more pressing problem with the left ear, operated on that ear instead. Did the plaintiff's consent cover the surgeon's action? A bold lawyer might assert that the plaintiff's consent to the operation on 'the right ear' is ambiguous: it could refer to the right

[37] Typically, the default rules of the 'law of contract' will provide for performance to be excused where the circumstances are radically different from those contemplated at the time of agreement; and, in long-term commercial contracts, the parties will incorporate standard provisions for 'force majeure' and the like.

[38] It might even be that the language of the consent is perfectly clear, but its application produces, as some see it, an unjust hardship. For instance, in *Evans v Amicus Healthcare Ltd* [2003] EWHC 2161 (Fam), consent to the use of sperm, eggs, and embryos was on the express basis that the parties were being treated together. After the parties split up, the question of whether the stored embryos could be accessed and used by the female (ex-)partner arose. To deny access and use (particularly where the partner was otherwise unable to have her own children) would cause hardship, but the terms of the consent were clear.

[39] (1905) 95 Minn 261; cf *Bennan v Parsonnet* (1912) 83 NJ Law 20, where the plaintiff, having consented to an operation for a rupture in his left groin, sued the defendant surgeon who operated on what he judged to be a more serious rupture in the plaintiff's right groin.

as opposed to the left ear; or it could refer to either ear depending upon which one the surgeon found to be problematic. Of course, if the plaintiff had authorised the surgeon to operate on 'the problematic ear', the argument that the authorisation was not specific as to the right or left ear as such might look more plausible. Similarly, if the authorisation conferred a broad discretion on the surgeon (for instance, by authorising the surgeon to take reasonable steps to improve the plaintiff's auditory problems), it might have been even easier to argue that the plaintiff's consent covered the operation on the left ear. However, with a consent expressly referring to the patient's right ear, and only to that one ear, the surgeon would need a different strategy, one relying less on the letter of the consent and more on its spirit and intent. Such an argument would thus become one about whether the consent, by implication, could be construed as licensing surgery on the left ear in circumstances that had not been foreseen at the time the consent was given.

For our purposes, it is not essential to draw a distinction between questions that turn on resolving the meaning of vague or ambiguous terms (interpretation, as some might have it, in the narrow sense) and questions of scope; for questions of scope are questions of interpretation in the broad sense; and questions of interpretation in the narrow sense, once determined, fix the scope of the consent. The point is that these questions are of great practical importance; for, like the surgeon in *Mohr v Williams*, in the absence of any other kind of justifying reason, an agent who appeals to a consent needs to have acted within the scope of its covering terms.

The principle of fidelity to an agent's will gives us our starting point. In this light, consider a pair of Canadian cases, *Marshall v Curry*,[40] and *Murray v McMurchy*,[41] designed to puzzle students of medical law. In the former, a surgeon removed a diseased testicle that he discovered during the course of carrying out an operation to repair a hernia; while, in the latter, a surgeon carrying out a Caesarean section found fibroid tumours in the patient's uterine wall and, fearing the risks associated with a further pregnancy, tied the woman's Fallopian tubes. Whereas, in the former case, the additional surgery was held to be justified; in the latter case it was not.

The position taken in *Murray v McMurchy* is very clear. According to Macfarlane J, the default position is that surgery must be justified by reference to the patient's consent or as a matter of necessity. With regard to the latter, responding to the argument put in support of the defendant that 97 per cent of patients would be annoyed if the additional procedure had not been undertaken, Macfarlane J said:

> I do not think that is the point. The point is whether such an emergency existed, whether it was *necessary* that the operation be done, not whether it was then more

40 [1933] 3 DLR 260.
41 [1949] 2 DLR 442 (BCSC).

> *convenient* to perform it. It must be remembered that the effect of the procedure here was to deprive the plaintiff of the possible fulfilment of one of the great powers and privileges of her life. The possibility of her exercising that power or privilege may be subject to risk but where is the necessity for an immediate decision? Where is the urgency? . . . There is . . . no evidence that these tumors were presently at the time of the operation dangerous to her life or health. The evidence is only that they *might* constitute a hazard in the event of a further pregnancy.[42]

But, if the additional procedure could not be justified as a matter of necessity, could it be brought within the scope of the consent? In fact, this seemed to lead to the same answer, because the husband signed a consent for his wife to have a Caesarean section together with 'any further surgical procedure found necessary by the attending physician.'[43] Unless 'necessary' in the context of the consent meant something different to 'necessary' in the context of a defence based on necessity, the defence was in no better shape when it relied on the terms of the consent. Assuming that the reference to 'any further surgical procedure found necessary' simply copied in the common law defence of necessity, the principle of fidelity pointed towards the finding that tying the Fallopian tubes was not within the terms of the consent. Or, to put this slightly differently, the additional procedure was not necessary in the sense that it was logically entailed by the terms of the consent; nor was it necessary in the practical sense that the agreed procedure could not be carried out without also undertaking the additional procedure; and nor was the additional procedure necessary in the sense that its performance was a matter of emergency.

In *Marshall*, at the time of the operation at issue, the defendant surgeon had already carried out running repairs on the plaintiff seaman on several occasions; and, indeed, he continued to do so after the operation. On the evidence, however, Chisholm CJ found that there was neither express nor implied consent to the removal of the testicle, but he accepted the defendant's evidence that, in his professional medical opinion, removal was reasonably necessary to avoid the risk of gangrene and blood-poisoning. On these premises, he said:

> It seems to me that [the] justification must be found either in an assent implied by the circumstances which arose or in some other principle—broader than and outside of any consent—founded on philanthropic or humanitarian considerations.[44]

Having reviewed the authorities, Chisholm CJ concluded:

> I find that the defendant after making the incisions on [the] plaintiff's body, discovered conditions which neither party had anticipated, and which the defendant

[42] [1949] 2 DLR 442 (BCSC), at 445.

[43] *Ibid*, at 443.

[44] [1933] 3 DLR 260, at 264.

> could not reasonably have foreseen, and that in removing the testicle he acted in the interest of his patient and for the protection of his health and possibly his life. The removal I find was in that sense necessary, and it would be unreasonable to postpone the removal to a later date. I come to this conclusion despite the absence of expressed and possibly of implied assent on the part of the plaintiff.[45]

Although the judgment in *Marshall* is much longer than that in *Murray*, and its review of the case-law far more extensive, its conclusion seems less satisfactory. Whilst Chisholm CJ is quite right in recognising that there might be a justification lying beyond consent, there are indications that he is influenced by what he sees as the merits. Clearly, he does not like the idea of a well-respected surgeon, trying to patch up an ancient mariner, being called to account for his best efforts. In consequence, the idea of necessity is stretched and there is even a hint that necessity might be misleadingly represented as an implied assent.

Following the thinking in *Marshall* and *Murray*, justification will turn on whether there is a consent and, if so, how it is interpreted; or, failing that, an appeal to necessity. Our interest is in the former interpretive question. That question brings together the regulative principles of fidelity and transactional expectation coupled with the law's two standard responses, which are to rely on either a literal or a purposive style of interpretation.[46] This prompts two questions. First, in relation to interpretation, how is the principle of fidelity to be accommodated with the principle of transactional expectation? Secondly, is the literal or the purposive style better designed to achieve the required accommodation of regulative principle?

Typically, disputes concerning the scope or interpretation of a consent arise where the parties' understanding is not co-extensive. Often, the recipient agent's reading is more extensive than that of the consenting agent. For example, the pregnant woman in *Murray* who consents to a Caesarean section and additional necessary procedures does not share the recipient's understanding that this covers tying her Fallopian tubes; and the seaman in *Marshall* who consents to an operation on his hernia does not share the recipient's understanding that, by implication, this covers the removal of a testicle. Again, in the context of research, pregnant women who agree to donate tissue for research might not share the recipient's understanding that this extends to commercial exploitation of the research[47]—indeed, a relative who consents to the retention of 'tissue' might not share the recipient's

[45] *Ibid*, at 275–76.

[46] In the context of the interpretation of a rule, where a 'literal' approach is adopted, the interpreter will be guided by the 'plain meaning' of the language used; by contrast, where a 'purposive' approach is adopted, the language used will be read in the light of the assumed spirit and purpose of the rule. See, further, John N Adams and Roger Brownsword, *Understanding Law*, 3rd edn (London, Sweet and Maxwell, 2003), ch 4.

[47] Compare *HOWARD FLOREY/Relaxin* [1995] EPOR 541.

understanding that this extends to the retention of whole organs.[48] And, in a different context, a vendor who consents to the sale of a pub (The Ship) and an adjoining shop might not share the purchaser's understanding that the consent includes the sale of a garden lying behind The Ship and the shop.[49] Assuming that these are all honest misunderstandings, how does the law resolve the conflict of interest between the agents? How is the principle of fidelity to the consenting agent's subjective will to be reconciled with the principle of reasonable transactional expectation? Such is our first question.

When we considered the same conflict of principles in relation to the signalling of consent, we concluded that the principle of fidelity should yield only where the consenting agent intentionally or recklessly misleads the recipient, or where the consenting agent has failed to take reasonable care and the recipient honestly and reasonably misreads the former's intentions. Broadly speaking, in the present context, this general approach seems to be on the right track.[50] It follows that, if we are to deviate from the consenting agent's honestly held subjective understanding, the relevant test is (i) whether the consenting agent's interpretation is reasonable, coupled with (ii) whether the recipient's interpretation is both honest and reasonable. If the consenting agent's interpretation is not reasonable, it is no longer privileged and it must give way to the recipient's honest and reasonable interpretation. However, if the consenting agent's interpretation is reasonable, then this determines the scope of the consent; and the recipient's honest and reasonable interpretation operates as an excuse rather than as a procedural justification. Clearly, given such guiding principles, the reference point for what constitutes a reasonable interpretation bears a considerable weight.

Occasionally, there might be a case where, from the standpoint of any rational person, a particular interpretation is (un)reasonable. For instance, if the express terms of a consent entail some extended application as a matter of logical necessity, it must be reasonable to read the consent as having this extended scope. However, where the claimed necessity is of a practical nature, or where the extension is based on a certain custom and practice, perfectly rational agents, with different spheres of practical experience and customary knowledge, might reasonably differ in their interpretation of the consent. Such a disagreement prompts our second question: namely, is the reasonableness (or unreasonableness) of an interpretation to be judged by reference to the language in which the consent is expressed (as advocated by a literal approach) or by reference to the purpose to which the consent was directed (as advocated by a purposive approach)?

48 See Margaret Brazier, 'Retained Organs: Ethics and Humanity' (2002) 22 *Legal Studies* 550.

49 See *Tamplin v James* (1880) 15 Ch D 215.

50 For the same pattern, see our discussion of informed consent in chs 5 and 6.

There is a huge jurisprudence debating the respective merits of literal and purposive styles of interpretation, particularly in the context of settling disputes relating to the meaning of constitutional and legislative provisions. However, in the context of a transaction between contemporaneous and specifically identifiable agents, our problems are eased in two respects. First, we do not have to address questions arising from the sometimes anachronistic reference to the originating will (for example, the will of the founding fathers back in the eighteenth century or even that of a legislative assembly in the earlier part of the twentieth century)—we need not choose between hard and soft originalism;[51] and, secondly, we do not have to reduce the many individual wills of a legislature to a collective operative intent.[52] Moreover, there will often be an opportunity for the recipient agent to go back to the consenting agent for clarification and confirmation as to the scope of the consent. Nevertheless, even in our simpler case, it is not at all clear which approach, literal or purposive, is the more appropriate.

In favour of literalism, it can said that it acts as an incentive to agents (both the consenting agent and the recipient) to be clear and precise as to the scope of the consent. Moreover, the more specific and comprehensive the articulation of the consent, not only is it less likely that there will be a genuine gap between the parties' understanding, it is more likely that the court will read down the consent in way that is faithful to the parties' actual and reasonable understanding. Even in a straightforward case such as *Mohr v Williams*, the parties could have put the matter beyond all doubt by specifying that the consent was to an operation on 'the right ear, and *only the right (not the left) ear*,' or some such form of words. Literalism might or might not have its intended effect. Where it does not have its intended effect—in other words, where consents are given without a great deal of thought and attention to the language employed—literalism becomes an unreliable indicator of the consenting agent's understanding; and the fidelity principle is imperfectly realised. If, on the other hand, literalism has its intended effect, the giving of consent becomes an exercise in lawyer-like

[51] See, eg, Cass R Sunstein, *Designing Democracy* (Oxford, Oxford University Press, 2001), at 87–89. Sunstein's remarks are framed by the view that the mission of a constitution is to steer a community towards the practice of deliberative democracy (which we discuss in ch 10). Thus, at 89, he says:

> Constitutional rights, as Americans understand them, are very much a product of interpretive practices that begin with the original understanding but do not end there. If a proposed method of constitutional interpretation would make a constitutional democracy worse, why should anyone adopt it? Courts do far better with soft originalism [ie treating the original understanding as relevant but not decisive], alongside incompletely theorized agreements, analogical reasoning, a general posture of humility, and concern for the goal of ensuring a well-functioning system of deliberative democracy. (our addition in brackets)

[52] Seminally, see GC MacCallum, 'Legislative Intent' (1966) 75 *Yale Law Journal* 754.

drafting. This is not always practicable and, indeed, in relationships predicated on trust such attention to the precise contours of the consent might be wholly counter-productive. However, the most serious objection to literalism (where it has its intended effect) is that, in many transactions, the recipient (repeat-players and the like) will have drafted the consent form, typically in terms that spell out the consent in a way that protects their interests, and then the form will have been simply presented to the consenting agent. In such circumstances (which are by no means uncommon), to permit the recipient to plead the reasonableness of its interpretation and the unreasonableness of the other agent's reading by reference to the language of the consent form is unattractive. Once again, literalism does not reliably indicate the consenting agent's will.

Such considerations might lead us to think that a purposive approach is a better bet and, certainly, the tendency of the common law has been to move away from literalism towards more purposive styles of interpretation. The attraction of purposivism is that it allows for some correction of the language by reference to the context. For example, if, in *Mohr v Williams*, it was clear from the context that an operation on the right ear was in contemplation, purposivism would correct for any slips in the paperwork suggesting that the consent was for an operation on the left ear. Similarly, if the consent forms were presented for signature without the patient having a clear sense of what the paperwork said he was agreeing to, purposivism could override the language of the consent form in favour of a contextual reading of what the patient was really agreeing to. In other words, purposivism draws a distinction between the 'paper' consent and the 'real' consent—or, as Stewart Macaulay has put it in a contractual context, the 'paper deal' and the 'real deal'.[53] In principle, this promises to be a more reliable indicator of the consenting agent's will. However, such a well-intentioned strategy can develop into a highly speculative approach, and it sends out the possibly counter-productive message that agents need not over-concern themselves with the language of consents. Most seriously, purposivism seems to put recipients in difficulty because it deprives them of what looks like the best evidence of the terms of the consent. To the extent that purposivism has such an impact, the law fails to do justice to the principle of transactional expectation.

If neither literalism nor purposivism recommends itself as an across-the-board approach, might we operate instead on a contextual case-by-case basis? Or, is it plausible to treat literalism as the default approach unless the circumstances indicate that it is inappropriate, in which event purposivism becomes the appropriate approach?

[53] Stewart Macaulay, 'The Real and the Paper Deal: Empirical Pictures of Relationships, Complexity and the Urge for Transparent Simple Rules' (2003) 66 *Modern Law Review* 44.

Let us try to reverse engineer a situation in which a literal approach would be appropriate—that is, appropriate to determine the reasonableness of both the consenting agent's and the recipient agent's understanding. What we are looking for is a context in which what the consenting agent says captures exactly what that agent means, one in which the terms of the consent have been carefully considered by the consenting agent. It is not essential that the language of the consent has been drafted by the consenting agent. However, formal reflection on the letter of the consent is not sufficient. Crucially, to be confident that the language accurately reflects the agent's will, the interpretive question now at issue needs to have been addressed and resolved. For example, in *Murray*, it is arguable that the language of the consent is ambiguous. The reference to additional 'necessary' surgical procedures might simply copy in the common law defence (which presupposes a severe or life-threatening condition that must be dealt with immediately) or it might authorise surgery that is essential (perhaps presupposing a serious condition that is better dealt with sooner rather than later) or at least highly desirable. This interpretive choice invites a familiar argument between those who contend that the former reading cannot be right because it adds nothing to the consent (the common law already provides this authorisation) and those who contend that the latter reading is too vague and that the former is meaningful as a precautionary notice. Unless the question of just how far the authorisation to undertake additional surgery extends has been addressed and resolved by the consent, the language is not a wholly reliable indicator—and neither side can rely on it to argue for the reasonableness of their particular interpretation.

This suggests that literalism will be an appropriate approach in relatively few situations. Some situations will be relatively informal; others will be more formal but will involve loose drafting or inattention to the detail that really matters; and others will disclose recipient-sided dictation of the consent. In these cases, a purposive approach is the fall-back. Indeed, in the case of one-sided dictation, purposivism makes good instrumental sense; for, if repeat-players and the like know that their standard forms will not be mechanically applied in accordance with their literal terms, they will have reason to enrich the context in a way that both raises the awareness of the other contracting party and brings them more fully into the transaction.

We can follow through the implications of a purposive fall-back position by considering how this might work in a case such as in *Greenberg v Miami Children's Hospital Research Institute*.[54] There, Greenberg and others offered to assist with a research project designed to locate the gene for Canavan's disease.[55] The initial approach and offer of assistance with the research was

[54] See 2002 WL 1483266 (ND Ill); 02-22244-CIV-MORENO (Miami); and Graeme Laurie, *Genetic Privacy* (Cambridge, Cambridge University Press, 2002) at 322–23.

[55] We set out the background more fully in ch 8.

probably expressed in an informal and relatively expansive manner. The research proposal came from the Canavan families and they were obviously eager to co-operate. Without any decisive articulation of consent, literalism has nothing to latch on to and a purposive interpretation is the only option. The problem in *Greenberg* is not so much that we must resort to purposivism but that, relative to its own sphere of understanding, each side has its own particular objectives and its own reasonable interpretation of the scope of the consent. From the side of the Canavan families, it is reasonable to view the consent as a vehicle for research (that is, for research 'pure and simple'); from the researchers' side, however, the culture of research and development suggests that it is reasonable to view the consent as a vehicle for research possibly extending through to commercial exploitation. If, relative to its own sphere, each side is taking a reasonable view, the upshot is that we do not have consent to exploitation. The principle of fidelity demands that we keep faith with the honest and reasonable understanding of the consenting agents; but we must also excuse the reliance of the researchers who have acted on a reasonable reading of the consent.

Let us suppose that the researchers in *Greenberg* entertained some doubt about whether the families had consented to commercial exploitation. Given the close working relationship between the researchers and the families, there would seem to be little practical difficulty in seeking clarification. Indeed, in such circumstances, double-checking the scope of the consent would surely be the natural precaution. If the researchers went ahead without confirming that they were still acting within the scope of the consent, they would no longer have reasonable grounds for believing that they were acting under the cover of the consent and we should not permit the consent to be pleaded as justification. As we remarked with reference to 'opt-out' schemes, legal regimes should resist any tendency towards lazy reliance on consent; if the researchers have such good reasons for going ahead without confirming consent, they should be required to justify their activities by reference to those (non consent-reliant) reasons.

Where the original consent does not expressly provide for the circumstances in question, it might be feasible for the relevant agent to the transaction to clarify the scope of the consent or to issue a fresh covering consent. Hence, in cases such as *Greenberg* and *Relaxin*,[56] the researchers might have gone back to their sources for express authorisation; and, provided that the sources' confirming or fresh consents met the usual criteria of validity, all would be well. Even where the circumstances are of a kind or degree that was wholly unforeseeable at the time the original consent was given, the parties might be able to cure the limitations of the original consent by fresh agreement. And, again, provided that the usual criteria of validity are satisfied, consent continues to give (procedural) justificatory

[56] Note 48 above.

cover. What if, however, the parties to the original transaction cannot reach agreement on how to proceed in the new circumstances?

Let us suppose that, in *Greenberg*, the researchers go back to the families to seek their approval for commercial exploitation of the research but the families refuse to consent. If the families have a non-contractual right (say, some species of property right) that the research is not commercially exploited, then the researchers will commit a private wrong if they proceed without the families' consent. This does not mean that the researchers might not be able to justify proceeding, all things considered (by reference to competing rights); but consent will not be their justificatory platform.[57] If the families contracted with the researchers, then (in the absence of express provision) their relationship with the researchers will be regulated by the institutional default rules (such as the doctrines of force majeure and frustration that are triggered by unforeseen and unprovided-for circumstances). Typically, these default rules will provide for the unravelling of the relationship, releasing the parties from further performance and adjusting the balance of benefit and expense between the parties. As we suggested earlier, we can trace the justification for the operation of these default rules to the parties' initial originating consent in engaging the particular institutional set.[58]

## IV Withdrawal and Refusal of Consent

In this final part of the chapter, we consider briefly two cases of the negation of consent. We start with withdrawal, which, ex hypothesi, only becomes an issue where consent has already been given. If consent, properly interpreted, was not given, a subsequent 'retraction' is not so much a withdrawal as an assertion of the limits of the earlier authorisation or, possibly, of what was actually a refusal. In the case of a refusal, of course, there has never been a 'yes'; the party who refuses says 'no'—and it is fundamental to Gewirthian theory that the will of an agent who says 'no' is respected equally to the will of an agent who says 'yes'.

### *(i) Withdrawal of Consent*

The possibility of a consent being withdrawn is a matter that we have raised already in this chapter. In some contexts, we have said, it will be understood that a consent may be withdrawn; in others, it is understood that a consent, once given, is not open to unilateral revocation. Consent to undergo a medical procedure or to participate in a research trial exemplifies the former; consent to a binding contractual agreement exemplifies the latter. Sometimes, too, the question of timing is critical—we gave the examples of

[57] See further ch 8.

[58] Likewise the justification for employing the general rules for the interpretation of agreements within the rule-set of the particular 'law of contract' that has been consensually engaged.

engagements (leading to marriage) and wills (leading to final dispositions) as consents that are revocable but that are capable of maturing into arrangements that are beyond simple unilateral withdrawal. Is there any underlying pattern to such examples?

As a matter of principle, it is tempting to think that fidelity to the will of the consenting agent entails that it is always open to an agent who consents (at time 1) to withdraw that consent when (at time 2) such reflects the will of that agent. However, we know that such a licence to withdraw at will would undermine much of the practical utility of consent as a procedural justification; for the recipient of a consent would hesitate to rely on it in such circumstances. Although this line of reasoning benefits from the counterweight of the principle of reasonable expectation, it surely sets off on the wrong foot. Fidelity to the will of an agent does not signify that agents may will whatever they like and have the law secure their wishes. Rather, agents may, if they so will, consent to some variation within the terms of the background scheme of rights and duties, or they may, if they so will, consent to the creation of a new relationship. Where agents thus consent to a change of position or to the engagement of some rule-set or the like, their will should be respected. However, fidelity demands that it is the will of agents within the overarching Gewirthian framework that is to be respected, not the will of agents at large. It follows that, if there is a pattern in relation to an agent's right to withdraw, we might begin to detect it by focusing on the two principal contexts in which consent will operate: first, where consent signals an agent's willingness to a change of position; and, secondly, where it signals the creation of a new relationship.

For the sake of illustration, we can recall a case hypothesised in our introductory chapter. Here, B, who is in need of storage space for his car, asks A whether he (A) would allow B to store his car in A's garage. A consents to this arrangement. The question arises when A decides that he no longer wishes to continue with the arrangement and signals to B that his consent is withdrawn. What then?

### (a) Withdrawal in Relation to an Agreed Change of Position

To begin with, let us suppose that the arrangement between A and B is entirely gratuitous. B does not pay for the privilege of storing his car in A's garage; and nor is there any implicit expectation of reciprocation. Formally, what we have here is that A is consenting to a change of position in relation the background property rights that hold as between himself and B. Were it not for A's consent, B would be trespassing (violating A's property rights) by using the garage. On the face of it, the position with regard to withdrawal is entirely straightforward: A may withdraw his consent. To this, we should note three qualifying remarks.

First, our assumption is that A retains full property rights in the garage (and access to it). A is waiving part of the benefit that he has by virtue of his property rights, but no part of the rights themselves are being transferred to B (by gift or exchange). This is not to say that there might not be cases in which the nature of the transaction is disputed or open to interpretation; and there might be cases in which A's long-standing acquiescence in B's *unauthorised* use of his garage is treated as a transfer of property rights. However, our hypothetical has none of these complications.

Secondly, our assumption is that A may withdraw at will, without having to give any particular reason for his withdrawal. Once again, this is not to deny the possibility that A may consent on terms that specify that withdrawal will take place only if certain contingencies arise (most obviously if A needs the garage space for his own car); or that there might be disputes about what was implicitly understood between the parties, or what is normal practice in such cases, or the like. However, we are treating our hypothetical as brutally simple: the understanding is that A may withdraw at will.

Thirdly, our assumption is that A may withdraw without giving B a special period of notice. This means that, once B has been notified of the withdrawal and has had a reasonable opportunity to remove his car from A's garage, B will be violating A's rights if the car has not been removed. Once again, this is not to deny that there might be all manner of disputes about the period of notice; and, indeed, even on our straightforward assumptions, there is inevitably some interpretive leeway in relation to B's 'reasonable opportunity'. Nevertheless, in the absence of contrary indication from A, the default assumption applies: A may simply notify B that his consent is withdrawn and B must accept that the garaging of the car is no longer authorised.

Allowing that the waters might often be muddied by particular questions of interpretation and understanding, is this simple case generalisable? It seems to us that it is. In other words, where A consents to a change of position, relaxing the benefit of a right that A has in relation to B, the default rule is that A may withdraw the consent at will. This is perfectly consistent with the principle of reasonable expectation (B must understand that A's authorisation is revocable) and it does not undermine the utility of A's consent (B enjoys the privilege of using A's garage for the time being and, of course, it is always open to B to ask A to give longer notice of an intention to withdraw, and so on).

### (b) Withdrawal in relation to the Consensual Creation of a New Relationship

Now let us change the hypothetical so that A either gives or sells the garage to B or contracts with B for the use of the garage. Where the background regime of rights and duties puts A in the position of owner of the garage, then A is empowered, if he so wills, to activate various kinds of transaction involving the creation of a new relationship with B with regard to the garage. If A gives or sells the garage to B, the effect of the transaction is to install B as the new owner of the garage. If A enters into a contract with B under which B agrees to pay a sum of money for the use of the garage, then the effect of this transaction is not to install B as owner of the garage but merely to purchase for B (within the terms of the contractual licence) a right for the time being to use the garage.

Where a new relationship is so created, A's right to withdraw is not reserved by the background regime as such; for rights held under the background regime are transferred or, in the case of a contractual licence, powers are exercised. Whether or not A has a right to withdraw in such circumstances will depend upon the terms and conditions that apply to the transaction in question. So, for example, one would normally expect a 'gift' to be irrevocable. If A says to B that he is giving the garage to B but that he reserves the right to revoke the gift, this seems to be a contradiction in terms. If, however, A stipulates that he reserves the right to revoke the gift within the next seven days (or some such period), then we might treat this as a gift once the period has elapsed without revocation—but, then, properly analysed, the gift itself (which only comes into effect once the period for revocation has elapsed) is not revocable. In the case of a sale or a contractual licence, A's originating consent will bring into play the governance regime represented by the local law of sale or contract. Unless explicitly signalled by A, the originating consent will not be revocable, and any right to withdraw will be determined by the local law that has been engaged. Such local law might grant to sellers or licensors a cooling-off period within which they may change their minds and unilaterally cancel, but, in the ordinary way of things, the default rules within such rule-sets will not countenance unilateral withdrawal. Accordingly, if A wants to withdraw from the arrangement with B, it will need to be by mutual agreement.

Is this example generalisable? Again, we suggest that it is. Where A's consent signals the creation of a new relationship, the authorising consent will be taken as binding unless A explicitly reserves the right to withdraw (in which case, as with the example of a 'gift', we might need to think twice about how to characterise the transaction). In the absence of such an explicit reservation, A's right to withdraw will be governed by the particular rule-set that has been engaged: some rule-sets might permit unilateral revocation, others will not.

It remains only to say that where a contractual relationship is created, A and B will have rights and duties against one another that arise under the terms of the contract made. For example, B might have a contractual right to use A's garage for 24 months in return for paying A a monthly sum of $100. Just as A may consent to a modification of background rights and duties, so too A may consent to a modification of the contractual rights and duties. For instance, A might consent to B paying only $50 each month while B has some unexpected financial difficulties.[59] If A then wishes to

[59] Compare the seminal approach of Denning J (as he then was) to just such a situation in *Central London Property Trust v High Trees House Ltd* [1947] KB 130.

withdraw this concession and reinstate the agreed contractual terms, the law of contract will make provision for this possibility (including what constitutes reasonable notice and the like). Such provision for withdrawal of a contractual concession might look very much like that governing the withdrawal of an agreed change of position with regard to background rights and duties, but, where the rule-set has been consensually engaged, it takes on a life of its own allowing it to make its own distinctive provision for withdrawal.

Once this underlying pattern is uncovered, it becomes rather easier to determine whether the consenting agent has the right to withdraw. However, these cases are still context-dependent and open to dispute about whether the right to withdraw has been qualified or reserved and, if so, in what terms. This takes us back to the questions of scope and interpretation that we have been dealing with and which we can pick up again as we turn to cases of refusal of consent.

### *(ii) Refusal*

Where the justificatory function of consent is abused, where it is assumed that 'consent' will be given, where the taking of consent is routine, perfunctory, and casual, where recipients will not take 'no' as an answer, and where consent operates as a convenient justificatory rationalisation, an agent's refusal might be viewed as pathological. In such catch-22 contexts, those who consent will be treated as having the capacity to say 'yes' or 'no'; but those who refuse will not. From many ethical perspectives, such practices will seem perverse. From a Gewirthian perspective, such practices—to put the point as dispassionately as possible—make the mistake of thinking that the giving of consent is more significant than the withholding of consent. According to the fidelity principle, the agent's subjective will should govern: if that will is to consent, so be it; if it is to refuse, again, and no less, so be it.

Once refusals of consent and the giving of consent are understood to be equally significant, it follows that the questions of signalling and of scope and interpretation that we have been discussing in this chapter are to be resolved in a common way. The way that we have suggested essentially involves prioritising the consenting or refusing agent's subjective will unless that agent has contributed to the recipient's misunderstanding. We can state quite shortly what this means in the particular case of a subjectively willed refusal of consent.

With regard to signalling, if A subjectively intends to refuse to consent to X, then a legal regime should normally treat A as signalling a refusal to B. Provided, however, that if A is responsible for misleading B (by apparently signalling consent, whether intentionally, recklessly, or carelessly) and subject to the honesty and reasonableness of B's reading of A's signals, A may be treated as having signalled consent.

Disputes concerning the scope and interpretation of a refusal might centre on a simple refusal (for example, the patient who refuses to submit to examination or treatment *tout court*) or on a refusal that is more specific and by way of a qualification to a consent (for example, the patient who consents to surgery on the right ear but not to surgery on the left, or the patient who consents to surgery using local but not general anaesthetic). Where the explicit refusal is set against a background of refusal, it is difficult to find a basis for consent; but where the refusal is by way of qualification to a consent, there is more room for debate. At all events, the governing approach once again is that legal regimes should be guided by the fidelity principle, seeking to give effect to the originating agent's honestly held subjective understanding. If that understanding is that a refusal has been given, then legal regimes should treat this as a 'no' unless the 'refusing' agent's understanding is unreasonable and the recipient's interpretation is both honest and reasonable.

Finally, it is worth cautioning against any misunderstanding of these short remarks on refusal. The brevity of our discussion does not indicate that there is little of interest or concern here. On the contrary, to violate a right in the teeth of the right-holder's refusal is as disrespectful of agency as to ignore a right-holder's consent. Once it is understood that refusals and consents are simply different, but equally significant, expressions of a right-holder's or a power-holder's will, it is axiomatic that refusals, like consents, must be taken seriously.

## V Conclusion

Legal regimes that aspire to be compliant with Gewirthian principles will recognise the importance of keeping faith with the will of an agent. Whether the agent is operating rights or powers, whether it is the agent's will to give, to withdraw, or to refuse consent, the fidelity principle demands that the law stays close to the agent's intentions and understanding of the situation. However, the interests of recipient agents must also be given some weight, for agents who are unable to rely on transactions are hindered in the exercise of their generic freedom. The tension between these regulative principles is a recurring theme of our discussion. Wherever legal regimes seek to set the conditions for an adequate consent or to adjudicate disputes such as those concerning the signalling of consent (or refusal) and the scope or interpretation of consent (or refusal), the tension must be addressed.

With regard to the issues raised in this chapter, we have suggested that the key to resolving this tension is to develop principles of responsibility on the originating agent's side, coupled with standards of honesty and reasonableness on the part of the recipient agent. Elaborating this scheme, legal regimes will find that signalling disputes cannot be addressed by taking a strict 'subjective' or a strict 'objective' approach; it is not a matter of choosing one or the other. Similarly, where questions of scope and interpretation arise, legal regimes should not respond by choosing a literal or a purposive approach for all cases. To do justice to Gewirthian principles, simple choices will not suffice; more complex accommodations are required. Some of these accommodations will be controversial, but, as ever, we can ask no more of legal officials than that they take account of the right considerations, that they think straight, and that they make an honest and good faith attempt to apply the relevant regulative principles.

Part Three

# CONSENT IN THE LAW I: QUESTIONS OF NECESSITY AND SUFFICIENCY

# 8

# The Necessity, Sufficiency, and Relevance of Consent I: Private Wrong and Private Empowerment

## I Introduction

In our introductory overview, we remarked that modern legal systems, reflecting the importance attached to individual (human) rights, increasingly identify consent as a relevant consideration. Indeed, this might be an understatement. Where consent is regarded as focal rather than merely relevant, the seeds are sown for an emergent 'cult of consent': for, just as there is a tendency to view doctrines of human rights in isolation from their foundations in respect for human dignity,[1] so there is a temptation to view consent in a way that is detached from its essential ties with human (or, more accurately, agency) rights (and their foundations in human dignity).[2] If our perception of consent is evolving in this way, it needs to be corrected. For it is a fallacy to view consent as a free-standing ethical or legal requirement. To the contrary, consent assumes relevance only as a derivative of a prior rights-based will theory.

Those (characteristically, modern) legal regimes that recognise the relevance of consent might reflect its significance by according it various degrees of justificatory weight. At strongest, the actual giving of consent (or, as a second-best surrogate, making every possible effort to obtain consent) will be the only justificatory reason recognised—the giving of consent (or its second-best surrogate), and nothing but the giving of consent (or its second-best surrogate), will do; procedural justification alone is recognised. At weakest, the giving of consent will have some justificatory bearing but it will

[1] On the linkage between human dignity, human rights, and the context of vulnerable agency, see Deryck Beyleveld and Roger Brownsword, *Human Dignity in Bioethics and Biolaw* (Oxford, Oxford University Press, 2001). See, too, ch 9 below.

[2] Consider, for example, the way in which the principle of consent features as one of the Human Genetic Commission's (HGC's) core ethical principles, see *Inside Information* (London, May 2002) at 35–40. Here, from an overarching principle of respect for persons, the HGC derives secondary principles of privacy, confidentiality, non-discrimination, *and consent*. However, consent is not a free-standing principle (on the same level as privacy, confidentiality, and non-discrimination), and not even a free-standing derivative principle; rather, it is implicated in the right to privacy, the right to confidentiality, and the right against discrimination.

be just one consideration in a range of recognised justificatory elements. To put this more formally, we can say that, in principle, and assuming that we are dealing with an agent (or agents) having both the capacity and competence to consent,[3] a legal system might—relative to the distinctive (justificatory and empowering) functions of consent—treat the giving of a valid consent[4] properly signalled[5] as:

(i) both a necessary and a sufficient condition;
(ii) a sufficient but not a necessary condition;
(iii) a necessary but not a sufficient condition; or
(iv) neither a necessary nor a sufficient condition (albeit still a relevant condition).

We start this chapter (in section II) with some preliminary remarks on the distinction between (i) the necessity and (ii) the sufficiency of consent as a justificatory reason. Having undertaken this groundwork, we are able to focus on questions concerning the necessity and sufficiency of consent in the domain of private law, dealing first with *private wrong* (in section III) and then with *private empowerment* (in section IV).

## II The Necessity and Sufficiency of Consent: Some Groundwork

Consider the hypothetical case of John who will die unless he receives a heart transplant. Alas, demand for organ transplants far exceeds supply. In desperation, John asks whether there are any other options. He is told that a research group that has been working on modifying organs taken from pigs to render them suitable for transplantation into humans is recruiting volunteers. John duly volunteers for the trial and he consents to the transplantation procedure. In such circumstances, provided that the surgery actually carried out remains within the scope of the patient's consent (and provided that there is no suggestion of professional negligence),[6] we would expect a modern rights-orientated legal regime to hold that there is *no private wrong* as between the parties. That is to say, we would expect such a

[3] On which, see ch 4.

[4] On the conditions of validity, see chs 5 and 6. On the 'giving of consent', it is to be noted that this might be restricted (quite literally and without exception) to the actual giving of consent or it might be broadened to allow, exceptionally, for second-best surrogate consent justification. Such second-best justifications might be very narrowly defined (as where *every possible* effort to obtain consent is the test) or defined more broadly to include all reasonable efforts or such efforts as are reasonably practicable. On paper, such broader formulations remain connected to the primary justification (viz, the actual giving of consent), but, in their application, such tests might depart from the spirit and intent of consent-centred justification.

[5] On which, see ch 7.

[6] On the scope and interpretation of consent, see ch 7. On the distinction between intentional and negligent private wrong, see our introductory remarks below.

legal regime to treat the patient's consent as at least a sufficient justificatory condition, as at least a sufficient procedural justification for the surgeon's intervention should the patient subsequently complain of a violation of (private) right.[7] In practice, however, legal regimes are guided by many background considerations; and, in principle, a particular system might take any of the four positions indicated in our Introduction to this chapter.

First (as in (i) above), a legal system might decree that the patient's consent is not merely sufficient but that it is also a necessary condition for the avoidance of private wrong. Where such significance is attached to the patient's consent, the surgeon's intervention will be justified if, and only if, the patient has duly consented.

Secondly (as in (ii) above), the legal system might regard the patient's consent as sufficient (for the purpose of negating private wrong), but not necessary. If so, reasons other than the patient's consent (that is, reasons other than the primary 'actual giving of consent' or one of its consent-centred surrogates)[8] will be recognised as justifications. For example, a surgeon might be able to respond to a patient's complaint of private wrongdoing where (notwithstanding that the patient has the capacity and competence to consent, but either has not done so or has actually explicitly refused to consent) it is judged that the intervention is in the patient's best interests.[9] In such a setting, a medical team that carried out a xenotransplantation in order to save John's life, but without his consent to such a procedure, might nevertheless have a defence.

Thirdly (as in (iii) above), the legal system might always require the patient's consent (rendering it a necessary condition) but without treating it as sufficient. Before we conclude that a legal system takes such a position, however, there are two distinctions that we need to bear in mind. One distinction is that between *private* wrong and *public* wrong, typically between the commission of a tort and the commission of a crime. The other distinction is that between an *intentional* private wrong and a *negligent* private wrong.

With regard to the first of these distinctions, it is important not to fall into the trap of assuming that there is a simple symmetry between the adequacy of consent for the purpose of negating a *private* wrong and its adequacy in relation to responding to a charge of *public* wrong.[10] For instance, where

[7] Of course, the fact that John consents to the procedure is no answer to a non-consenting third party who is infected as a result of the xenotransplantation.

[8] See n 4 above.

[9] Of course, whether or not such a legal position is coherent or rationally defensible is another matter.

[10] If A does no *private* wrong to B because B consents, it does not follow that A and B do no *private* wrong to C. The fallacy that we are highlighting in the text, however, is different: it is that, if A does no *private* wrong to B or C or any other agent, it does not follow that A does no *public* wrong.

xenotransplantation is judged to be a public health hazard, a legal system might decree that such a procedure may be lawfully carried out only if (a) the patient consents and (b) the procedure is specifically authorised by a regulatory body that maintains oversight of experimental medicine. On closer analysis, however, this statement of the legal position might prove to be elliptical, compressing the position taken in relation to both private and public wrong. Fully stated, the legal position might be (i) that the surgeon does no *private* wrong vis-à-vis the patient, provided that the patient has consented, and (ii) that the surgeon does no *public* wrong, provided that the patient has consented and that the regulatory body has licensed the particular xenotransplantation. If this is an accurate statement of the legal position then, for the purposes of responding to alleged *private* wrongdoing, the consent of the patient is at least a sufficient condition, possibly a necessary and sufficient condition, but definitely not a necessary but not sufficient condition; while, for the purpose of responding to an alleged *public* wrong, the patient's consent is a necessary but not a sufficient condition. To find a pure example of consent being treated as a necessary but not sufficient condition for the purposes of private wrong, we need a case in which, to respond to the patient's complaint of private wrong, the surgeon must show that the patient consented and must also meet some other condition (for example, that the patient was counselled, or required to take a second opinion, or something of that kind—although some such conditions may be seen as derivative of the (sole) consent requirement).

With regard to the second distinction, that between intentional and negligent private wrong, modern tort regimes will recognise that patients can be wronged by both intentionally inflicted harm and by professional negligence. The fact that a patient consents to a proposed medical intervention might suffice to negate an accusation of intentional wrongdoing but it does not necessarily cover the negligent strand of the surgeon's conduct. However, this should not be taken to indicate that consent is a necessary but not a sufficient justificatory condition. There are several ways in which a physician might do a prima facie wrong to a patient—for example, wrongs within the trespass group are intentional and, as such, they are distinguishable from negligent wrongs, which might concern the selection of the treatment option, the execution of the treatment, or the quality of information supplied to the patient. In principle, a patient might have a specific right relating to each of these wrongs. Accordingly, before we conclude that a legal regime treats the patient's consent as a necessary but not a sufficient condition, we must follow the right line of inquiry. The question to be asked is *not* whether a consent that is necessary in relation to an intentional wrong is sufficient in relation to some other kind of (eg negligent) wrong. The questions to be asked are: (i) whether a consent that is necessary in relation to an intentional wrong is also sufficient in relation to that wrong; and (ii) whether a consent that is necessary in relation to a negligent wrong is also sufficient in relation to that wrong. We shall have a little more to say about this later in the chapter.

To return to the four basic positions that a legal system might adopt, there is a final possibility within this set. Here (as in (iv) above), again for the purpose of responding to a charge of private wrong, a legal system might treat the patient's consent as neither a necessary nor a sufficient condition. This signifies that (a) even if the patient has *not* consented, surgical intervention may still be justified (perhaps, in a paternalistic culture, where the physician judges that intervention is in the patient's best interests), and (b) even if the patient has consented, this alone will not justify surgical intervention. In other words, where (iv) is the case, this amounts to saying that, consent-based justification is not the only recognised justificatory reason and that, insofar as a consent-based justification is recognised, the giving of consent is not the only requirement. In this fourth scenario, the legal system takes quite a complex approach to consent but, in both dimensions of necessity and sufficiency, the position adopted apparently signals a diminution in the weight and significance attached to consent.

Although the position that we have just hypothesised treats consent as less important, it still allows some room for consent-based justification, at any rate where consent is accompanied by whatever other considerations are stipulated. A further possibility, however, is that consent-based justifications simply are not recognised; that is, a legal regime might deem it irrelevant to plead consent as a purported justification for what is regarded as a private wrong. Whilst it would not be incorrect to say that, where consent is treated as *irrelevant*, it is treated as neither a necessary nor a sufficient justificatory reason, nevertheless such a statement might be misleading. For, quite clearly, there is a significant difference between allowing consent to justify in some circumstances (but not treating it as either a necessary or a sufficient condition) and rejecting it as irrelevant for justificatory purposes. If a regime systematically rejects the relevance of consent where a private wrong is alleged, it cannot be founded on respect for human rights and the autonomy of agents.[11]

As we have pointed out, we need to be careful to distinguish between consent as a response to an alleged private wrong and consent as defence to an alleged public wrong. This is not to suggest that one may not attempt to construct a consent-based defence to a charge of public wrong by relying on the consensual nature of the alleged criminal conduct—in other words, although it is not usually expressed in quite this way, one may

[11] Such systematic rejection of the relevance of consent should not be confused with the insistence that, unless there is a prima facie private wrong (as judged by recognised private rights), consent is not relevant. Such an insistence is perfectly proper in a rights-centred regime. It is a fallacy to suppose that what is not otherwise a private wrong can be transformed into one by dint of an absence of consent. See below at 242.

contend that, if it is conceded that the consent of the participants would suffice to answer any charge of *private* wrong, then it should also suffice to negate any charge of *public* wrong. Thus, in legal systems around the world, we encounter a much-debated question where agents who are alleged to have committed a *public* wrong seek to defend themselves by reference to the consent of the parties involved (such consent negating any *private* wrong). For example, in France, we find it being argued that *consensual* dwarf-throwing should not be treated as contrary to ordre public;[12] in England, we have heard the argument that *consensual* sado-masochism should not be treated as involving criminal offences against the person;[13] in North America and Europe, it has been argued that *consensual* assisted suicide should not be classified as a criminal offence;[14] and, on both sides of the Atlantic, there is a major body of jurisprudence concerning the legal treatment of consensual homosexuality.[15] In some cases, the consent justification has been rejected, whether because it is treated as irrelevant (the ruling legal paradigm not being rights-based) or because it is not sufficient; in other cases it has been accepted. Discussion of such cases, however, will be postponed until the next chapter, in which we consider a number of matters concerning the necessity and sufficiency of consent in relation to *public* wrongs.

In the present chapter, our focus is on the *private* domain, on such fundamental legal building blocks as tort, contract, and property. In this domain, the background framework for private right and wrong is laid out by the regime of tort law (or delict, in civilian legal systems), in which recognised interests, relating to such matters as person, reputation, and property, are protected. If tort is designed to stabilise social relations by protecting interests as they currently stand (that is, to preserve the status quo),[16] contract introduces the dynamic for change.[17] Contract, as it were, sets the framework for private empowerment, typically being employed to

[12] Conseil d'Etat (October 27, 1995) req nos 136–727 (Commune de Morsang-sur-Orge) and 143–578 (Ville d'Aix-en-Provence).

[13] *R v Brown* [1993] 2 All ER 75; and *Laskey, Jaggard and Brown v United Kingdom* (1997) 24 EHRR 39.

[14] In North America, see *Washington v Glucksberg* 117 S Ct 2258; and *Re Rodriguez and Attorney-General of British Columbia* (1993) 107 DLR 4th 342. In Europe, see *Regina on the Application of Mrs Dianne Pretty v DPP and Secretary of State for the Home Department* [2001] UKHL 61; *Case of Pretty v The United Kingdom* (2002) ECHR 2346/02, April 29; [2002] 35 EHRR 1.

[15] Starting with the classic exchange between Patrick Devlin, *The Enforcement of Morals* (Oxford: Oxford University Press, 1965) and HLA Hart, *Law, Liberty and Morality* (London: Oxford University Press, 1963); and continuing in the courts with, for example, *Bowers v Hardwick* 106 S Ct 2841 and, most recently, *Lawrence v Texas* 123 S Ct 2472.

[16] Compare the category of 'non-subtractive' interests in the Gewirthian hierarchy of generic goods.

[17] Compare the category of 'additive' interests in the Gewirthian hierarchy of generic goods.

facilitate the exchange of goods and/or services. The institution of private property intersects with both tort (where property-based interests are protected) and contract (where contract is used to effect the transfer of a property-based interest) and, in this sense, property is implicated in both private wrong and private empowerment. Indeed, the standard conception of property as comprising a 'bundle of rights' (the right to exclude, the right to use and control use, the right to alienate, and so on) points to the range of proprietary rights, some relating to private wrong (such as the claim-right to deny access to others), others relating to private empowerment (such as the power of sale).

With this groundwork in place, we can move on to consider the necessity and sufficiency of consent in private dealings of the kind covered by the law of tort, property, and contract. In particular, we can highlight three kinds of mistake: one is thinking that consent is *not* sufficient for the purposes of negating a wrong; a second is thinking that consent is necessary in the sense that to act without consent must be to do a wrong; and a third is to think that consent is necessary in the sense that it is the only possible justification where a right is infringed. These latter two mistakes are constituent aspects of what we will refer to as the Fallacy of Necessity.

## III Private Wrong: The Necessity and Sufficiency of Consent as a Relevant Justificatory Condition

In her Gifford Lectures, Onora O'Neill remarks on the 'triumph' of autonomy in modern bioethics. Insightfully, she sets this development alongside the more general phenomenon of the importance attached to consumer choice in modern societies. In such societies, where the culture of consumerism prevails, we find that 'informed consent requirements are often seen not only as necessary but also as sufficient for ethical justification.'[18] Thus:

> If we abstract from all the fundamental ethical principles that structure the institutional background of consumer choice—such as those that shape and justify economic and legal institutions—we may well think that informed consent is both the necessary and the sufficient justification of all economic transactions in the everyday life of a consumer society.[19]

According to O'Neill, once medical decision-making is placed in this same framework of consumerist thinking, we will find that medical ethics becomes fixated with just one idea: 'informed consent is seen as offering *necessary and sufficient ethical justification*.'[20] If we accept O'Neill's account

[18] Onora O'Neill, *Autonomy and Trust in Bioethics* (Cambridge, Cambridge University Press, 2002) at 47 (the Gifford Lectures were delivered at the University of Edinburgh, 2001).

[19] *Ibid.*

[20] *Ibid*, at 48 (emphasis in original).

of the ascendancy of notions of autonomy and consent in modern ethics, and if we accept that the law will reflect a background culture of consumerism, then we will not be surprised if modern legal regimes treat an agent's (informed) consent as a necessary and sufficient condition for both the denial of *private wrong* (for instance, in medical transactions) as well as the assertion of *private empowerment* (in economic transactions).

On the face of it, a consumerist ideology that puts consent at the heart of its private law regime would be in line with the pattern of a rights-based approach. As we have said, assuming rights-based theory, the principal function of consent is to signal some concession in relation to the benefit covered by a right, the giving of consent being the procedural justification for what would otherwise be a violation of the right in question. We have also said that consent operates as the pre-condition of private empowerment, consent signalling that the parties are assuming a new set of rights and obligations. On this analysis, the idea that consent offers a necessary and sufficient legal justification for what would otherwise be a private wrong and that it is the necessary and sufficient basis of private empowerment has an air of plausibility. However, we need to check this claim more carefully against the specific features of Gewirthian rights-theory, for we must not make the mistake of skimming consent off the surface and forgetting that it is one aspect of a larger body of theory.[21]

Three aspects of that larger theory are material and guiding. First, if there is no violation of right, there is no wrong, and no call for justification (procedural or substantive). Secondly, if there is a violation of right, then in the absence of the rights-holder's consent there is a wrong (in other words, unless there is a procedural justification, the violation of right entails that a wrong is done). Thirdly, even if there is such a wrong, it might be substantively justified all things considered—for example, in circumstances of the kind found in the well-known case of *Tarasoff v Regents of the University of California*,[22] agent A might be justified in breaking a confidence concerning agent B if disclosure of the information is necessary for the protection of agent C's life.

Given these general bearings, we can say that consent seems to be at least a sufficient response to an alleged private wrong (at any rate, where the response is directed to an agent who, having consented, now complains that a wrong has been done). To this extent, to proceed with consent is to do no wrong. However, we must beware the Fallacy of Necessity that comes with a fixation with consent. The Fallacy is a composite of two mistakes.

[21] Similarly, as we cautioned in our introductory remarks, we should not make the mistake of skimming rights off the surface of a larger theory that presupposes the dignity and vulnerability of agency and the special features of the context in which agents can operate as a community of rights. See further ch 9.

[22] (1976) 131 Cal Rptr 14 (Cal Supreme Court).

First, we should not think that to proceed without consent is (in itself) to do a wrong: this is not so; and it is not so because the wrong is constituted by the violation of a right, not by the lack of consent as such. Secondly, having corrected for the first error, we should not jump to the conclusion that to violate a right without consent is *necessarily* to act in a way that cannot be justified: procedural justification is one thing, substantive justification quite another.

Although this chapter focuses on the private domain, it should be said that the shape of private right and wrong, consent and justification, applies equally to cases in which agents complain that they have been wronged by public bodies. Hence, a complainant will not get to first base unless a right has been infringed. If a right is engaged, then the complainant's consent will give the public body a procedural justification and no wrong will have been done. In the absence of consent, however, the public body will need a substantive justification of the kind offered by overriding rights. So, for example, in *Peck v United Kingdom*,[23] where Peck's complaint related to the distribution of local authority CCTV footage that showed him attempting to commit suicide in a public place, the first question was whether any relevant right was engaged. The court ruled that Article 8(1), the privacy provision of the European Convention on Human Rights, was engaged.[24] Had Peck consented to the local authority's use of the footage, there would have been no wrong. However, in the absence of Peck's consent, the local authority needed a substantive public interest justification of the kind provided for by Article 8(2) of the Convention.[25] The court ruled that, on the facts, no such justification could be made out.

Our discussion in this section of the chapter is in five stages. First, we cast doubt on the proposition that consent is correctly viewed as a necessary and sufficient condition—from a Gewirthian perspective, consent might well serve as a (procedural) justification but so, too, might overriding rights (qua substantive justification). Secondly, we underline the point that, from a Gewirthian (or, indeed, any rights-centred) perspective, it is a fallacy (one aspect of the Fallacy of Necessity) to suppose that any kind of justification is called for in the absence of a prima facie violation of an agent's rights. This leads to the third stage of our discussion in which we comment on a trio of cases in which the claimants asserted contested proprietary rights to establish that, in the absence of consent, they had been

[23] (2003) 36 EHHR 719.

[24] Article 8(1) provides: 'Everyone has the right to respect for his private and family life, his home and his correspondence.'

[25] Article 8(2) provides: 'There shall be no interference by a public authority with the exercise of this right except such as is in accordance with the law and is necessary in a democratic society in the interests of national security, public safety or the economic well-being of the country, for the prevention of disorder or crime, for the protection of health or morals, or for the protection of the rights and freedoms of others.'

wronged. Fourthly, we deal with the other aspect of the Fallacy of Necessity, sketching the kinds of defences recognised by regimes of tort law. In practice, consent (volenti or assumption of risk) is not the only recognised defence, implying that consent is not treated as a necessary justification in response to alleged private wrong. However, this raises the question of whether further defences (such as necessity, privilege, and Act of God or whatever) are properly recognised: for, from a Gewirthian viewpoint, if consent is not the root justification, it must be a PGC-sensitive substantive justification, such as the need to respect overriding rights. Finally, we address any lingering doubts that consent should be viewed as a sufficient (if not a necessary) justification.

### *(i) Viewing Consent from a Gewirthian Perspective*

From a Gewirthian perspective, there seem to be only two kinds of reasons (antecedent justifications, such as self-defence, apart) that pass muster in response to a prima facie private wrong (the facts not being contested). One reason (by way of a procedural justification) is that the agent who has been prima facie wronged has consented to the offending action by the wrongdoing agent. The other reason (by way of a substantive justification) is that the agent who is the prima facie wrongdoer has acted in this way in order to protect or respect more compelling rights. Because procedural justification, unlike substantive justification by reference to overriding rights, serves to *negate* the wrong, we have suggested that the former has priority (the principle of the 'priority of consent'). These points bear a little more elaboration.

First, the agent who apparently has been wronged might have consented *directly* to the act in question. Such a *direct* consent might have been signalled in person, or it might have been signalled by a third party agent on behalf of the principal. As we have already said, the more remote the expression of consent from the agent who has been wronged, or the more implicit the signalling, the more problematic the procedural justification.[26] However, the general principle of direct consent is clear enough even if its application is taken beyond the paradigm of explicit personal consent.

Secondly, the agent who apparently has been wronged might have consented *indirectly* to the act in question. For example, the agent might have consented to a scheme of governance under which he accepts rules which immunise authorised agents against what would otherwise be private wrongs. This is a principle of indirect consent; it is critical to a consent-based theory of public governance; and we will discuss it fully in chapter ten.

Thirdly, in relation to substantive justification, where the purpose of the supposedly wrongdoing agent is to serve overriding rights, these rights

[26] See ch 7.

might be of the agent to whom the apparent wrong has been done or they might be rights of third party agents.

In the light of these rudimentary principles, the obvious question raised by treating consent as a necessary condition for all justificatory purposes is this: where a legal system holds that some particular action can be justified if, and only if, it has the consent of the agent whose rights are prima facie violated, how can this be squared with the case of the agent (such as the confidant in *Tarasoff*) who acts without such an authorising consent but who does so for the sake of overriding rights? Some space for overriding rights reasons, some space for substantive justification, surely must be found.

The Gewirthian three-level hierarchy of rights, it will be recalled, provides that those rights that relate to basic goods take priority over those rights that relate to non-subtractive or additive goods, and those rights that relate to non-subtractive goods take priority over those rights that relate to additive goods. Broadly speaking, then, physical interests take priority over mere property interests which, in turn, take priority over mere economic interests.[27] As a rule of thumb, this suggests that, with regard to the necessity of obtaining the rights-holder's consent, a legal system will be on the right track if:

(i) consent of the rights-holder is treated as a *necessary* condition for justified interference with such physical interests as are protected by basic rights;
(ii) in the absence of overriding basic rights, consent of the rights-holder is treated as a *necessary* condition for justified interference with such proprietary interests as are protected by non-subtractive rights; and
(iii) in the absence of overriding basic or non-subtractive rights, consent of the rights-holder is treated as a *necessary* condition for justified interference with such economic interests as are protected by additive rights.

The reason for insisting that nothing other than consent will do is that the action to be justified impinges on a benefit (a basic, non-subtractive, or additive good) protected by the right. To take the right seriously, we must restrict the kind of practical reason that will suffice to 'trump' the right—in the Gewirthian scheme, the restriction is severe, rights holding good against all reasons other than more compelling rights considerations. With no such overriding reasons in play, the right holds good. The only way in which interference can be justified is if the rights-holder (under a will theory) licenses it by consent.[28]

[27] See n 31 in ch 2 above.

[28] In this part of our discussion, it should be remembered, we are putting to one side the possibility of antecedent justification.

In short, then, where agent A seemingly commits a private wrong by violating the prima facie rights of agent B, Gewirthian principles indicate that:

(i) in the absence of an overriding rights justification, agent B's consent is the necessary (and sufficient) justifying condition for A's action;
(ii) where an overriding rights justification is available to A, B's consent (even if not a necessary justifying condition) will still suffice to justify A's action; and
(iii) in a case such as (ii), even if A is able to rely on an overriding rights justification, the principle of the 'priority of consent' dictates that, where practicable, A should first seek B's consent (thereby avoiding the unauthorised violation of B's right).

### *(ii) One Aspect of the Fallacy of Necessity: Without Consent there is a Wrong*

It is a fallacy to suppose that, because (in some cases, anyway) consent is necessary for the avoidance of private wrong, there is necessarily a private wrong in the absence of consent. This is not so. To invoke a legal figure of speech, just because consent operates as a shield (as a defence) it does not follow that it (that is, its absence) operates as a sword (as a cause of action).

To appreciate why the above is a fallacy, we need to understand the distinctive way in which any rights-centred regime will view the following proposition, namely: *Agent A, by doing X, has perpetrated a private wrong against agent B because agent A has not obtained the consent of agent B for the doing of X.* A rights-centred approach will view this proposition as a shorthand for (the more accurate) following proposition: *Agent A, by doing X, has prima facie violated right R held by agent B. Not having obtained the consent of agent B for the doing of X, agent A has perpetrated a prima facie private wrong against agent B.*' The emphasis of this is very important: first, there is a prima facie violation of a right; it is only if there is such a rights-violation that consent becomes a relevant issue; consent, to repeat, is not a free-standing consideration. To put this from the complainant agent's [B's] perspective, if A's doing X violates no prima facie right of B, A does no wrong, and A does not need to appeal to B's consent to justify the doing of X. Or, if B has no relevant right, B cannot establish a wrong simply by pleading lack of consent. Thus, in the context of an alleged private wrong, arguments about consent are immaterial in the absence of an established violation of a prima facie right.

By contrast, where a legal regime is influenced by non rights-centred thinking, the proposition and the significance of consent will tend to be viewed rather differently. For instance, where the approach is utilitarian, A's failure to obtain B's consent might be regarded as wrong, not because B has a right that is otherwise violated by A, but because getting consent is simply the best available option as judged by the usual utilitarian criteria (such as the transaction and opportunity costs saved (or incurred) by A, the satisfaction experienced by (or the distress occasioned to) B, the preferences of other agents having an interest in the matter, and so on). If the approach is communitarian, the group might be committed to the ideal that 'we simply do not do things without getting the consent of others'; in which case, by failing to get B's consent, A fails to respect the community's standards. Or, again, in a Kantian-influenced regime, where performance in accordance with one's duties to others is categorically required, A may be judged to have done wrong by failing to get B's consent, but the judgement is made without invoking a consequential utilitarian calculation, a community-defining duty, or (other than as reflex of A's duty) B's prima facie right.[29]

Bearing these preliminary remarks in mind, we can move on to discuss a trio of controversial cases,[30] each one lying at the margins of recognised property rights. In each case, the allegation of private wrongdoing relies on the fact that the action in question has not been authorised by the complainant—that is, that the action has been taken without the complainant's consent. Although these claims imply that, in the absence of the complainant's consent, there must be a private wrong, we know that this proposition is suspect—even if the complainant has not consented, the action might simply involve no wrong because no relevant rights are violated. This is the critical point in our trio of illustrative examples.

### *(iii) Commercial Exploitation Without Consent*

If, where agent A is the proprietor of X, agent B exploits X, then this is a prima facie violation of A's property rights over X. A has a claim-right against B that B should not exploit X without A's permission. If A has consented to B's exploitation of X, B has a response to the prima facie wrong. If A has not consented, B has no ready answer and the prima facie wrong remains a prima facie wrong. So much is straightforward. However, where the X in question is A's body or A's body parts (including already removed body parts) or tissue containing genetic information about A, or the like, things are less clear-cut. For the question of whether, in principle, an agent can have property rights in his or her own body, or its parts, or the genetic information therein, is deeply contested in both legal and philosophical circles. For example, one of the leading commentators, Stephen Munzer,[31]

[29] Compare the Kantian-inspired, duty-driven theory of principled autonomy advocated by O'Neill, n 18 above.

[30] Namely, *Moore v Regents of the University of California* 793 P2d 479; *Greenberg v Miami Children's Hospital Research Institute, Inc* 208 F Supp 2d 918 (ND Ill 2002), 02-22244-CIV-MORENO (Miami); and *R v Department of Health ex parte Source Informatics Ltd* [1999] 4 All ER 185, [2001] QB 424 (CA).

[31] Stephen R Munzer, *A Theory of Property* (Cambridge, Cambridge University Press, 1990), especially at 37–58.

rejects the 'imperial' view that all body rights are property rights. Rather, he divides body rights into 'personal rights' and 'property rights', the latter then being divided into weak and strong property rights.[32] Transferability, Munzer maintains, is the key to property rights; and transfer for value (rather than gratuitous transfer) is the key to strong property rights. Thus:

> Most body rights are personal rather than property rights; examples are rights not to be murdered, not to be searched without a warrant or just cause, not to be compelled to testify against oneself, not to be libeled or slandered, to speak freely, and to exclude others from sexual or other physical contact. Some body rights are property rights—whether weak, such as the right to donate an organ upon death, or strong, such as the right of publicity or the right to sell blood or semen.[33]

To place these remarks in the present context, we can proceed on the following basis. First, a legal regime guided by Gewirthian principles will clearly recognise that agents have claim-rights relating to their physical integrity. If agent A lops off agent B's arm, this is certainly a violation of B's prima facie rights (B's consent, of course, would negate the private wrong). Secondly, we can agree with the sceptics that it does not follow from the fact that agents have claim-rights to their bodily integrity that these claim-rights are *property* rights. Indeed, on a Gewirthian analysis, claim-rights to bodily integrity fall within the class of basic rights rather than non-subtractive (property) rights.[34] To this extent, we can agree with Munzer. Thirdly, we can also agree with the sceptics that it does not follow from the fact that agents have claim-rights to their bodily integrity that they have *property* rights to their removed body parts.[35] In other words, even if agent A does wrong by lopping off agent B's arm, this does not entail that agent B has proprietary rights over the removed arm. Fourthly, however, we believe that a defensible Gewirthian case can be made out for the institution of private property in general,[36] and for the application, in particular, of property rights to agents' body parts.[37] While this is not the place to rehearse the argument, the basic idea is simple enough. It is that, if we understand a *proprietary* right as being distinctively 'preclusionary', in the sense that the right-holding agent may claim the benefits of proprietorship (such as use and access, and so on) without having to justify such enjoyment by reference either to his own needs or to the requirements of others—

[32] Stephen R Munzer, *A Theory of Property* (Cambridge, Cambridge University Press, 1990), especially, at 48–49.

[33] *Ibid*, at 57.

[34] See n 31 in ch 2 above.

[35] Cf JW Harris, 'Who Owns My Body?' (1996) 16 *Oxford Journal of Legal Studies* 55.

[36] See Alan Gewirth, *The Community of Rights* (Chicago, IL, University of Chicago Press, 1996), especially at 166–213.

[37] See Deryck Beyleveld and Roger Brownsword, *Human Dignity in Bioethics and Biolaw* (Oxford, Oxford University Press, 2001), ch 8; and 'My Body, My Body Parts, My Property?' (2000) 8 *Health Care Analysis* 87.

in other words, it suffices to say, 'This is mine,' preclusion signifying that no further reason is required—then why should our body parts not be appropriate objects of property rights? Indeed, our position is that if a case for preclusionary property rights can be made in relation to anything, then our own bodies and body parts are surely the most eligible objects for such protection. Granted, the recognition of such rights would be controversial and it would be moot how many of the characteristic entitlements that make up the property bundle should be enjoyed in relation to body parts. Nevertheless, there is undoubtedly a decent basis for this kind of claim in Gewirthian theory. Against this background, we come to the first of our illustrative examples, the famous Californian case of John Moore.

The story in John Moore's case began in 1976 when he started having treatment for hairy cell leukaemia. During the course of this treatment, the doctors removed Moore's spleen and other samples of his tissue. These procedures were clinically justified and, in themselves, gave rise to no allegation of wrongdoing. However, Moore's doctors realised at an early stage that a cell-line established from his T-lymphocytes might be valuable commercially (but they did not inform Moore about this). Having obtained further samples, the doctors duly developed this cell-line and, in 1981, it was patented (by the University of California). When Moore discovered what had happened, he asserted that the doctors' conduct was wrongful. The essence of Moore's complaint was that his consent to the removal of his spleen and to the post-operative removal of further blood and tissue samples was on the basis that this was clinically indicated not that any of this was for the purpose of research and development leading to commercial exploitation.

In 1984, Moore commenced legal proceedings against the doctors and the University of California, pleading: (1) breach of fiduciary duty or lack of informed consent; and (2) conversion (wrongful interference with his property), with the object of asserting a claim to a share in the profits generated by the patent. At first, his legal action was unsuccessful. However, the California Court of Appeal held in Moore's favour, ruling by a majority that he did own his cells.[38] The reasoning was:

(a) that the recognised rights and interests that persons have in their bodies are so akin to property that to call them anything else would be 'subterfuge'[39]; and
(b) that not to grant persons the right to control what happens to their tissue would lead to violations of rights to privacy and human dignity.[40]

[38] See (1988) 249 Cal Rptr 494.
[39] *Ibid*, at 504–5.
[40] *Ibid*, at 508.

On further appeal, however, the Supreme Court of California took a different view, ruling that Moore had no property rights in his cells, but that he had a case for breach of fiduciary duty.[41] The main reasons given by the Supreme Court against Moore's property rights (again by a majority) were:

(a) that it was not necessary to recognise Moore's property rights to provide him with the appropriate remedy[42] (and, indeed, it would not be appropriate for the courts as against the legislature to decide on Moore's proprietary interest);[43]
(b) that there was nothing unique about Moore's cells. Everyone has cells that produce lymphokines;[44] and
(c) to grant Moore a property right would inhibit medical research.[45]

The case went no further, the parties settling in the light of the court's ruling that there was a breach of fiduciary duty.

Put simply, Moore's contention was that the doctors had done him wrong because they had acted without his consent (and, to obtain a valid consent from him, they would have had to have informed him as to their intentions). If the doctors had informed Moore, he might well have consented to the proposed attempt to develop the cell-line (possibly on the understanding that he would share in the profits of any commercial exploitation) and there would then have been no private wrong. Without Moore's consent, however, all bets were off. Does it follow, then, that Moore's consent was a necessary condition for the avoidance of what would otherwise be a private wrong? To answer this question, we must separate out that part of Moore's claim relating to the basis on which he was treated from that part relating to his claimed share in the profits of exploitation.

With regard to the basis on which he was treated, Moore's claim had solid foundations. Plainly, he had a right that the doctors' medical interventions, including their taking of blood and tissue samples, should not be made under false pretences. In a fiduciary relationship, false pretences would include both active and passive deception. Insofar as the doctors acted under false pretences, they did a wrong to Moore. If Moore had consented to being treated on such a basis (admittedly, a pretty implausible scenario), this would have been a different matter; it would at least have been a sufficient justification for withholding information from him concerning the commercial potential of his T-lymphocytes. For it to be a *necessary* condition, however, the doctors would have to have no other justificatory avenue. But, what else could they say? They might have said that they thought it

[41] See (1990) 271 Cal Rptr 146, (1990) 793 P2d 479; cert denied (1991) 111 S Ct 1388.
[42] (1990) 271 Cal Rptr 146, at 168.
[43] *Ibid*, at 160.
[44] (1990) 793 P2d 479, 490.
[45] (1990) 271 Cal Rptr 146, at 161–63.

best not to tell Moore the whole story in case he objected to the research and development or in case their relationship with Moore was soured and this interfered with his recovery. Clearly, however, such a self-serving purported justification would not do. Where consent is required, it is precisely to secure the right to object (to stand on one's rights if one so wills); and the idea that the physician's therapeutic privilege justifies non-disclosure for commercial reasons is risible.

The other part of Moore's claim, the part that did not succeed, was problematic. Moore's assertion was that he was wronged if he was excluded from sharing in the profits of the commercial venture in which his tissue had played a part as a source material. Without a contractual right to support this claim, Moore relied on a property right in his tissue. If he had such a right, it was at least arguable that the right reached through to a share in the profits. If he had such a property-based right to a share of the proceeds, the patent proprietors did him a wrong by excluding him from his share. If Moore had consented to forgo his share of the profits, the wrong would be negated. However, Moore's failure to succeed with this part of his claim should not be seen as turning on any question of consent; it is explained by his failure to persuade the court that he had the originating property right. Without this right, there was no wrong. To be sure, it was not quite as simple as that because the non-recognition of the right was (and still is) controversial and we can detect a fair slice of utilitarian reasoning in the court's policy. Nevertheless, if we take the court's sceptical approach towards the extension of property rights, it *was* as simple as that. Moore's consent was not necessary because, so far as the profits of the venture were concerned, Moore had no rights.

More recently, a variation on *Moore* has been presented for determination in *Greenberg v Miami Children's Hospital Research Institute*.[46] Briefly, in the late 1980s, the lead claimant, Greenberg, approached one of the defendants, Matalon, who at that time was a research physician in Chicago, to request his involvement in a project designed to locate the gene for Canavan disease. Matalon agreed and, for some seven years (during which time Matalon moved the research to Miami), Greenberg supplied the project with tissue and blood samples from members of his family, including samples from the brain and other organs of his deceased son who had been afflicted with the disease. More generally, the researchers enjoyed considerable co-operation from families affected by the disease—samples were collected and information was gathered from the disease registers, and so on—and the National Tay-Sachs and Allied Diseases Association supported the research by making financial contributions. However, when the gene was duly identified the researchers took patent protection, as a result of

[46] See 2002 WL 1483266 (ND Ill); 02-22244-CIV-MORENO (Miami); and Graeme Laurie, *Genetic Privacy* (Cambridge: Cambridge University Press, 2002) at 322–23.

which access to a test for the disease was available only under licence. The plaintiffs, representing the families, objected strongly to this commercialisation of the research, for they contended that they had participated on the understanding that this was a research project for the public benefit and in the expectation that there would be ready access to any carrier and pre-natal tests developed. The plaintiffs felt betrayed and, filing a six-count complaint against the defendants, they sought to restrain the latter from enforcing their patent.[47]

As in *Moore*, one of the causes of action pleaded was conversion (based on alleged property in the samples and the genetic information therein). Greenberg, however, is distinguishable from *Moore* in at least two respects. First, unlike *Moore*, where the objection was not to commercialisation per se, but to commercialisation without the tissue source's consent, *Greenberg* raises a subtly different question: namely, should the researchers be permitted to commercialise their work when key participants in the project objected in principle to such steps being taken (and would not have participated had they thought this might happen)?[48] Secondly, whereas Moore did not know that his tissue samples were being used for research, those who donated material in *Greenberg* understood that this was the principal purpose of the project. Arguably, then, whilst the consent to the donation was under-informed in both cases, the degree of under-information in *Greenberg* was significantly less (raising an issue about the scope and interpretation of the consent). The case having come on, initially, before a District Court in Illinois, it was transferred to Miami for a hearing on the merits.[49] There, in response to the defendants' application to strike out the claim, District Judge Moreno ruled that (as in *Moore*) conversion was not arguable, and, indeed, it was held that the only claim that could survive the defendants' motion to dismiss was that alleging unjust enrichment.[50]

The general normative shape of *Greenberg* is as in *Moore*: unless the claimants can assert and establish a wrong by reference to a recognised right, they cannot get to first base; and pleading either a lack of consent or

[47] The plaintiffs alleged (i) breach of informed consent, (ii) breach of fiduciary duty, (iii) unjust enrichment, (iv) fraudulent concealment, (v) conversion, and (vi) misappropriation of trade secrets.

[48] One can readily think of other scenarios of this kind: for example, parents who donate an embryo to a cell bank for stem cell research, on the understanding that the project will be exclusively of a research nature, might object if cell-lines derived from the embryo are then made available to pharmaceutical companies for a fee.

[49] See n 46 above: Gettleman J held that Illinois had no jurisdiction to hear the case but that, in the interests of justice, it would be transferred to Florida rather than dismissed.

[50] Stated shortly, the elements of an action for unjust enrichment are that the plaintiff has conferred a benefit on the defendant, who has voluntarily accepted that benefit, such that it would now be unjust for the defendant to retain the benefit without paying for it.

conduct going beyond the cover of consent is no short-cut.[51] To this extent, the moral of *Greenberg* is the same as that in *Moore*: even if a right plus absence of consent adds up to a wrong, it does not follow that an absence of right plus an absence of consent also adds up to a wrong—one and one adds up to two, not three.

There were, however, other possible angles in *Greenberg*. As we have said, District Judge Moreno treated a claim for unjust enrichment, which is a close cousin of contract, as arguable; and some might have counselled pleading the case in contract rather than property. With the case so pleaded, a court that is sympathetic to the claimants might read in a contract between the contributors (let us avoid saying 'donors' since this suggests gift rather than contract) and the researchers, thereby allowing the former to retain control under the terms of the agreement. But if a contract can be constructed or implied in this way, this suggests that the consent of the contractors is not a necessary condition (that is, that consent is not a necessary condition for private empowerment). After all, the researchers would hardly concede that they had consented to such a contract. What we should make of this is not yet clear. Here, it suffices to note that courts will sometimes overcome the absence of one kind of right (property) by finding another kind of right (contract in this example). In so doing, there might be some distortion of the ground rules concerning consent but this is a matter that we need to reconsider later in this chapter, in the context of private empowerment.

In the third of our examples, *Source Informatics*, we again see the importance of the rights on which the claimant's case rests. As in *Moore* and *Greenberg*, the availability of property rights is contested but, in *Source Informatics*, it is at least common ground that a privacy interest of some sort is implicated. However, privacy interests are themselves contested and varied (not least with regard to their character as proprietary or non-proprietary)[52] and a protective right might stake out a broader or narrower set of interests for protection.

In *Source Informatics*, the applicant company planned to collect data about the prescribing habits of general practitioners, thinking that such information would be of commercial value to drug companies. Its intention was to supply pharmacists with software enabling them to download onto disk the name of the general practitioner together with the identity and quantity of the drug prescribed. Importantly, the software was designed in such a way

[51] Those rights-driven legal regimes that take a conservative approach towards pleading offer some resistance to the notion that 'no consent' qualifies as a cause of action. However, this is not an unqualified good, for the danger with such a conservative culture is that the courts will be slow to recognise rights that, from a Gewirthian perspective, should be recognised.

[52] Compare, eg, Anita L Allen, 'Genetic Privacy: Emerging Concepts and Values' in MA Rothstein (ed), *Genetic Secrets: Protecting Privacy and Confidentiality in the Genetic Era* (New Haven, Yale University Press, 1997) at 31.

that patients could not be identified. Unexpectedly, however, the Department of Health issued guidance advising that, because '[t]he patient would not be aware of or have consented to the information being given to the data company . . . [a]nonymisation of the data (with or without aggregation) would not obviate a breach of confidence.' Faced with this difficulty, the company sought a declaration that this guidance was in error.

At first instance, Latham J dismissed the application, taking a strongly protective approach towards any unauthorised use of confidential information. Even if anonymity could be guaranteed for the patients, even if there was no obvious harm to patients, Latham J was troubled by the prospect of unauthorised processing. Whilst some of Latham J's comments[53] might be interpreted as implying a longer-term and pragmatic utilitarian calculation, a great deal of what he says indicates a concern with the rights of patients. Even if, because of anonymisation, patients cannot be harmed in the sense that another will have identifiable information about them, Latham J is reluctant to allow that there is, therefore, no breach of right. Yet, if this is so, what right might this be? The obvious answer is that Latham J's position presupposes some species of proprietary right (in which case, unauthorised use indeed would be a prima facie violation of the patient proprietor's right).

On appeal, the Court of Appeal reversed Latham J's decision, saying that, once the information was anonymised, no harm could be done to the patients, no rights could be violated. Having reviewed the case-law on breach of confidence, Simon Brown LJ articulated the focal question as follows:

> To my mind the one clear and consistent theme emerging from all these authorities is this: the confident is placed under a duty of good faith to the confider and the touchstone by which to judge the scope of his duty and whether or not it has been fulfilled or breached is his own conscience, no more and no less. One asks, therefore, on the facts of this case: would a reasonable pharmacist's conscience be troubled by the proposed use to be made of the patients' prescriptions? Would he think that by entering Source's scheme he was breaking his customers' confidence, making unconscientious use of the information they provide?[54]

With the qualifier 'reasonable' signalling that this is not simply a matter of a clear conscience, subjectively speaking, the question becomes: relative to what would a pharmacist reasonably so believe? To which the answer is: if the processing of the information infringes no rights (or interests) of the patient, then the pharmacist could reasonably believe that, even without the former's consent, no wrong is done to the patient. It is at this stage of the reasoning that Simon Brown LJ departs most obviously from the line

[53] Eg his comments concerning the public interest: see [1999] 4 All ER 185, at 196.
[54] [2000] 1 All ER 786, at 796.

taken by Latham J. In response to the question, 'What interest of the patient is the law seeking to protect?', Simon Brown LJ says:

> In my judgment, the answer is plain. The concern of the law here is to protect the confider's personal privacy. That and that alone is the right at issue in this case. The patient has no proprietorial claim to the prescription form or to the information it contains. . . . [The patient has] no property in the information and no right to control its use provided only and always that his privacy is not put at risk.[55]

According to Simon Brown LJ, therefore, because privacy (construed narrowly) is the relevant right, anonymisation sufficiently protects the patients' interests, and their lack of knowledge or consent is immaterial.

This decision has attracted considerable criticism.[56] As Graeme Laurie has pointed out, the Court of Appeal, by treating privacy (narrowly understood) as the only interest at stake,

> ignores other perfectly valid claims that individuals might make over their personal information. These might emerge either as part of a richer concept of privacy, or as an aspect of individual autonomy, or indeed as a reflection of a property interest that individuals might have in their own information. But, having delivered a minimalist view of privacy, the court rejected out of hand any prospect that individuals might have a property interest in personal information, or that there might be wider autonomy issues at stake.[57]

If (contrary to the Court of Appeal) we were to take a proprietary approach, such as we might attribute to Latham J, we would need to distinguish between information that fell within a person's proprietary right and information that fell outwith that right. If a person has a proprietary right in the information first put into circulation, then the patient must have the right to control the subsequent use of that information, *including the right to control whether or not the information is anonymised.* To say, as Simon Brown LJ holds, that the patient cannot be harmed once the information is

[55] *Ibid*, at 797.

[56] See especially Deryck Beyleveld and Elise Histed, 'Betrayal of Confidence in the Court of Appeal' (2000) 4 *Medical Law International* 277.

[57] *Ibid*, at 225–26. Laurie treats confidentiality as a cousin of privacy. As for privacy, this

> has its roots in a moral value system which places considerable emphasis on the protection of the rights and interests of individuals and presupposes such social norms as respect for individuals. In this it is allied to the related concepts of liberty and autonomy, and all three combine to perform essentially the same function—they prescribe the way in which individuals are to be treated in Western society, and they operate to establish and maintain boundaries between the individual and society. *These constructs are all adjuncts to a view of human dignity that is prevalent in our society.*

(*Ibid*, at 84, emphasis added)

Such a prevalent view of human dignity, it seems, is what we have characterised as 'human dignity as empowerment'; see Deryck Beyleveld and Roger Brownsword, n 1 in ch 1 above.

anonymised is, from a proprietary perspective, to miss the point: if information which is subject to a proprietary right is anonymised without the patient's consent, the right has been infringed and the harm has already been done. Furthermore, if (contrary to the Court of Appeal) we were to take a broader privacy perspective, we might also find that anonymisation does not exhaust the content of a person's privacy rights in relation to the flow of their personal information.

To turn *Source Informatics* around, let us suppose that a claim were to be made by a patient who did not wish to be given information about his or her own genetic make-up. The claimant agent protests, 'I did not consent to this; I did not wish to know.' To get such a claim to first base, the claimant must focus, not on the absence of consent, but on the underpinning right not to know. The challenge is to persuade the court to recognise this right directly or to include it within an established right such as that protecting privacy (or autonomy). In a jurisdiction where privacy rights are freely recognised, it might be plausible to argue that the right to control the *outward* flow of sensitive personal information implies a right, too, to control the *inward* flow of such information. Even in such a legal regime, there might be hesitation about recognising such a right. However, this is the way to present the claim, not to major on the absence of consent. We must always remember: no right plus no consent adds up to no claim.

Briefly, to take stock, the lesson of all three cases is that, where there is no consent, but also no covering right, the facts do not stack up to a private wrong; and the argument for the missing right is not improved by labouring the absence of consent. However, this is not to say that the denial of right is justified. In our view, the courts in these cases are far too ready to dismiss the claimed covering proprietary right and, in *Source Informatics*, the privacy interest is unjustifiably narrowed—but, of course, we acknowledge that the existence and scope of property and privacy rights is a matter for debate. Our essential point is that the lack of consent in these cases does not offer the claimant a short cut to success. Having said this, if the court judges that the merits lie with the claimant, then the missing right might be fashioned by reinterpreting the existing repertoire of rights or, as we suggested in relation to *Greenberg*, by constructing a contract to support the claim. Although this bypasses one problem, it hints at a different concern for those who take consent seriously: namely, that the complaint about the lack of consent is transferred from the now successful original claimant to the now unsuccessful original defendant.

### *(iv) Defences to Private Wrong and a Second Aspect of the Fallacy of Necessity*

Regimes of tort law recognise a variety of defences to claims—for example, absolute and qualified privilege might be available to a defendant in a defamation action, or Act of God to a defendant in a nuisance action, or self-defence to a defendant in an action for trespass to the person, and so on. Amongst these defences, the significance of consent is reflected in the defence of volenti non fit injuria (or, as it might sometimes be put, assumption of risk or incurred risk).

At one time, the defence of volenti had something of a bad name because, during the earlier years of industrialisation, there was a tendency to apply it for the protection of employers faced with claims by employees who had been injured at work.[58] However, the paradigmatic statement of this defence is fully in line with a Gewirthian view of consent in the law. Thus, according to Prosser:[59]

> In its simplest and primary sense, assumption of risk means that the plaintiff, in advance, has expressly given his consent to relieve the defendant of an obligation of conduct toward him, and to take his chances of injury from a known risk arising from what the defendant is to do or to leave undone. The situation is then the same as where the plaintiff consents to the infliction of what would otherwise be an intentional tort, except that the consent is to run the risk of unintended injury, to take a chance, rather than a matter of the greater certainty of intended harm. The result is that the defendant is relieved of all legal duty to the plaintiff; and being under no duty, he cannot be charged with negligence.[60]

Of course, to qualify as a valid consent, an advance assumption of risk must satisfy the dual conditions of unforced choice and informed choice; and, in line with this reservation, the jurisprudence of volenti does indeed attend to the requirement that the relevant agent was aware of, and appreciated, the risk being assumed and that it was assumed voluntarily.[61] Tort regimes, however, do not limit volenti to cases of explicit assumption of risk; they also allow, quite extensively, for the implied assumption of risk. To be sure, an implied assumption of risk, no less than an express assumption of risk, must satisfy the dual conditions of validity; and this does have some

[58] Generally, see Morton J Horwitz, *The Transformation of American Law 1780–1860* (Cambridge, MA, Harvard University Press, 1977).

[59] William L Prosser, *The Law of Torts*, 3rd edn (St Paul, MI: West, 1964). To similar effect, see Dan B Dobbs, *The Law of Torts* (vol 1) (St Paul, MI, West, 2001), at para 95:

> One who consents or apparently consents to acts that would otherwise count as an intentional tort cannot recover damages for those acts. . . . For example, a sexual touching would be a battery if it is not effectively consented to, but if the plaintiff effectively consents to the touching, there is no battery. . . . An analogous rule applies in some but not all negligence cases under the name of assumed risk.

The consent principle is general in its scope, firm in its acceptance, and central in its significance. It makes the plaintiff's right of self-determination or autonomy the centrepiece of the law on intentional torts and to some extent other torts as well.

[60] *Ibid*, para 67, at 450.

[61] See *ibid*, para 67, at 461–68.

confining influence on the implied version of the doctrine.[62] Nevertheless, once we move from express to implied consent, we encounter signalling questions, as well as questions of scope and interpretation in a more aggravated form.[63]

If volenti largely fits the pattern of Gewirthian procedural justification, the existence of further defences indicates that consent is not the only recognised response to wrongdoing. What this implies is that legal regimes do not treat consent-based procedural justification as the exclusive response to a private wrong. And, quite rightly so, for it is another aspect of the Fallacy of Necessity to suppose that, in the absence of consent, there can be no (substantive) justification. Even so, there remains the question of whether recognised defences, other than volenti, fit the required pattern of Gewirthian (substantive) justification.

The defence of necessity is an interesting case in point. In *Mouse's Case*,[64] where a barge was caught in a storm, the passengers jettisoned a number of items of property to lighten the load. Mouse threw out a casket belonging to the plaintiff. His defence, that his action was necessary in order to save life, was accepted. Three and a half centuries later, in *Southport Corporation v Esso Petroleum Co Ltd*,[65] necessity was pleaded once again to justify damage caused by jettisoning. Here, the defendants, having discharged oil into the sea in order to lighten their tanker when it was grounded in bad weather, were sued by the Corporation, whose land was fouled by the drifting oil slick. Although Devlin J was not convinced that necessity would be available to a defendant in an action in nuisance where one form of property damage (to the Corporation) was inflicted in consequence of action taken to avoid another kind of property damage (to the tanker), he conceded that:

> The safety of human lives belongs to a different scale of values from the safety of property. The two are beyond comparison and the necessity for saving life has at all times been considered a proper ground for inflicting such damage as may be necessary on another's property.[66]

Again, the ranking of human life above mere property is in line with the Gewirthian hierarchy of generic goods; but how far should necessity be recognised, bearing in mind that the actions to be justified are prima facie wrongs and taken without the authorising consent of the rights-holder?

[62] The baseline questions that we discussed earlier, in ch 5, are also relevant to the determination of whether an alleged implicit choice to assume a particular risk is unforced. So, for example, we find the case-law showing a distinct reluctance to treat rescuers as implicitly assuming the risk of perils created by a negligent defendant.

[63] See our extended discussion in ch 7.

[64] (1608) 12 Co Rep 63.

[65] [1953] 2 All ER 1204.

[66] *Ibid*, at 1209–10.

In *London Borough of Southwark v Williams*,[67] the council sought possession of houses that were occupied by squatters. The squatters admitted that they had no title but they sought to justify or excuse their actions on the grounds, inter alia, of necessity. The circumstances in which the squatters had occupied the (temporarily vacant) houses were sufficient to attract the court's sympathy—these were homeless and desperate people. However, in the court's view, this was not a case of imminent danger to life, and the circumstances, dire though they were, did not suffice to bring the defence of necessity into play. As Lord Denning MR said:

> If homelessness were once admitted as a defence to trespass, no one's house could be safe. Necessity would open a door which no one man could shut. It would not only be those in extreme need who would enter. There would be others who would imagine that they were in need, or would invent a need, so as to gain entry. Each man would say his need was greater than the next man's. The plea would be an excuse for all sorts of wrongdoing. So the courts must, for the sake of law and order, take a firm stand. They must refuse to admit the plea of necessity to the hungry and the homeless; and trust that their distress will be relieved by the charitable and the good.[68]

The court duly made the order for possession in favour of the council.

There are several ways of reading the court's restriction of the defence of necessity in *Williams*. On the one hand, we might applaud it as a stout defence of individual right. The court's firm stand is not so much 'for the sake of law and order' but for the sake of the background scheme of rights, and the principle that it should only be in exceptional circumstances that rights-holders should suffer unauthorised (ie non-consensual) harm to their protected interests. On the other hand, we might criticise the court for attaching too little weight to the basic goods of the squatters and too much weight to the property interests of the council. However, as the court emphasises, defences need to be workable and not wide open to abuse. We might conclude, therefore, that the instincts of the court in *Williams* are sound in its concern to protect private (property) rights; that the court is correct in allowing that, where life is at risk, such rights may justifiably be overridden; and that no court can be entirely confident about striking the right balance between principle and practice where the defence of necessity is pleaded in a context that falls short of life-threatening emergency.

When we discussed the case of John Moore earlier in this chapter, we rejected any suggestion that Moore's doctors could have argued 'therapeutic privilege' as a defence to their non-disclosure. Generally, such a defence is seen as a legacy of a paternalistic culture and, in a culture of patient autonomy, it is nowadays regarded with some suspicion. However, within a

[67] [1971] 2 All ER 175.
[68] *Ibid*, at 179.

rights regime, the defence of 'therapeutic privilege' may be read as a variation on the theme of necessity (in the sense that the doctor's failure to disclose may be justifiable by reference to the patient's basic interests in making a full recovery or avoiding a life-threatening setback). In this light, it is fairly easy to dismiss any such defensive argument by Moore's doctors as abusive—they stood to profit by non-disclosure and, quite clearly, they were not motivated by considerations concerning Moore's recovery. But, in cases of good faith medical judgement, there must be room in principle for 'therapeutic privilege'. Again, however, finding the right practical balance in which the lines are drawn clearly for the guidance of both doctors and patients is a challenge for any legal regime.

### *(v) The Sufficiency of Consent*

If it is accepted that consent is not *necessary* in the way just indicated, then it is, as we have said, a fallacy to believe that to violate a right without consent is beyond (substantive) justification. Even if there is a prima facie wrong, this overstates the justificatory significance of an absence of consent. Nevertheless, where a rights-holder consents to an action that impinges on the interest protected by the right, it is axiomatic that consent precludes complaint by the rights-holder in relation to that action. In other words, in private law, it is axiomatic that consent, if not a necessary justification, is at least a *sufficient* justification as between the rights-holder and the recipient of the consent.[69]

This being so, it can only be muddled or misdirected thinking that tricks us into wondering whether consent is a sufficient justification. We can give three short examples of such misguided thinking.

First, recalling the distinction between intentional and negligent private wrongs that we pointed to in our introductory remarks, it might be thought that, where agent B remains liable for a private wrongdoing despite agent A's consent, this speaks against the sufficiency of consent as a justification. However, as we have intimated already, this is simply muddled thinking. If agent A consents to an intentional act by agent B that would otherwise constitute a private wrong against agent A, it is axiomatic that A's consent provides agent B with a sufficient justification *in relation to that particular intentional act*. Equally, if agent A consents to the risk of a negligent act by agent B that would otherwise constitute a private wrong against agent A, it is axiomatic that A's consent provides agent B with a sufficient justification *in relation to that particular negligent act*. However, A's consent in relation to the risk of a particular negligent act does not signify consent in relation to an intentional act, and nor does A's consent in

[69] This does not, of course, exclude the possibility that the recipient of the consent might do a wrong to a third party. Even if consent is a sufficient justification between the first-party rights-holder and the second-party recipient of the consent, it is not a comprehensive justification.

relation to a particular intentional act signify consent to the risk of all kinds of negligent conduct by B. Provided that we remember this, we should not slip into thinking that B's potential exposure to other kinds of claims by A indicates that A's consent in relation to a particular act is not a sufficient justification for B in relation that particular act (and in relation to such a claim by A).[70]

Secondly, following on from this first example of misdirection, we can say that it is vital to remember that a consent is only a sufficient justification so far as the terms of the particular consent go. In other words, a consent only sufficiently justifies where the particular act of wrongdoing falls within its scope and where the particular wrongdoer is the beneficiary of the consent. Thus, we misdirect ourselves if we think that, where A consents to a particular risk of negligence by B, but where B is nevertheless liable for some other act of negligence or where C is liable for negligence, this speaks against the sufficiency of consent as a justification. Such supposed counter-examples might raise issues concerning the scope and interpretation of a consent, but they do not in any way challenge the justificatory sufficiency of consent.

Thirdly, as we have seen, there are several conditions to be satisfied before we can say that a particular consent has been given by a competent agent and that it is a valid and properly signalled consent. If, in a particular case, consent fails to justify because there is a problem about competence or signalling or validity, this in no way speaks against the sufficiency of consent as a justificatory reason. The axiom, correctly stated, is that a valid consent, properly signalled by a competent agent, serves as a sufficient justification (according to its particular terms) in relation to what would otherwise be a private wrongdoing.

## IV Private Empowerment: The Necessity and Sufficiency of Consent as a Relevant Justificatory Condition

In the late nineteenth century, despite the availability of a variety of medicinal products, flu epidemics took their toll. One such product was the Carbolic Smoke Ball. In an advert placed in the *Pall Mall Gazette*, its manufacturers claimed that, if the smoke ball was used as prescribed three times daily for a fortnight, the user would not contract influenza. So confident were the manufacturers that, in this advert, they promised to pay £100 to anyone who, having used the smoke ball as instructed, nevertheless succumbed to the flu. One Mrs Carlill, the wife of a London solicitor, having read the advert, purchased the smoke ball from her local chemist. She used the smoke ball as prescribed; but then caught influenza. In the event, she survived this particular bout of flu to go on living well into her 90s when,

[70] See n 69 above.

predictably, flu finally did bring her life to an end.[71] However, long before this was to happen, Mrs Carlill had unfinished business with the manufacturers of the smoke ball. She wanted her £100; but the company refused to pay. So began one of the most famous episodes in the common law of contract. And, *Carlill v Carbolic Smoke Ball Company*[72] conveniently provides us with a test case on the necessity and sufficiency of consent as the basis of private empowerment.

The court clearly believed that the merits were with Mrs Carlill and, one way or another, her claim was destined to succeed. However, the difficulty was that Mrs Carlill's claim pleaded that the manufacturers were in breach of contract with her. But what contract was this? No one denied that Mrs Carlill had a contract with the chemist from whom she purchased the smoke ball, but, in the absence of any direct negotiation or dealing between herself and the manufacturers, on what basis could it be argued that Mrs Carlill's relationship with the manufacturers was contractual? Treating the manufacturers' advert as akin to an offer of a reward, the court was able to identify a framework for agreement between the parties. However, according to the English doctrine of consideration, to qualify as 'contractual' (in the sense of an agreement enforceable at law), the transaction between the manufacturers and Mrs Carlill would need to involve some reciprocation on her side. What, then, was her side of the bargain? Mrs Carlill was not promising to use the smoke ball and nor was she paying the manufacturers any money. The court gave a fairly unconvincing answer suggesting that consideration could be found in the inconvenience suffered by Mrs Carlill when she used the smoke ball (a relatively unpleasant procedure) or in the indirect benefit enjoyed by the company through the sale of its products. Modern commentators would find the latter ground more promising than the former, reworking it to construe a so-called 'collateral contract' (between Mrs Carlill and the manufacturers) alongside the main contract of sale between Mrs Carlill and the chemist. Under the collateral contract, in return for the company's offer of £100 insurance against the risk of the smoke ball's failure, Mrs Carlill made her offer (to the chemist) to purchase a smoke ball. Even with the assistance of this modern approach, however, there is a sense that, for the sake of achieving the right result, the facts are being forced into a contractual matrix.

Without yet having fully clarified our thoughts about the necessity and sufficiency of consent as the basis of contractual empowerment (and as the justifying reason for enforcement), *Carlill* prompts two (possibly naïve) questions. First, if contracts can be construed or implied, or if the facts can be moulded into a collateral contract, to what extent are we treating con-

[71] For a fascinating account of the background to this case, see AWB.Simpson, 'Quackery and Contract Law: the Case of the Carbolic Smoke Ball' (1985) 14 *Journal of Legal Studies* 345.

[72] [1893] 1 QB 256.

sent as a *necessary* condition for the exercise of private empowerment (and, concomitantly, as the justifying reason for treating the new relationship as binding)? Is the promisor's consent truly necessary? Secondly, if a promise (such as a manufacturer's promise) is seriously made, why not treat it as *sufficient* for contractual obligation? Why insist that only the restricted class of promises made in a certain form (for example, under seal) or comprising a reciprocal exchange (as required by the doctrine of consideration) is contractual? Or, if contract is to be so restricted, why not recognise a background (tortious) right where a promise is seriously made and detrimentally relied on?

### *(i) The Necessity of Consent*

The paradigm of private empowerment involves an agent freely and with relevant knowledge consenting to the creation of a new relationship. The change of relationship might involve something as simple as a gift or a promise or the consent might signal a willingness to be bound by the rules of a game or the outcome of a voting process, or the like. If a particular agent, having opted to create a new relationship, subsequently claims that the promise, or the rules of the game, or the outcome of the vote should not be enforced, the obvious response is that this is not a complaint open to the agent because the agent consented to the new relationship (or to the process giving rise to it). The whole idea of private empowerment is that the agent holds a key (namely, the key of free and informed consent) that may be used to open the door to new relationships but, having turned the key, the agent is estopped from pleading that the newly created rights and duties should not be enforced.

As legal systems become more sophisticated, they offer privately empowered agents a variety of options represented by institutional sets such as contract, trust, partnership, marriage, and so on. In each case, the Gewirthian threshold condition is that agents invoke and participate in the chosen institutional set on the basis of consent (and to be Gewirthian-compliant, a legal regime should copy in this condition). Moreover, because such consent must be both free and informed, a consensual invocation of one of the institutional options presupposes a self-conscious awareness that one is engaging a particular institutional set. Should an agent, having brought into effect a new relationship by invoking a particular institutional set, subsequently plead that the rules of the set should not be enforced, then the obvious response once again is that the agent's threshold consent precludes such a plea. Accordingly, *if* consent is a good reason for holding an agent to a newly created relationship in simple cases of private empowerment, then it seems to be equally so in the more complex cases associated with the invocation of institutional legal sets.

Our immediate concern, however, is not with the *sufficiency* of consent as a justification for enforcing newly created relationships but with the *necessity* of consent in this context. Our question is whether, in the absence of an initial consenting act of private empowerment, an agent can justifiably be held to the terms of a new relationship.[73] In one sense, it seems to be an analytical truth that an adequate originating consent is a necessary condition because a proposition of the form 'By virtue of private empowerment, agent A has created a new relationship with agent B' presupposes a consensual act by A: without consent, there is (analytically) no act of private empowerment and no new relationship so created. However, the court's approach in *Carlill* raises a suspicion that, on occasion, the law might treat parties 'as if' they have a contract—the contrast there being between the clearly invoked contract between Mrs Carlill and the chemist from whom she purchased the smoke ball and the 'as if' or deemed contract between the manufacturers of the smoke ball and Mrs Carlill. If this suspicion proves well founded, and if enforcement of the new relationship is justifiable, it means that an agent's threshold act of consent is not necessarily the justification for holding the agent to the terms of a new relationship. In other words, even if the concept of private empowerment presupposes a consensual opting-in or opting for a new relationship, the law might not treat an agent's threshold consent as a necessary condition for enforcing a new relationship.

The form of this analysis bears comparison with what we have already said about private wrongdoing and its possible (substantive) justification, all things considered. At one level, we have the questions, 'Has agent A, whose rights have been infringed, been the victim of a wrong?' and 'Has agent A, whom we are treating as having created a new relationship, exercised a power to create such a relationship?'. If agent A, whose rights have been violated, has not consented to the act in question, a wrong has been done to A. With so much talk of fallacy in the air, it is worth emphasising that it is *no* fallacy to hold that consent is a necessary condition to neutralise a violation of prima facie rights. In the same way, if agent A has not consented to the creation of a new relationship by the exercise of his powers, we misrepresent the position if we treat him as having exercised the relevant powers—this is a fiction. Once again, it is *no* fallacy to insist that, without consent, new relationships are imposed rather than self-generated. At another level, however, we have the questions, 'Is there nevertheless a (substantive) justification for infringing A's rights?' and 'Is there nevertheless a (substantive) justification for treating A as bound by the terms of a new relationship?'. In such cases, the fact that A has not consented entails that a wrong is done and a power not exercised; but it does not conclude our inquiry into justification, all things considered.

[73] Of course, *within a particular set* (whether an informal set such as a game or a more formal legal set), the ground rules of the set will determine how far consent is necessary. Such rule-sets, as we have said many times, enjoy relative autonomy.

Let us focus on the case of contract. In a broad sense, and generally speaking, contracting is a bilateral exercise of private empowerment designed to strike a bargain (and, with that, to put in place a new relationship between the parties). In this broad sense, contracting might be informal, the agents' bargain not being recognised by the law as 'contractually enforceable'; and, correlatively, the agents might or might not intend to invoke the legal institution of 'contract' (that is, the institutional set comprising the particular class of bargains that the law will enforce). Or, of course, contracting might be formal, the agents' intention being to engage the institutional set of contract. We take it that if the phenomenon of 'constructed' or 'as if' contracts is to be found, then we will find it in this latter category of formal contracting.

Even if it should transpire that consent is not treated as a necessary condition for treating agents *as if* they have engaged the legal institution of contract, there is nevertheless plenty of evidence that, in the ordinary run of transactions, legal regimes are sensitive to the need for authentic consensual engagement. Characteristically, legal regimes put in place safeguards against non-consensual (including inadvertent) contracting—for example, by regulating inertia selling and by declining to enforce agreements that have supposedly crystallised by virtue of the offeree's silence or inaction. However, away from the ordinary run of things, we find a different story. Exceptionally, we find the law resorting to compulsion (such as with the compulsory purchase of land or the compulsory licensing of a medicine); we find hybrids, such as 'quasi-contract' (prior to the explicit recognition of restitution), being resorted to; and we find ex post facto 'construction' (the constructive trust, for instance) and 'invented' (as some would have it) contracts. Where the law resorts to such exceptional measures, it cannot rely on consent as anything more than a fiction, and, if there is a justifying reason for enforcement, it must lie elsewhere. In a general sense, that reason must be 'the doing of justice', and, if it is to be justice according to Gewirthian principles, it must be for the sake of respecting prima facie or competing rights. For example, if a compulsory purchase order is placed on agent A's land for the sake of safeguarding the supply of water to a nearby city, the form of justification for this compulsory contract is not A's consent (even if there is an 'agreement' signed off by A), but the basic rights of the agents who live in the city and who need water. To do justice to the complexity of 'the doing of justice' as a justifying reason would take another book. Here, a couple of indicative examples from the law of contract must suffice.

A common problem (the so-called problem of pre-contractual reliance) arises where parties incur costs during the negotiation of a contract which are then wasted if the expected contract does not materialise. In many contexts, such wasted costs are quite fairly and properly at the risk of the negotiating parties, and justice requires no rectificatory steps to be taken.

However, there are cases in which one party encourages the other party to incur the expenses, or at any rate acquiesces in what it knows will prove to be wasted expenditure.[74] The Wisconsin case of *Hoffman v Red Owl Stores Inc*[75] is a famous example of this particular problem. In *Hoffman*, the claimants, who were small-town bakers, approached the defendant with a view to acquiring a franchise to operate a Red Owl Store. They were encouraged to believe that they would be given a franchise for a particular store and, with the defendant's knowledge, they sold up their house and business, and relocated to the site of the new store. However, at the eleventh hour, the claimants were told that the agreed up-front payment for the franchise was being revised and, in consequence, the deal fell through, leaving the claimants with considerable wasted expenditure. A rigid regime of contract law would reject the claimants' action for an indemnity against their wasted expenses (their so-called 'reliance loss') and a fortiori any claim for loss of anticipated profits (their so-called 'expectation loss').[76] However, a more flexible regime would have a number of ways of responding sympathetically to the Hoffmans' claim.

One way, borrowing the idea from *Carlill*, would be to construct a collateral contract under which the defendant would undertake at least to indemnify the Hoffmans against their wasted expenses if they would proceed as if the formal contract for the franchise were already in place. Another way—an approach favoured in civilian legal systems—is to treat a failure to negotiate in good faith (*culpa in contrahendo*) as an actionable tort (or delict).[77] In *Hoffman* itself, the court drew on paragraph 90 of the *American Restatement of Contracts 2nd* to find in favour of the claimants. According to paragraph 90:

> A promise which the promisor should reasonably expect to induce action or forbearance on the part of the promisee . . . and which does induce such action or forbearance is binding if injustice can be avoided only by the enforcement of the promise. The remedy granted for the breach may be limited as justice requires.

The first of these approaches (construing a collateral contract) purports to be squarely contractual; the second is explicitly non-contractual; and the third (as provided for in the *Restatement*) is ambivalent, accepting detrimental reliance as a ground for recovery within a conceptual framework that treats an exchange of promises as the paradigm of contract—famously moving Grant Gilmore to pronounce the 'death of contract'.[78] If we rely on

[74] Cf *Waltons Stores (Interstate) Ltd v Maher* (1988) 76 ALR 513.

[75] 133 NW 2d 267 (1965).

[76] Seminally, see Lon L Fuller and William R Perdue, 'The Reliance Interest in Contract Damages' (1936) 46 *Yale Law Journal* 52 and 373.

[77] See Friedrich Kessler and Edith Fine, 'Culpa in Contrahendo, Bargaining in Good Faith and Freedom of Contract: A Comparative Study' (1964) 77 *Harvard Law Review* 401.

[78] Grant Gilmore, *The Death of Contract* (Columbus, OH, Ohio State University Press, 1974).

the first approach, we seem to be paying little more than lip service to the necessity of consent; the driving force behind the decision is the perceived unfairness of leaving the Hoffmans to pick up the bill for their wasted pre-contractual expenses. If we rely on the second approach, the case is removed from the category of private empowerment; the negotiating relationship is governed by background rights and obligations, and consent is no longer a contentious issue. If we follow the third approach, provided that the promisor has given his promise freely and with the knowledge of potential liability under paragraph 90, the requirement of consent is satisfied and nothing hinges on whether the liability is characterised as essentially tortious or as essentially contractual.

Another context in which there is a temptation to put in place a 'constructed' contract is that in which a third party, C, will not otherwise be entitled to take the benefit of a contract between A and B (this contract being intended to be for the benefit of C). For example, A promises B that, in return for some service provided by B, A will pay an agreed sum of money to C. B intends that the contract with A is to be for the benefit of C, but A renders his promise to B. In some legal regimes, the contract might be treated as exclusively between A and B, with B being the only party recognised as having the right to enforce A's promise. Where this is the legal position, it can give rise to questionable results. If, say, B dies and A declines to pay the promised sum to C, it is arguable that the 'doing of justice' requires that C should be able to enforce A's promise. Such an argument might rest on the principle that (B not having consented to non-performance by A) A's promise should be enforced, or it might be based on a perceived need to protect C against misleading indications given by contractors or something of that kind. Following the pattern of responses to the problem of pre-contractual reliance, there are again several ways in which a result in favour of C might be achieved. For example, a collateral contract of some kind might be constructed between A and C; or an unjustifiable failure to perform a contract for the benefit of a third party might be treated as a tort;[79] or, if C has detrimentally relied on the agreement between A and B, A's failure to pay might be treated as actionable.[80]

In each of these instances, just as in *Greenberg* (which we discussed earlier in the chapter), a court might construct a contract ex post facto as a way of securing what it perceives to be a just result. Where this occurs, the real justification for enforcement is not that the agent against whom

[79] Compare the so-called 'disappointed beneficiary' cases, such as *White v Jones* [1995] 2 AC 207 and its equivalents in other jurisdictions. In these cases, the head contract between the testator and the professional will-drafters is designed to benefit third parties. Where the professionals fail to exercise due care or act with due speed, as a result of which the will fails to deliver the expected benefit, the beneficiaries might frame their claim in tort.

[80] This by no means exhausts the list of possible strategies for the protection of C. For example, trusts or agency relationships might be constructed.

enforcement is ordered has consented to enter into the constructed contract but that such remedial measures are called for if justice is to be done. Consent, as the Realists might have put it, is more by way of conclusory than justificatory reasoning. Assuming that there would otherwise be an injustice (relative to Gewirthian standards), this is not an entirely satisfactory state of affairs. By way of mitigation, it can be pleaded on behalf of particular legal regimes that they become locked in their own history and jurisprudence. In some regimes, contract has, so to speak, a broader 'protective umbrella' than is found in others; in some, torts is more flexible than in others; in some, the principle has crystallised that unjust enrichment should be reversed by way of a restitutionary remedy but in others it has not; and, in some regimes, property rights are more extensive than in others. It follows that, where a court sees the need to do justice but does not have to hand a direct and appropriate legal tool, it will go for the next best resource in the toolbox.[81] So it is that, *in extremis*, we find contract being relied on (for the sake of doing justice) when a better-equipped regime would be in a position to rely instead directly on a tort or a restitutionary or a property right.

What we should conclude, therefore, is that, while consent is a necessary condition for the exercise of private empowerment as such, it is not a necessary condition for the justifiable enforcement of an 'as if' or constructed contract. What needs to be justified here is precisely the enforcement of a new set of rights and duties created *without* the consent of the relevant agents. Moreover, if legal regimes are to bring their remedial actions and their ostensible remedial justifications more closely into alignment, they need to develop direct and explicit remedial resources rather than resorting to fictions.

### *(ii) The Sufficiency of Consent*

While discussing the necessity of consent, we did not firmly contend that the threshold consent of agent A is at least a sufficient justification for holding A to the newly created arrangement of rights and obligations. However, it seems to us that the sufficiency of consent in such circumstances is so plain as to be axiomatic. If so, it follows that in the domain of private law an agent's consent is a *sufficient* justification for (a) holding the consenting agent to a modification of the position obtaining under existing background rights and duties (thereby precluding the agent from asserting what would otherwise be a private wrong) and (b) holding the consenting agent to the normative consequences of an act of private empowerment (thereby precluding the agent from denying the binding nature of the newly created

[81] This next best resource is not always contract, for this is a matter that depends very much on the configuration of the particular legal regime: see Basil Markesinis, 'An Expanding Tort Law—The Price of a Rigid Contract Law' (1987) 103 *Law Quarterly Review* 354.

rights and obligations). Again, if it is correct to treat it as axiomatic that consent is sufficient in relation to private empowerment, any train of thinking that suggests otherwise must involve misdirection or muddle.

When we discussed *Carlill*, one of the questions prompted was this: why not simply treat the manufacturer's promise as contractually binding; why require consideration from the promisee? At first blush, this question seems to imply that where legal regimes decline to treat a promise as contractually enforceable unless it complies with certain formal requirements (seal, written evidence, notorial authentication, or whatever) or it is supported by consideration, they do not treat the promising agent's consent as a sufficient justification for enforcement. However, this line of reasoning runs into confusion unless we distinguish between the sufficiency of a consensual promise for the purpose of engaging the formal institutional set of contract law, and the sufficiency of bare promises as provided for by the governing rule-set. In other words, we must distinguish between originating consents (or promises) to engage a set of rules and consents (or promises) within the engaged rule-set. The doctrinal requirement of consideration is internal to the 'law of contract' (or, at any rate, some versions of it) and it does not speak to the consensual exercise of a power (whether to make a gratuitous promise, or to engage a rule-set of some description). Given that institutional sets such as the 'law of contract' enjoy relative autonomy, there is no Gewirthian consent-related reason for condemning the doctrinal requirement of consideration. Nevertheless, one might wonder why legal regimes adopt such a requirement—that is, one might wonder why the consideration requirement is thought to be functional.

In fact, although legal regimes rarely treat a bare promise, without more, as contractually binding, their reasons for requiring formalities or for requiring consideration in support of an informal promise are somewhat murky.[82] In the case of formalities, it is arguable that legal regimes should not waste their resources on disputes that centre on whether or not a promise was actually made—hence the adoption of formal requirements that ease this evidential question; or it is arguable that suitably designed formalities serve to protect promisors against improper pressure or undue influence by the promisee.[83] However, the desire to give promisors an opportunity to resile from informal promises that they have freely made but which they now regret seems at odds with an institutional set that aspires to promote transactional security. With regard to consideration, there is again the possibility that this additional requirement serves as a surrogate for a requirement that is actually contained within the notion of a free and informed consent.

[82] See, eg, James Gordley (ed), *The Enforceability of Promises in European Contract Law* (Cambridge, Cambridge University Press, 2001).

[83] Whether as a corrective measure if the originating consents are deficient, or as a free-standing matter of institutional design under relative autonomy.

Certainly, there is reason to think that, prior to the modern articulation of a doctrine of economic duress, the doctrine of consideration covered for cases of this kind—for example, in the famous case of *Stilk v Myrick*,[84] where the captain promised the crew additional wages, while one report of the case indicates that duress (qua public policy) was the reason for non-enforcement of the promise, another report suggests that it was for want of consideration that the promise was not enforced. Similarly, consideration might operate as an indirect way of inquiring as to the precise nature of the promisor's intention, its function being to check (somewhat disingenuously) whether the promisor truly intended to make a gratuitous promise.[85] That a legal regime has not yet evolved to the point where it can give clean doctrinal expression to what it is doing is a matter of regret, and, as we remarked earlier, legal regimes should strive to bring into alignment their judicial actions and their covering doctrines. Nevertheless, the lack of alignment or obliqueness of legal doctrine should not mislead us into thinking that consent is not a sufficient justification.

What do these observations add up to? We suggest that consent is a sufficient condition for acts of private empowerment, whether or not the act is directed at a formal institutional set. If an agent consents to the creation of a new set of rights and duties, that consent suffices to justify enforcement of the newly created rights and duties. Where institutional sets, such as the 'law of contract', are consensually engaged, the design of these sets enjoys relative autonomy. Accordingly, the puzzle about a doctrinal requirement such as that of consideration is not so much whether it fits with a consensual approach to contract (this being covered by the originating consents) but whether it is functional given the aims of the particular institutional set.[86] If the set aims to mimic consent, then doctrines that are so directed make sense (relative to the aims of the set). However, if this is not what the set aims to achieve, then a different kind of functionality is what we are looking for. In the case of formalities, such a functionality might be that efficiency and economy are served by minimising disputes about whether or not consent was given. However, in relation to consideration, it is much more difficult to understand why it is judged to be functional to protect competent agents against those consequences of their acts of private empowerment that they come to regret. Still, we need not agonise about this because relative autonomy screens it off from fundamental issues of consent.

[84] (1809) 2 Camp 317.

[85] Compare the more direct approach of the civilian doctrine of *causa*.

[86] Of course, if the originating consents are deficient, the doctrinal requirements for formality and consideration must be evaluated relative to a corrective function.

## V Conclusion

In the private domain, what can we say about the general shape of a legal regime if it is to be compliant with Gewirthian principles?

First, it must be recognised as axiomatic that consent is a sufficient (procedural) justificatory reason; and that this axiomatic principle holds with regard to both private wrongdoing and private empowerment. Relative to private wrongdoing, consent, so viewed, operates to preclude the consenting agent from alleging private wrong where the offending action falls within the scope of the authorising consent and, relative to private empowerment, consent operates to preclude the consenting agent from denying the binding force of a set of rights and duties newly created by the agent's own act of private empowerment. In all cases, of course, the consent should be treated as effective for these preclusionary purposes only if it satisfies the several conditions of adequacy.

Secondly, although consent is a sufficient justificatory condition in relation to private wrong, it is not also necessary. To be sure, if the rights-holder has not consented, the violation of right will involve a wrong; and we should be mindful of the principle of the 'priority of consent'—namely, that it is always better to act with the rights-holder's authorisation (to avoid any wrongdoing) rather than to rely on the wrong that is done being the lesser of two evils. Having said this, however, it remains the case that, from a Gewirthian perspective, an agent's prima facie private rights may be justifiably infringed for the sake of more compelling rights (to overlook this is to make one of the errors associated with the Fallacy of Necessity). Whilst legal regimes might not always articulate their private law defences in a language that copies cleanly onto Gewirthian principles, this is not the most important issue; what really matters is that illicit reasons—for example, paternalistic or utilitarian reasons—are not covertly resorted to under cover of recognised defences.

Thirdly, in relation to private empowerment, consent (while necessary for an act of empowerment) is again not a necessary condition for the enforcement of a new set of rights and duties (modifying the existing set of background rights and obligations). Such measures might be required for the sake of achieving justice between the parties. However, legal regimes do not always articulate their remedial responses in a way that cleanly and accurately reflects Gewirthian principles that would justify their actions. Instead, they resort to constructing contracts, and the like, 'as if' the agents concerned had consented to an exercise of private empowerment. This is a fiction, and we should not equate a justification that rests on a consent given by an agent with a justification that employs the rhetoric of consent ('as if' there had been an exercise of private empowerment) but which relies on a justification other than consent given by an agent. If substantive justification is called for, we should settle for nothing less and certainly not for a *faux* procedural justification.

Finally, although in many cases the only plausible justification for acting in a particular way will be that the relevant agent has authorised the action by giving consent, no legal regime should fall into the trap of thinking that it is necessarily wrong (or beyond justification, as in our second concluding remark above) to act without consent (this is another trap set by the Fallacy of Necessity). In each case, we need to be guided by the Gewirthian scheme of rights; in some cases, the scheme will indicate that, absence of consent notwithstanding, the action (albeit involving the doing of a wrong) is justified; and, in other cases, it will indicate that there is no need to justify the action because, no prima facie right having been violated, there is simply no wrong.

# 9

# The Necessity, Sufficiency, and Relevance of Consent II: Public Wrong

## I Introduction

In this chapter, our focus moves to the way in which consent operates in the context of *public* wrong. Modern legal regimes will set out their basic catalogue of public wrongs in their criminal code, but this scheme will be supplemented and refined in various ways. For example, where conduct that is otherwise prohibited may be permitted under licence, the regulatory (licensing) body will draw the line between prohibition and permission on a case-by-case basis. The two questions that are focal for our discussion are: first, whether the consent of the participants is a *sufficient* justification in relation to an alleged public wrong; and, secondly, whether the consent of the victim (of the alleged public wrong) is the *necessary* justification.

With regard to the first of these questions, our discussion links back to what we have said about *private* wrong. For, if agents do no *private* wrong to one another because their transaction is consensual, they might still do a *private* wrong to a non-consenting third party (whose rights are infringed by the transaction—recall, for instance, the case of xenotransplantation, where non-consenting third parties are put at risk) and there might still be a *public* interest in regulating their conduct where it has such 'externalities'. To suppose otherwise is to commit one of the several fallacies of consent. However, if the agents do no private wrong inter se or to any third party (because all agents are consenting), it becomes more difficult to see how a public interest argument for intervention might be made out. Of course, if we recoil from sado-masochism, dwarf-throwing, or the kind of dinner party that Armin Meiwes notoriously arranged with Bernd Brandes, or the like, we might think that, to the contrary, it is actually very easy to formulate a public interest reason for intervention. Accordingly, to put the point more carefully: the proposition is that, where all participating agents are consenting, it becomes more difficult to see how a public interest argument for intervention might be squared *with rights theory*. Is consent not a sufficient justification in such circumstances?

In the first part of this chapter, we will pursue this question of the *sufficiency* of consent (as a response to an alleged *public* wrong) by considering two landmark cases concerning the substantive due process jurisprudence of the Fourteenth Amendment—*Washington v Glucksberg*[1] and *Lawrence v Texas*[2]—together with a third (English) case, *Comment on Reproductive Ethics*,[3] concerning access to state-of-the-art embryo-screening technology. Whereas, in *Glucksberg* (on assisted suicide), the consent of the participants was argued unsuccessfully as a sufficient response to an alleged public wrong, in *Lawrence* (on homosexuality) the same form of argument succeeded. In *Comment on Reproductive Ethics*, similar questions of consent and public wrong were at issue; the court upheld the legal permission; but the case is not a straightforward triumph for liberalism, for it prompts some troublesome concerns about the need for autonomy-limitation and restraint. If, as we suggest, there are public interest reasons that justify intervention, the consent of the participants notwithstanding, it is not just the Fallacy of Necessity that need concern us; we must also avoid the Fallacy of Sufficiency (in the sense of falling into the trap of believing that consent is a sufficient response to a charge of public wrong).

In the second part of the chapter, we will turn to the *necessity* of consent as a justification in the domain of public wrong. Where agent A commits a public wrong against agent B, in principle, does A have any defence other than B's consent (if, indeed, B's consent is a defence at all)? Typically, legal regimes recognise several defences, not always distinguishing clearly between those defences that are regarded as full justifications and those that are merely excusing conditions, as well as mitigating circumstances. We will particularly focus on the defence of necessity where it is argued in the context of an absence of consent, a defence famously rejected in the historic case of *R v Dudley and Stephens*,[4] but tentatively accepted in the recent case of *Re A (Children) (Conjoined Twins: Surgical Separation)*.[5]

## II Public Wrong and the Sufficiency of Consent

To declare that some conduct constitutes a public wrong, notwithstanding (i) that the participants have engaged in the conduct on the basis of free and informed consent, and (ii) that there is no private wrong of any kind, is seemingly to discount the significance of an agent's autonomy and to violate the canons of Gewirthian morality. In this part of our discussion, we

[1] 117 S Ct 2258 (1997).

[2] 123 S Ct 2472 (2003).

[3] *R (Quintavalle on behalf of Comment on Reproductive Ethics) v Human Fertilisation and Embryology Authority* [2002] EWHC 2785 (Admin), [2003] EWCA Civ 667. The decision of the Court of Appeal was unsuccessfully appealed to the House of Lords: see *Quintavalle v Human Fertilisation and Embryology Authority* [2005] UKHL 28. See, further, Roger Brownsword, 'Happy Families, Consenting Couples, and Children with Dignity: Sex Selection and Saviour Siblings' [2005] *Child and Family Law Quarterly* 435.

[4] (1884) 14 QBD 273.

[5] [2000] 4 All ER 961.

will consider, first, *Washington v Glucksberg*[6] and *Lawrence v Texas*[7] as representative of a litany of well-known cases involving restrictions on lifestyle autonomy, such restrictions being imposed for the sake of the 'public interest'. Insofar as the public interest is simply a token of the intolerance of the local 'moral majority', it will fail to justify the State's action. However, if the public interest represents a principled strand of Gewirthian thinking, it might be possible for the State to make out a defence of its restriction. We will, then, focus on *Comment on Reproductive Ethics*, in which the court (paradoxically) might be thought to attach too much weight to the particular-occurrent exercise of agent autonomy and to pay too little attention to the sustainability of the context of a community of rights on which Gewirthian thinking is predicated.

Formally, we can say that, to justify treating conduct that, of itself, involves no private wrong as a public wrong, the State must be able to show: (a) that it has recognisable Gewirthian rights-related reasons for intervention; and (b) that its intervention is a necessary and proportionate measure in the circumstances. As general guidelines, we suggest that there are just three categories of Gewirthian rights-related reasons, as follows:

Class (i) reasons: in order to secure respect for the rights of fellow agents in the community—covering:

- interventions that are designed to discourage violations of rights;[8]
- interventions that aim to co-ordinate the community's activities so that responsibilities to rights-holders are discharged more effectively;
- interventions that are designed to assist with the enforcement of rights.

Class (ii) reasons: in order to preserve the context in which autonomous agents will enjoy the opportunity to flourish as members of a community committed to human rights and responsibilities—such a context is multi-layered and includes:

- interventions that are designed to make essential community choices between morally optional conduct or forms of life

[6] 117 S Ct 2258 (1997); 138 L Ed 2d 772.

[7] 123 S Ct 2472 (2003).

[8] This is a broad reason authorising public intervention in order to protect vulnerable agents (as argued, for instance, in the assisted suicide cases) but also to pre-empt actions that might generate rights-violating consequences. For example, in the *Laserdrome Decision* (24 October 2001, BVerwGE 115, 189), the Federal Administrative Court in Germany was concerned that 'playful killing' at the Laserdrome (a shooting arcade) tended to trivialise violence and might, thus, weaken respect for the well-being of other agents. Against this consideration, the fact that participation was voluntary and the consent of the players was mutual was irrelevant. Quite possibly, such reasoning might support a prohibition on consensual cannibalism (of the Meiwes and Brand variety); and, similarly, a legal regime might intervene to prevent cruelty to animals for fear that agents might otherwise become desensitised to the infliction of physical damage in a way that might then be copied across to transactions with fellow agents. Clearly, such slippery slope arguments need to be handled very carefully. To justify intervention, the steps must be necessary and proportionate.

- interventions that provisionally settle the community's position on a morally contested matter (whether relating to the interpretation of rights principles or their application)
- interventions that aim to preserve those features of the context from which agents take their identity as members of a community committed to respect for rights and, concomitantly, their responsibilities.[9]

Class (iii) reasons: in order to give effect to prohibitions that have been expressly authorised (under strict conditions of consent) by members of the community.

Because 'public interest', like 'consent', is open to abuse as a lazy justification (or, even worse, as a rhetorical defence of the indefensible),[10] these special cases should not be viewed as a blank cheque. It is worth repeating, therefore, that even if the State is able to defend its prohibition by reference to one of the above reasons, its particular intervention must be a necessary and proportionate measure in the circumstances.

### *(i) Autonomy-limitation I: The Regulation of Assisted Suicide and Homosexuality*

To focus our discussion of *Washington v Glucksberg* and *Lawrence v Texas*, a thumbnail sketch of the ground rules for constitutional challenge under the Fourteenth Amendment is necessary. Under the Fourteenth Amendment, it may be argued that legislation is unconstitutional either because it offends against the principle of equal protection or because it violates due process. Where violation of due process is alleged, the failure might be argued to be of a procedural or a substantive nature. For present purposes, we can put procedural due process questions to one side. Whereas arguments about equal protection tend to be concerned with suspect classifications (and distinctions), arguments about substantive due process involve a weighing of the liberty interests of citizens against the countervailing interests of the State. Thus, it is substantive due process that invites the kind of consent-based challenge that we are contemplating.

The jurisprudence of substantive due process draws an important distinction between a *fundamental* liberty interest (or fundamental right) and a liberty interest that is *not fundamental*. If those who challenge are able to

[9] Arguably, intervention to regulate embryonic sex selection might be so viewed—at any rate if one sex (historically, male) was disproportionately favoured and if this then had a negative impact on the way that the disfavoured sex regarded itself; but the more obvious concern, perhaps, is that members of the favoured sex will show less respect for the rights of members of the disfavoured sex, see n 52 below and the accompanying text. Whether the case for intervention rests on class (i) or class (ii) reasons, or a mixture of such reasons, prohibition is by no means the only form of regulatory response and a less drastic measure might suffice: see Owen D Jones, 'Sex Selection: Regulating Technology Enabling the Predetermination of a Child's Gender' (1992) 6 *Harvard Journal of Law and Technology* 1, at 52–61 (sketching a tax-based approach).

[10] See Roger Brownsword (ed), *Law and the Public Interest* (Stuttgart, Franz Steiner, 1993).

point to a fundamental liberty interest on which the contested statute impinges, then the level of review involves a so-called 'heightened scrutiny'; the State will be able to justify deprivation of a fundamental liberty only if required so to act for the sake of a compelling State interest. However, if the liberty interest is classified as non-fundamental, constitutional review will be at a lower 'rational basis' level. Here, the State will succeed in defending the constitutionality of its statute provided only that the statutory curtailment of liberty can be shown to be rationally related to a legitimate State interest. In neither case is it for the court to substitute its judgment of a reasonable balance between the competing interests; provided that the State's position is within the range of reasonableness, the contested law will survive constitutional review for substantive due process.[11]

(a) Assisted Suicide

In the parallel cases, *Washington v Glucksberg*[12] and *Vacco v Quill*,[13] the US Supreme Court rejected Fourteenth Amendment challenges to the constitutionality of State prohibitions against assisted suicide. Whereas argument in *Glucksberg* centred on questions of substantive due process, in *Quill* they centred on equal protection. As we have said, it is substantive due process that opens the Constitution to the argument that a prohibition unlawfully impinges on consensual activities. In what follows, therefore, we will concentrate on *Glucksberg*.

In *Washington v Glucksberg*,[14] the State of Washington's prohibition against assisted suicide was challenged by a group comprising four doctors (who averred that they would be prepared to assist terminally ill patients to end their lives but for the legal prohibition), three terminally ill patients (all of whom died before the case reached the Supreme Court), and the non-profit organisation Compassion in Dying. The District Court ruled in favour of the plaintiffs; a panel of the Court of Appeals of the Ninth Circuit reversed the lower court before the Ninth Circuit rehearing the case en banc reversed the panel's decision; finally, the Supreme Court reversed the Ninth Circuit thus leaving Washington's prohibition intact. Stated shortly, the Supreme Court ruled that the asserted right to assistance in committing suicide was not to be treated as a fundamental liberty interest. Hence, it sufficed for Washington to show that its ban on assisted suicide reasonably related to the protection and promotion of a legitimate State interest. In the court's judgment, Washington comfortably met this standard because there were a number of such interests to which its prohibition was referable.

[11] For a full account of the jurisprudence of the substantive due process clause, including his views on the element of judicial restraint, see the concurring opinion of Souter J in *Glucksberg*.

[12] 117 S Ct 2258 (1997); 138 L Ed 2d 772.

[13] 138 L Ed 2d 834.

[14] 117 S Ct 2258 (1997); 138 L Ed 2d 772.

Stated equally shortly, the fundamental question raised by a consent perspective is this: why is the consent of the terminally ill, but competent agent, not sufficient to license the doctor *to assist* with the desired suicide? Since the central holding in *Glucksberg* is that there is no generalised right to commit suicide including a right to assistance in doing so, we seem to be channelled by both *Glucksberg* and the consent perspective towards the same questions: namely, what rights do agents have in end of life contexts and how do acts of assistance relate to whatever rights are held? Is the key to this an articulation of the generally recognised right to life[15] or an application of a claimed 'right to die'?

Let us start with the right to life (RL). Paradigmatically, this right protects an agent against the intentional deprivation of life. We can extend the paradigm to include protection against reckless or careless conduct that is life-threatening. However, even as extended, this fundamental negative claim-right does not exhaust the possible articulations of the right. A fuller set, addressing acts of assistance as well as positive rights, might be articulated to include the following:

RL(a): a negative claim-right that other agents do not act in ways that are intended to terminate one's life (ie the basic right, possibly extended to cover reckless and careless conduct);

RL(b): a negative claim-right that other agents do not take steps to assist others to terminate one's life or to assist one to terminate one's life;

RL(c): a positive claim-right that other agents act in ways that are designed to save or sustain one's life;

RL(d): a positive claim-right that other agents act in such a way as to assist in saving or sustaining one's life.

Each of these claim-rights encompasses a benefit for the rights-holder and places other agents under a duty—in RL(a) and RL(b), a duty not to perform life-terminating acts (or to assist with such), and in RL(c) and RL(d), a duty to perform life-saving acts (or to assist with such). If the rights-holder consents to non-performance of the duty, the benefit (the rights-holder's life) is placed in jeopardy and, in the standard way, the effect of the consent is to estop the rights-holder (or any representative on behalf of the rights-holder) from asserting a violation of right—as between the (consenting) rights-holder and the duty-bearer, consent operates to modify the background relationship; no wrong is done; the latter's act of killing (or assisting with such) or neglect of life-saving is justified. Accordingly, if an agent consents to a physician taking active steps to terminate the agent's life,

[15] In one of the leading European cases, *Regina on the Application of Mrs Dianne Pretty v DPP and Secretary of State for the Home Department* [2001] UKHL 61; *Case of Pretty v The United Kingdom* (2002) ECHR 2346/02, April 29; [2002] 35 EHRR 1, it was argued that '[t]he right to die is not the antithesis of the right to life but the corollary of it' [2001] UKHL 61, para 4 (per Lord Bingham).

or if an agent refuses the offer of life-sustaining treatment or consents to it being withdrawn, then the consent gives (procedural) justificatory cover to these life-terminating acts.[16]

This articulation of the right to life does not directly speak to the agent's right to commit suicide. The Gewirthian view is that agents are under no duty to sustain their own lives where their will is to bring an end to the life that supports their agency (and, indeed, which is essential for them to form and carry through their agency-terminating suicidal purpose). It follows that, for Gewirthians, suicide is permissible and that it is impermissible for other agents to interfere with an agent whose freely chosen and informed purpose is to commit suicide. If we articulate these principles under a right to suicide (RS), an agent's entitlements include:

RS(a): a permission to take one's own life; and
RS(b): a negative claim-right that other agents do not act in ways that are intended to interfere with an agent's exercise of permitted suicide under RS(a).

Treating this couplet as a supplement to the right to life set, we can return to the question of where the right to life takes us in relation to the question of physician-assisted suicide.

If it is submitted in cases such as *Glucksberg* or its European equivalent, *Dianne Pretty*,[17] that assisted suicide (whether the assistance is given by a physician or by some other agent) may be justified by reference to the right to life, the argument might be put in two ways. One argument, the direct argument, is that RL(b) is engaged; this right protects an agent against unwilled assistance with life termination; but where, as in these specimen cases, the rights-holder consents to (indeed, requests) the assistance, the assisting agent does not violate this right. The other argument, an indirect argument, starts with RL(a), reasoning perhaps that RL(a) looks more familiar (and certainly more fundamental) than RL(b). The argument is that, if the rights-holder would consent to being killed by another agent (so

[16] Where an agent consents to life-sustaining treatment being withdrawn, it might be said that the agent exercises 'a right to die' and that withdrawal of the treatment is permissible. However, this so-called right to die is nested within a specific claim-right under the right to life; so it is advisable to eschew characterising this as a right to die—it is a corollary of a particular aspect of the right to life. Even more misleadingly, although withdrawal of treatment is permissible, this is entirely in the context of the (private) transaction between the agents. Permissibility here means that no private wrong is done to the agent whose life is terminated by the consensual withdrawal of the treatment. That is all.

[17] Note 15 above. The specific question in *Pretty* was whether the Director of Public Prosecutions acted lawfully in refusing to grant an advance immunity against prosecution to Dianne Pretty's husband, should he assist with her suicide. However, the case, both in the English courts and at the European Court of Human Rights, involves extended consideration of whether, and how, various rights (under the European Convention on Human Rights) might be engaged by a person, such as Mrs Pretty, who seeks assistance with suicide.

that there would be no violation of RL(a)), then this must entail that the rights-holder consents also to assistance (so that there is no violation of RL(b)). Assuming that this entailment holds, this indirect argument is restricted to those cases where the rights-holder would consent to a termination that would otherwise be a violation of RL(a). In practice, this is probably so in the majority of assisted suicide cases. However, there might be cases where the agent, while needing assistance, wishes to administer the final life-terminating act personally (or, at least, to maintain control for the time being over that final act), in which event the justification for assistance rests on the direct argument. Can the direct argument bear the weight of justification?

Let us concede that the substance of RL(b) is somewhat unfamiliar. Scenarios in which an agent would violate this right by offering or putting in place unwilled-for life-terminating assistance (for example, an unsolicited suicide kit being delivered to one's home) are largely hypothetical. Nevertheless, the proposition that agents have RL(b) is plausible enough. If they did not have this negative claim-right, such unwanted acts of assistance would be permitted. And, certainly in a culture that treats the right to life as fundamental, it would seem incongruous not to recognise RL(b). So far as the applicants in cases like *Glucksburg* and *Dianne Pretty* are concerned, however, nothing hinges on this. For if, contrary to the direct argument, life-terminating acts of assistance are permitted—that is, such acts are permitted irrespective of whether they are wanted by the agent-to-be-assisted—then such acts must be treated as lawful (ie as at least involving no private wrong). Whereas if, applying the direct argument, life-terminating acts of assistance are permitted only where they are supported by the consent of the agent-to-be-assisted, then where there is consent such acts must also be treated as lawful (ie as at least involving no private wrong). Of course, in the former case, consent is not relevant to the justification because we start from a position of permission; it is only where acts of assistance constitute a prima facie violation of a right (namely, of RL(b)) that consent becomes relevant to the justification. Given that the former lacks the plausibility of the latter, we will proceed on the basis that the best argument drawing on the right to life is the direct invocation of RL(b) and, concomitantly, the giving of consent by the rights-holder.

If we accept this analysis, agents, including the terminally ill, have a specific claim-right (under the general rubric of the right to life) that others do not (against the will of rights-holding agents) assist or aid and abet their suicide. Where an agent consents to such assistance, then such acts constitute no *private* wrong. To protest that Washington's prohibition overlooks the parties' consent (or, similarly, to challenge the State's refusal to confer immunity on the assisting agent, as in *Dianne Pretty*), is to plead the absence of that particular private wrong and to put the onus on the State to justify its restriction.

Let us suppose that, instead of starting with a right to life, the right to die (RD) is taken as axiomatic. On the face of it, this is a strange kind of right—because, quite simply, we will all die anyway. However, if we treat this death-wish right as relating to life-threatening acts by others (such acts being required) and life-saving acts by others (such acts being prohibited), and if we articulate such a right in the way that we articulated the right to life, then we have the following set of claim-rights:

- RD(a): a positive claim-right that other agents act in ways that are intended to terminate one's life (ie the basic right, possibly extended to require reckless and careless life-threatening conduct);
- RD(b): a positive claim-right that other agents take steps to assist others or oneself to terminate one's life;
- RD(c): a negative claim-right that other agents do not act in ways that are designed to save or sustain one's life (including the claim-right that others do not interfere with one's own attempted suicide);
- RD(d): a negative claim-right that other agents do not act in such a way as to assist in saving or sustaining one's life.

Assuming that such rights are covered by the will theory, then they operate with life-threatening effect only where the rights-holding agent so wills. So, for example, the positive right to be killed by others RD(a) would only apply with terminal effect where the agent rights-holder so willed. Nevertheless, as a default position, the right to die would constitute a strange community in which the burden would lie on agents to signal a will to live. Where the burden was not discharged, and in the absence of a dereliction of duty, the expectation of rights-holders would be for a short life. Nevertheless, for the avoidance of doubt, we should read in alongside the right to die, the two suicide entitlements RS(a) and RS(b), the latter of which is already contained within the broader right RD(c).

For at least three reasons, we need take this thought-experiment little further. First, while such a rights regime (or some part of this regime) might make some kind of sense for members of a suicide club, or for gladiators, or the like, it makes little or no sense for members of societies of the kind that we are presupposing. Secondly, whilst the applicants in cases such as *Glucksberg* and *Dianne Pretty* argue that their consent authorises the life-terminating assistance of others, they do not argue for a positive claim-right of the kind articulated by RD(b). Their contention is not that, say, physicians would do wrong if they did not give life-terminating assistance as and when required. Even if it is arguable within Gewirthian theory that there are positive *obligations* to assist, the applicants do not need to put the case so strongly. It suffices to contend that physicians and other authorised agents do no wrong when, supported by consent, they give life-terminating assistance. Such a contention, however, draws on RL(b), coupled with consent; that is, it draws on a claim found in the *right to life* set. Thirdly, underlining this last point, if applicants in cases such as *Glucksberg* and *Dianne Pretty* were to argue that they had a positive claim-right to assistance with life termination, they would not need to plead the significance of the agent's consent: if the agent is exercising a positive claim-right (as a corollary to RL(b)),[18] the assertion of the claim-right (not consent) does all the justificatory work.

But, what about the line of argument in *Glucksberg* that, if we recognise a right to suicide, such a right must include a right to assistance with suicide? If this argument is predicated on a negative claim-right to suicide of the kind represented by RS(b) or RD(c), the court in *Glucksberg* will not allow it to get off the ground. For, whilst the court accepts that suicide has been largely decriminalised, it does not equate this with an acceptance of suicide. Rather, the softening of the criminal law reflects the view that it is unfair to exact punishment on the suicide's family; suicide itself is still viewed with disapproval. On this account, the permissibility of suicide (as in RS(a)) is not yet conceded and, if morality recognised a category of grudging permissibility, the court in *Glucksberg* might just about buy it. At all events, any idea that there is a duty not to interfere with an attempted suicide (correlative to RS(b) or RD(c)) let alone a duty to assist (correlative to RD(b)) must be firmly rejected. To repeat, of course, if one were to recognise the latter right, consent would be irrelevant because the agent would be calling on a positive right to assistance, and, if the former right were recognised, not only would consent be irrelevant, the substance of the claim-right would not reach to assistance. Accordingly, on the *Glucksberg* analysis, the strongest claim that might be made is that the act of suicide is (grudgingly) permissible, that requesting assistance with suicide is permissible, and that responding to such a request by assisting is also permissible.

In contrast to the court in *Glucksberg*, Gewirthians have less hesitation in recognising that an agent has entitlements in relation to the will to end one's own life (to undertake, as it were, one's final act of agency). Those entitlements are RS(a) and RS(b), which supplement, as we have said, the agent's right to life set. It follows that an agent's 'right to suicide' amounts to a permission to take one's own life RS(a), coupled with a claim-right that others do not interfere with such a life-taking act RS(b). It is also the case that, where an agent seeks assistance with suicide, it is permissible for another agent to respond to that request. The permissibility of assistance might be argued to derive from RS(a), but we have derived it already from RL(b)—and, indeed, we have even contemplated an extension to RL(b) that would

[18] The corollary to RL(b) would be to the effect that, where the agent rights-holder requests assistance with suicide, there is then a duty to assist. This is to be distinguished from RD(b), according to which there is a duty to assist with suicide attempts unless the agent signals that assistance is against his or her will. In the former, the default position is a right against life-threatening acts; in the latter, it is a right to be subjected to life-threatening acts—in both cases, unless the agent rights-holder wills otherwise.

make assistance a matter of requirement.[19] Accordingly, the argument that the right to suicide entails a right to assistance with suicide takes us to the point that we have reached already: namely, that where agent A consents to B's assistance, B is permitted to assist. In such a case, there is no private wrong between the parties, and the onus once again is thrown onto the State to justify its prohibition on B's act of assistance.

Taking stock, we suggest that an axiomatic right to die is not the obverse of an axiomatic right to life. Even with a will theory of rights, a community that is orientated towards the former is a very different community to one orientated towards the latter; and no community can be sensibly orientated towards both axiomatic rights at the same time. For our purposes, the axiomatic right is the right to life, not the right to die. Moreover, we can say all that we want to say about the assisted suicide cases by reference to articulations of the right to life, the justificatory force of consent, and the right to suicide that sits alongside the right to life. Where an agent exercises a particular articulation of the right to life in a way that puts his or her life in jeopardy (and, of course, this includes not only agents who request assistance with death but also agents who, like Bernd Brandes, volunteer for death) the agent has chosen death, or the risk of death, over life, and we might be tempted to refer to this choice in terms of a right to die. However, this is liable to confuse. The agent is not relying on a free-standing right to die; indeed, the agent is not relying on any kind of right to die. The only right in play is a right to life; and the default operation of particular articulations of this right are modified by the rights-holder's consent.

Now that we have the axiomatic right to life articulated and its relationship to a right to die clarified, we can see that the issue presented by the assisted suicide cases runs parallel with that presented by the arguments concerning active euthanasia. With regard to active euthanasia, RL(a) (an agent's protection against unwilled life-terminating or life-threatening acts by others) is focal; with regard to assisted suicide, RL(b) (an agent's protection against unwilled assistance with life-terminating acts) is focal; and, in both instances, the argument is that the consent of the rights-holding agent authorises (and justifies) what would otherwise be a violation of duty by the agent who terminates, or who assists with the termination of, the former agent's life. If consent is treated as a sufficient justificatory reason, assisted suicide and active euthanasia should be held to be lawful. Yet, in one test case after another, the highest courts in North America and Europe have rejected the pressure to relax the legal position in relation to assisted suicide, and, for most legal systems, the prohibition against active euthanasia is where the regulatory line is most clearly drawn in the sand.

From a Gewirthian perspective, is there any way that such a refusal to recognise the sufficiency of consent might be justified? Viewed as a

[19] See n 18 above.

free-standing transaction between two agents, the one consenting and the other acting on the basis of the consent, the latter does no *private* wrong to the former—on this point, the consent is conclusive. However, the standard reason given by rights-committed legal regimes for their refusal to recognise the *public* lawfulness of assisted suicide or active euthanasia is that such recognition would potentially undermine the right to life of third parties, particularly of vulnerable third party agents. So, for example, in *Washington v Glucksberg*, we find Chief Justice Rehnquist, delivering the opinion of the Court, saying:

> [t]he State has an interest in protecting vulnerable groups—including the poor, the elderly, and disabled persons—from abuse, neglect, and mistakes. The Court of Appeals dismissed the State's concern that disadvantaged persons might be pressured into physician assisted suicide as 'ludicrous on its face.' . . . We have recognized, however, the real risk of subtle coercion and undue influence in end of life situations. . . . Similarly, the New York Task Force warned that '[l]egalizing physician assisted suicide would pose profound risks to many individuals who are ill and vulnerable. . . . The risk of harm is greatest for the many individuals in our society whose autonomy and well being are already compromised by poverty, lack of access to good medical care, advanced age, or membership in a stigmatised social group.' . . . If physician assisted suicide were permitted, many might resort to it to spare their families the substantial financial burden of end of life health care costs.
>
> The State's interest here goes beyond protecting the vulnerable from coercion; it extends to protecting disabled and terminally ill people from prejudice, negative and inaccurate stereotypes, and 'societal indifference.' . . . The State's assisted suicide ban reflects and reinforces its policy that the lives of terminally ill, disabled, and elderly people must be no less valued than the lives of the young and healthy, and that a seriously disabled person's suicidal impulses should be interpreted and treated the same way as anyone else's. . . .
>
> Finally, the State may fear that permitting assisted suicide will start it down the path to voluntary and perhaps even involuntary euthanasia. . . .
>
> This concern is further supported by evidence about the practice of euthanasia in the Netherlands. The Dutch government's own study revealed that in 1990, there were 2,300 cases of voluntary euthanasia (defined as 'the deliberate termination of another's life at his request'), 400 cases of assisted suicide, and more than 1,000 cases of euthanasia without an explicit request.[20]

This battery of counter-arguments raises two sets of questions: one set of questions concerns the adequacy of these reasons when pitched against the consent of the applicant agents in such test cases; and the other set concerns the way in which a legal regime might best give effect to lawful assisted suicide or euthanasia (whether by way of general rule, exception, special procedure, or other means).

From a Gewirthian consent perspective, the general issue raised by the prohibitions against active euthanasia and assisted suicide can be put in the following terms: where (test case) agent A is quite clearly consenting to

[20] 117 S Ct 2258; 138 L Ed 2d 772, at 795–96.

agent B acting in a way that would otherwise be a violation of the relevant aspects of A's right to life (the protections secured by (RLa) and (RLb) in the right to life set listed above), why does this clear consent not take priority over the concern that we might have about the validity of ostensible consents given in the general run of life-terminating cases? Or, assuming that, because of A's consent, B does no private wrong to A, how can the State defend a public prohibition on B's acts by reference to a diffuse concern about the possibility of private wrongs taking place between other agents? We suggest that if a public interest defence is to be made out, then the best justification runs along the following lines.

First, it is arguable that there is a difference between removing the prohibition against active euthanasia and removing it against (physician-) assisted suicide. Without more (ie without some kind of procedural safeguard), to remove the prohibition against actively terminating the life of another provided that the latter has consented truly would be a hostage to fortune. The defence of consent is problematic enough where it is asserted by the defendant and denied by the victim, but, if the court were to hear only the defendant's version of events, this would be a licence to kill. Arguably, to remove the prohibition against (physician-)assisted suicide would be less drastic. In principle, if events stopped at this point, supposedly consenting agents could put their side of the story; in practice, however, if assistance with suicide was followed by suicide (as it often would be), the defence of consent would again be a hostage to fortune. At all events, whether or not one accepts that there is a material distinction to be drawn between consent as a defence to active euthanasia and consent as a defence to assisted suicide, it is undeniable that the former is a hostage to fortune and that no rational legal regime could accept such a change to the general prohibition against homicide.

Secondly, if consent cannot be contemplated as a general defence to active termination of life, might a special exception be made for active termination at the hands of a physician? Again, this would be a hostage to fortune and no such exception could be sensibly adopted in this form.

Thirdly, to avoid the defence of consent operating as a hostage to fortune, it needs to be hedged with procedural safeguards designed to confirm that a valid consent is in place. Such safeguards might be developed within the medical profession (for example, by way of provision for counselling, delays, cooling-off periods, independent second and third medical opinions, and so on) and, indeed, they might be reinforced by the need to obtain advance judicial authorisation for the particular termination.

Fourthly, if a State were to refuse to entertain such procedural safeguards, it could rightly be accused of being lazy;[21] and it might be open to

[21] In *Glucksberg*, 138 L Ed 2d 772, at 801, Justice O'Connor (likewise the minority in *Re Rodriguez and Attorney-General of British Columbia* (1992) 107 DLR 4th 342) allows for such

the same kind of criticism if it fudged the issue in an ad hoc way.[22] Moreover, if, subject to a special procedure, a legal regime already permits the life-terminating withdrawal of treatment and support from patients who are diagnosed as being in a persistent vegetative state, it must be inconsistent not to permit assisted suicide (or active euthanasia) subject to a special consent-confirming procedure. Indeed, from a consent perspective, it must be conceded that it is absurd that a State should permit the withdrawal of treatment and support from patients who are unable to indicate their consent and yet prohibit life-terminating acts or assistance therewith requested by an agent who can and does consent. Surely, it is only in Wonderland that the fiction of consent is to be preferred to the fact.

Fifthly, accepting that the onus is on the State to justify not putting in place a special procedure for lawful active euthanasia, it must also be accepted that the justification cannot be that the agent's standing on the negative right to life is to be treated as more important than the agent's consenting to an act that would otherwise violate that negative right. In other words, it cannot be asserted by way of justification that the agent's will to live is more important than the agent's will to die.[23] The agent, as Ronald Dworkin would put it, has critical interests at stake whichever way we go with this life or death dilemma.[24]

a possibility: '[A] decision upholding a general statutory prohibition of assisted suicide does not mean that every possible application of the statute would be valid. A State . . . must acknowledge that there are situations in which an interest in hastening death is legitimate. Indeed, not only is that interest sometimes legitimate, I am also convinced that there are times when it is entitled to constitutional protection.' And, again (at 804–6), Justice O'Connor says: 'The State interests supporting a general rule banning the practice of physician-assisted suicide do not have the same force in all cases. . . . I do not, however, foreclose the possibility that an individual plaintiff seeking to hasten her death, or a doctor whose assistance was sought, could prevail in a more particularized challenge. Future cases will determine whether such a challenge may succeed.'

22 For example, by a judicious but non-transparent exercise of prosecutorial discretion after the event. Or, again, when Annie Lindsell (having motor neurone disease) asked the High Court in England to authorise physician-assisted suicide for her, the court advised that no such authorisation was required, provided that the physician was administering drugs for the primary purpose of the relief of her pain and suffering. More generally, the recognition of double effect as a defence means that, in practice, physicians can assist death by over-prescription of pain-relieving drugs.

23 As Justice Brennan emphasised in his dissent in *Nancy Beth Cruzan v Director, Missouri Department of Health* 111 L Ed 2d 224, at 268:

> An erroneous decision to terminate artificial nutrition and hydration, to be sure, will lead to failure of that last remnant of physiological life, the brain stem, and result in complete brain death. An erroneous decision not to terminate life support, however, robs a patient of the very qualities protected by the right to avoid unwanted medical treatment. His own degraded existence is perpetuated; his family's suffering is protracted; the memory he leaves behind becomes more and more distorted.

24 See Ronald Dworkin, *Life's Dominion* (London, Harper Collins, 1993).

Sixthly, having accepted that an agent's will to live is no more important than the agent's will to die, it is nevertheless the case that the State should ensure that there is no doubt that the agent's consent to giving up the protection of the negative right to life is genuine. A State would let its agents down very badly if, in relation to the most fundamental of rights (the right of an innocent agent not to be killed against its will), it did not make absolutely sure that the agent's ostensible consent was authentic. It follows that any special procedure for confirming that agents have consented to the active termination of their lives must be foolproof.

Seventhly, where a State (seeking to defend its refusal to recognise consent as a defence to unlawful killing, even in the restricted area of active terminations by physicians) argues that it is not satisfied that special consent-confirming procedures will prove foolproof in practice, its defence is not yet complete. To complete the case for the defence, the State must make a comparative judgement about the estimated number of frustrated wills in two situations: (a) where a special procedure is not recognised; and (b) where a special procedure is recognised.

Eighthly, the State may aver that, in good faith, it judges that the number of agents whose will (to live or to die as the case may be) is frustrated in situation (a) is less than would be the case in situation (b). And, given the speculative nature of this judgement, it is hard to quarrel with a State that generally governs in good faith.

Or, ninthly, the State may say that it finds the comparative judgement impossible to make. On the one side, it does not really know the extent of frustrated wills occasioned by its prohibition, and on the other side, even with the benefit of some empirical evidence (such as that in the Netherlands), it cannot begin to estimate the extent to which the obtaining of consent would become routinised and unreliable under a special licensing procedure. Faced with such uncertainty, the State would like to be able to resort to a default position to resolve the dilemma, but, whichever default position one adopts, either the will to live or the will to die will be privileged, and this, the State accepts, is not legitimate. Accordingly, the State declares that, for want of a better option, it will maintain its prohibition.

Turning specifically to the refusal to recognise consent as a defence to physician-assisted suicide, it might be argued that the State has less cause for concern—it is, after all, acts of assistance rather than life-terminating acts that are at stake. However, this is to assume that there is a relatively robust line dividing mere acts of assistance from acts of life termination. In practice, however, especially where we are dealing with vulnerable agents, Chief Justice Rehnquist might well be correct in alerting us to the dangers of fine distinctions and slippery slopes. Certainly, we should not think that we can afford to regulate less stringently for the validity of purported consents in the context of assistance with suicide. This being so, the problem again presents itself as one of finding the pattern of regulatory overview that least frustrates the legitimate will of agents (whether their will is in favour of or against assistance). Accordingly, the State's best justificatory strategy looks parallel to the one we have outlined in relation to active euthanasia.

Gathering together the strands of this argument, the State's best justificatory position is that it maintains its *public* prohibitions against active euthanasia and physician-assisted suicide in order to minimise the number of *private* wrongs perpetrated in the area of the right to life. In principle, the absence of private wrong would be a complete defence, but, in practice, procedures cannot be put in place that reliably identify the cases of private wrong from the cases of no private wrong. Somewhat crudely, therefore, the State resorts to its general prohibitions. As Robert Nozick aptly remarked:

> [T]he statement that a particular piece of legislation makes some persons unfree to perform some acts they should not be unfree to perform (according to what is thought to be the optimal pattern of freedom and unfreedom), even if true, is not by itself a *conclusive* objection to the legislation. For it may be that no feasible and acceptable pattern of freedom and unfreedom is more optimal . . . than the one yielded by this legislation.[25]

In some jurisdictions, of course, a less crude approach has been adopted. Recently, Belgium has followed its neighbour, the Netherlands, in relaxing its prohibitions in end of life cases; and 'death with dignity' has been licensed in places as different as Oregon and the Northern Territories of Australia. However, in a cosmopolitan world, cultures vary significantly and it is difficult for even enlightened lawmakers to be confident that they have achieved the optimal pattern of Gewirthian freedom, ensuring that the will of agents—those whose will is to live as well as those whose will is to die—has the best chance of being realised (or not frustrated).

After this long haul, therefore, we find that the public interest justification upon which the State may rely is a class (i) reason (to put in place a regulatory regime that best secures the rights of agents) but that, because the pattern of the required regime is contestable, the State must arbitrate for the time being and thus it invokes a class (ii) reason to support the prohibition. In other words, it is not so much the prohibition per se that is justified; the prohibition is justified, following class (ii) reasoning, as the choice made by the State in provisional settlement of a question about which Gewirthians may reasonably disagree, namely whether the practical consequences of replacing a general prohibition with a special procedure would be more or less supportive of agency.

Finally, our sketch of a public interest argument for the prohibitions against active euthanasia and assisted suicide should not be misunderstood. From a Gewirthian perspective, when the State intervenes to prevent an

[25] Robert Nozick, 'Coercion', in Peter Laslett, WG Runciman and Quentin Skinner (eds), *Philosophy, Politics and Society* (4th Series) (Oxford, Basil Blackwell, 1972) 101, at 126.

agent from exercising a fundamental right (and no right is more fundamental than the right to life), it has some explaining to do. To point to some risk to other agents is nowhere near enough. The State must show that its good faith and conscientious judgement is that a general prohibition represents the least unsatisfactory of a number of unsatisfactory regulatory options. Judged by these criteria, the decision in *Pretty* falls well short of the mark; *Glucksberg* might be judged to be closer to the mark; but, whatever we make of these particular rulings and the shape of their justificatory arguments, we must allow for the possibility that, in some social settings, a public interest argument for prohibition might be made out.

(b) Homosexuality

In two landmark decisions, *Bowers v Hardwick*[26] and, more recently, *Lawrence v Texas*,[27] the US Supreme Court has found itself divided on the vexed question of whether it is legitimate to criminalise consensual adult homosexual acts. In the former, the majority upheld the constitutionality of a Georgia statute proscribing sodomy (whether or not the participants were of the same sex). In the latter, the majority (overruling *Bowers*) struck down a Texas statute proscribing sodomy (this statute, unlike the Georgia statute, being drafted more narrowly to cover acts of sodomy only between parties of the same sex). In both cases, the real issue concerned the application of the sodomy statute to consenting adult homosexuals.

In *Lawrence*, the police, responding to a reported weapons disturbance, entered Lawrence's apartment. There, they found Lawrence and another man, Garner, engaged in 'deviate sexual intercourse' within the terms of the Texas Penal Code. As their case unfolded, however, Lawrence and Garner challenged the constitutionality of the Texas sodomy provision arguing that it violated both the equal protection and the due process clauses of the Fourteenth Amendment. Essentially, their argument was that the Texas law, by targeting sodomy between same-sex parties, denied to homosexuals the equal protection of the law; and that the statutory deprivation of homosexual liberty was not consistent with the substantive dimension of due process. Although O'Connor J ruled against the statute on equal protection grounds, and thereby found a way of distinguishing rather than overruling *Bowers*,[28] the majority opinion (and the minority dissent) centres on the due process point.

According to the jurisprudence of the Fourteenth Amendment, if Lawrence and Garner could point to a *fundamental* liberty interest on which the sodomy provision impinged, then Texas would be able to justify its law only if required so to act for the sake of a compelling State interest.

[26] 106 S Ct 2841.
[27] 123 S Ct 2472.
[28] *Ibid*, at 2486–88.

However, if Lawrence and Garner's liberty interest was non-fundamental, constitutional review would be at the lower 'rational basis' level. Here, Texas would be able to defend the constitutionality of its sodomy statute provided only that it could be shown to be rationally related to a legitimate State interest.

The majority opinion in *Lawrence* leads off by criticising *Bowers* as failing to grasp the breadth and depth of the liberty interest at stake.

> To say that the issue in *Bowers* was simply the right to engage in certain sexual conduct demeans the claim that the individual put forward, just as it would demean a married couple were it to be said marriage is simply about the right to have sexual intercourse. The laws involved in *Bowers* and here are, to be sure, statutes that purport to do no more than prohibit a particular sexual act. Their penalties and purposes, though, have more far-reaching consequences, touching upon the most private human conduct, sexual behavior, and in the most private of places, the home. The statutes do seek to control a personal relationship that, whether or not entitled to formal recognition in the law, is within the liberty of persons to choose without being punished as criminals.
>
> This, as a general rule, should counsel against attempts by the State, or a court, to define the meaning of the relationship or to set its boundaries absent injury to a person or abuse of an institution the law protects. It suffices for us to acknowledge that adults may choose to enter upon this relationship in the confines of their homes and their own private lives and still retain their dignity as free persons. When sexuality finds overt expression in intimate conduct with another person, the conduct can be but one element in a personal bond that is more enduring. The liberty protected by the Constitution allows homosexual persons the right to make this choice.[29]

In these remarks, the majority come about as close as they can to asserting that a fundamental liberty is at stake, emphasising that these are intimate personal choices, central to personal dignity and autonomy, and warranting the utmost respect under the Constitution.[30] Moreover, the majority reason that, if the Constitution protects heterosexual autonomy in relation to such matters as marriage, procreation, contraception, family relationships, and the like, then it should treat persons in a homosexual relationship in the same way.[31] Yet, the majority do not quite push the liberty interest across the line dividing the non-fundamental from the fundamental. Instead, they rest their case on the importance of the interests implicated in recognising the freedom of same-sex parties coupled with the lack of legitimate State interest. Thus, sweeping things up, the majority opinion concludes:

[29] Robert Nozick, 'Coercion', in Peter Laslett, WG Runciman and Quentin Skinner (eds), *Philosophy, Politics and Society* (4th Series) (Oxford, Basil Blackwell, 1972) 101, , at 2478.

[30] See, too, *ibid*, at 2481 (drawing on *Planned Parenthood of Southeastern Pa v Casey* 112 S Ct 2791).

[31] *Ibid*, at 2481–82.

> The present case does not involve minors. It does not involve persons who might be injured or coerced or who are situated in relationships where consent might not easily be refused. It does not involve public conduct or prostitution. It does not involve whether the government must give formal recognition to any relationship that homosexual persons seek to enter. The case does involve two adults who, with full and mutual consent from each other, engaged in sexual practices common to a homosexual lifestyle. The petitioners are entitled to respect for their private lives. The State cannot demean their existence or control their destiny by making their private sexual conduct a crime. Their right to liberty under the Due Process Clause gives them the full right to engage in their conduct without intervention of the government. . . . The Texas statute furthers no legitimate state interest which can justify its intrusion into the personal and private life of the individual.[32]

Attention to consent (the full and mutual consent of the participants), it will be noted, aids the argument that a liberty interest (albeit non-fundamental) is at stake and, at the same time, weakens the argument that the State has a legitimate interest in regulating the relationship between the parties. To put this another way, where there is no private wrong (because the parties have consented), it becomes more difficult to assert a public wrong, and, in the view of the majority, Texas has no basis for treating Lawrence and Garner's conduct as a public wrong.

The minority is scathing of the majority opinion, accusing it of playing fast and loose with precedent in order to promote the homosexual agenda as part of a broader liberal manifesto. On the fundamental question, however, its rejection of the majority position is blunt:

> I turn now to the ground on which the Court squarely rests its holding: the contention that there is no rational basis for the law here under attack. This proposition is so out of accord with our jurisprudence—indeed, with the jurisprudence of any society that we know—that it requires little discussion.
>
> The Texas statute undeniably seeks to further the belief of its citizens that certain forms of sexual behavior are 'immoral and unacceptable' . . . the same interest furthered by criminal laws against fornication, bigamy, adultery, adult incest, bestiality, and obscenity. *Bowers* held that this *was* a legitimate state interest. The Court today reaches the opposite conclusion. . . . The Court embraces instead Justice Stevens' declaration in his *Bowers* dissent, that 'the fact that the governing majority in a State has traditionally viewed a particular practice as immoral is not a sufficient reason for upholding a law prohibiting the practice' . . . This effectively decrees the end of all morals legislation. If, as the Court asserts, the promotion of majoritarian sexual morality is not even a *legitimate* state interest, none of the above-mentioned laws can survive rational-basis review.[33]

On this view, even if it is conceded that there is no private wrong, the majority may still decree, via normal democratic processes, that the conduct

[32] *Ibid*, at 2484.
[33] *Ibid*, at 2495.

constitutes a public wrong. Hence, while homosexuals are free to argue for changes in their local law, it is another matter altogether to force through such changes in the absence of democratic majority will:

> I would no more *require* a State to criminalize homosexual acts—or, for that matter, display *any* moral disapprobation of them—than I would forbid it to do so. What Texas has chosen to do is well within the range of traditional democratic action, and its hand should not be stayed through the invention of a brand-new 'constitutional right' by a Court that is impatient of democratic change.[34]

Accordingly, for the minority, the Constitution permits States to enact their own local moral preferences, the regulation of homosexuality falls within this category, and if it is judged that it is time for a change in the law, 'those judgments are to be made by the people, and not imposed by a governing caste that knows best.'[35]

At first blush, the minority opinion speaks the language of pluralistic tolerance and local democracy. However, this approach maintains the right of States to enact morals legislation; and this allows for intolerant majorities to enact repressive local prohibitions. Is there any way that such an approach can be squared with Gewirthian consent principles? Or is the majority on the right track in centring its reasoning on the absence of private wrong between Lawrence and Garner?

If we take it that there is no private wrong between the participating agents, the onus is on the State to show good reason for nevertheless prohibiting the conduct in question. One reason would be that of the form that we saw in *Glucksberg*, namely that the public prohibition is required in order to minimise the risk of private wrongdoing, thereby achieving the pattern of regulation that best provides for the realisation of agents' wills. For example, if it were argued that a relaxation in the Texas law would put at risk minors or vulnerable agents whose consent could not be assured, this might have the makings of a case for some level of restriction if not for a full justification of the statute itself. Again, if it were argued that the activities of the participants impinged on the private rights of third parties (for example, by constituting a nuisance), and that a *public* prohibition was required in order to secure respect for those *private* rights, this might have some justificatory potential. Yet, while the majority try to forestall such lines of justification (by pointing to the absence of both minors and any public manifestation of the activity), the minority do not even attempt to mount such a defence of the legislation. For the minority, the argument turns on whether or not States are permitted to enact their own local moral preferences. What should we say to this?

[34] Robert Nozick, 'Coercion', in Peter Laslett, WG Runciman and Quentin Skinner (eds), *Philosophy, Politics and Society* (4th Series) (Oxford, Basil Blackwell, 1972) 101, , at 2497.

[35] *Ibid*, at 2498.

In a seminal essay, Ronald Dworkin tried to weaken the argument that communities are entitled to prescribe according to their own moral lights by unpacking the restrictions contained within the very idea of a 'moral' position.[36] Such a counter might well suffice to invalidate the Texas statute, for, in the light of Dworkin's analysis, the enactment of laws against homosexuality might well be exposed as local prejudice masquerading as local morality—and not even the minority in *Lawrence* would wish to defend the right of States to enact their own local prejudices. However, if we assume that we are dealing with local preferences that cannot be so easily disqualified, what room is there for local morals legislation?

According to Gewirthian principles, some acts are to be classified as morally optional. The PGC does not *directly* prescribe that, for example, we should wear trousers or skirts, that we should drive on the left or drive on the right, that we should have two or three witnesses if we wish to make a will, that we should call time on personal injury claims after three, six, or 12 years, that married couples should observe the rules of monogamy or polygamy, and so on. However, where settlement of options is essential for the good order of a community, an election must be made and it must then be treated as binding on agents within the community. It follows that an act which involves no private wrong, as judged by a direct application of the PGC, may nevertheless be justifiably decreed a public wrong by virtue of the *indirect* application of Gewirthian principles (such as one of the class (ii) public interest reasons identified earlier). For example, where local moral preference is for heterosexual relationships, nuclear families, and marriage, those agents who elect to enter the institution of marriage might find that they are subject to restrictions (bigamy is a case in point) that would not otherwise apply. In this limited sense, local morality has a legitimate role to play in setting public standards, and this might involve some impingement on sexual or familial relations.

However, it is important to remember that, although the basic regulatory positions are to prohibit, to permit, or to require, a local legal regime may fine-tune its permissions in various ways.[37] For example, some permissions may be glossed with State encouragement (as is the case, for instance, with transactions that are recognised as legally enforceable and research and development that leads to patentable inventions), others with State discouragement (simply by withholding legal recognition or, more actively, as is the case, for instance, with the preconditions for a lawful abortion). In this light, it becomes apparent that there is an important difference between

[36] Ronald Dworkin, *Taking Rights Seriously* (revised edn) (London, Duckworth, 1978) ch 10, at 248 et seq.

[37] On the regulatory range in general and the fine-tuning of permissions in particular, see Roger Brownsword, 'Regulating Human Genetics: New Dilemmas for a New Millennium' (2004) 12 *Medical Law Review* 14, at 15–18.

the community preferring to support and sustain a particular type of familial or sexual relationship (such as heterosexual monogamy) and prohibiting all other familial or sexual relationships. So long as the formally supported (and, quite possibly, financially incentivised) forms can co-exist with the non-legally recognised alternatives (in which, let us remind ourselves, no private wrong is done), a permissive approach should be maintained. Hence, while a community might prefer heterosexual to homosexual familial relationships, it is wholly unclear why it should be necessary to support the former by *prohibiting* the latter.

Another kind of class (ii) reason arises, not in relation to moral optionality, but where there is a genuine and reasonable moral disagreement upon which a public position must be taken. This might arise where there is a plausible and sincere difference of local opinion as to the interpretation of Gewirthian principles, or their application. However, even if we concede that the local disapproval of homosexuality is formally speaking a 'moral' judgement of some kind, when expressed as a prohibition it cannot be viewed as a plausible articulation of Gewirthian rights-led morality. This is quite simply not a matter about which Gewirthians might reasonably disagree. It follows that it is wholly unclear how the minority might justify its position by reference to this justificatory strategy.

Turning to the majority's view, it is not enough to rely on the absence of private wrong between the test case parties. For the purpose of scrutinising general rules, test case circumstances cannot be isolated from the general run of cases or from their community context. If the agents in question do no private wrong between themselves and if there is no broader question about potential private wrong (as in *Glucksberg*), then, from a consent perspective, the fundamental question becomes: what sort of regime of public governance have these agents consented to? If we assume a rights-respecting regime of governance, the constitution will reflect the following two principles:

(a) that the State may not restrict the exercise of generic rights directly derived from the PGC (including the exercise of consent in relation to such rights) unless (i) the agents concerned specifically consent to such a restriction or (ii) it is for the sake of equivalent or overriding rights of other agents (this is the sphere of compelling State interest); and
(b) that the State may regulate conduct that, while permissible in itself under a direct application of the PGC, nevertheless necessitates settlement for the sake of good community order, and, similarly, the State may intervene to settle a genuine moral disagreement as to the permissibility of conduct (this is the sphere of legitimate State interest).

Applying these criteria (which, it will be appreciated, draw on all three classes of public interest reasons), we can allow that there might be some room for local morals legislation (for example, where a decision must be made about the permissibility of abortion; or, where monogamy is opted for, there would be a public interest in regulating bigamy and (possibly) adultery). However, it is difficult to see how the minority in *Lawrence* could find the Texas statute constitutional.

Once again, the thrust of these remarks should not be misunderstood. We believe that the majority made the right decision in *Lawrence*. However, this is but an illustrative case. The larger point is that, whether the decision in *Lawrence* was correct or incorrect, we must allow for the possibility of a public interest justification overriding the consideration that the agents whose conduct is to be regulated have consented to the acts in question.[38]

### *(ii) Autonomy-limitation II: The Regulation of Access to Reproductive Technologies*

Shahana and Raj Hashmi live in Leeds in the North of England. One of their children, their son Zain, was born with the blood disorder, beta thalassaemia major. To rectify this disorder, Zain needs a stem cell transplantation, using the cord blood or bone marrow of a donor who is free of the thalassaemia gene as well as being a tissue-match with Zain. Having tried unsuccessfully to find a suitable donor for Zain, including giving birth to a further child (alas, not a tissue-match) by natural reproduction, the Hashmis sought advice from Dr Simon Fishel, the Managing and Scientific Director of Centres for Assisted Reproduction Limited (CARE), the largest single provider of IVF (in vitro fertilisation) services in the United Kingdom.

Dr Fishel advised the Hashmis that a procedure pioneered at the Reproductive Genetics Institute in Chicago might assist them. This procedure involves: removing a single cell from the early embryo by a biopsy; using pre-implantation genetic diagnosis (PGD) to check that the embryo is free of the thalassaemia gene; using a similar process, Human Leukocyte

[38] Interestingly, compare the remarks of Cass Sunstein in *Designing Democracy* (Oxford, Oxford University Press, 2001) at ch 8. Writing before *Lawrence*, Sunstein assumes that the ruling in *Bowers* renders it unlikely that local sodomy legislation will be held unconstitutional under the substantive due process clause (he thinks that equal protection is a more promising avenue for challenge). However, at 186, Sunstein addresses the unlikely in the following terms:

> Maybe these are largely technical difficulties. Substantive due process is well established in a number of privacy cases, and perhaps the relevant tradition should be read at a sufficient level of abstraction to include consensual relations between homosexuals. If a state is going to forbid people from engaging in consensual sexual activity, it should certainly have to come up with a good reason for the ban. In the case of people who are under age, it can point to the absence of real consent. In the case of incest among adults, it can point to psychological harms and to risks to the children who might result. In the case of adultery, it can perhaps refer to the need to protect the marital relationship. It is hard to find a similar justification for bans on consensual sodomy among adults. In these circumstances, a decision to overrule *Bowers v Hardwick* should be counted as a cause for celebration.

Antigens (HLA) tissue-typing, to confirm a tissue match; and then implanting an embryo that satisfies both requirements. However, Dr Fishel's view was that, before such a procedure could be lawfully undertaken in the UK, it would need to be specifically authorised by the Human Fertilisation and Embryology Authority (the relevant regulatory body). For, although there was nothing new about PGD being carried out as part of IVF treatment licensed by the Authority, tissue-typing had not previously been carried out as part of such treatment.[39] Accordingly, on behalf of the Hashmis, CARE made the appropriate application to the Authority, seeking clarification as to whether a licence to administer IVF treatment might also include authorisation for tissue-typing. In December 2001, the Authority announced that, in principle, it would be prepared to license tissue-typing but only where PGD was already being licensed for a serious genetic disorder. Such licences (for PGD plus tissue-typing) would be granted only exceptionally. In a blaze of publicity, in February 2002, the Authority gave the go-ahead for the Hashmis, granting a licence to Park Hospital, operated by CARE in Nottingham, to carry out the treatment.

The chances of the treatment being successful are not good. In the first round of treatment, 15 embryos were produced; only one was a tissue match but it carried the thalassaemia gene. For the second round, the Hashmis travelled to Chicago, where 10 embryos were produced. Two of these embryos seemed suitable; one was implanted, but no pregnancy resulted. At this juncture, however, the Hashmis' efforts were interrupted when Comment on Reproductive Ethics (CORE), a group for whom absolute respect for the embryo is axiomatic, sought a judicial review of the Authority's December 2001 announcement and, by extension, the licence granted the following February. CORE argued that the Authority had no power to issue a licence permitting the use of HLA tissue-typing to select between healthy embryos.

Whether or not the Authority has power to license the testing of embryos (whether by PGD, HLA, or both) essentially turns on the provisions in Schedule 2 of the Human Fertilisation and Embryology Act 1990. Here, it is provided in a general clause that a licence 'cannot authorise any activity unless it appears to the Authority to be necessary or desirable for the purpose of providing treatment services,'[40] 'treatment services' being defined in the main body of the Act as 'medical, surgical or obstetric services provided to the public or a section of the public for the purpose of assisting women to carry children.'[41] Closing this up, we can say that the Authority

[39] Neither the framework legislation, the Human Fertilisation and Embryology Act 1990 nor the Authority's own (then current) Code of Practice (5th edition, 2001) deals explicitly with this issue. However, para 9.5 of the Code articulates the precautionary principle that procedures carrying the risk of harm to the development of an embryo should be avoided.

[40] Human Fertilisation and Embryology Act 1990, sch 2, para 1(3).

[41] *Ibid*, s 2(1).

is empowered (as a matter of necessity *or* desirability) to license only such activities as are designed to assist women to carry children. Schedule 2, para 1(1) lists a number of essential IVF activities, such as creating embryos in vitro (item (a)) and placing them in the woman (item (e)). The particular question raised by CORE, however, pointed to the relevance of item (d) in this list, which refers to 'practices designed to secure that embryos are in a suitable condition to be placed in a woman or to determine whether embryos are suitable for that purpose.'[42] Fairly obviously, these provisions are so slack as to offer considerable interpretive leeway.

At first instance, the Authority argued that tissue-typing on a biopsied cell did not amount to the 'use' of an embryo (and, thus, did not need to be authorised by licence).[43] Failing that, it was argued that tissue-typing could be licensed, under the general clause, as an activity designed to assist women to carry children. On both points, Maurice Kay J ruled against the Authority.[44] Before the Court of Appeal, the Authority effectively abandoned its first argument,[45] and the appeal hinged on the second argument. On this second point, the Court of Appeal unanimously reversed the High Court, ruling that the Authority acted within its powers in licensing the procedure.[46] Whereas, on this second point, Maurice Kay J gave the legislative provisions a fairly literal and restrictive reading, the Court of Appeal[47] gave the legislation a much broader purposive reading,[48] holding that the Authority had been given the responsibility by the framework legislation for making precisely such difficult ethical decisions.

The case (which was unsuccessfully appealed to the House of Lords, the Law Lords unanimously dismissing the appeal)[49] raises a host of important

[42] *Ibid*, sch 2, para 1(1)(d).

[43] Section 3(1)(b) of the Act prohibits, inter alia, the 'use' of an embryo except in pursuance of a licence.

[44] *R (Quintavalle on behalf of Comment on Reproductive Ethics) v Human Fertilisation and Embryology Authority* [2002] EWHC 2785 (Admin).

[45] In the instant case, this concession was not decisive but its import has been underlined in the subsequent conjoined cases of *Evans v Amicus Healthcare Ltd and others; Hadley v Midland Fertility Services Ltd and others* [2003] EWHC 2161 (Fam), especially at paras 163–65. For, if PGD involves the 'use' of an embryo, it follows that an embryo may be 'used' before it is implanted. And, if a consent may not be withdrawn or varied after an embryo has been 'used', this implies that the cut-off point for withdrawal or variation may be prior to implantation.

[46] [2003] EWCA Civ 667 (Lord Phillips MR, Schiemann and Mance LJJ).

[47] Following the approach in *R (Quintavalle) v Secretary of State for Health* [2002] EWCA Civ 29 (18 January 2002); [2003] UKHL 13 (13 March 2003).

[48] In the modern law, the seminal guidance is Lord Wilberforce's opinion in *Royal College of Nursing of the United Kingdom v Department of Health and Social Security* [1981] AC 800, at 822.

[49] See *Quintavalle v Human Fertilisation and Embryology Authority* [2005] UKHL 28; and, for analysis, see Roger Brownsword, 'Happy Families, Consenting Couples, and Children with Dignity: Sex Selection and Saviour Siblings' [2005] *Child and Family Law Quarterly* 435.

questions about such matters as (what Lawrence Lessig terms) the 'regulability' of new technologies,[50] the appropriate way of reading framework legislation where the technology has raced ahead of the strict terms of the regulatory provision, and the optimal institutional design for handling such controversial issues. However, for our purposes, the only question is whether there is a legitimate public interest in restricting access to reproductive technologies when couples such as the Hashmis do so on the basis of free and informed consent.

First, given that we are addressing this question from a Gewirthian rights perspective, we can summarily dismiss the dignitarian objection. The dignitarian alliance, as we know, condemns many practices as compromising human dignity; it sees dignity being compromised in the Hashmis' case; it thinks that the State should prohibit the deselection of healthy embryos; but this is precisely the kind of intervention that a Gewirthian (or, indeed, general human rights) perspective resists.[51]

A second argument is much more tricky. Taking a rights-led perspective, some might assert that there is a problem about the Hashmis' actions at the level of private right and wrong. In other words, it is not so clear that they do no private wrong. This argument hinges on what we make of the status and interests of the saviour sibling. In a robust but raw rights-led paradigm, the embryo will have no entitlements. However, in a more sophisticated view that allows for the possibility of agency (such as in the precautionary approach outlined in chapter four) or the futurality of the embryo, this could be a problematic case. The point is that the planned donation of the embryo's cord blood is without the embryo's consent; and the actual taking and donation of the cord blood (which, of course, takes place at a later stage) is without the consent of the newly born child. To be sure, this does not constitute a wrong in itself. But, if the embryo or the newly born child has rights (or possibly has rights), that is a different matter.

Thirdly, and most significantly for our discussion, there is an objection that invites consideration of the broader context in which a Gewirthian community of rights can flourish. It recognises that public intervention, in relation to conduct that of itself might not seem to be a private wrong, may be justifiable in order to prevent corrosion of (or the compromising of) this context. Consider, against a generally prohibitive background, the following process of incremental relaxation of the law:

(i) PGD to screen against serious disease is permitted (in the way that the Authority has read the implicit intent of the Act);

50 See Lawrence Lessig, *Code and Other Laws of Cyberspace* (New York, Basic Books, 1999).

51 See, further, Roger Brownsword, 'Bioethics Today, Bioethics Tomorrow: Stem Cell Research and the "Dignitarian Alliance"' (2003) 17 *Notre Dame Journal of Law, Ethics and Public Policy* 15.

(ii) PGD to screen against sex-related disease is permitted;
(iii) tissue-typing, as an add-on to PGD under (i), is permitted (as the Court of Appeal has ruled);
(iv) free-standing tissue-typing in order to treat a serious disease in a child already born is permitted;[52]
(v) PGD to screen against less serious disease is permitted; and
(vi) PGD for social sex selection is permitted (contrary to the attitude currently taken by the Authority).[53]

Let us stop there—before we get to other forms of positive selection or the genetic manipulation of embryos or reproductive cloning. Let us assume that couples do no *private* wrong if they avail themselves of any of these procedures. May the State nevertheless justifiably prohibit access to such technologies?

The significance of (i) and (ii) is that unhealthy embryos will be deselected. If a State already permits abortion of seriously damaged fetuses, this does not seem additionally problematic. However, at (iii) and (iv) an embryo is being selected, not for its own health, but for the sake of the health of a third party. We can, and should, debate the ethics of this—and, arguably, the Court of Appeal passes too quickly over these questions[54]—but it is difficult to see how such choices corrode the context in which agents make sense of their identities as bearers of rights and responsibilities. With (v), as with (vi), it will be argued that permitting such procedures signals a lack of respect for, respectively, the disabled and the disfavoured sex. Once again, these are issues that merit debate. Certainly, public regulation might be necessary if screening against disability or sex has indirect and longer-term effects that undermine respect for rights. However, although

[52] The Human Fertilisation and Embryology Authority declined to license free-standing tissue-typing for the Whitakers, whose son Charlie suffers from the rare blood disorder, Diamond Blackfan anaemia: see Rebecca Allison, 'New Designer Baby Row as Watchdog Rejects Family's Plea for Treatment' (2002) *The Guardian*, 2 August, p 3. However, in July 2004, in response to a case on all fours with that of the Whitaker family, the full 18-member Authority announced its intention to relax the restriction that barred the way to authorising free-standing tissue-typing. The Chair of the Authority, Suzi Leather, explained that, in the light of the latest evidence, the Authority was satisfied that there was no increased risk to the embryo arising from the tissue-typing procedure: see Sarah Boseley, 'Green Light for 'Designer Babies' to Save Siblings' (2004) *The Guardian*, 22 July, p 1.

[53] Human Fertilisation and Embryology Authority, *Sex Selection: Options for Regulation* (London, 12 November 2003). More recently, challenging the Authority's view, the House of Commons Science and Technology Committee has controversially reported in favour of permitting couples to select their children by sex for family balancing: see Jeremy Laurance, 'Child's Welfare Should not be a Factor in IVF Therapy, say MPs' (2005) *The Independent*, 22 March, p 6.

[54] See Roger Brownsword, 'Reproductive Opportunities and Regulatory Challenges' (2004) 67 *Modern Law Review* 304.

there is a sense in which such screening might compromise the context, any intervention by the State is more for class (i) than class (ii) reasons.[55]

To get to the kind of justification that we are looking for, we need to move on to the cases of positive selection and genetic manipulation (or enhancement) of the embryo that lie further up the track.

Let us suppose that there comes a time when reliable procedures for selection and manipulation are available. At that point, there might still be disagreement about how far we may legitimately close off options for agents-to-be, that is to what extent we must allow to such agents-to-be an 'open future';[56] and, for class (ii) reasons, the State will need to take (and will be justified in taking) a position. Even if this issue is settled, however, there might yet be concern about the possibly corrosive effect that selection and manipulation might have in relation to the kind of social context presupposed by a Gewirthian community of rights. From a Gewirthian agency perspective, consent (or its absence) assumes significance precisely because it represents the free and informed choice of a rights-bearer or power-holder. This is why consent justifies and why consensual acts (involving no private wrong) may only exceptionally be prohibited. Yet, if the cumulative effect of so many consensual acts of reproductive specification is to devalue the perceived importance of choice (because the choice is less that of the present individual than that of that person's genetic selectors or specifiers), it is arguable that we threaten the very context in which, inter alia, the choice to consent assumes significance.[57]

To allow that regulatory steps may be required in order to maintain a context in which individuals conceive of themselves as having the capacity for choice and as bearing the responsibility that goes with being in control is to invite bad faith governance and abuse. For defenders of Gewirthian principles, this is dangerous ground. Nevertheless, in principle, we suggest that a further public interest reason for denying that consensual acts are necessarily justified (and that they should be immune from public prohibition) is that we must take care not to undermine the very context in which a culture of consent can flourish.

[55] An outright prohibition ab initio, however, seems like a measure that is neither necessary nor proportionate. Provided that the State is aware of the risk, it can monitor the situation or, say, limit sex selection to special cases where families are otherwise dramatically unbalanced. See, too, n 9 above.

[56] For discussion, see Dena S Davis, 'Genetic Dilemmas and the Child's Right to an Open Future' (1997) 28 *Rutgers Law Journal* 549, especially at 561–67 (arguing that a reflexive application of autonomy values will set limits to parents' reproductive autonomy); and Roger Brownsword, 'An Interest in Human Dignity as the Basis of Genomic Torts' (2003) 42 *Washburn Law Journal* 413, at 440–44.

[57] See, eg, Jürgen Habermas, *The Future of Human Nature* (Cambridge, Polity Press, 2003); Francis Fukuyama, *Our Posthuman Future* (London, Profile Books, 2002); and Bill McKibben, *Enough: Genetic Engineering and the End of Human Nature* (London, Bloomsbury Publishing, 2003), especially at 47 and 195.

### *(iii) Taking Stock*

We have suggested that where agent A does no private wrong by doing X to (or with) agent B, the onus is on the State to justify treating X as a public wrong. To make out a justificatory case, the State will need to demonstrate that its prohibition is a necessary and proportionate measure appropriately related to the protection of the rights (equivalent or overriding) of fellow agents or to the preservation of the context in which a community of rights is viable. Regrettably, it is too easy to make light of consent where it is an inconvenience, and appeals to the 'public interest' are too easily a cover for improper motives or reasons. Nevertheless, we cannot discount the possibility that a proper, Gewirthian-compliant, defence can be made out.

## III Non-consensual Justifications and Excuses

Legal systems commonly make special provision for 'rights-violations' that arise in the context of self-defence, as a matter of necessity, or under the pressure of duress or provocation, or the like. What should we make of such provisions? Are they simply misguided; or do we need to supplement our governing Gewirthian principles?

Where an agent acts with an authorising consent or where overriding rights are in play, Gewirthian principles allow for the possibility of *justified* 'rights-violations'. Such an act of justified rights-violation is to be regarded as at least morally permissible (and, in some cases, it might be morally required). It follows that anything that falls short of justification as permissibility does not challenge the importance of consent. In this light, we can recall the standard distinction drawn between justifications and excuses. According to Hart,

> In the case of 'justification' what is done is regarded as something which the law does not condemn, or even welcomes. But where killing (eg accidental) is excused, criminal responsibility is excluded on a different footing. What has been done is something which is deplored, but the psychological state of the agent when he did it exemplified one or more of a variety of conditions which are held to rule out the public condemnation and punishment of individuals.[58]

Fairly straightforwardly, we can relate this distinction to what we have said about justification as permissibility (or even requirement): if an act, when *justified*, is not condemned, it must at least be permitted, and if welcomed then this fits with the performance of a required act; but if an act, when merely *excused*, is deplored, then it is neither permitted nor required. It follows that excuses are conceptually distinct and do not signal a departure from the central place accorded to consent as an authorising act. And this

[58] HLA Hart, *Punishment and Responsibility* (Oxford, Clarendon Press, 1968) at 13–14.

applies a fortiori to mitigation, where the pleaded circumstances serve only to reduce the seriousness of the offence or the severity of the punishment.

Perhaps the clearest case of justified 'rights-violation' is the case where the agent acts in self-defence. Where agent A acts against agent B's rights, and B responds by way of self-defence, B has an antecedent justification for his defensive acts. If asked to elaborate, we might say that A has forfeited the benefits which apply under the primary scheme of rights or that the baseline regulating the relationship between A and B has been disturbed by A's attempted violation of B's rights: either way, a secondary scheme of entitlements comes into play. Under the secondary scheme, B is entitled to make a proportionate defensive response, impinging on the benefits ordinarily covered by A's primary rights. Proportionality is assessed relative to the Gewirthian hierarchy of goods—for example, if B's basic rights are under threat, a self-defensive measure aimed at A's basic rights will not be disproportionate, but such a self-defensive measure will be much more difficult to justify if it is B's non-subtractive or additive rights that are under threat.[59]

What, then, of the defence of necessity (assuming that we are dealing with agents who are competent and capable of consenting or refusing)? In the historic case of *R v Dudley and Stephens*,[60] the court rejected necessity as a defence to a charge of murder, the defence being put in terms that 'in order to save your own life you may lawfully take away the life of another, when that other is neither attempting [to take] nor threatening yours, nor is guilty of any illegal act whatever towards you or anyone else.'[61] There, it will be recalled, the shipwrecked defendants began to discuss their options some 18 days after they had been cast adrift off the Cape of Good Hope (by then probably more than 1,000 miles from land), and when they had been seven days without food and five days without water. In their desperation, they slit the throat of the cabin boy, Richard Palmer, who was in a seriously weakened condition, and, having fed on his body and blood for some days, they were picked up by a passing vessel. The court's judgment, delivered by Lord Coleridge CJ, is unclear as to whether necessity should be considered as a possible justification or as an excuse;[62] but, whichever way it was regarded, the court was satisfied that morality did not dictate an

[59] There are some intriguing questions about the 'reasonableness' of acts of self-defence by over-protective property owners. However, we must pass over such questions because they do not throw any light on our analysis of consent.

[60] (1884) 14 QBD 273.

[61] *Ibid*, at 281 (Lord Coleridge CJ).

[62] At 286–87, Lord Coleridge says:

> Now it is admitted that the deliberate killing of this unoffending and unresisting boy was clearly murder, unless the killing can be justified by some well-recognised excuse admitted by the law. It is further admitted that there was in this case no such excuse, unless the killing was justified by what has been called 'necessity'.

absolute or unqualified necessity to preserve one's life, and that the law should follow suit by rejecting any such justifying or excusing doctrine. Although the death penalty handed down by the court was subsequently commuted to a term of six months' imprisonment, indicating that the circumstances allowed for some mitigation,[63] this landmark of common law jurisprudence establishes that necessity, in the form pleaded, is to be recognised as neither a justification nor an excuse. Given that the defendants went ahead with the killing without consulting the cabin boy, to recognise a defence based on necessity in such circumstances would be to drastically devalue the significance of consent. Moreover, to recognise such a defence would be to diminish the importance of the victim's rights, confirming the common suspicion that necessity as a defence fits more comfortably within a utilitarian paradigm.

From a consent perspective, it seems pretty clear that necessity should not be recognised as an alternative justification in a bilateral transaction such as that in *Dudley and Stephens* where the party pleading necessity has acted to advance its own agency interests. However, in a rather different kind of case, tested recently in *Re A (Children) (Conjoined Twins: Surgical Separation)*,[64] the argument against recognising a defence of necessity is less clear-cut; and, in fact, it was accepted by one judge in the Court of Appeal. Put shortly, the question for the court was whether the medical team could lawfully attempt to separate the conjoined twins Jodie and Mary where: (a) the girls' parents did not consent to the separation; (b) without the separation both girls would die; and (c) if the separation were attempted, Mary would certainly die but there was a reasonable prospect that Jodie would survive. According to Brooke LJ, if the medical team were to carry out the separation of the twins, they would do so under the cover of necessity, because the purpose of the separation was to avoid inevitable and irreparable evil (the death of Jodie), separation was necessary for this purpose, and the evil inflicted on Mary (her death) was not disproportionate to the evil to be avoided (the death of both twins). Can this be squared with consent theory?

As expressed by Brooke LJ, the defence of necessity applies where the defendant has acted in a way that is necessary and proportionate to avoid the greater of two evils. So stated, the defence is compatible with more than one moral theory (including utilitarianism), each having its own version of what counts as an 'evil'. If the defence is to be an articulation of Gewirthian rights theory, it needs to be restated along the following lines: where a

[63] For the background, see AWB Simpson, *Cannibalism and the Common Law: The Story of the Tragic Last Voyage of the Mignonette and the Strange Legal Proceedings to which it Gave Rise* (Chicago, IL, University of Chicago Press, 1984).

[64] [2000] 4 All ER 961. For a cross-section of academic opinion, see the six papers in (2001) 9 *Medical Law Review* 201–98 (a special issue dedicated to *Re A*).

defendant, agent A, has acted without the consent of agent B and in a way that violates agent B's prima facie rights, then agent A will have a defence of necessity where the action is necessary and proportionate for the avoidance of a more serious harm to *B*'s agency goods, or those of third party agent C. Under cover of such a doctrine of necessity, agent A may (at least temporarily) bar the path of agent B, who is (seemingly unknowingly) heading for Mill's rickety bridge, or enter B's property in order to prevent the spread of fire to C's and D's land, or apply force to B where B is interfering with a procedure designed to save B's own, or C's life, and so on. In all these cases, however, the pattern that we are looking for is that A, faced with competing obligations (whether conflicting obligations owed to just one other agent, B, or to several agents, B, C, and D), appeals to necessity (for the sake of performing the higher obligation) in order to justify breaching the least important obligation.

So understood, it remains moot whether Brooke LJ was right in applying the doctrine of necessity to the case of the twins. In the standard emergency case, a doctor who acts to save the life of one who is not able to consent will be covered by necessity, but, in the case of the twins, this would only shield the doctors against a subsequent complaint by Jodie, whose life they saved. The controversial question is whether necessity would cover the medical team in relation to their taking of Mary's life without her consent and in the face of the parents' refusal to consent. Putting the position of the parents to one side, it is arguable that the actions of the medical team were permissible (if not required) relative to Gewirthian theory. For the team made its choice between the neonates, neither of whom was an ostensible agent, believing that it was not possible to save both girls and that, in the light of the medical prognosis for each child, it was only Jodie who was viable. However, once the parents' refusal to consent to the separation is brought back into consideration, the puzzle becomes more complex.[65] The fact that separation is against the will of the parents (the fact they do not consent) is relevant only so long as it relates to a particular right that the parents have. Once the particular right is identified and specified, the defence of necessity has to overcome (i) the non-consensual harm to Mary's basic goods (the loss of life that she does not consent to) and (ii) the non-consensual harm to the parents' agency goods (whatever, on analysis, this might prove to be). If Mary were already an ostensible agent, with the developed capacity to consent, it would be easy to argue that the non-consensual harm under (i) ranks higher than that under (ii) (the parents'

[65] In general, on the legitimate sphere of parental choice and control, compare Joseph Goldstein, 'Medical Care for the Child at Risk: On State Supervention of Parental Autonomy' (1977) 86 *Yale Law Journal* 645. And, specifically in relation to *Re A*, see John Harris, 'Human Beings, Persons and Conjoined Twins: An Ethical Analysis of the Judgment in *Re A*' (2001) 9 *Medical Law Review* 221.

lives are not being threatened), and we would be back then to the simpler question of whether it is permissible (or required) to inflict such non-consensual harm on Mary in order to save Jodie's life. Such is not the situation, however: it is the parents who are the ostensible agents, not Mary and, indeed, not Jodie. In another context, we have suggested that this conflict between the interests of ostensible and non-ostensible (albeit potential) agents, where the latter plead rights that rank higher than those argued for by the former, if not intractable, is at least moot.[66] Whilst, for moralists, judgement may be suspended in such circumstances, for a court of law a reasoned justification must be offered and a public judgment must be made.[67]

From a consent perspective, the best guidance that we can give is this: first, necessity will not justify (or excuse) agent A violating (ostensible) agent B's rights, without agent B's consent, where A so acts in order to advance A's own interests (*Dudley and Stephens* is quite correct on this point); secondly, necessity may justify (or excuse) agent A violating (ostensible) agent B's rights, without agent B's consent, where A's action is necessary and proportionate for the avoidance of a more serious harm to B's own agency goods, or those of third party agent C; and, thirdly, if, exceptionally, the situation does not fall within either of these guidelines (as in the case of the twins), then the court must be guided by the default principle that, in the absence of an authorising consent, an agent cannot justify violating the prima facie rights of another without reference to competing overriding rights. Where the position is morally contestable (where, from a Gewirthian perspective, agents may reasonably disagree), and where a decision must be made, then it falls to the State to declare in good faith its best (albeit provisional) judgement on the matter.

Turning from necessity to duress, we have already discussed the way in which duress bears on the validity of a supposed 'consent'.[68] Now, the

[66] Deryck Beyleveld and Roger Brownsword, *Human Dignity in Bioethics and Biolaw* (Oxford, Oxford University Press, 2001) at 254 et seq. See, too, our remarks on commensurability in ch 4 above, at 103–104.

[67] We have some sympathy with Barbara Hewson, 'Killing Off Mary: Was the Court of Appeal Right?' (2001) 9 *Medical Law Review* 281, where it is argued that the case should not really have come to court (it was driven by the technology of separation), that the courts should have declined to decide (declaring the case moot), and that the decision made by the court was wholly unsatisfactory. However, we could scarcely disagree more strongly with Hewson's despairing conclusion that the 'decision would have been less troubling if the judges had constructed a case for separation based on implied consent . . .' (at 298). This would have compounded whatever sins the court committed. The twins were not subjects of consent; they could not give any kind of consent; and to rest the argument for separation on such a procedural justification is a non-starter. If we think that the judges were deluding themselves in treating the separation as in Mary's best interests, this would be equally so if they resorted to the fiction of consent.

[68] See chs 5 and 6.

question is rather different. It is whether agent A may justify, or be excused, violating (ostensible) agent B's rights, without the latter's consent, on the grounds that agent C has applied (or threatened to apply) duress either to A or to some other agent D. This is a complex question and a few short comments must suffice.

The first point to make is the obvious one that any rational legal order will want to be satisfied about the credibility of the threat to A. Assuming that the appropriate evidential burden is met, a consent-conscious legal regime might be attracted by the following guidelines. First, duress is not a justification for A where A violates B's rights (without B's consent) in order to avoid the effect of the duress *upon A* as applied or threatened by C. In such a scenario, C does wrong to A, A does wrong to B, and the former wrong does not justify the latter. However, it should not be forgotten that C is the originating wrongdoer and that A does not freely choose to violate B's rights. It is arguable, therefore, that A should be excused if the wrong done to B is of a lesser order than the wrong that would be done to A.[69] In effect, on this analysis, C would be treated as responsible for the wrong done to B. Secondly, duress (analogously to necessity) may justify, or excuse, A violating B's rights (without B's consent) where A so acts in order to protect the more compelling rights of D against the duress applied or threatened by C—for example, A may appeal to duress to justify stealing money from his employer, B, where C has threatened to kill D if A does not steal the money and hand it over to C.

Although the first of these guidelines seems sound enough, the second will not do, for it leaves unclear the relationship between duress and necessity where agent A violates the rights of B (without B's consent) in order to protect the more compelling rights of D. In the case of duress, A so acts only under pressure from C; in the case of necessity, A acts freely. What this suggests is that, in the present context, a legal regime should never regard duress as anything more than an excusing condition. By contrast, where agent A is faced with competing obligations (one relating to B's rights, the other to D's rights), and where D's rights are more compelling, A is required to meet the obligation to D rather than B; and the doctrine of necessity applies to justify A's violation of B's rights. On this analysis, necessity might still serve as an excuse (rather than a full justification) where agent A is judged, in good faith, to have acted out of a misplaced duty (in other words, where the court holds that A has mistakenly taken his duty to D to be more compelling than his duty to B)—but, having said this, a legal regime would be more focused conceptually if it recognised a defence of mistaken necessity for such an error.

[69] Or, if excuse seems inappropriate, at least the duress applied by C should operate as a mitigating factor.

## IV Conclusion

Consent is a sufficient procedural justification to negate what would otherwise be a private wrong. However, as we saw in the previous chapter, it is not a necessary justifying condition in relation to private acts; and now we see that it is not a necessary justification either in relation to public wrong. To this extent, there is some symmetry between consent in the private and the public domain.

Where there seems to be no private wrong, because the participants have given their consent, it is not only those who are fixated with consent who might reason that the acts are immune against public regulation. Nevertheless, so to reason is to commit the Fallacy of Sufficiency; for, consent notwithstanding, the State might be able to justify treating the conduct in question as a public wrong. This burden of public justification is considerable, but Gewirthian theory invites public interest justifications that refer to the protection of the larger scheme of rights (and consents) (as in *Glucksberg*), or to the need for settlement of morally optional or morally contested matters (within a Gewirthian framework of moral principle), or to the need for precautionary measures lest the context for agency be compromised, or to the explicit authorising consent of the agents whose private rights are now restricted (albeit an unlikely contingency). However, we must be careful not to allow 'public interest' justifications to be abused, or used as a pretext for non-Gewirthian interventions, and no public restriction is justifiable beyond the point at which it is a necessary and proportionate response.

Part Four

# CONSENT AS THE BASIS OF LEGAL (POLITICAL) AUTHORITY AND OBLIGATION

# 10

# Consent and the Stability and Authority of Law

## I Introduction

Thus far, everything that we have said speaks to the importance of keeping consent, conceived as a procedural justification, on a tight rein. If we loosen the reins, consent (like 'public policy' in the law) is liable to become an unruly horse. Before we know it, the integrity of consent as a procedural justification is liable to be challenged by fiction, with consent being constructed, imputed, or presumed as and when decision-makers find it convenient to do so. Accordingly, our account of consent presupposes a specific and identifiable transaction with, on the one side, a consenting agent (who is a subject of consent) and, on the other, an agent who is the recipient of the consent. Emphasising the importance of fidelity (to the will of the former agent), we have been led by the subjective view of the consenting agent in relation to such matters as information, interpretation, and signalling. In this account, it is axiomatic that we do agents a serious wrong if we attribute to them the will 'to authorise X' when either it is not their will to consent at all or, if it is their will to give some kind of authorisation, then it is not to authorise 'X' as such. Of course, this is not to say that, in the absence of an authorising consent to X, there can never be a (substantive) justification for doing X. What the absence of consent signifies is that there is no procedural justification.

Although our procedural justificatory conception of consent presupposes a tight connection between the will of the consenting agent and the consent that legal regimes will treat as fit for reliance (by way of claim or defence), we have not excluded the possibility of the consenting agent acting through a third party agent representative. Such a representative might be a proxy or an 'agent' in the technical sense employed by the law of agency. However, the terms on which such representative agency may generate a procedural justification are restricted, the conditions for direct dealing (between a consenting agent and a recipient) being copied across. In other words, the transaction between the consenting agent (or principal) and the third party representative agent must meet the criteria for direct dealing; essentially, if the third party representative agent is to be authorised 'to consent to X' (on behalf of the principal), then this must be in line with the will of the principal. It follows that procedural justification will break down if the supposed principal is not actually a subject of consent[1] or, where the principal is a subject of consent, the conditions for a valid and effective consent are not satisfied.[2]

Where a third party representative agent is duly authorised, the scope of that agent's authority is determined by the will of the principal. In principle, the scope of the authorisation might lie at any point on a range that runs from highly specific to relatively open-ended. For example, if the principal authorises the representative agent to make an offer of $500,000 for Green Gables, there is only one act open to the representative, and, concomitantly, there is only one act that can be procedurally justified. However, if the principal authorises the representative to make an offer of $500,000 for Green Gables or any similar property in the area (an authorisation, it should be said, that looks suitably vague to be a hostage to fortune and an invitation to litigation), or for any property within 10 miles of Green Gables, or for any property in the United States, the discretion given to the representative expands with each further band of authorisation. Provided that the representative agent acts within the terms of whatever extended authorisation has been conferred, the principal is bound and the justification for holding the principal to the deal is procedural. Even if the principal did not consent to the representative's particular action in the sense that the purchase made by the agent was, as it were, foretold or determined in advance by the principal, the representative agent's action is covered by the terms of the authorisation—and there is an identifiable consenting agent who is the source of that authorising consent.

This model of representative agency, based on consent, is applicable to a broad range of activities including 'governance' activities, such as casting a vote. For example, the principal might authorise a third party representative (or proxy) to vote on its behalf. The authorisation might be specific or relatively unspecific. For example, it might be limited positively ('Vote for X') or negatively ('Do not vote for Y'), or it might accord some discretion to the representative (for example, where the authorisation is to vote for X or Y or, much more openly, to vote for the best person). As with the previous property-purchasing authorisation, provided that the representative agent acts within the scope of the particular vote-casting authorisation, the principal is bound by the representative agent's acts; and consent-based procedural justification is, again, the reason for the principal being so bound.

We should not think, however, that this model of procedural justification applies only exceptionally to governance activities. Private governance, so called, is predicated on consent and procedural justification.[3] For example,

[1] For example, as in the substituted judgement cases that we discussed in ch 4.

[2] The relevant conditions being those that we discussed in chs 5, 6, and 7.

[3] See, eg, Julia Black, 'De-centring Regulation: Understanding the Role of Regulation and Self-Regulation in a "Post-Regulatory" World' (2001) 54 *Current Legal Problems* 103.

it is common practice for disputes in labour relations or commercial contracting to be settled by an arbitrator whose appointment and authority rests entirely on the consent of the disputants. When the disputants authorise the arbitrator to settle the dispute, they can set some parameters for the arbitrator's work but they will not know what the outcome of the arbitration will be. Nevertheless, the successful party has good reason to hold the other party to the result handed down by the arbitrator, and that reason is consent-based procedural justification.

Consent-based procedural justification is also the basis of rule-making in schemes of private governance. For example, within clubs, particularly larger clubs, various executive and rule-making decisions will be delegated to committees. On some substantive matters, members will be invited to vote, and they will have some say in who is appointed to which committee. However, to a considerable extent, the governance of the club will rest with the members of the committees rather than with the members of the club at large. Why are the latter members bound by the decisions of the former? Why are members bound by this scheme of governance? In both cases, the answer goes back to the originating consent given by members when they applied to join the club. Club membership is optional. However, having opted to join, members have consented to the club's constitutive rule-framework, and it follows that, provided the club is run in accordance with these rules, members have no cause for complaint. The scheme of governance at the club is procedurally justified (which is not to say, of course, that the scheme, or decisions made thereunder, can be justified to non-members).

Having, thus far, applied this account of consent (within the larger framework of Gewirthian moral theory) to evaluate the way that consent functions within the law (as a defence to criminal charges, as a response to tort claims or claimed infringements of property rights, as the basis for empowerment by engaging institutional sets such as the law of contract, and so on), we now turn to a much larger question. This is the question of how Gewirthian theory in general and consent in particular relate to the entire doctrinal sets of legal regimes together with their regulatory apparatus. In other words, in this chapter, we turn from the role of consent in authorising modifications to one's position *under the law* or creating new relationships *under the law*, to the role of consent in authorising the legal framework itself. To what extent is procedural justification the key to the authority of law? Or, to put the same question in the language of obligation, to what extent is the consent of citizens the justificatory reason for holding them bound by the larger politico-legal regime and its determinations? In short, how far is the model of procedurally justified consent-based private governance applicable to public governance?

Our discussion in this chapter is in three parts. First, we make some introductory remarks about the claimed authority of legal regimes, about the distinction between 'legitimate' and 'legitimating' authority, and about the 'procedural turn' as a move made by those who aspire to legitimate regulation as well as by those who seek legitimation for the regulatory positions taken by a regime. We also draw a fundamental distinction between the problem of politico-legal authority in a community that is morally homogeneous, all members of the community subscribing to the same general moral principles (ideal-typically, a community of rights that we will call Gewirthia), and the problem in communities that are morally divided or pluralistic in the sense that members subscribe to rival sets of general moral principles (or associated beliefs). Drawing on this distinction, in the second section of our discussion, we consider what we term 'the internal problem of authority', this being the problem set in the context of a community whose members share the same general moral commitments. Even here, there will be contested interpretations and applications that require authoritative public settlement. In the third section of the chapter, we turn to what we call 'the external problem of authority', where the setting is a community that is morally divided. Of course, the extent of moral pluralism in any community is a matter of degree, but, even where just one dissenting citizen believes that the legal regime is making a fundamental moral error (by reference to principles that the dissenter accepts but the regime rejects), it is incumbent on those who support the regime to explain why the dissenter is bound—that is, why even the dissenter should regard the legal regime as having authority. In both cases, our particular interest is in clarifying how far we can run with a procedural justification to 'bind in' those who dispute the authority of law or who claim to be free to follow their consciences rather than the legally authorised rules or determinations. After all, *if* the relationship between representative governing agents and citizens can be assimilated to that between a principal and a representative agent or treated as analogous to private governance within a club, citizens (just like principals and club members) will be bound by acts taken by their representatives or delegates within the scope of their authority. The fact that citizens did not know in advance what particular decision would be the outcome of the process, or that they would now prefer some other rule or determination, will not release them from their procedural bond.

Stated broadly, the conclusion that we will reach is that the model of consent-based private governance does not copy across readily to public governance. Although public governance must take what we describe as a procedural turn, the underlying justification for schemes of public governance (constitutions), as for particular legislative and judicial acts, lies in the requirements of the PGC rather than the consent of agents. In this sense, the justification is substantively derived from the PGC rather than procedurally authorised by agents; rather than consent authorising legitimate public governance, it is legitimate public governance that commands assent and that gives agents the opportunity to participate in consensual processes of governance.

## II Law's Claim to Authority

Whether we are guided by Lon Fuller's pre-theoretical identification of law with the enterprise of subjecting human conduct to the governance of rules,[4] or Karl Llewellyn's non-institutional law-jobs theory,[5] or HLA Hart's institutionalised view of law as the intersection of primary and secondary rules,[6] we get to pretty much the same place. First, law is about establishing order, about channelling behaviour, and settling disputes; in essence, law is a means to resolve disputes by providing a framework of rules for determining permissible and impermissible conduct, just and unjust allocations of resources, and so on. Secondly, it is about establishing who has the say and sway in carrying out these regulatory functions. Thirdly, law strives to impress its authority on social life. Law, as Hartians never fail to insist, is not about citizens being obliged to comply; law is an affair of obligation; law is about giving reasons for obedience to rules, and justifications for imposing sanctions for violations of rules.[7] Or, to put this point that law is not merely *a* framework for resolving disputes slightly differently, an appeal to the law is an appeal to exclusionary reasons for acting, reasons or rules that purport to override other reasons or rules that might come into conflict with them or each other.[8] As such, to appeal to the law is to appeal to what purports to be the final arbiter, not only in disputes about how agreed rules are to be applied, but in disputes about which framework of rules is to be applied.

Since the law is itself a framework of rules, this raises the question of the conditions under which claims for a framework to have the status of 'final arbiter' are justified. In asking this, however, it is important to distinguish the following three different questions:

(1) What are the conditions under which a framework of rules can or will effectively serve as the final arbiter in disputes? In other words, what are the conditions for a framework to operate de facto as the final arbiter?
(2) What are the conditions for a framework to operate as the final arbiter in a secure or stable manner?
(3) What are the conditions for making good the claim that a framework does in fact provide exclusionary reasons for acting, and that it actually has the authority it claims?

[4] Lon L Fuller, *The Morality of Law* (New Haven, NY, Yale University Press, 1969), passim.

[5] Karl N Llewellyn, 'The Normative, the Legal, and the Law-Jobs: The Problem of Juristic Method' (1940) 49 *Yale Law Journal* 1355.

[6] HLA Hart, *The Concept of Law* (Oxford, Clarendon Press, 1961).

[7] *Ibid*, at 82 and 88.

[8] Joseph Raz, *Practical Reason and Norms* (London, Hutchinson, 1975).

The first question makes no necessary reference to either the legitimacy or the legitimation of the rule framework, the second concerns legitimation, and the third concerns legitimacy.

As regards the first question, the ability to enforce a framework of rules is surely sufficient, even if it is not necessary. However, might is not right (might does not come warranted for its legitimacy), and, whilst might cannot be ignored, it offers no reason for respect (might is not, without more, legitimated). Moreover, given the propensity of human beings to fight for—indeed, to die for—things that they hold dear, a framework that is imposed on those who are to obey its rules against their will is very unlikely to be secure or stable.

If the rule framework is to operate as a final arbiter in a secure and stable manner, it needs to be respected. It is a truism that compliance with legal rules will be more faithful and smoother where the authority of law has been internalised than where there is a resistance of some kind (moral, cultural, economic, or otherwise). Or, as Jürgen Habermas has put it:

> [T]hough modern law requires from its addressees nothing more than norm-conformative behavior, it must nevertheless meet the expectation of legitimacy, so that it is at least open to people to follow norms, if they like, out of respect for the law.[9]

Legitimation, thus, is a process of responding to the expectation that those in power can articulate reasons for citizens to respect the governing rule-framework. In response, it will not do for those in power simply to restate that they are in power and that deviance will not be tolerated. However, what else might they say by way of legitimation? Appeals of a formal kind to the generality of the rules of law, or to their equal application, cut little legitimating ice. For, while it is arguable that such formal characteristics are necessary for an order to qualify as a *legal* order,[10] they are a long way from sufficient where it is the material provisions of the rules that are at issue. This invites an attempt at substantive legitimation. However, in divided moral communities, this strategy has limited prospects, and the rule-framework is heading for a legitimation crisis. It is with these legitimating avenues blocked that many commentators have seen considerations of fair process as the key to legitimating law. Whether we are focusing with Rawls[11] and Habermas on deliberative democracy, public reason, and the quest for an overlapping consensus at the commanding heights of the regime, or with Teubner[12] on reflexive law within areas such as employment

[9] Jürgen Habermas, 'Introduction' (1999) 12 *Ratio Juris* 329, at 330.

[10] See, eg, Fuller, n 4 above.

[11] John Rawls, *Political Liberalism* (New York, Columbia University Press, 1993).

[12] Gunther Teubner, 'Substantive and Reflexive Elements in Modern Law' (1983) 17 *Law and Society Review* 239. See, too, Philippe Nonet and Philip Selznick, *Law and Society in Transition: Toward Responsive Law* (New York, Harper & Row, 1978).

and consumer law, legitimation theory has taken a procedural turn. In this context, it is natural to wonder how far a theory of consent as procedural justification aligns with such a legitimating strategy. On the face of it, where there is consent to a framework, it should be at least a factor in promoting security and stability.[13]

The third question is about the legitimacy of the rule-framework rather than its legitimation. To be sure, there is a supportive relationship between these ideas in that, where a rule-framework is legitimate, it would be precisely by reference to its legitimacy that one would normally seek to legitimate it. In practice, however, as we have said, substantive legitimation (appeal to the substantive legitimacy of the rule-framework) runs into trouble in divided moral communities—and, hence, the turn to proceduralism.

If we approach the relationship between legitimacy and legitimation in the opposite direction, the supportive connection breaks down, for it is clear that successful legitimation does not entail legitimacy. Indeed, those who favour a procedural strategy accept that the success of such a strategy hinges on the willingness of agents to give up those very ideas of legitimacy that are the cause of their disunity and that destabilise public governance. So, legitimating consent does not necessarily imply that legitimacy rests on consent. Nevertheless, from Locke onwards, a raft of theories in the social contract tradition is predicated on the idea that consent is the justifying condition for the authority of law, as non-consent is the justifying condition for revolutionary rejection of tyranny.[14]

At first blush, there is something inherently implausible (not to say, unpromising) about the turn to proceduralism. The problems of stability and authority, it is conceded, are most acute when the law takes sides on opposed moral positions. It is in just these circumstances that a legitimation crisis is prompted, and it is in just such a context that proceduralism is advanced as the best practical response. Yet, if the protagonists and pluralists are to bargain their way to a solution, where the only force (to use Habermassian rhetoric) is the force of the better argument, then something has to give. Broadly speaking, what the proceduralists ask of the disputants is nothing less than that they abandon their deepest (but incompatible) moral convictions—that is, those very beliefs that are the source of the instability, and which, if insisted upon, would fatally obstruct a consensual accommodation of all reasonable viewpoints, or of principles that could not

[13] It is only a factor because the fact that someone has consented to something does not absolutely guarantee that he or she will not object to it being done.

[14] See, eg, Hanna Pitkin, 'Obligation and Consent' in Peter Laslett, WG Runciman and Quentin Skinner (eds), *Philosophy, Politics and Society* (4th Series) (Oxford, Basil Blackwell, 1972) at 45.

be reasonably rejected.[15] This is quite a price, and the question is: why would it be rational for morally divided agents to accept such a procedural demand? For, it is surely an unstated premise of proceduralism that, given the right bargaining situation, it can be rational for persons to consent to being governed by a framework that might produce rules and decisions that go contrary to what the persons believe to be morally acceptable. While we will offer a general analysis of the extent to which this is possible, we are, of course, specifically interested in the implications that this has for a PGC-ruled theory of justification and for the role that the PGC might play in creating a consensus that contributes to a stable legal order.

Despite these reservations, we have elsewhere argued that part of the solution to the problems of stability and authority lies in a procedural turn, which places the focus on agreed procedures to resolve disputes rather than on the content or substance of the decisions,[16] and we will do so again here.

From a Gewirthian viewpoint, there are at least three types of politico-legal context in which a turn to proceduralism might be contemplated.

First, there is Gewirthia, a community fully committed to Gewirthian moral principles. If we suppose that we live in such a legal order guided by adherence to the PGC as its universally agreed upon fundamental constitutional principle, disputes can still occur about what the PGC permits or requires that bear on the authority of the decisions. The problem of authority within such a context is controlled by the universal commitment to the PGC. What we have in Gewirthia is an 'internal problem of authority'. Secondly, there is a community in which some agents are committed to Gewirthian moral principles, but others are not. Thirdly, there is a

[15] Compare Scanlon's contractualist approach. In TM Scanlon, 'The Aims and Authority of Moral Theory' (1992) 12 *Oxford Journal of Legal Studies* 1, at 5, Scanlon conceives of a moral wrong in the following terms: '[A]n act is morally wrong just in case it would be disallowed by any principles that no one could reasonably reject if they were seeking principles which could be the basis of informed, unforced general agreement.' Then, at 11:

> According to my version of contractualism, for example, we have reason not to be cruel to people or to break our promises to them because such actions would not be allowed by principles that they could not reasonably reject.

Despite the multiple negatives in these formulations, the governing principles seem to be those that we could not reasonably reject if we hoped to achieve a consensus as to our governing principles. This is saying something more than that we are bound by reasonable principles, but, so long as the test hinges on disputants having a reasonable attitude (in the context of a desire to achieve consensus), it is not altogether clear precisely what or how much is being asked of parties, except that it is a great deal.

[16] See Deryck Beyleveld and Roger Brownsword, *Law as a Moral Judgment* (London, Sweet and Maxwell, 1986) (reprinted Sheffield, Sheffield Academic Press, 1994). A procedural turn is also involved in what Gewirth calls 'the method of consent' in 'the indirect applications of the PGC,' which he sees as the justificatory basis for the supportive welfare state: see Alan Gewirth, *Reason and Morality* (Chicago, IL, University of Chicago Press, 1978) at 272–365, especially at 304–12.

community in which no one accepts Gewirthian moral principles, but it is a divided moral community (for example, one where utilitarians and Kantians are at moral war with one another). In these latter two communities, we have an 'external problem of authority'. This background typology, with its distinction between the two kinds of authority problem, structures our discussion in the remainder of this chapter. Before we proceed, however, three short related observations can be made.

The first comment concerns the substantive anchoring point for any turn to proceduralism. In Gewirthia, all operations, including procedural operations, are subject to the substantive regulation of the PGC. If the procedural turn is to commend itself to rational agents in Gewirthia, it must make sense relative to substantive Gewirthian principles. Once we move beyond Gewirthia, those who are committed to Gewirthian principles will continue to view procedural options in the light of the PGC and the generic values of agency. However, it is less clear what connection proceduralism has with prior substantive views where the problem is one of external authority and where the procedural strategy involves renouncing either a foundationalist moral epistemology or fundamental moral convictions or both.[17]

Following on from this first comment, the second point is that the demand made by the procedural turn in Gewirthia seems to put agents under much less strain than is the case in other contexts. In Gewirthia, proceduralism (under what Gewirth calls the 'method of consent')[18] involves consenting to abide by disputed but not unreasonable interpretations of one's own moral principles. One might not agree with the interpretation but at least it is an interpretation of one's own moral principles. By contrast, agents elsewhere are asked to make a major sacrifice, being asked to consent to obey decisions that go contrary to their own moral principles and that conform, in effect, with moral principles with which they do not agree.

Finally, we should say that we see no reason why the same regulatory question cannot be as much a problem in Gewirthia as outside it. For example, agents in Gewirthia, acting on their own interpretations of the precautionary principle under the PGC, might come to different views about the correct regulatory position in relation to both abortion and the use of human embryos for research. These differences might be quite nuanced, concerning not just whether such activities should be permitted, but whether public funds should be applied in support and whether there should be incentivisation (in the case of embryo research) through the patent regime, and so on.[19] Outside

[17] See, eg, the sceptical remarks in John Finnis, 'Natural Law and the Ethics of Discourse' (1999) 12 *Ratio Juris* 354.

[18] See n 16 above.

[19] See, further, Deryck Beyleveld and Shaun Pattinson, 'Globalisation and Human Dignity: Some Effects and Implications for the Creation and Use of Embryos' in Roger Brownsword (ed), *Global Governance and the Quest for Justice: Human Rights* (vol 4) (Oxford, Hart Publishing, 2004) at 185–202.

Gewirthia, moral horns might be locked, too, over precisely the same regulatory issues, albeit that divisions of opinion can be traced more straightforwardly to first (but opposed) moral principles. In the absence of a real world instantiation of Gewirthia, this kind of pluralistic community (with its external problem of authority) is where procedural solutions must be tested in practice. However, because the internal problem of authority has fewer complicating features than the equivalent external problem, we will begin with it.

## III The Internal Problem of Authority

Suppose then, the existence of our imaginary country, Gewirthia. In supposing Gewirthia, suppose that the PGC is, as we contend, dialectically necessary, and also, to simplify matters as much as possible, that everyone in Gewirthia agrees that this is the case. In consequence, the legal system of Gewirthia is guided by the fundamental and completely overriding constitutional principle that all activities and laws must be in conformity with the PGC. In Gewirthia, the external problem of authority will not arise in the State's dealings with its own citizens. However, it might arise when outsiders are required to obey Gewirthia's laws and it will need to be referred to in the education of Gewirthian children. Where it arises, it will be answered by reference to the dialectical necessity of the PGC. Alongside this, the fact that all are agreed upon the dialectical necessity of the PGC will contribute greatly to the stability of Gewirthia's legal system. Nevertheless, because the dialectical necessity of the PGC does not mean that rational Gewirthian citizens can never disagree about what the PGC requires or permits, such disputes can create problems of authority and stability.[20]

There are at least three reasons why the applications of the PGC leave room for rational and not unreasonable disagreement.

First, application of the PGC might involve a decision between two or more answers that the PGC leaves optional, but between which a choice must be made. For example, the PGC does not (without more) have a preference for the rule of the road to be that cars must drive on the left rather than the right.[21] However, the PGC will not permit persons to drive on whichever side of the road they wish. The result would be mayhem, injury, and death to many, which the PGC would not permit unless all affected persons had consented freely to this arrangement. The PGC, therefore,

[20] The history of religion shows us that internecine disputes can be just as bloody (or even more so) than those between different faiths.

[21] We say 'without more' because there are, in theory, things that could render the choice non-optional under the PGC. One of these would be the finding that, because most persons are right-handed and left-brained, it is safer for them to drive on the right. However, as far as we know, there is no reason to suppose that this is the case.

requires that there be a general rule that all persons driving in the same direction must drive on the same side of the road, but it is neutral over which side this should be.

Secondly, the PGC gives different weight to different generic conditions of action (to be determined by the criterion of needfulness for action). However, actions differ in the probability with which they affect the generic conditions of agency as well as in the extent to which they impact on the generic conditions. For this reason, application of the PGC to cases where the generic rights of agents are in conflict will generally involve not only assessing the importance of the generic conditions affected in the conflict but also the probability of actions having effects on the generic conditions.[22] However, as we have already pointed out in chapter two, there does not seem to be any good reason for regarding scales of probability and scales of importance of a generic condition as commensurable in a way that permits a specific probability of a generic harm X to agent A to be discounted by a specific lower importance of generic harm Y to agent B. Consequently, unless the conflict involves variation in only one variable, the PGC does not directly enable the calculus that must be used in resolving conflicts of generic rights to be operationalised.[23]

Thirdly, even if there is, unlike in the previous two examples, a dialectically necessary answer to an application of the PGC, the application might be so complex that it leaves room for rational doubt about the correct answer.[24] For example, judgements employing the criterion of needfulness for action clearly require knowledge about human biology and psychology, and while it is clear that life is more needful than, say, accurate information, the ranking of other generic conditions will be more difficult, and quantification of the need even more so. These matters will be open to scientific dispute and no less open to rational disagreement than scientific judgements generally.

The fact that the PGC does not directly yield answers to disputes of these three kinds, does not, however, mean that the PGC does not tell us (a) that it is more important that these disputes are settled than that they are left unsettled and (b) how such disputes are to be resolved. According to Gewirth, the PGC directs answers in these cases indirectly, by providing that answers arrived at by procedures that the PGC directly authorises are to be applied and obeyed. It is important to observe, however, that to the

[22] Recall our comments, in ch 9, on the difficulty of comparing the impact of a general prohibition on active euthanasia with the impact of a special authorising procedure.

[23] Compare, too, our discussion of *Re A (Children) (Conjoined Twins: Surgical Separation)* [2000] 4 All ER 961, in ch 9.

[24] See the excellent treatment of the correlative point that controversiality does not imply the absence of a right answer by Ronald Dworkin in 'Can Rights be Controversial?' in *Taking Rights Seriously*, revised edition (London, Duckworth, 1978), ch 13, at 279–90.

extent that these are procedures that the PGC directly and specifically authorises, they are not procedures that bind agents for the free-standing reason that they have consented to submit their disputes to them.[25] However, as we shall see shortly, matters become less clear if the PGC recognises more than one procedure as appropriate or if the particular procedure to be used involves agents participating in the decision-making by casting a vote or indicating their consent.

Why might it be more important, indeed necessary, that a public choice be made between permissible or arguable articulations of the PGC rather than leaving the matter unresolved or unregulated? If it is possible for the disputants to co-exist without any settlement or regulatory intervention, that is fine. If motor cars are designed so that they will avoid contact with one another no matter on which side of the road they are driven, there is no pressing need to establish a rule of the road (or some other regulatory response that will serve the same purpose). However, this might not be the case. The setting, instead, might be one where not to reach agreement on matters of import under the PGC is either not to defend the interests that the PGC protects (in the rule of the road example, resulting in mayhem on the roads) or to positively invite persons to take matters into their own hands when they have disputes (resulting in animosity and ultimately resort to force that run directly contrary to the PGC). It is in settings of this kind that agents are required to settle their differences. It is in such cases that, if the citizens of Gewirthia are to guide themselves by the PGC, they must accept a procedural turn. But, of course, whilst this general line of argument indicates why citizens are required to make a procedural turn, it does not yet indicate which procedural turn they must make.

There are a number of procedures that persons use to decide questions when there is disagreement between parties. One tactic is to resort to chance, such as the flip of a coin ('heads I win, tails I lose'). Another is to delegate the decision to a third party. It is vital to the acceptability of a procedure that it be free from bias, that it enable decisions to be reached dispassionately or fairly, whichever of these ideas is applicable. The nature of the dispute will also influence the acceptability of a procedure. Thus, for example, where the choice between options is a choice between things over which the PGC is neutral, a random unbiased procedure seems acceptable. However, where the issue is one of complexity, then it is not a random answer that is called for but one that can attend to the evidence in an expert, good faith way (transparently, accountably, reviewably, untainted by con-

[25] In the same way, if the PGC requires an agent to consent to X, although the giving of consent will entail that no wrong is done by the recipient to the consenting agent, it is the PGC's requirement that does the basic justificatory work. The standard case of procedural justification, it must be remembered, is one in which the giving of consent is optional rather than required.

flicts of interest, sincerely, etc). In principle, the PGC might identify one particular procedure as uniquely appropriate, and thus required, for the decision-making purpose; or it might identify one general type of procedure (say, third party adjudication) as appropriate, while leaving some optionality as to the particular specification (say, adjudication by a judge sitting alone, or by a judge sitting with a jury (of eight, ten, or 12 lay persons)); or it might identify more than one general type of procedure as appropriate (say, third party adjudication or legislative decision).

Let us pause to review how far, if at all, consent and procedural justification is implicated in these steps towards determinative processes and their binding outcomes. First, we are saying that citizens in Gewirthia are required by the PGC to resolve certain practical matters by establishing a rule or making a decision (whether it be a rule or decision about property or about road traffic, it is a matter of some importance relative to the values protected by the PGC). Where it is reasonable to believe that more than one answer is compatible with the PGC, a determination must be made because, relative to the values of the PGC, leaving the matter unresolved is less satisfactory than resolving it (even allowing that the final resolution might be incorrect and that some agents in Gewirthia will view it as misconceived). At this first level, therefore, agents have no choice; they are required to resolve the matter; it is a matter of obligation that steps are taken to make a determination.

Secondly, however, there is, ex hypothesi, a choice about which determination is made. Let us suppose that the contested question is about the use of human embryos for research. Some Gewirthians, let us suppose, believe that human embryos should not be used for research after they have developed for 12 days. Against this view, other Gewirthians take the more permissive line that research is permissible until the appearance of the primitive streak or 14 days (after the first cell division), whichever is earlier. Given the present state of embryology, let us suppose that both views are defensible relative to Gewirthian standards. Which rule is it to be, 12 days or 14 days? And, let us suppose, a determination must be made; this is not a case where there can be peaceful or orderly co-existence. At this point, if the protagonists cannot agree upon a resolution, the PGC dictates that a process for determination must be brought into play. However, whilst the PGC might identify one process as uniquely suitable for this purpose, as we have said, it might also allow that more than one process will suffice. If the former, then the matter is straightforward: the question must be submitted to the indicated process for determination, and the answer is binding. On these premises, agents are required to make a determination (rather than leave the issue unresolved), and they are required to submit the issue to a particular procedure for determination. It is requirement all the way; procedural justification by way of consent is not relevant. If, however, more than one procedure is suitable, the analysis is pushed to a third level.

Thirdly, imagine that (i) a determination of the 12- or 14-day limit must be made, and (ii) that the protagonists have the option of submitting the matter to a tribunal comprising either experts only or a mix of expert and lay members. If the protagonists consent to refer the matter to, let us say, the expert-only panel, then their consent is the reason why they are bound by the determination of the panel; this is akin to a model of private governance (albeit driven by the background requirement to settle the matter); and we do have a procedural justification. However, if they cannot agree on which of the panels should be charged with making the determination, we are taken to yet a further level.

Fourthly, where the PGC allows for a choice between one or more decision-making procedures, there is a problem if the agents concerned cannot agree upon which procedure to use. Proceduralism thus throws up its own questions for determination, and we seem to need a further level of proceduralism to resolve the matter. However, this threatens to become an infinite regress of one layer of proceduralism on another. At this level, we can say that the procedural turn that best serves the PGC is one to which agents consent. Failing this, at some point, the PGC must call time, and agents will be required to resolve their principal substantive differences. If they do so by consent, they are bound under a procedural justification; if they do not do so by consent, but because the PGC directly requires them to make a determination in a particular way, then the justification for holding them to the outcome is substantive.

In the light of this, what should we make of the processes of representative government that are typical of large modern democracies? We need to decompose such processes into three key elements. First, there is the basic institutional structure of public governance (the constitution and the primary organs of governance); secondly, there are the officials, the legislators and the judges, who are the principal authorised players in that structure; and, thirdly, there are the rules and decisions made by using this process. To be sure, there are procedures for decision-making here, and, periodically, citizens are invited to cast their vote, but how plausible is it to present the outcomes of the process as binding on agents by virtue of their authorising consent? That is, how plausible is it for decision-makers to argue that the rule framework, together with the decisions made thereunder, are procedurally justified (by reference to authorising consent)?

For most agents, the basic politico-legal structure of their community is simply there as a social fact. It is not meaningfully engaged by agents in the way that they might engage optional sets such as the law of contract or the law of marriage. Crucially, it is not comparable to the originating consents that bind members to the private governance structures that are distinctive of their club. In practice, we are born into the club that is the nation state and, for the most part, we simply we do not consent to our membership in any meaningful way. In consequence, as many critics of social contract theory have pointed out, with the exception of special applications for citizenship, it is a fiction to rest legitimate governance on consent, historic or present. Rather, in the words of Hanna Pitkin: 'The only "consent" that is relevant is the hypothetical consent imputed to hypothetical, timeless, abstract, rational men.'[26]

With regard to the officials, agents have a little more involvement. There are elections for many official positions. However, political elections are very different from the process of authorising a representative as one's political agent. When one authorises another agent as one's representative, it is that nominated agent alone who is authorised to speak for the principal. When an agent casts a vote in a political election, the elected representative might be one for whom the agent did not vote. So, we have a process to which one has not given an originating consent, and a representative person whose election is not necessarily authorised by one's consent.

Much the same applies to the outcomes produced by the scheme of public governance. Occasionally, outcomes are determined by public referenda. However, the majority view will prevail. For agents who take the minority view, this is again a process that has not been authorised by one's originating consent and that produces a result that is contrary to one's will. To be sure, participation in a referendum, like participation in an election, might be optional. Having participated, one has no complaint that one's vote has been counted in the way that one has indicated. To this extent, those who count the votes have a procedural justification for the returns they make. However, this is a long way from saying that the outcome of the process is procedurally justified on the basis of consent.

This point should not be misunderstood. Our point is not that public governance will only be procedurally justified where it operates on the basis of direct democracy, citizens having a vote on every issue. This is not the case in private governance (where delegated or representative decision-making may be consensually authorised), and nor is it the case in public governance. In order for consent to justify a procedure for decision-making it is not necessary that consent be given to procedures on a dispute-by-dispute basis. In a complex society this is not feasible. In such a society, it is acceptable for routine kinds of disputes that consent be given for certain types of determinative procedure, that consent be given for certain classes of disputes to be processed in a standard way, and even for dispute resolution procedures to be decided by a body to whom this decision is delegated (which, characteristically, will be the legislative body or executive arm of government). In effect, a referendum is not essential on every issue, but should be reserved for very exceptional decisions that have far-reaching implications about how the PGC is to be applied.

[26] Note 14 above, at 57.

What, then, can be said to those citizens of Gewirthia who find themselves on the losing side at an election, or who complain that they have not consented to the delegated authority that grounds procedures for dispute resolution under the PGC? What matters here is that they have the opportunity to participate and that the process of appointment of government and legislature (which will ultimately determine specific dispute resolution procedures) be a reviewable one that is itself transparent, fair, and so on. The reason why this is enough is because the citizens of Gewirthia respect the generic rights of all agents and understand that no agent is infallible, thus that they are not infallible. They also presume (unless presented with direct evidence to the contrary) that other agents are sincere in their beliefs and preferences when these differ from their own. They do, not, therefore, insist on their own views at all costs. To do so is to place the most basic values that the PGC protects under threat, both at the level of likely effects and at the level of respect for the autonomy of other agents. Thus, the citizens of Gerwirthia must, and do, recognise that the method of consent, as expressed in the larger scheme of public governance, involves the optimal compromise of their views within their commitment to the PGC itself.

If the citizens of Gewirthia are required to submit themselves to democratic public governance, nevertheless this is not a licence for either simple majoritarian rule or for an elective dictatorship.

First, because the procedural turn is guided by the PGC, it is also limited by the PGC. Thus, the PGC polity only permits decisions to be reached that do not run contrary to the PGC (or, in practice, do not run clearly contrary to the PGC). In effect, the PGC polity has the form of a constitutional democracy, in which the generic rights are trumps over decisions of the majority. Implicit in this thinking is the idea that there are some values that the PGC protects that limit the results that can be left to democratic processes, local or national, State or federal, values that cannot be overridden by decisions reached using the method of consent.[27] What these are will be dealt with below, but in the abstract they are the values that must be presupposed by the supposition that the method of consent can provide justification for rules and decisions arrived at by its procedures. It follows, furthermore, that these values are values that may (indeed, ought to) be imposed, regardless of consent.

Secondly, because the generic rights, in principle, trump any decisions that the procedures yield, it is necessary for there to be a body entrusted with scrutiny of the results achieved by the method of consent. Typically, this will be a constitutional or supreme court, which must be able to operate with some distance from majority decision-making, whether this is exercised directly or indirectly through the elected legislature, the executive, or lower courts/tribunals, etc. However, because no one is infallible and

[27] Compare our discussion of *Lawrence v Texas* 123 S Ct 2472 (2003), in ch 9.

even supreme court judges can be corrupt, this body cannot be wholly above external accountability. How accountability to, yet independence from, the majority is to be achieved presents one of the most difficult problems for constitutional design in Gewirthia, and this is not the place to discuss its intricacies. However, it would seem that limited terms of office, some degree of representation of the different interest groups/political factions in Gewirthia, and the continual possibility of review of decisions of this body are features that, at least in principle, can contribute to achievement of the desired goals.

We conclude, therefore, that the key to the internal problem of authority in Gewirthia is not procedural justification on the basis of consent in the way that agents may authorise schemes of private governance or arbiters of private disputes. The reasons why Gewirthians are bound by their procedural turn is because they are not omniscient super-beings and this is their best practical strategy for defending and promoting the values of the PGC. Gewirthians are fortunate enough to have a good government; they are bound to respect it; but they are not bound because they have consented but because their basic scheme of governance is right.[28]

## IV The External Problem of Authority

The external problem of authority arises in pluralistic societies. In some such societies, the PGC will not be universally, or even widely, accepted; in others, it will not be accepted at all; but in all such societies, citizens will subscribe to competing moralities. Where the pluralistic society is one in which the PGC is not accepted at all, a Gewirthian commentary on its problem of authority will be guided by the values of the PGC but it will be offered as a prescription for that society from the outside. Where the pluralistic society is one in which the PGC enjoys some degree of acceptance, a Gewirthian commentary on its problem of authority, once again, will be guided by the values of the PGC. However, it is now much more an insiders' commentary as those Gewirthian agents within the society address its authority problem. It is this (Gewirthian) insiders' view of the external problem of authority that is our focus.

Let us suppose that, in our hypothetical pluralistic society, the persons who believe in the PGC are very powerful. Indeed, they are powerful enough to impose the PGC on the society against the will of those who object. Does it follow that, because the PGC is dialectically necessary, this is permissible? Perhaps it might be thought that because agents contradict

[28] For a similar inversion, see Pitkin, n 14 above. And, with a focus specifically on Kant's version of social contract theory, compare Onora O'Neill, 'Kant and the Social Contract Tradition' in François Duchesneau, Guy Lafrance, and Claude Piché (eds), *Kant Actuel: Hommage à Pierre Laberge* (Montreal, Bellarmin, 2000) at 185–200.

that they are agents if they do not accept the PGC, actions that require them to act in accordance with the PGC cannot be against their will. If they do not accept the PGC then they deny that they are agents, and since agents are beings who have the capacity to act voluntarily to achieve their purposes, they thereby deny that they are such beings, thereby denying that they have the capacity to consent or withhold consent. However, this is not valid because it does not follow from the fact that a being who acts contrary to the PGC, or who fails to accept it as the supreme guide to action, denies that it is an agent that this being is not an agent. Indeed, in order to deny the PGC, to contest its dialectical necessity, to oppose its values, and so on, the disputant must be an agent. Furthermore, recognising the fallibility of all agents, those who uphold the PGC must accept the possibility that they are mistaken in the reasoning that leads them to believe in the dialectical necessity of the PGC.[29] Propositions that are certainly true are not necessarily necessary truths, and those that are necessary truths are not necessarily certain, if by certainty we mean that they cannot be doubted by rational persons acting in good faith. For this reason, those who accept the PGC must accept that at least some respect must be given to the views of those who do not accept the PGC in good faith. In addition, whether or not those who deny the PGC are, as deniers of the PGC, to be respected, those who accept the PGC must recognise that they may not impose the PGC on others if this requires them to interfere with the generic interests of agents against their will in a way that is disproportionate to the generic interests that trying to impose the PGC is intended to protect. Not all generic interests carry the same weight under the PGC. Thus, where it is the case that persons who disagree with the PGC might be prepared to fight (violently) for values contrary to some PGC values, this is a factor that those who would impose the PGC on them against their will must take into account. The implication of this is that, in the real world, PGC values must, to some extent, be compromised by those who uphold the PGC in order to optimally protect the PGC. A PGC-maximising approach might not be the optimal one. The crucial question, however, is to what extent the PGC in its maximal application (its application in Gewirthia) can be compromised.

We will address this question, to begin with, not directly through the PGC, but through the general approach taken by social contract theories. In general, social contract theory, like the internal applications of the PGC, rests on the proposition that, when it is not possible to resolve an issue or reach agreement on the basis of given or agreed principles, it might be possible to resolve the issue or reach agreement by an appeal to agreed procedures. The difference is that, whereas in the internal application of the

[29] For further discussion of the implications of human fallibility and vulnerability, see Deryck Beyleveld and Roger Brownsword, *Human Dignity in Bioethics and Biolaw* (Oxford, Oxford University Press, 2001), especially ch 6.

PGC or any other principle that governs the internal problem of authority, the agreed principle can be assumed, this is not the case in social contract theory. Thus, if recourse to a procedural turn is to justify decisions, there must be justification for accepting solutions that are incompatible with the principles held by at least some of the parties to the contract. Social contract theory, therefore, essentially involves a specification of the conditions under which it is rational for persons to accept decisions that run counter to what their moral principles actually require. As we have remarked already, this differs from the procedural turn involved in internal applications of a principle where the burden on the procedural turn is merely to justify decisions that are under-specified by the principle supposed or that are reasonably open to doubt on the basis of the given principle.

If the first generation of social contract theories addressed the conditions under which it would be rational to become a member of an organised society, the current generation of procedural theories assumes that the context for rational choice is already one of membership of organised societies (and, what is more, organised societies with a democratic commitment). For this latter group, the turn to proceduralism is prompted by three considerations: first, by the rejection of 'force' as any kind of legitimating reason; secondly, by the insufficiency of formal equality under the law (rules that treat like cases alike might still be unjust or oppressive); and, thirdly, by the inescapable fact that, in pluralistic societies, the content of rules or decisions cannot always command the respect of the many moral constituencies that comprise such a society.[30] Although John Rawls' later writing has become something of a beacon for this mode of thinking, the seminal idea goes back to the 'ideal speech' situation elucidated by Jürgen Habermas.[31] Here, Habermas gives an account of a set of conditions that are purely procedural

[30] Compare Cass R Sunstein, *Designing Democracy* (Oxford, Oxford University Press, 2001) at 49–50:

> In most democratic nations, citizens must proceed in the face of conflict and disagreement on the most fundamental matters. The existence of diverse values—of pluralism and even multiculturalism—seems to threaten the very possibility of a constitutional order. People disagree on rights, on the good life, on equality and liberty, on the nature and the existence of God. How can constitutionalism be feasible in these circumstances?

In response, stated shortly, Sunstein supports deliberative democracy as a constitutional design that aims to encourage reflection and reason-giving, in fact as a democratic design that aspires to create a framework for a republic of reasons. Thus (at 239):

> Deliberative democracies do not respond mechanically to what a majority currently thinks. They do not take snapshots of public opinion. A deliberative democracy requires the exercise of governmental power, and the distribution of benefits and burdens, to be justified not by the fact that a majority is in favor of it but on the basis of reasons that can be seen, by all or almost all citizens, as public-regarding.

[31] See, seminally, 'Toward a Theory of Communicative Competence', in HP Dreitzel (ed) *Recent Sociology No 2* (New York, Macmillan, 1970) at 114–48.

under which he claims that it is rational for persons to accept decisions/judgements about which they do not agree.

In essence, Habermas contends that if answers to moral problems are arrived at in an 'ideal speech situation', then these answers are to be accepted as binding (although he even more controversially states that they are to be accepted as true).[32] The ideal speech situation is defined by a number of purely procedural conditions: in particular, the disputants must be able to present their viewpoints in a way that is free of disparities of power that preclude each of them from having an equal say; the debate must be conducted sincerely, orientated towards the truth without ulterior motives; it must be governed by rules of logical consistency; the disputants must be prepared to yield from their starting position; and answers must be reviewable when new 'facts' come to light, etc. In short, the ideal speech situation is one in which all parties operate in nothing less, and also nothing more, than complete good faith.

But, precisely because the results of an ideal speech discourse are not limited by any rules relating to the substance of the decisions reached (there is no agreed overarching principle, no comprehensive theory), this is surely overly formalistic. A social contract that it is rational for someone to enter into from their own value-perspective (and specifically a rational acceptance of the results of the procedural turn that it involves) is limited by the proviso that persons bound by the contract not be placed in a worse position by its terms or results than they would be by being excluded from the contract altogether.[33] Now, precisely how 'being worse off' is to be measured will be a matter of dispute, and social contract theories vary to a large extent according to how they assess the relative value of being in the contract as against being excluded from it. However, in general terms, either there must be some way of determining this in a way that all contractors must accept or else the determination must be purely relative to the values held by the individual parties. The whole point and promise of the procedural turn to resolve intractable disputes over matters of substance derives from the idea that the values that persons espouse might require them to compromise other values they espouse in order to protect the values they hold most dear or rationally ought to hold most dear. Consequently, social contract theory, in general, must observe the proposition that it is only rational for persons to compromise their values to the extent that this is necessary for the optimal achievement (the best achievement possible in practice) of their most prized values or those that they rationally ought to prize most highly.

[32] For discussion of this, see TA McCarthy, 'A Theory of Communicative Competence' (1973) 3 *Philosophy of the Social Sciences* 135–56, at 150.

[33] This is one interpretation of what is generally known as the 'Lockean proviso'. For an illuminating discussion of this, see David Gauthier, *Morals by Agreement* (Oxford, Clarendon Press, 1986) at 190–232.

It follows that, if any particular version of proceduralism is to be plausible, it must pass muster relative to this general condition.

On this basis, it is clear that the ideal speech situation does not unconditionally provide sufficient reason for persons to accept its conclusions. It only does so for those who believe that there are no substantive values that persons rationally must accept *and/or* for those who do not attach more importance to any of the substantive values they espouse than they attach to the value of simply reaching a consensus agreement (and who thereby attach absolute value to reaching a consensus).

Another 'procedural model' is, in effect, to be found in Ronald Dworkin's elucidation of what he calls 'a discriminatory moral position'.[34] Such a position is one:

(1) for which reasons are given, but which excludes:

  (a) prejudices (postures that take into account considerations excluded by 'our conventions');
  (b) mere emotional reactions (feelings presented in a way that makes them immune to support by reasons);
  (c) rationalisations (which include: appeals to false or irrational beliefs; considerations that cannot be plausibly be connected to their conclusions; and considerations that the proponent would not be prepared to countenance if proffered by others); and
  (d) parroting (repeating what others have said without critical understanding);

(2) that is held sincerely;
(3) that is consistent with the other beliefs of the proponent; and
(4) that is not held arbitrarily (ie not presented as self-evident when it is generally accepted that reasons for it are required).

This model is not, however, purely procedural, because there is a substantive element built into the exclusion of prejudice by the notion that 'our conventions' must not be violated. However, this merely serves to highlight the fact that the real problem might be that there may be no consensus over 'our conventions'. This is seriously problematic if 'our conventions' refers not only to shared rules of reasoning but also to at least a range of substantive beliefs, *if* the model is intended to provide neutral reasons for accepting answers that *everyone* who is rational must accept. Thus, the existence of 'conventions' (equivalent to a degree of consensus) should be viewed merely as setting limits to the possibility in practice of a rational solution of ethical disputes.

[34] See Ronald Dworkin, *Taking Rights Seriously*, revised edition (London, Duckworth, 1978) at 248–53.

As already noted, it is important to distinguish the social contract as a basis for justifying rules or decisions produced by agreed procedures (a question of legitimacy) from the social contract as a means of securing a willingness to abide by the decisions or rules produced by agreed procedures (a question of legitimation). However, in theories of the social contract that disavow the idea of a set of values to which persons must, if they are to be rational, adhere, either the idea that the social contract be justificatory must be abandoned or else the distinction between justification and political legitimation must be denied, for all that the social contract can then do is produce a willingness to abide by rules/decisions produced by agreed procedures. From what is essentially the perspective of political legitimation, the efficacy of the social contract is strictly limited by whatever degree of consensus there is about core values that represent the values that those party to it are not prepared to sacrifice for other values. From this perspective, nothing can be said to 'the fanatic' who is willing to sacrifice everything to achieve whatever he or she values. Furthermore, unless there are values that must be adhered to as rational values, there is nothing that can be said to the fanatic that has the force of justifying these values as against the values of the fanatic.

Now, clearly, if we are right that the PGC is dialectically necessary, then there are values that all agents (hence, including all agents as social contractors) rationally must accept on pain of denying that they are social contractors by denying that they are agents. The PGC, as a structure of values, thus constitutes a rationally necessary core consensus to ground the social contract as a mechanism of justification of a procedural turn. However, as already noted, decisions and rules that the PGC ideally requires cannot simply be imposed on those who do not accept it, simply because this might entail violating more important values within the structure of values enshrined within the PGC. Thus, to a degree, the need for political legitimation requires a compromise of the values that the PGC requires. Now, within the structure of the PGC, the general rule for compromising values supported by the PGC is given by the criterion of needfulness for action. This, however, is too vague for practical application in the context of the problems with which the social contract is designed to deal. The criterion needs to be focused on the social contract, but how is this to be taken forward?

Illumination is provided by David Gauthier's suggestion that the most important civil and political rights are not to be viewed as products of the procedures agreed as a result of the social contract, but as conditions for the Lockean proviso to be satisfied.[35] The idea is that there are (pre-contract) rights (civil and political) that persons must be granted if they are not to be worse off as a result of being bound by the contract than if they were

[35] See David Gauthier, *Morals by Agreement,* (Oxford, Clarendon Press, 1986) at 227.

excluded from it. But, surely, if the generic conditions of action are indeed generic, then they must be conditions that all agents must have, to at least some extent, to be contracting *agents*, and some of these will be necessary in order to be *contracting* agents. But which are these latter? The answer to this, we suggest, is the basic generic conditions. These are conditions interference with which impacts negatively on the very possibility of action. They are differentiated from additive and non-subtractive generic conditions[36] in that the latter are conditions of successful action in general rather than of action as such. Now, precisely because entering into the social contract requires distance from success in achieving one's particular-occurrent purposes, it requires distance from the conditions of successful action, and this indicates strongly that the core of values that should set limits on the social contract are the basic generic conditions. However, if this is correct, then these values should not merely play this role in the thinking of Gewirthians. They should play this role also in the thinking of all who make claims that the social contract is capable of fulfilling a justificatory role in relation to decisions/rules arrived at by agreed procedures.[37]

Even from the perspective of political legitimation plain, pure, and simple, attention to the generic conditions of agency is instructive. From this perspective, what matters is not whether values are rationally necessary but whether or not they are widely enough shared to be a core that must be attended to and limit decisions and rules arrived at by agreed procedures if the society is to be stable. Now, in modern societies, particularly Western societies, there is such a core of values. These are enshrined in the Universal Declaration of Human Rights, the United Nations Covenants, and the regional human rights instruments, such as the European Convention on Human Rights that give effect to the Universal Declaration. Thus, for example, we can remove some of the idiosyncratic/culturally relative tone of Dworkin's reference to 'our conventions' by giving this a legalistic interpretation, where these refer to the fundamental rights and freedoms enshrined in the human rights instruments (and particularly those dealing with civil and political rights). However, once we do so, then it again becomes clear that the generic conditions of agency must form part of this core simply because, as we have argued,[38] they are conditions necessary for the exercise of any rights and, logically, fundamental rights must be granted to conditions that are necessary for the exercise of any rights whatsoever.

This said, we should again point out that protection of the values enshrined within the PGC (namely, the generic *conditions*) is not the same

[36] See our earlier comments on this point in ch 2.

[37] In general, human rights instruments that deal with civil and political rights cover basic conditions, whereas those that deal with social, economic and cultural rights go beyond these, although they sometimes still include what we consider to be basic conditions.

[38] See ch 2.

as protection of the generic *rights* within the PGC. This is because the PGC operates with the generic rights as rights under the will conception that are both positive and negative. In order to argue that the PGC itself is implied within social contract thinking generally or within the jurisprudence of human rights law, reasons must be given for regarding rights to the generic conditions as rights under the will conception and as positive as well as negative. While we have argued (see chapter 2) that the jurisprudence of the European Court of Human Rights makes it plausible to attach these features to the rights of the European Convention on Human Rights, we make no claim that these features must be attached to other human rights conventions or as rights to the generic conditions of action viewed as necessary conditions of the enterprise of social contracting (except as a consequence of the dialectical necessity of the PGC). However, to those who accept the dialectical necessity of the PGC, most of these additional thoughts are redundant.

How far, then, may Gewirthians insist upon the values of the PGC in their dealings with non-Gewirthians? To what extent is it permissible for Gewirthians to compromise when addressing the external problem of authority? Second-best Gewirthian responses, like first-best responses, are governed by the values of the PGC. Applied to a social contract approach to the external problem of authority, we suggest that this indicates that Gewirthians should not treat everything as negotiable. The generic conditions of agency, the conditions that enable the parties to identify themselves as social contractors, the conditions that enable agents to form the judgement that bargaining is better than fighting, that co-operation and compromise are better than conflict, are simply non-negotiable.

## V Conclusion

According to Hanna Pitkin, a traditional consent theorist will found politico-legal obligation on consent in the following terms:

> [Y]ou are obligated to obey if and only if you have consented. Thus your consent defines the limits of your obligation as well as the person or persons to whom it is owed. Legitimate authority is distinguished from mere coercive power precisely by the consent of those subject to it. And the justification for your obligation to obey is your own consent to it; because you have agreed, it is right for you to have an obligation.[39]

Pitkin is critical of such an account and, in the light of our analysis, we can add that it commits two fundamental errors. First, it commits the Fallacy of Necessity. Consent-based procedural justification is not the only source of rights and obligations. Secondly, it commits the sin of fictionalis-

[39] Above n 14, at 51.

ing consent—or, at any rate, it will quickly do so if the consent theorist argues that the scheme of governance in question is an instance of legitimate authority. For, while the scheme of governance might, indeed, be an example of legitimate authority, its credentials as such do not rest on consent, either in principle or in practice. In principle, the most that a consent-based procedural justification can achieve (as in private governance) is that the recipients of the consent have a justificatory response to the consenting agent. More is required if the scheme is to be justified *tout court*. In practice, agents simply do not consent to schemes of public governance.

Having said this, in Gewirthia, where there is an internal problem of authority, as in pluralistic communities where there is an external problem of authority, a procedural turn makes sense. In Gewirthia, the sense of proceduralism is that it improves the chances of aspirant communities of right conducting their business, private and public, in ways that are legitimate. In other words, proceduralism here is ultimately for the sake of legitimacy. Where the problem is one of moral pluralism, legitimacy tends to give way to legitimation. Where sights are set lower, proceduralism appeals as a legitimating strategy. To the extent that proceduralism, in either context, fits the model of authorised private governance, it is based on consent; and, in the usual way, consent precludes complaint. However, if it is a theme of this book that we should not be seduced by the rhetoric of consent as a justifying reason in private life, this applies equally in public affairs, and perhaps most of all where it is suggested that the authority of the politico-legal system rests on consent.

Whatever the merits of 'governance by consent'—for example, in rejecting brute force in favour of due process and the rule of law, as well as signalling an inclusive attitude on the part of the governing bodies, and in general easing the process of legitimation—it should not be readily equated with governance that is justified by consent. For the most part, what justifies public governance (where it is legitimate) is that it conforms to the values of the PGC, not that it derives its authority from agents who have consented to be bound by its operations. For the most part, it is a fiction (a very large and endemic fiction) to claim that government is authorised by consent; and it is always a fallacy to fetishise consent to the point of believing that, unless government is authorised by consent, it cannot possibly be legitimate.

# 11

# Consent as Procedural Justification: Concluding Remarks

## I Introduction

At the outset, we remarked that, notwithstanding its familiarity, there is a great deal to understand about the idea of consent. Without such an understanding, it is too easy for the law to endorse the systematic abuse or misuse of consent in practice (whether by over- or under-reliance), and it is too easy to criticise the law for taking up seemingly arbitrary positions (for example, in relation to the requirement that consent should be free and informed) or for adopting doctrines that are over- or under-protective of the 'consenting' parties. Modern communities of rights, which at the same time are communities of consent, deserve better than this.[1]

Having sharpened our appreciation of consent, we are better placed to cut our way through a range of abusive, opportunistic, or misguided practices that variously undervalue or overvalue consent, that fictionalise it or that are fixated by it, and that treat it too casually or too cautiously. Consent, in principle, is a distinctive and an elegant procedural justification; however, the very familiarity of consent in practice, and particularly consent in the law, engenders confusion and contempt, mess and muddle. In these concluding remarks, we endeavour to pick out those aspects of our discussion that should enable us not only to make some sense of consent in the law but to give this important procedural justification a more coherent application.

We start with some methodological remarks, emphasising the Gewirthian vantage point that informs our analysis of consent. We then move on to the functions of consent and the pattern of justification within a will theory of rights (such as Gewirthian theory). This takes us on to the questions of who can consent (subjects of consent) and under what conditions consent will be judged to be adequate (when it is properly signalled, free and informed, and so on). We deal next with the important idea of the 'relative autonomy' of consent within institutional sets, before speaking to the justificatory power and province of consent. This takes us to some remarks about 'legitimation' and 'legitimacy', leading to the important question in morally

[1] For development of the idea of such a community governed by the PGC, see Alan Gewirth, *The Community of Rights* (Chicago, IL, University of Chicago Press, 1996).

divided societies of the potential and limits for 'governance by consent' as the basis of politico-legal authority. We conclude with a short comment about law and consent in the global order after 9/11.

## II Methodology

The approach employed in our essay on 'consent in the law' has been, as Ronald Dworkin would term it, 'outside in' rather than 'inside out'.[2] We have not attempted to construct a map of consent by basing ourselves on observations of positive legal practice or by analysis of legal discourse. Had we done this, our map would have shown that consent is caught up in a range of competing ideological perspectives that drive the discourse, doctrines, and outcomes of modern, complex, legal systems. We would have found that consent is variously judged to be relevant or irrelevant, central or marginal; we would have found varying tests for the capacity to consent; and we would have found the requirements for a valid consent being stated and applied with varying degrees of stringency. Sometimes, the explanation for the way that consent is handled will be found in a proximate local legal ideology—for example, that lawyers should defer to medical practice, or that contract is an essentially adversarial activity, or that labour markets need light regulation, or that crime must be controlled, and so on, each of which would generate a thin theory of consent, making it easy to hold that patients, contractors, employees, and suspects or defendants in the criminal justice system have 'consented'. Sometimes, these local legal ideologies will be reinforced by background ethical commitments—for example, a background commitment to a utilitarian perspective will generate a much less principled approach to consent than will be the case with a rights view of the kind that we have elaborated in this book. Again, law has its own culture of relative restraint: in some courts in some jurisdictions, precedents and 'the jurisprudence' will be treated with the utmost respect; some appellate courts will be extremely reluctant to interfere with the exercise of trial court discretion; the judicial branch will see fit to defer to the executive and the legislative branches; and so on. But, in other courts in other jurisdictions, some or all of these restraints will be less faithfully observed; in some courts, the imperative is to get the right result.[3] Accordingly, how the court understands its role in the overall regulatory array is another important factor in explaining the way that consent is handled in practice.

Without doubt, an 'inside out' theorisation of consent in the law would shed some reflexive light on legal practice(s). However, even allowing for the globalisation of law, each legal system studied would operate by

[2] Ronald M Dworkin, *Life's Dominion* (London, HarperCollins, 1993) at 29.

[3] Generally, see Karl N Llewellyn, *The Common Law Tradition* (Boston, MA, Little, Brown, 1960).

reference to its own distinctive culture and its own particular ideological composition. Such theorisation, therefore, would not be so much about *consent*—it would be more about the influence of ideology in the law; and, indeed, such a study could do equally well with other pervasive legal concepts. Neither would such theorisation generate an account of consent *in the law universally* so much as an account of the way consent is viewed and applied in a range of different legal systems. At all events, such an essay in 'lexicography with local history, or even . . . lexicographies conjoined with all local histories'[4] has not been our project.

Our project has been to address consent in the law 'outside in', our outside starting point being Gewirthian moral theory. For two reasons, as we explained in chapter two, we believe that this particular theory is the most appropriate vantage point for any essay in practical reason (which we take to be the proximate context for our essay on consent, whether it be consent in moral reason or consent in legal reason). First, we believe that, by applying the dialectically necessary method to the concept of agency, rational beings must accept Gewirthian principles as the most defensible ethic for their community. Quite simply, the PGC sets the required ethical standard. Secondly, we believe that, employing a dialectically contingent approach, the same Gewirthian principles are presupposed by a community of rational beings committed (contingently) to human rights. Although the latter is a weaker argument for Gewirthian principles, the contingency upon which it relies (acceptance of human rights) is widely accepted in those communities that take consent seriously. Communities of rights, as we have said, are communities of consent. Given this approach, it is fundamental to our thinking that, before we can understand consent in the law, we must understand how consent fits and functions in a Gewirthian will theory of rights.

## III The Functions of Consent

If, within Gewirthian theory (or any cognate moral theory), rights are 'trumps' (in the sense that rights outrank other moral suits), then the most obvious function of consent is to operate, as it were, as a 'counter-trump'. The recipient of a valid and effective consent has an answer to what would otherwise be a wrong, an act that would otherwise violate an agent's generic rights. Consent, however, can go beyond authorising particular acts. By consenting, power-holders may authorise acts that are in accordance with a newly created relationship or that are in compliance with a rule-set that has been engaged. Whether in relation to particular acts that have been authorised or acts under rule-sets that have been authorised, the recipient of consent has a procedural justification, and, whilst this does not present an

[4] John Finnis, *Natural Law and Natural Rights* (Oxford, Clarendon Press, 1980) at 4.

answer to all-comers, it suffices as against the consenting party—in this sense, consent as a justification is both personalised and, so to speak, privatised.

In this light, we can see that, within Gewirthian-regulated relationships, consent operates as a dynamic having two principal functions. Consent functions, first, as a reason for holding a rights-holder to a change of position and, secondly, as a reason for holding a power-holder to the terms of a new relationship (or to the terms of a rule-set that has been engaged).

Placing these two functions within the larger scheme of Gewirthian principles, the following general guidelines can be stated.

A *Consent as the reason for holding a rights-holder to a change of position (consent as a defence to wrongdoing)*

- Where A, the rights-holder consents to B doing X (an act that would otherwise violate A's right), then B, the recipient of the consent, does no wrong to A by doing X. The function of consent is to license B to do X; B is permitted to do X; X involves no wrong as between A and B. B has a procedural justification for doing X, A's consent negating or nullifying what would otherwise be a wrong.
- Where A, the rights-holder has not consented to B doing X (an act that violates A's right), then B has no procedural justification for doing X. Nevertheless, B might have a substantive justification for doing X.
- Such substantive justification, appealing to the general principles of the PGC by which A and B are bound rather than to A's consent, might be of more than one type. For example:

  —B might rely on an antecedent (substantive) justification of the kind that would be applicable if B were himself responding by way of self-defence to a wrongful act by A, or if B's act was designed to rectify a past injustice; or

  —B might rely on an overriding rights (substantive) justification. In this latter case, while the doing of X might be justified by reference to rights that override A's right, there is nonetheless a wrong to A. In other words, unlike a procedural justification, an overriding rights substantive justification does not negate the wrong to A; it simply justifies B's act all things considered.[5]

[5] Of course, there might be cases in which A's right is so basic that it cannot be justifiably overridden. Here, consent by A is the only defence for B. Ironically, this is just the situation where many legal systems are least willing to follow the logic of procedural justification and recognise the authorising effect of A's consent. See ch 9 for our discussion of physician-assisted suicide and euthanasia.

B *Consent as the reason for holding a power-holder to the terms of a new relationship (consent as the reason for entitlement)*

- Where A, a power-holder, consents to X (a new relationship, a new set of rules, or the like), then B, the recipient of the consent, has a procedural justification for holding A to X; A is bound by X.
- Where A, a power-holder, has not consented to X, then B has no procedural justification for holding A to X. Nevertheless, it might be justifiable to hold A to X all things considered, not by reference to A's consent but by reference to a substantive rights-sensitive justification.

If we are to maintain the integrity of consent, it is important to respect the distinction between procedural and substantive justification. To be sure, Gewirthian principles allow for both types of justification, but the right kind of justification has to be applied in the right kind of way. Three points, in particular, bear repetition.

First, according to the principle of the 'priority of consent', it is better to obtain the rights-holder's consent for what would otherwise be a violation of that right than to justify wrongdoing by reference to overriding rights—if evil is avoidable, it should be avoided rather than justified as the lesser of two evils. In this light, where legal regimes present a rights-holder's consent as one of several justifying reasons, but without prioritising consent, they are defective. For example, one of the objectionable features of the European Directive on Data Protection[6] is that the data subject's (rights-holder's) consent to the processing of personal data is presented as one of a number of reasons that will suffice to render the processing of data legitimate, but without consent being prioritised as a justifying reason.[7] Read literally, the Directive treats each of the listed reasons as equal to any other, each being sufficient, and all reasons being, as it were, on the same plane. In the case of the Directive, not only is this out of kilter with the principle of the 'priority of consent', it is a hostage to fortune, inviting the side-stepping of consent in ways that might depart altogether from a rights-respecting approach—for example, if the justifying reasons are open to a utilitarian reading[8]—or that might accept too quickly that the case for overriding rights is made out.[9]

Secondly, whilst it might seem perfectly obvious that, where A has *not* consented, then we should not resort to a procedural justification, one of

[6] Directive 95/46/EC.

[7] See Arts 7 and 8 of the Directive.

[8] In Art 7(c), for example, the justifying reason is that processing is necessary for compliance with legal obligations; in Art 7(d), that it is necessary to protect 'the vital interests' of the data subject; and, in Art 7(e), that it is necessary 'for the performance of a task carried out in the public interest.'

[9] Notoriously, there is a danger that the judicial branch might defer to the executive view that overriding (ostensibly rights-based) public interest justifications are in play.

the recurrent themes of our discussion has been that legal systems are prone to 'fictionalise' consent, that is, to proceed as though A has consented when this manifestly is not the case. This is much worse than a distortion of the facts or sloppy practice; it avoids addressing the need for substantive justification—and, of course, the most worrying case is where a faux procedural justification is offered in lieu of a failed substantive justification (or one that would fail).

Thirdly, where it is claimed that an action is *not* justified, we should not pretend that this claim rests on the procedural ground that there has been a failure of consent when the real (but undeclared) reason is that we simply disapprove of the action in question. If our disapproval translates into a plausible substantive argument, then we should be more direct in articulating the real basis of our objection, but if there is no such plausible substantive reason, then we have a faux denial of procedural justification covering what would be a failed substantive objection. To this extent, falsifying the absence of consent is as bad as fictionalising its presence. As we have said repeatedly (if not always in these precise words), consent should operate as a *transparent* procedural justification; false accounting, whether by way of assertion or denial of consent, simply will not do.

## IV From a Simple Community of Rights to a Legal Community of Rights

When a 'simple' Gewirthian community of rights evolves into what is commonly thought of as a modern municipal legal system,[10] the basic functions of consent remain the same, the basic guidelines continue to apply. No doubt, the complexity of modern legal regimes tends to obscure the legitimate role for consent. However, in a legal regime that is committed to Gewirthian principles, the ground rules for procedural justification remain unaltered.

*First*, the generic basic interests of agents are protected by a mix of public (criminal law) and private law measures. Whereas the criminal law (and its associated apparatus of prevention, detection, and enforcement) will aim to protect (representative agent) A's generic physical and psychological interests against injury inflicted *with intent* by other agents, the private law of tort will provide for compensation where such injury is inflicted *unintentionally* (sometimes only on proof of fault, at other times on a strict liability basis). Such measures for prevention, protection, and compensation extend beyond physical interests to interests in property, reputation, personality, and the like.

[10] That is, an institutionalised and integrated system of primary and secondary rules of the kind famously sketched in HLA Hart, *The Concept of Law* (Oxford, Clarendon Press, 1961).

Typically, the form of such private law protective measures is that A has a right that B (and other agents) should not do X (against A's will). However, in line with the guidelines sketched above, if A consents to B doing X, B has a procedural justification for the doing of X and, in principle, this will be a recognised defence against any private law claim by A. Accordingly, we find legal regimes recognising consent, or voluntary assumption of risk, or their cognates, as defences to claims in tort.

Where the protective measures are provided for by the criminal law, typically, the form of the law will be to create an offence which, in the first instance, places a duty on agents not to do X with intent. However, the Gewirthian reason for the duty not to do X is that A and fellow agents have rights that X not be done against their will. It follows that, in principle, A may consent to the doing of X and, thereby, provide procedural justification for the recipient of the consent. However, whether or not A and the recipient of A's consent are then immune against criminal charge or conviction hinges on a number of further considerations relating to the functioning of the community of rights.[11]

*Secondly*, over and above the basic protections of generic interests in person and property, legal regimes will empower agents to enter into transactions that create new relationships or engage various rule-sets. Some aspects of empowerment will be immanent within the bundle of property entitlements (such as the power to alienate by gift), others will be of a supplementary nature (such as the power to alienate by contract). This is not to say that the simpler Gewirthian community will be unable to regulate for gifts, exchanges, or marriage, and the like; optional transactions of this kind will be regulated through ordinary custom and practice. However, with a centralised civil system of law, these options are regulated in a way that is usually much more detailed and formal than is the case with customary standards.

The role of consent in relation to such optional transactions is to signal that one's will is that a power is to be exercised in a particular way. Having so consented, having given an 'originating consent' as it were, an agent is 'bound in'. Now, the critical point here is that consent, whether in a simpler Gewirthian community or in a legal system committed to Gewirthian principles, operates as a threshold (or entry) condition in relation to optional sets. It is as though agents must first pass through a consenting chamber, for the purpose of checking and clearing their authorisations before they are admitted to whatever activity is governed by the particular rule-set. In the paradigmatic case, this is where the procedural justification is located. In other words, no matter whether we are considering the binding effect of, say, the rules of an informal market (regulated by local custom) or of a formal market (regulated by the law of contract), the

[11] See our discussion in ch 9, and below at 356–357.

procedural justification that we are looking for is located at the point at which those rules have been consensually engaged. It is this originating consent that bears the weight of the procedural justificatory burden.[12]

Provided that we can identify an entry point at which an agent consensually submits to the relevant rules, we have a procedural justification for holding the agent to those rules. We will say more about the relative autonomy of such rule-sets later in these concluding remarks but, at this point, two qualifying comments are in order. First, even if an adequate originating (authorising) consent is in place, a community might wish to incorporate consent into the rule-set itself. Let us suppose, for example, that the rule-set for marriage permits husbands to insist upon having sexual intercourse with their wives even against the will of the latter. In other words, let us hypothesise a rule-set for marriage that, in effect, gives husbands a licence to rape their wives.[13] Provided that the originating consent is adequate, a woman who enters marriage on these terms has given her husband this licence, and she is bound by the terms of the marital relationship. 'Rape in marriage' is, thus, procedurally justified. Nevertheless, a community might feel that such a rule-set is no longer functional or appropriate, and, for this reason, it changes the rules of the set so that wives in marriages have the right to say no to sex as they would if they were unmarried women. Secondly, if the flux of social life makes it unrealistic or difficult to isolate or monitor originating consents, a legal regime might incorporate surrogate consents within the rule-set itself. On this basis, the rule-set for marriage might be modified to protect the generic interests of wives (so that the procedural justification is internal to the rule-set itself rather than external to it at the point of entry). Similarly, the rule-set for contract (at any rate, covering everyday routine contracts of consumption) might adopt formation criteria that mimic the conditions for an originating consent (so that, to some extent at least, procedural justification is internally secured).[14]

*Thirdly*, in principle, just as agents might consent to submit to rules that have already been made, they might also consent to submit to rules that are to be made by agents who act on their rule-making authorisation. In a simpler Gewirthian community, the time might come when the group realises that it needs some (public) rules to regulate a particular matter for the good governance of the group. For example, the group might realise that, unless access to land is regulated, a tragedy of the commons is waiting to happen. Accordingly, it is agreed that some member or members of the group should be authorised to make the rules. In such a case, the relationship

[12] And, it is this consent that authorises the 'relative autonomy' of so-called consensual doctrines within the rule-set engaged. See below at 351–355.

[13] Compare *R v R* [1991] 2 All ER 257 (CA); [1991] 4 All ER 481 (HL).

[14] Alternatively, procedural justification might be abandoned. If we were to go down this track, we might reject consent as the justification for applying much of the consumer law of contract, and, instead, we would need to support the doctrinal set on substantive grounds.

between the members of the group and the recipient(s) of their consent is precisely as we would have it in a private transaction: the recipient or recipients have a procedural justification; they can point to the consents given by the members of the group as conferring their personal authority to make the rules; and, provided that they act within the terms of the authorisation, they can point to the same consents to justify the rules actually made. To this extent, we can maintain that the root of public empowerment, like that of private empowerment, is the consent of citizens. To this extent, the public mirrors the private.

However, once we presuppose a move from small group governance to modern big government, the paradigm of procedural justification is less readily instantiated. In fact, even in the context of small group governance, the ideal-type of procedural justification soon breaks down. Suppose, for example, that the group realises that it needs public rules not just to regulate access to land but to co-ordinate a whole range of matters. Instead of authorising certain agents to act on behalf of the group each time a rule-making need arises, it is agreed that a standing rule-making body would be more efficient. The group is now on the way to institutionalising a legislature and, although the agents who consent to this move and their recipients are still related as in the simple case of one-off rule-making authorisation, this will soon change. Soon, there will be agents who have not personally consented to this standing body being so authorised, and those who are members of the body will not necessarily have been recipients of anyone's consent (other than through voting procedures, for what they are worth as procedural justifications).

The bigger that government becomes, the more distant the authorising relationship between citizens and officials in legal regimes, the less plausible it becomes to rest justification for acts of public governance on the consent of agents. For the most part, to resort to procedural justifications in such cases is to resort to a fiction. This does not mean that, in modern legal regimes, the constitution, the structure and form of public governance, and the particular regulatory enactments cannot be justified. What it means is that the justification has to be a substantive one demonstrating that governance is in line with the principles of the PGC; there is no short cut to procedural justification via citizens' consent. In a modern legal regime, when public decisions about, say, land use planning are made (not so much to avert a tragedy of the commons as to impose a sensible zoning policy), we must ask whether they impinge upon the generic rights of agents and, if so, whether an overriding rights justification can be made out. To claim that anything goes because the government has a mandate is to abuse the idea of consent. No doubt, where a substantive justification is available, it might be said that rational citizens would consent to such measures (as, indeed, they would)—but, then, if public acts are substantively justifiable, a procedural justification is redundant.

The fact of the matter is that, in a modern legal regime, public governance is institutionalised in a way that sets it apart from the simpler Gewirthian community. It is still a community of rights in the sense that those charged with public responsibility must act in accordance with the PGC and the regime of rights that flows directly from the master principle. However, in such a regime, the key to the justification of public measures is largely substantive rather than procedural. We will have more to say about this in due course.[15]

## V Who can Consent?

It is only subjects of consent who can give a consent; without subjects of consent, procedural justification cannot get off the ground. Ideal-typically, subjects of consent are those who have the *developed* capacity (dispositional and particular-occurrent) to form a will about the giving or refusing of consent. Since the consent will relate to the exercise of a right, privilege, power, or immunity, it is essential that the will to consent is exercised with a relevant understanding of what is at stake. Parties on the dominant side of a relationship must, thus, appreciate that the giving of consent is optional, and that, once consent is given, the recipient of the consent is authorised to act in ways that would not otherwise be available.

Alongside these conditions for an ideal-typical subject of consent, procedural justification requires a subject of consent with particular-occurrent communicative competence (the proviso for communicative competence, as we termed it). Paradigmatically, then, the sources of procedural justification are subjects of consent in settings that meet the proviso for communicative competence.

In relation to these matters, legal regimes might operate in a manner that is sometimes over-protective, at other times under-protective. The risk of over-protection arises where determinations of the capacity of those who are near-agents or intermittent agents fall to be made. In practice, precautionary reasoning requires, and enables, a legal system to hedge its bets in relation to the possible agency of such persons—at least the law can see to it that their generic interests (as possible agents) are shielded against harm. However, there is no such safe option with regard to their consenting capacity and it must be recognised that these are often very difficult cases. If parties are treated prematurely as subjects of consent, they might be held bound by authorisations that are adverse to their interests, but if subjects of consent are denied the opportunity to exercise their will, this evinces a lack of respect for their agency. Instinctive paternalism is no better than instinctive liberation. Decision-makers must make good faith judgements, and

[15] See below at 359–361.

those judgements must be respected even though we suspect that they will sometimes be in error.

In general, there is a risk of under-protection where the law is dealing with those who are judged *not* to be subjects of consent. Given that those who are not subjects of consent have no relevant will to exercise, the employment of best interests tests, or substituted judgements, or proxies does not involve a lack of respect for agency. Nevertheless, precautionary reasoning under the PGC regulates transactions with such beings (who are not subjects of consent), and they can be wronged in two ways. First, agents who deal with such beings might fail to discharge their duties (under precaution), in which event the transaction is not substantively justified. Best interests justifications are notoriously slippery and they need to be scrutinised carefully lest they under-protect the interests of those who are not subjects of consent. Secondly, agents who deal with such beings might claim that the transaction is procedurally justified. This is a serious misrepresentation, and we need to ensure that substituted judgements and proxies are not so abused.

There is also a risk of over- or under-protection in relation to those who *are* subjects of consent. Legal regimes over-protect consenting agents if they over-prescribe the conditions for a valid consent; whereas, if they under-prescribe the conditions, they under-protect such agents and accept procedural justification too readily. At the same time, of course, if consenting agents are over-protected, their recipients are under-protected, and vice versa. As we shall see in the next section of our concluding remarks, getting the right protective balance is a major challenge for a legal regime as it strives to set the appropriate conditions for an adequate consent.

## VI Disentangling the Requirements of an Adequate Consent

If a subject of consent purports to consent to X, what else do we need to consider before we accept that the recipient of the consent has a procedural justification for acting in reliance by doing X (or acting in accordance with X where X is a rule-set)? Essentially, we need to consider whether the consent was properly signalled, whether it was given as a matter of unforced and informed choice, and whether the scope of X covers the particular act that the recipient claims it does. Because consent takes its significance in the context of a transaction between agents, it is another recurring theme of our discussion that the law must strive to balance the legitimate interests of both parties to the transaction, the consenting agent and the agent who is the recipient of the consent.

### *(i) Signalling*

When we discussed the signalling requirement in chapter seven, we suggested that legal regimes should be guided by a principle of fidelity (to the consenting agent's will) and by a principle of reasonable transactional expectation (to protect the interests of the recipient). If we ignore the former, we under-protect the consenting agent, but if we ignore the latter, we over-protect the same agent. Conversely, if we ignore the former, we over-protect the recipient while, if we ignore the latter, we under-protect the recipient. How should legal regimes address the challenge of giving these guiding principles due weight?

We suggested that legal regimes should start with the fidelity principle, with the principle that every effort must be made to keep faith with the agent's will. To treat an agent as consenting (with all that this entails) when this is not the agent's will is to do a serious wrong to the agent. If possible, this must be avoided. Accordingly, legal regimes should start by seeking out the supposedly consenting agent's *subjective* intention to signal consent; they should require that such intent is signalled distinctly and definitely, personally, and unequivocally; and, where there is a significant delay between the signalling of the consent and its implementation (or reliance upon it), there should be a double-check that the intent to consent has been maintained. However, we also recognised that the consenting agent has a responsibility not to mislead the recipient; and that, where the consenting agent intentionally, recklessly, or negligently misleads the recipient, who in good faith relies on the consent, the principle of reasonable transactional expectation takes priority.

While unpacking these principles, we were particularly critical of the use of opt-out schemes. To be sure, we are not alone in thinking that there is something dubious about such schemes—and, indeed, in arguing that opt-outs under-protect those who are deemed to have consented. However, we can now see precisely why there is a problem with opt-outs. First, assuming that an agent is not required (under the principles of the PGC) to participate in the particular scheme (that is, assuming that it is permissible not to donate one's blood, organs, DNA samples, or similar), then we should not treat the agent as consenting to participate unless we have a clear and reliable signal that this is the agent's will. To act on any other basis is to discount the fidelity principle—which is precisely what opt-outs do, and do so, moreover, on a systematic and organised basis. Secondly, lazy reliance on opt-outs means that the premise that agents are not required to participate is not seriously examined. If it is clear that non-participation is permissible then, procedural justification aside, a substantive overriding rights justification is called for. But, of course, it might be the case that participation is required as a matter of positive moral obligation, in which event no attempt at procedural justification need be made. At all events, rubber-stamped procedural justifications such as those associated with opt-out schemes are not only a fiction, they divert attention from possibly crucial questions concerning substantive justifications.

We have just said that consents by opt-out are a fiction; agents are, conveniently, deemed to will to participate. The parallels with the fiction of consent in a substituted judgement are obvious. Recall the case of Jerry Strunk, who, of course, was *not* a subject of consent.[16] Let us suppose (counter-factually) that another close relative in the Strunk family is also an adequate tissue-match for Tommy; and let us suppose that this close relative (let us call him Billy) is a subject of consent but that he is on his deathbed. Now, if the imperative is to get a life-saving kidney for Tommy, it matters not whether it comes from Jerry, who is not a subject of consent, or from Billy, who is a subject of consent. However, while Jerry does not have the capacity to say yes or no, Billy does; if Billy says yes, all well and good, but he might say no. To guarantee the required result, we deem (note, *deem*) Jerry to consent by way of a substituted judgement that purports to speak for him; and we deem (again, note, *deem*) Billy to consent by way of an opt-out that he has not activated. Transparently, however, in both cases, the purported procedural justification is functionally equivalent and it is a fiction. Legal regimes should not play such games.

### *(ii) Unforced Choice*

Where consent is taken seriously, it is axiomatic that the agent's will to consent is not coerced, that it is an unforced choice. However, the implementation of this principle runs into difficulty as soon as we ask at which point the line is to be drawn between a forced (or unfree) and an unforced (or free) choice. Is there not an element of arbitrariness in drawing this line? In which case, how can a legal regime be confident that it is striking the right balance, neither under-protecting nor over-protecting agents who purport to consent?

In chapter five, we suggested that legal regimes should start by developing an ideal-type of forced choice. Such an ideal-type, we argued, would build on three conditions as follows:

(i) the baseline relationship between the intervening agent and the target agent is compliant with Gewirthian moral principles (the parties, thus, come to the transaction with clean hands, neither having previously wronged the other);
(ii) the intervening agent intends its power-play (the force or pressure applied) to have a negative bearing on the generic interests of the target agent, and the target agent so apprehends the intervention; and
(iii) the force or pressure applied is a causative factor in eliciting the consent of the target agent.

The effect of the first of these conditions is twofold. So far as the *intervening* agent is concerned, if it does not come to the transaction with clean hands, we need to look carefully at the nature of the pressure applied—otherwise, we might be tempted to think that an 'offer' of a reduced level

[16] See ch 4, at 114–117.

of threat is a case of positive pressure when it should be characterised as negative; a threat, even a reduced threat, to the target agent's generic interests is nonetheless a threat. So far as the *target* agent is concerned, if it does not come to the transaction with clean hands, the acts of the intervening agent might be antecedently justifiable.[17] Although the effect of the first condition is to screen off questions of antecedent justification (leaving the judgement of antecedent justification to be made independently), the ideal-type leaves open the possibility of the intervening agent having a substantive overriding rights justification. What it precludes, where it is instantiated, is the intervening agent having the support of a procedural justification. To be quite clear, even if the intervening agent has a substantive overriding rights justification for applying negative pressure to the target agent's generic interests, the negative pressure applied disqualifies any reliance on a procedural justification. In short, where the consent ostensibly given by the target agent does not meet the requirement of being an unforced choice, the so-called 'consent' does not satisfy the ideal-typical conditions for a valid consent, and no procedural justification is possible. Such a benchmark, however, has to be defended against the charge, on the one side, that it is over-protective and, on the other side, that it is under-protective of agents who are subjects of consent.

Minimalists will argue that, unless the will of an agent is overborne (in whatever extreme and exceptional circumstances this is conceded to arise), the ostensible consent of agents is to be treated as free and unforced. From this perspective, our ideal-type is too protective. We disagree. To be sure, there is a difference between an agent being so coerced that its will is overborne and an agent acting 'against its will' in the face of a negative power-play against its generic interests. However, this does not seem to us to reflect a defensible distinction between a forced and an unforced choice so much as a distinction between a breakdown in the agent's will (a non-expression of will) and a forced articulation of will. The reason why the latter is significant for the purposes of procedural justification is that such a consent is procured by the application of pressure against the target agent's generic interests. Even if there is an 'all things considered' justification for the application of such negative pressure (for example, a small measure of physical harm is threatened in order to obtain a 'consent' that will lead to the saving of a life), the target agent is wronged, and it would be improper to allow that an ensuing 'consent' qualifies as a procedural justification. Hence, our ideal-type specifies that agents who seek to rely on a procedural justification must not only come to the transaction with clean hands, they must also respect one another's generic interests when eliciting consent—of all agents,

[17] If the intervening agent has an antecedent justification for acting against the generic interests of the target agent, the action is substantively justified. Procedural justification would then be unnecessary. But, in any event, it would be unavailable.

the recipient who has applied negative pressure to obtain the consent is least well placed to argue that an unforced choice to consent was made.

Approaching the ideal-type from the opposite direction, it might be criticised as being under-protective. It is true that our ideal-type follows the familiar liberal line of distinguishing between threats (which are illegitimate) and offers (which are legitimate), as a result of which we are too ready, our critics might argue, to characterise an offeree's 'consent' as an unforced choice. How can we permit reliance on procedural justifications where impoverished agents contract to sell valuable resources or where plea-bargains are struck by vulnerable defendants in the criminal justice system, and so on? But this tries to get a procedural justification to run before we even have it walking. If the ex ante relationship between the parties is not morally clean, particularly if the agent who makes the 'offer' is already in breach of obligations to the offeree, all procedural bets are off. And, if the ex ante relationship between the parties is morally clean, there is still a long way to go before we can conclude that the consent is valid and effective. In particular, it must be given by a subject of consent, it must be properly signalled, it must be made on an informed basis, and so on.

This analysis resists two sources of misdirection. First, we should not view the requirement of a freely given consent (or consent as an unforced choice) in isolation; rather, it must be viewed in the context of the normative principles set by the PGC. If the recipient of the 'consent' is in violation of those principles, it does not matter how emphatically the target agent 'consents', there can be no procedural justification. Secondly, we should not be seduced by the idea that freedom is relative, a matter of degree, into thinking that no defensible line can be drawn between forced and unforced choice. Granted, if consent is detached from the normative scheme of rights and duties flowing from the PGC, we might be tempted by this idea—and legal regimes are certainly prey to criticism of this kind if consent is so detached. However, provided that consent is viewed in a transactional context governed by the PGC, we can develop perfectly coherent ideal-types of forced and unforced choice (in each case, centring on the presence or absence of a negative power-play against the target agent's generic interests), and no apology needs to be made for a regulatory position that is so determined.

### *(iii) Informed Choice*

The requirement that consent must be made on the basis of an informed choice raises similar doubts as those already summarised in relation to the requirement of unforced choice. Essentially, how can the law avoid arbitrariness in setting the limits of disclosure? And can it have any confidence that its regulatory requirements are neither over- nor under-protective of the 'consenting' agent? What is more, in the case of this informational condition, doubts about the coherence of the concept are compounded by the development in the courts of a doctrine of informed consent in medical law. Thus, we have two major questions: one is whether a coherent ideal-type of informed consent can be constructed; the other is whether we can read such an ideal-type through the legal doctrine that takes it name.

First, the construction of an ideal-type of informed consent starts with the principle of fidelity which, in this case, translates as a subjectivist view of the relevance of particular items of information. In other words, it is the consenting agent's (subjective) view of what is relevant or material that matters. If there is an informational deficiency that the consenting agent views as material, fidelity indicates that this is not an informed consent. Fidelity, however, is again qualified by a measure of personal responsibility. To the extent that the consenting agent has failed to take reasonable care with its own informational field, it bears the responsibility for consenting on a deficient informational basis.

So far as the recipient of the consent is concerned, the pattern of reasoning is similar to that concerning unforced choice. The idea of informed consent is not free-standing; it must be viewed in the context of a transaction governed by Gewirthian principles. Those principles put agents under various informational duties, of both a negative and a positive kind. Provided that the recipient of the 'consent' has clean hands in relation to those informational duties, there is nothing yet to preclude a procedural justification.

This leaves the following situation as a hard case. On the one side, the consenting agent has exercised due diligence in gathering and acting on relevant information; on the other side, the recipient of the consent has clean hands. Nevertheless, there is material information of which the consenting agent is unaware (and could not reasonably, or even possibly, be aware). The fidelity principle indicates that this omission matters; but the principle of reasonable expectation demands that the recipient's interests be given due consideration. How is the law to avoid over-protecting or under-protecting the consenting agent?

When we discussed the parallel question in relation to signalling, we suggested that the lack of a subjective will to consent entails that no consent is given; but that the recipient's interest should be protected by a principle of reasonable mistake. Much the same applies here. However, the jurisprudence surely must distinguish between informational deficits concerning (i) future and (ii) present facts. Let us suppose that the agent consents to a medical procedure that, unknown to the parties, either (i) will be overtaken by a superior procedure in a year's time or (ii) is already being replaced by such a procedure in some areas and could be made available to the consenting agent. So far as an unknown future development is concerned, this surely must be the consenting agent's risk (unless the agent makes special provision for some sort of insurance against this risk). However, where the informational deficit concerns present facts, it is arguable that, in principle, we should treat the consent as withdrawn once the facts become known. In practice, this means that the recipient will have a procedural justification until the consent is withdrawn, by which time it might or might not be entirely academic.

What, then, of the doctrine of informed consent in medical law? In the modern law, the emphasis of this doctrine is less on consent than on the duty to inform. Whether a doctor advises surgery or, say, a course of antibiotics or antidepressants, professional due diligence is now interpreted as requiring the patient to be informed as to the risks associated with the treatment and as to alternatives. In the case of surgery, a physician will violate the patient's right to bodily integrity unless the intervention is authorised by the patient's consent; here, the duty to inform operates in a context of procedural justification. However, if the treatment is self-administered by the patient (on the physician's advice), there is no prima facie violation of the patient's rights and no need for procedural justification; here, the duty to inform (which, if breached, will give rise to an action for compensation by the patient) operates in a context in which there is no question of procedural justification. It follows that the development of the doctrine of informed consent needs to be scrutinised more for its compliance with Gewirthian positive informational duties than for its conformity with a Gewirthian analysis of consent.

When informed consent is carried across into contract law, there is yet more work required to bring the doctrinal development into focus. If contract law is engaged by an originating consent, the particular disclosure rules adopted within contract law will reflect the community's sense of what kind of institutional set is functional. If it is judged that a set designed for co-operative dealing is more functional than one designed for competitive dealing, the disclosure rules will be more demanding, and the rhetoric and requirements of informed consent will gain ground. However, this only holds so long as the originating consent bears the weight of procedural justification. If it does not, the informational obligations prescribed internally by the law of contract should be set to act as surrogates for what should be (paradigmatically) the externally secured authorising consent; and disagreements about disclosure and the like will reflect disagreements about the informational obligations that should attend the originating consent. We will return to such matters shortly when we speak to the idea of relative autonomy within institutional sets such as the law of contract.[18]

### *(iv) Interpretation*

Where there is a dispute about the scope of a consent, while a restrictive reading will tend to protect the consenting agent, a broad reading will tend to protect the recipient. But which approach should the law adopt? If the

[18] See below at 351–355.

law is to do justice to the principles of fidelity and reasonable expectation, neither approach should be adopted as a matter of course. Nor would it be appropriate for the law routinely to favour a literal reading over a purposive reading, or vice versa. How, then, is the law to handle the by now familiar dilemma of neither over- nor under-protecting the consenting agent?

Broadly speaking, the general approach that we suggested for signalling disputes applies also to interpretive questions. Thus, if we are to deviate from the consenting agent's honestly held subjective understanding, the relevant test is (i) whether the consenting agent's interpretation is reasonable, coupled with (ii) whether the recipient's interpretation is both honest and reasonable. If the consenting agent's interpretation is not reasonable, it is no longer privileged and it must give way to the recipient's honest and reasonable interpretation. However, if the consenting agent's interpretation is reasonable, then this determines the scope of the consent; and the recipient's honest and reasonable interpretation (that is, a good faith misunderstanding) should be treated as an excusing condition.

Clearly, the application of such principles turns on the criterion of reasonableness that is employed. Some interpretations are reasonable in the sense that they are logically or practically required, even if not self-evident on the face of the consent. But what about those differences of interpretation that cannot be so resolved? What about those hard cases where, standing in the shoes of the consenting agent, the interpretation argued for is reasonable, but the same is true of the recipient's interpretation relative to the latter's position? If this is the situation, then it breaches the principle of fidelity to hold the consenting agent to anything more than the terms of the consent reasonably interpreted within that agent's subjective sphere of understanding. To the extent that the recipient has relied on a different interpretation, but one that is reasonable relative to the recipient's sphere of understanding, the principle of reasonable expectation demands that the latter be excused. Such, then, is the basic pattern for the hard case: no consent on the one side, with excused reliance rather than procedural justification on the other.

### *(v) Taking Stock*

From the many points that can be made about the conditions for an adequate consent, perhaps three should be highlighted.

First, for the sake of clarity of thought, we need to disentangle and separately identify the conditions for an adequate consent. Assuming that the source of the 'consent' is a subject of consent, a purported consent might nevertheless fail for various reasons. In practice, a failed consent is a failed consent; a consent that is not properly signalled fails as much as one that is extracted by force or one that is not properly informed or one that is of inadequate scope, but clarity demands that we specify the particular reason for the failure.

Secondly, while each condition of adequacy has its own jurisprudence, an overarching theme is that the law must set the conditions in a way that protects the interests of both parties to the transaction.[19] On behalf of the consenting agent, we have articulated a principle of fidelity; on behalf of the recipient of consent, the balancing principle is that of reasonable expectation. Relative to these principles, it is sometimes easy to see how the law should respond. For example, opt-out schemes give insufficient weight to the fidelity principle, and, generally, no recipient who has applied negative pressure to the consenting agent's generic interests can reasonably expect to rely on that consent for the purposes of procedural justification. Other cases, however, are much more difficult, particularly those where the consenting agent has acted reasonably and responsibly and the recipient has acted in good faith and reasonably.

Thirdly, where legal regimes interpret the conditions of consent, especially in the hard cases, in ways that are open to question, it is essential that good faith and conscientious official decisions are respected. Indeed, this is simply a particular application of the more general requirement for restraint by agents whose governance is guided by the PGC and who aspire to maintain and strengthen their community of rights.[20]

## VII Relative Autonomy

As the various functions of consent are uncovered, one of the persistently puzzling features of the law is that consent seems to operate both outside and inside institutional sets. Where consent operates on background rights and duties (and privileges and no-rights), there is no such puzzle: a procedural justification will not wash unless the rights-holder has consented. However, where agents draw on their powers to engage institutional sets, such as the law of contract, we sometimes find an apparent duplication of consent. On our analysis, an originating consent is required if there is to be a procedural justification for the application of the rule-set; and yet, to some

[19] In our introductory remarks in ch 1, we raised the question whether, in principle, the conditions for an adequate consent should be adjusted depending on the nature of the interests at stake. Essentially, our analysis (in relation to background and originating consents) sets the same standards for adequacy whatever the interests (and whether an agent is purporting to consent to a change of position within a relationship or the creation of a new relationship). However, where these standards incorporate subjective elements (as in the case of the informational condition), there will be some variability in the application of the standards from one agent to another, and, in ch 7, we recognised that legal regimes might set evidential requirements for signalling that reflect the relative importance of the interests at stake. It is also the case that, under relative autonomy, a rule-set might adopt graduated or differential conditions for consent depending upon the significance of the interests at stake.

[20] For a general theory of official accountability and citizen restraint, see Deryck Beyleveld and Roger Brownsword, *Law as a Moral Judgment* (London, Sweet and Maxwell, 1986; reprinted Sheffield: Sheffield Academic Press, 1994), especially at chs 5 and 7–9.

extent, the rule-sets themselves also make consent a requirement. Consent, thus, seems to operate in two spheres, one external to the rule-set and the other internal to it. What is the relationship between these two spheres of consent?

For the sake of illustration, let us suppose that a court is seized of a dispute between two contracting parties. The contract, which is for the lease of a large warehouse, provides, inter alia, that the claimant-lessee is not to sublet any part of the premises without the consent of the defendant-lessor, which consent should not be unreasonably withheld. The claimant, having been denied permission to sublet, contends that the defendant is in breach because the latter is unreasonably withholding consent. Now, consider the following three different levels of defence that the defendant might offer:

(1) The defendant argues that he has good grounds for denying permission in this particular instance and that consent is not being unreasonably withheld; hence, there is no breach of contract (lease).
(2) The defendant argues that the contract (lease) is actually invalid because the formalities required by the local law for such transactions have not been complied with: there is no written record of the parties having consented.
(3) The defendant argues that he did not freely consent to submit to the local law of contract (leases). He contends that the claimant threatened to burn the warehouse down if negotiations for the lease (subject to the local law) were not opened.

Each of these arguments involves an issue of consent. The first is very familiar to contract lawyers, arguments about the interpretation of terms in commercial agreements being one of the most common causes of litigation. In this particular hypothetical, the dispute hinges on what the local law takes to be the test of a reasonable (or not unreasonable) refusal on the part of the lessor and then how that test applies to the facts of the dispute. In principle, each legal regime has relative autonomy in how it deals with such matters. Thus, it might have its own developed jurisprudence of reasonableness in the light of which the status of the owner's refusal is clear (one way or the other); or it might rely on the standards of reasonableness recognised and relied on by business people in the warehousing sector; or it might draw on the standards of the wider business community, or even society at large. At all events, there is no requirement that the test should be compliant with Gewirthian principles, in the sense that the test is directly derived or deduced from such principles.

The second argument is again familiar to contract lawyers. Where there is a failure to evidence consent in the way that local formalities require, different legal regimes will respond in different ways. Some might take an unyielding approach, insisting upon 'strict compliance'; others will be more relaxed about formalities, particularly if there is evidence by way of performance from which the parties' consent can be implied. In some jurisdictions, the crucial question might be whether the owner has acted in bad faith by waiting opportunistically to take this technical point; in others, good faith might not be a recognised doctrinal category.[21] Once again, however, legal regimes have relative autonomy in the way that they handle this issue that arises within the law of contract.

In the first two cases, the dispute is remitted to the rules of the relevant local institutional set (the local 'law of contract' as applied to leases), and, in each case, we have said that legal regimes enjoy relative autonomy in respect of the particular rules that they adopt. However, this degree of autonomy is predicated on the contractors having authorised the application of the local rule-set by way of an originating consent. With the defendant's third argument, however, a question-mark is raised precisely about the validity of the originating consent. Yet, the way in which the defendant puts the argument has a distinctly unfamiliar ring to it. It is as though the defendant is pointing to a definite entry point—a consenting chamber, as it were—where the parties consented to submit to the local law of contract for the purposes of negotiating the lease on the warehouse. It is as though the defendant is arguing that, at this point, he went through the motions of consenting but this was a sham because of the background duress applied by the claimant. But, if this model is out of touch with the ordinary experience of contracting, if there is no consenting chamber, then two things follow: one is that the court cannot arbitrate the defendant's argument (because it is not practically meaningful); and the other is that, without the linchpin of an originating consent, the relative autonomy of the rule-set can no longer be conceded.

Before we follow up these consequences, it should be said that there are rule-sets where there is a very deliberate process of consensual engagement, such that it is perfectly defensible to hold on to the idea of relative autonomy. In commerce, for example, there are various kinds of clubs (trading in both traditional and electronic environments), with their own distinctive rule-sets, and, before a new 'member' is permitted to join the club, an originating consent is required. We might view marriage in much the same way. And, where couples seek to enter into regulated schemes for assisted conception, at any rate in the United Kingdom, provision is made for their counselling as to the scheme's ground rules in a way that again fits the image of a chamber of consent. No doubt, such instances could be multiplied. Nevertheless, in many societies, these are exceptional breaks in the flow of everyday life, and the question is what we make of routine contracting in both consumer and commercial markets.

[21] See, eg, Roger Brownsword, Norma J Hird, and Geraint Howells (eds), *Good Faith in Contract: Concept and Context* (Aldershot, Dartmouth, 1999).

If we decide that the chamber of consent is a fiction in relation to a particular class of transactions, then it is a fiction to talk about originating consent, and it is misguided to concede relative autonomy to the particular rule-set. However, we do not yet have to give up on procedural justification. Instead of basing the procedural justification on the (fictitious) originating consent, we might incorporate consent requirements within the rule-set, where they are not so much duplicates for the (missing) originating consent requirement but surrogates for it. In this light, the development of doctrines such as duress and informed consent within the modern law of contract can be seen as a welcome substitute for originating consents—albeit focused on the adequacy of the consent in relation to the particular contract made rather than the adequacy of the prior consent to submit oneself to the governance of the rules of the law of contract. Even so, this seems to be progressive, for, as it becomes less plausible to view contracting as an optional activity preceded by an originating consent, the law rightly responds by copying in more stringent (surrogate) consent requirements.

Alternatively, instead of looking for an originating consent prior to each contracting activity, the law might base its procedural justification on an originating consent that authorises the application of the law of contract to a block of transactions. However, we must be careful here not to fictionalise consent. Just because consumers shop till they drop or business people enter certain markets does not mean that they signal an originating (and ongoing) consent thereby. If contracting zones were more decisively demarcated from the ordinary run of social life, this might be a plausible view, but, in most modern market societies, this would be just another fiction.

Having said all this, there remains the curious doctrinal requirement (internal to the common law of contract) that the parties should intend to create legal (or contractual) relations. Quite what this doctrine means is unclear; quite what its function is, equally, is a mystery. In practice, it conveniently allows courts to filter out unmeritorious individual claimants and to maintain the borders of contract law in the larger field of private law.[22] However, in principle, it seems to be asking the very question that would be addressed in the chamber of consent. It asks the parties whether they really wish to deal with one another in a way that will be governed by the rules of the law of contract. Do they so consent? In practice, the law presumes that consumer and business contractors do intend to create legal relations and, in this sense, consent. In other words, the legal presumption is that those agents who enter marketplaces intend to submit to the application of the rule-set represented by the local law of contract. Granted, this is a default presumption; it is rebuttable. Nevertheless, this smacks of a fiction. In practice, these agents do not pass through a chamber of consent; nor do they have a

[22] See, eg, Stephen Hedley, 'Keeping Contract in its Place—*Balfour v Balfour* and the Enforceability of Informal Agreements' (1985) 5 *Oxford Journal of Legal Studies* 391.

convenient way of signalling that they opt in or opt out. The doctrine of intention to create legal relations has the potential to serve as a surrogate for the originating consent; but it then co-opts parties into the law of contract without taking a hard look at whether the parties intended to engage that particular rule-set. For such parties, the law of contract takes some internal measures (particularly those doctrines that regulate against fraud and non-disclosure, and coercion and duress) to check the integrity of the consent on which the agreement is predicated, but the fundamental question of whether the agents consensually engaged the law of contract to govern their dealings is either not asked or it is answered unsatisfactorily.

## VIII The Justificatory Power and Province of Consent

If some communities undervalue and fictionalise consent, then others can overvalue it, becoming fixated with the twin ideas that consent is proof against any kind of wrong, and that an absence of consent is a cause for complaint. We suggested in chapters eight and nine that it is important not to get carried away with consent to the point where simple fallacies become written into our practical reason. The two principal fallacies are thinking, first, that consent is a necessary justifying reason (the Fallacy of Necessity) and, secondly, that consent is a sufficient justifying reason (the Fallacy of Sufficiency).

### *(i) The Fallacy of Necessity*

The first fallacy, thinking consent is a necessary justifying reason, encourages two mistakes. One mistake is to think that where there is no consent there must be a wrong (and, thus, there must be a remedy), and the other is to think that consent offers the only justification in response to a prima facie wrong.

To straighten out our thinking, it is as well to remind ourselves of the general pattern of Gewirthian reason, or indeed of any moral reason driven by a will theory of rights. First, acts by agents will be classified as prohibited, permitted, or required. The classification of a particular act will depend upon how it stands relative to the principles of the PGC. Secondly, what makes an act wrong is that it fails to conform to what is prohibited or required under the PGC. In both cases, the act fails to respect a right (negative or positive) that is protected by the PGC. Thirdly, acts that are 'comprehensively'[23]

[23] A's consent that B may do X gives B, the recipient of the consent, a limited or personal permission to do X. A, at least, has no complaint if B does X. However, by doing X, B might violate the right of C. Thus, A's consent does not, of itself, ensure that B's doing of X is comprehensively permitted. B's doing of X is only comprehensively permitted where the doing of X involves no private wrong to any agent, A, C, and others. Even if the doing of X is so permitted, there remains the question of whether it is immune against public regulation (see 'The Fallacy of Sufficiency' below at 356–357).

permitted by the PGC require no further justification. Fourthly, acts that are prima facie wrong under the PGC (because they fail to respect a right) might be justifiable by reference to the PGC if they are responses to some previous wrong or if they are designed to satisfy more compelling rights. We have referred to justifications of this kind as substantive (antecedent and overriding rights) justifications. Such is the basic pattern.

How, then, does consent and procedural justification fit into this basic pattern? Quite simply, an act that is prima facie wrong (because it seemingly violates a right) will be procedurally justified if the wrongdoer is the recipient of an adequate consent from the rights-holder. For present purposes, we need go no further—that is to say, we need not deal with consent and the exercise of agents' powers.

Provided that we keep in mind the basic pattern of reasoning, we should not commit the fallacy of thinking that an act done without the consent of the complaining agent must be wrong. Rights are the source of entitlement and the focus for wrongdoing. If a right is violated, a wrong is done. If the rights-bearing agent has consented, no wrong is done to that agent by the recipient of the consent. If, however, no right is violated, no wrong is done and there is no wrong for consent to cure.

Generally speaking, where legal regimes operate with a tendency towards procedural conservatism, requiring claimants to plead their cases by reference to established rights (or causes of action), there will be a resistance against this fallacy. Unfortunately, there might also be a resistance to recognising claims that should be recognised because they draw on Gewirthian rights. Accordingly, what legal regimes should open themselves to is the pleading of PGC-derived rights, even if such rights are not yet recognised in the jurisprudence; but, at the same time, they should not be drawn into the fallacy of thinking that new actions must be recognised simply because the defendant has acted without the claimant's consent.

As for the error of thinking that where a prima facie wrong is done to a rights-bearing agent the only justification is the latter's consent, legal regimes again offer resistance to this fallacy by virtue of recognising a range of defences other than consent. In other words, legal regimes tend to be geared for both procedural and substantive justification. Provided that the recognised substantive justifications (such as self-defence, necessity, or the like) fit with larger Gewirthian principles, and provided that the 'priority of consent' is respected, legal regimes are on the right track.

### *(ii) The Fallacy of Sufficiency*

There is no fallacy in thinking that, where A consents to act X by B that would otherwise infringe some right of A, then B does no wrong to A by doing X. There is no private wrong between A and B; act X is, at least, permissible between the parties, and, to this extent, A's consent is a sufficient justification. The major fallacy is to jump to the conclusion that the procedural justification that holds between A and B[24] is sufficient for the purpose of excluding the possibility of act X being treated as a public wrong. The fallacy is to think that the absence of private wrong is incompatible with there being a public interest case for intervention. In line with the pattern of Gewirthian reasoning, however, the public interest case must not only draw on the PGC, it must represent a more compelling application of the master principles than allowing A and B to engage in what (by reference also to the PGC) is personally permissible conduct.

Gewirthians, like other liberals, are nervous about licensing the State to interfere with conduct that is permissible in and of itself. On the premises that present this problem, it must remembered, the agents not only do no wrong between themselves, but at first blush they do no wrong relative to the PGC. For the State to turn this around into a justifiable case for intervention, compelling reasons are required. We suggested, in chapter nine, that the following three classes of reasons would be legitimate building blocks for a public interest case:

(1) measures that are taken in order to secure respect for the rights of fellow agents in the community;
(2) restrictions that are imposed in order to preserve the context in which autonomous agents will enjoy the opportunity to flourish as members of a community committed to human rights and responsibilities; and,
(3) measures that give effect to prohibitions that have been expressly authorised (under strict conditions of consent) by members of the community.

Other than in very small communities, it is hard to imagine the third reason being applicable in practice, in which case the burden of justification will fall on the first two classes of reason. Moreover, because 'public interest', like 'consent', is open to abuse as a lazy justification, these special cases should not be viewed as a blank cheque. If the State is to defend its intervention, in addition to having the right reason, the particular measures introduced must be necessary and proportionate in the circumstances.

## IX Legitimation and Legitimacy

Our Gewirthian methodology, with its rationalist foundationalism, makes it important to distinguish between a legal regime's aspiration to regulatory legitimacy and its aspiration to regulatory legitimation. For Gewirthians, the idea of regulatory legitimacy (in the sense of regulatory compliance with the PGC) has a hard edge to it; we are contemplating substantively rational justification in a strong sense. More generally, however, it is important to discriminate between 'legitimacy' and 'legitimation'. Even though these

[24] But, of course, not necessarily between A and C; or B and C; or both A and B, and C.

terms are sometimes used interchangeably, we want to draw out the distinction between getting (or attempting to get) the regulatory position right (relative to the regime's ultimate standards of legitimacy) and giving reasons in support of the claim that the regulatory position merits respect (which is a matter of stabilising legitimation for the regime).

What does it mean for a legal regime to aspire to regulatory legitimacy? Each legal regime will have certain fundamental value commitments, commitments to the protection of life and liberty, property and privacy, equality and dignity, welfare and happiness, or the like. Typically, these commitments will be written into basic documents at constitutional level. To the extent that a legal regime claims legitimacy for its operations, it claims, first, that its operations are consonant with such basic constitutional values and, secondly, that these values themselves are worthy of respect (as legitimate). In defence of its legitimacy, a legal regime might even be prepared to step outside the legal system itself to defend its basic values.[25] For example, the legitimacy of the new Constitution of the Republic of South Africa might be asserted on the ground that its values express the deepest commitments of post-apartheid South Africa; or the commitment to respect for human dignity as the paramount principle of the German Basic Law might be defended as expressing the deepest values of the new Federal Republic. Again, the step beyond the legal system might take defenders of its legitimacy, directly or indirectly, to a supporting moral theory—as would be the case, for instance, in the hypothetical community of Gewirthia.

At some point, the defence of a legal regime's legitimacy must come to an end, whether the terminus be the constitution, the community's commitments, or a particular moral theory. If the particular resting point is taken to be a rationally necessary one, the legal regime views legitimacy in a foundationalist way (as in Gewirthia), but if the particular resting point is viewed as optional in the final analysis, the legal regime takes a relativist view of legitimacy. This should not be taken to imply that, in practice, the one regime will strive for legitimacy more earnestly than the other. In practice, provided that there is a genuine commitment to the regime's values, the operators of the legal system will orientate themselves to those values. What this signifies is that, where a legal regime has basic commitments to a will theory of rights, it should view the legitimacy of its operations in the terms mapped out in this book.

A legal regime's aspiration to regulatory legitimation is another matter altogether. Each legal regime needs to maintain public confidence in its operations and respect for the regulatory positions that it takes. This is par-

[25] Although, often, appeals to the values of the constitution represent a strategy of avoidance, drawing a line on any further inquiry into legitimacy: see Frank I Michelman, 'Constitutional Legitimation for Political Acts' (2003) 66 *Modern Law Review* 1.

ticularly so in relation to the criminal justice system but it also matters on the civil side. Similarly, governments need to maintain public trust and confidence. In order to maintain confidence, citizens need to be constantly reassured that regulation is 'working' and that proper regard is being paid to the regime's values. It is not enough, for example, that the criminal justice system expresses a commitment to due process (as a sign of its legitimacy), the public must be persuaded that due process is actually respected (and, yet, at the same time, that crime is under control).

The operation of all aspects of a legal regime, however, is not under constant public scrutiny. As a result, the rhetoric of legitimation can become rather casual and loose. With regard to reliance on consent, we have seen that there is a danger that legal regimes fictionalise consent where they find it convenient to do so. As we have emphasised, where this happens the idea of procedural justification is abused and there is a question mark as to whether a substantive justification is available. Or, to put this in terms of legitimacy and legitimation, where consent is fictionalised, it is not clear that the legal regime is operating with legitimacy, and the idea of consent is employed (pathologically) as a legitimating device.

We should distinguish, then, between two very different kinds of legal regimes. On the one hand, there are legal regimes that operate in a principled way, that aspire to respect the rights of agents, and that rely on procedural consent-based justifications only where it is legitimate to do so; on the other hand, there are legal regimes that operate pragmatically, aspiring to a working level of effectiveness, and that rely on consent as their justification whenever it suits, that is, whenever legitimation so demands.

Bearing this caution in mind, we can move on to our penultimate remarks. These concern the idea of 'governance by consent'.

## X 'Governance by Consent' and the Authority of Law

From a Gewirthian viewpoint, a commitment to 'governance by consent' is to be welcomed. For, it proclaims a commitment to democratic processes, to respect for human rights, and to the eschewal of brute force, as well as signalling an open and inclusive approach to governance. However, this is not quite the same thing as suggesting that the authority of the law rests on consent in the procedural justificatory way that we have elaborated in this book. If the authority of public governance were to rest on consent in this procedural justificatory sense, it would resemble something like a fully enfranchised Greek city state, with direct democracy, a high level of moral consensus, and a willingness to compromise for the sake of public agreement. Nowadays, big representative government does not look much like that, and, equally importantly, modern democratised societies are divided rather than united by their moralities. In modern pluralistic communities, the social bonds tend to be commercial rather than cultural.

The moral pluralism of modernity presents a serious challenge to politico-legal authority. However, the challenge is of a different kind and order depending upon the nature and depth of the pluralism. In chapter ten, we drew a distinction between the internal problem of authority facing politico-legal regimes such as that of Gewirthia (where there is a shared commitment to the values of the PGC), and the external problem of authority facing politico-legal regimes that operate in a context of fundamental value pluralism. In Gewirthia, the shared commitment to the values of the PGC means that there is no deep difference of moral principle. Nevertheless, even in Gewirthia, there will be disagreements as to the application of the criteria in particular cases. Where general regulatory positions need to be taken (if only provisionally) or specific decisions must be made, the legitimacy of those positions or decisions will be contested. In such cases, we have said that contested regulatory determinations must be defended, and respected, as good faith conscientious efforts to apply the agreed criteria. Even if such determinations cannot be presented as authoritative by virtue of being legitimate in any straightforward or non-controversial sense, they are to be regarded as legitimate for practical purposes, and they will be legitimated by reference to the decision-making process. In Gewirthia, governance by consent requires that citizens respect contestable articulations of the PGC for the sake of the deeper values of the PGC.

Where communities are more deeply pluralistic, there will be disagreement that reaches right back to the basic commitments themselves. A number of writers, most famously perhaps John Rawls in his later work,[26] have thought that public decision-making in such contexts cannot be presented as authoritative if it simply mirrors one segment of opinion and presents it as the legitimate view. Instead, there has to be a process of public reason in which the participants effectively give up their own comprehensive criteria of legitimacy. Having set aside their fundamental differences, the parties might then find the way clear to agree regulatory positions that survive scrutiny for their reasonableness. In such a polity, regulation would be legitimated, not by reference to contested criteria of legitimacy, but (paradoxically and controversially) by reference to a process that puts the decision-makers' fundamental values out of play. As Jürgen Habermas has said, deliberative democracy of this kind leads to a 'process-conception of legitimation.'[27] In such a divided community, 'governance by consent'

[26] John Rawls, *Political Liberalism* (New York, Columbia University Press, 1993).

[27] Jürgen Habermas, 'Introduction' (1999) 12 *Ratio Juris* 329, at 333 (a special issue on Habermas' philosophy of law). Habermas continues:

> Legitimation depends on an appropriate legal institutionalisation of those forms of rational discourse and fair bargaining that ground the presumption of the rational acceptability of outcomes. (*ibid*)

requires citizens to respect not only contestable interpretations of principles to which they subscribe but the articulations of principles that they contest and flatly reject.

To what extent, however, in Gewirthia or beyond, does 'governance by consent' betoken procedurally authorised governance? In the absence of any meaningful originating consent, citizens are simply co-opted into the going scheme of governance. To say that citizens, by 'subjecting themselves' to that scheme of governance, or by occasionally participating as voters, give their authorising consent is to make a mockery of consent, and to put the point more cautiously in terms of the 'presumed' or 'tacit' or 'implicit' consent of citizens is only to confess to the fiction that this manifestly is. If, instead, it is claimed that, because rational agents would consent to the particular scheme of governance, there is a hypothetical consent, this might be correct. Whether or not it is correct will depend upon the credentials of the particular scheme of governance. But, then, this is just the point. The acid test for legitimate governance is whether the scheme meets the criteria of legitimacy, not whether it meets with the consenting approval of its citizenry. In Gewirthia, conformity with the PGC is the key to justifying the scheme of governance; the fact that citizens would consent to submit to such a scheme, if invited to do so, has no added justificatory value. Even with the procedural turn that we described in Gewirthia, what matters is the actual legitimacy of the framework for public governance, not the hypothetical consent of Gewirthian citizens.

Let us make no mistake: governance by consent is a progressive idea, but it is not to be confused with governance that is procedurally authorised by consent. And nor is this a matter for apology or regret. If the best that government can say to citizens is, 'You consented, so you have no complaint,' this is a long way short of a government that can say to its citizens, 'You have no complaint because the scheme is fully justifiable as legitimate.' Of course, to defend the politico-legal framework by reference to consent is more appealing where the full justification presupposed by the legitimacy defence is contested. However, where consent is a fiction or a fraud it is not the easier option; it is certainly not the only justificatory option (this is to succumb to the Fallacy of Necessity); and, where a decent fist can be made of the full substantive justification, the procedural justification is neither the right nor the better option.

## XI Law and Consent in the Global Order after 9/11

Globalisation presents something of a paradox. At the same time that pressure to commit to human rights and respect for the Rule of Law is increased, one senses that—certainly after the tragic events of 9/11—the weight actually accorded to the values represented by human rights has decreased.[28] Reflecting (critically) on this state of affairs, Helena Kennedy sees law and consent as the building blocks for the restoration of civilised society. Thus:

> Law is a cornerstone. And unless we are prepared to revert to the continuous use of force, law is the supreme regulator. Whether nationally or internationally, it is the glue that holds together the constituent parts of a society, a civilising force. Law is what makes the centre hold, the mortar that fills the gaps between people and communities, creating a social bond without which the quality of our lives would be greatly undermined. Just law is the invisible substance which sustains social well-being, moral consensus, mutuality of trust and interest. If we interfere with the principles which underpin law, fritter them away, pick them out of the crannies of our political and social architecture, restoration is impossible. Our only hope is an order governed by law and consent.[29]

Whilst we entirely endorse the spirit of these remarks, we can conclude by restating briefly the letter of the relationship between supreme regulative principles, law, and consent.

First, the supreme regulative principle is the PGC; no regulatory regime will be legitimate unless it aspires to order agent interactions in a way that is compatible with the PGC. Indeed, no positive regulatory order should be treated as an instance of a legal regime (or a legal system) unless it has this value orientation. Only in this qualified sense, should we treat law as the supreme regulator.

Secondly, in an order governed by law (properly conceived), human rights will be respected. Furthermore, the pattern of justification will be as given by a will theory of rights under the PGC. Substantive justification draws down the values of the PGC; procedural justification flows from the consent of agents who exercise their will in relation to their rights and powers in a particular way.

Thirdly, such a legal order will neither treat consent as a fiction but nor will it be fixated by consent. Whenever consent is presented as being 'deemed', 'imputed', 'implied', or the like, we need to take a hard look at it; otherwise, we might be ruled by fiction or fraud. Equally, whenever consent is presented as a free-standing justification, we need to check that it has not become detached from the framework of rights and duties to which it belongs. Over-egging consent might not be the worst of sins; but legal regimes with Gewirthian aspirations should not encourage such fallacies.

Fourthly, we should not think that operationalising consent in the law is a straightforward business. It would be too much to expect a legal regime to strike the right balance, all the time and each time, between the interests

[28] See, further, Roger Brownsword (ed), *Global Governance and the Quest for Justice: Volume 4, Human Rights* (Oxford, Hart Publishing, 2004); and Phillipe Sands, *Lawless World* (London, Penguin Books, 2006).

[29] Helena Kennedy, *Just Law* (London, Chatto and Windus, 2004) at 9.

of the supposedly consenting agent and the recipient. But at least we know what the challenge is—and our best hope is that those charged with responsibility in our legal regimes understand what the question is and make a good faith attempt to answer it. In practice, we cannot ask for more; but we certainly should not settle for less.

Finally, whilst we can agree with those critics of globalisation who believe that consent is an idea whose time has come,[30] we must not lose sight of the context from which consent derives its normative significance. It is not consent that demands that a precondition for global community is that the huge inequalities of resource and opportunity that divide the First and the Third World, the North and the South, must be eliminated; it is not consent that demands that governments must treat their citizens with equal concern and respect; it is not consent that demands that cultural diversity should be recognised or environments protected. Procedural justification matters but it counts for little unless the background is broadly compliant with the values of the PGC. What the world needs now is a real determination to promote the generic conditions of agents irrespective of historic national boundaries. There might or might not be an international consensus that such steps should be taken. However, the justification for taking the steps is not they are authorised by consent, but that, as a matter of right, agents are entitled to such attempts being made. The world might be a better place if there was an international consensus that it should become such a place, and the fact that there was such a consensus might help it to become a better place; but it is not consent alone that pushes for the world to become such a place.

[30] See, notably, George Monbiot, (London, Flamingo, 2003).

# Index

www.ingramcontent.com/pod-product-compliance
Ingram Content Group UK Ltd.
Pitfield, Milton Keynes, MK11 3LW, UK
UKHW020831290926
15470UKWH00009B/1846/J